THOSE WILD WYNDHAMS

THOSE WILD WYNDHAMS

Three Sisters at the Heart of Power

CLAUDIA RENTON

ALFRED A. KNOPF   NEW YORK   2018

THIS IS A BORZOI BOOK PUBLISHED BY ALFRED A. KNOPF

Copyright © 2014, 2018 by Claudia Renton

All rights reserved. Published in the United States by Alfred A. Knopf, a division of
Penguin Random House LLC, New York, and distributed in Canada by Random House
of Canada, a division of Penguin Random House Canada Limited, Toronto. Originally
published in hardcover in Great Britain by William Collins, an imprint of
HarperCollins Publishers, London, in 2014.

www.aaknopf.com

Knopf, Borzoi Books, and the colophon are registered trademarks of
Penguin Random House LLC.

Library of Congress Cataloging-in-Publication Data
Names: Renton, Claudia, author.
Title: Those wild Wyndhams : three sisters at the heart of power / by Claudia Renton.
Description: First edition. | New York : Alfred A. Knopf, 2018. | "This is a Borzoi Book."
| Includes bibliographical references and index.
Identifiers: LCCN 2017059932 (print) | LCCN 2017050326 (ebook) |
ISBN 9781101874301 (e-book) | ISBN 9781101874295 (hardcover)
Subjects: LCSH: Wyndham family. | Elcho, Mary, 1862–1937. | Adeane, Madeline, 1869–
1941. | Grey, Pamela, 1871–1928. | Sisters—England—Biography. | Aristocracy (Social
class)—England—History—19th century. | Aristocracy (Social class)—England—
History—20th century.
Classification: LCC DA562 (print) | LCC DA562.R45 2018 (ebook) |
DDC 941.081092/52 [B]—dc23
LC record available at https://lccn.loc.gov/2017059932

Jacket illustration: The Wyndham Sisters by John Singer Sargent, 1899.
Catharine Lorillard Wolfe Collection, Wolfe Fund © The Metropolitan Museum
of Art/Art Resource, NY
Jacket design by Carol Devine Carson

Manufactured in the United States of America
First United States Edition

For Mama.

Always.

LA CHANSON DE MARIE-DES-ANGES

Y avait un'fois un pauv'gas,
Et lon la laire,
Et lon lan la,
Y avait un'fois un pauv'gas,
Qu'aimait cell'qui n'l'aimait pas.

Elle lui dit: Apport'moi d'main
Et lon la laire,
Et lon lan la,
Elle lui dit: Apport'moi d'main
L'coeur de ta mèr' pour mon chien.

Va chez sa mère et la tue,
Et lon la laire,
Et lon lan la,
Va chez sa mère et la tue,
Lui prit l'coeur et s'en courut.

Comme il courait, il tomba,
Et lon la laire,
Et lon lan la,
Comme il courait, il tomba,
Et par terre l'coeur roula.

Et pendant que l'coeur roulait,
Et lon la laire,
Et lon lan la,
Et pendant que l'coeur roulait,
Entendit l'coeur qui parlait.

Et l'coeur lui dit en pleurant,
Et lon la laire,
Et lon lan la,
Et l'coeur lui dit en pleurant:
T'es-tu fait mal mon enfant?

JEAN RICHEPIN (1848–1926)

Do you know Richepin's poem about a Mother's Heart? It means something like this: "there was a poor wretch who loved a woman who would not love him. She asked him for his Mother's heart, so he killed his Mother to cut out her heart and hurried off with it to his love. He ran so fast that he tripped and fell, and the heart rolled away. As it rolled it began to speak and asked 'Darling child, have you hurt yourself?'"

GEORGE WYNDHAM TO PAMELA TENNANT, 11 MARCH 1912

CONTENTS

WYNDHAM FAMILY TREE

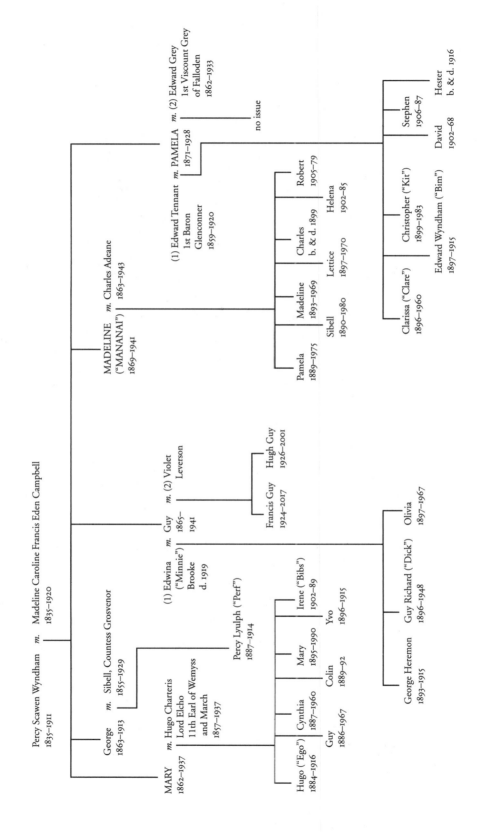

Percy Scawen Wyndham *m.* Madeline Caroline Francis Eden Campbell
1835–1911   1835–1920

MARY 1862–1937 *m.* Hugo Charteris Lord Elcho 11th Earl of Wemyss and March 1857–1937

George 1863–1913 *m.* Sibell, Countess Grosvenor 1855–1929

MADELINE ("MANANAI") 1869–1941 *m.* Charles Adeane 1863–1943

PAMELA 1871–1928 *m.* (1) Edward Tennant 1st Baron Glenconner 1859–1920

m. (2) Edward Grey 1st Viscount Grey of Falloden 1862–1933 — no issue

Guy 1865–1941 *m.* (1) Edwina ("Minnie") Brooke d. 1919

Percy Lyulph ("Perf") 1887–1914

m. (2) Violet Leverson

Francis Guy 1924–2017

Hugh Guy 1926–2001

Hugo ("Ego") 1884–1916

Guy 1886–1967

Cynthia 1887–1960

Colin 1889–92

Mary 1895–1990

Yvo 1896–1915

Irene ("Bibs") 1902–89

George Heremon 1893–1915

Guy Richard ("Dick") 1896–1948

Olivia 1897–1967

Pamela 1889–1975

Sibell 1890–1980

Madeline 1893–1969

Lettice 1897–1970

Charles b. & d. 1899

Helena 1902–85

Robert 1905–79

Clarissa ("Clare") 1896–1960

Edward Wyndham ("Bim") 1897–1915

Christopher ("Kit") 1899–1983

David 1902–68

Stephen 1906–87

Hester b. & d. 1916

THOSE WILD WYNDHAMS

PROLOGUE

On a cool February night in 1900, Pamela Tennant, the aristocratic wife of the industrialist Eddy Tennant, was dining at the London town house of her brother and sister-in-law, Lord and Lady Ribblesdale. The Season, the annual, months-long jamboree of social events that consumed the lives of the upper classes from late spring until the last day of July, had not quite started, but there was already a smattering of balls. By early summer that smattering would become a deluge, as seemingly every house in Mayfair echoed to the strains of bands and England's elite waltzed round and round camellia-filled ballrooms in what would prove to be the last year of Victoria's reign.

Pamela was not really looking forward to the Season that was to come, or to any Season, for that matter. In the five years since she had married, her refusal to play ball socially had provoked several spats with her sister-in-law. Charty Ribblesdale, one of the audacious Tennant sisters who had launched themselves into London Society twenty years before, could not understand why Pamela, whose birth afforded her entry everywhere, should willfully clam up when faced with new people. Pamela's refusal to play by any rules but her own and her often brittle social demeanor mystified Charty and her sisters Margot and Lucy. They thought it alien to the ethos of the Souls: their fascinating, chattering set who affected insouciant ease, no matter how frantically their legs paddled beneath the serene surface.

The delightfully haphazard Mary, Lady Elcho, Pamela's eldest sister, was a leading light of the Souls. Pamela, beautiful, brilliant, a master of the pointed phrase, had it in her to joust with the best of them. But she chose not to. Instead, she professed disdain for "those murdered Summers" of the Season, and openly expressed her preference for her home in rural Wiltshire, some hundred miles southeast of London, where she caravanned across the undulating chalk hills known as the Downs in the company of her children. It was a very peculiar attitude.

The burly American placed next to Pamela also seemed ill at ease among Society's hubbub. John Singer Sargent, whose *Carnation, Lily, Lily, Rose* had dazzled the Royal Academy of Arts, the imperious institution that dictated British artistic taste from Burlington House on London's Piccadilly, over a decade before, was establishing himself as a society portraitist *par excellence*, but he had little time for his sitters' chatter. He preferred quiet times in the Gloucestershire village of Broadway, in the dreamy Cotswolds with his sisters and nieces—incidentally, not far from where Mary Elcho lived at Stanway, the beautiful Jacobean manor house that had been in her husband's family for centuries. "He was very nice & simple, & . . . very shy & not the least like an American," Mary's friend Frances Horner reported to the artist Edward Burne-Jones after meeting Sargent (for Sargent, although an American by parentage, had been born and raised on the Continent), "& he wasn't very like an artist either! . . . he hated discussing all his great friends . . . & talking about his pictures."

Perhaps Charty took a certain pleasure in seating Pamela next to Sargent that evening. It was a taste of her own medicine—and Charty could justify the placement because Sargent was currently working on a portrait of Pamela and her sisters. It had been commissioned the year before by their father, Percy Wyndham, who, with his wife, Madeline, had built Clouds House in Wiltshire—really, more a mansion—which was little over a decade old and already famous as a "palace of weekending" where the great and the good, from artists to actors, generals and politicians, gathered. Pamela, Mary and sweet-natured Madeline Adeane (who so unluckily after a whole brood of girls had finally succeeded in giving birth to a boy only for the premature infant to die the same day) had been sitting to Sargent ever since then.

There was plenty to talk about. No mention was made of the Boer War's disastrous progress, or Pamela's elder brother George, a rising political star, Under-Secretary in the War Office, whose triumphant speech in the House of Commons a few weeks before had singlehand-edly seemed to redeem the Government's conduct of the war. All Sargent's talk was of the portrait. The first sittings had taken place over a year before, in the splendid, high-ceilinged drawing room of the Wynd-hams' London house, 44 Belgrave Square. Yet just recently, Pamela, in the thick of preparations for one of the tableaux of which she was so fond, received a letter from Percy suggesting that Sargent's portrait might still not be finished in time for this year's Summer Exhibition at the Royal Academy, one of the highlights of the Season each year, and at which the painting was intended to be first displayed to the masses. What with the uncertain light at this time of year, and the fact that the Wyndhams would not be in London until after Easter, "perhaps this is better," he concluded. To Pamela's mind, this was not better. At this rate, she replied ominously, there was the danger that "we shall all be old and haggard before the public sees it."

Pamela in the flesh made the shortcomings of Pamela in oils all too clear. Sargent told Pamela in his deep, curiously accentless voice (the leg-acy of his Continental upbringing) that he "felt *sure*" that Mr. Wyndham "would not mean it to be as it is." "He is very anxious for some more sit-tings from me and enquired my plans most pertinaciously," Pamela told Percy the next day. Her very presence had seemed to prove an inspiration: " 'and now I see you oh it must be worked on'—squirming & writhing in his evening suit—'no finish—no finish'—he got quite excited."

As agreed, Pamela made her way to Sargent's studio on Tite Street in still-bohemian Chelsea at half past two the following Saturday. Three or four days was all that Sargent, a phenomenally fast worker, required before she could thankfully flee London once again. "He has not repainted the face . . . He worked on little corners of it and has much improved it I think," Pamela said. He had remodeled her nose, taken "a little of the color out of my cheeks, this improves it," and transformed her hair from "all fluffy and rather trivial looking before" to swept back, which "has strengthened it, and made it *more* like my head really."

There was one loss. The front of Pamela's dress, an eye-catching blue, had, Sargent said decisively, to go. It was, she explained to her parents, "disturbing to the *scheme* . . . And much as I regret my pretty blue front I *quite* see it was rather preclusive of other things in the picture as a whole. For instance both sisters seem to *gain* by its removal—one's eye is not checked & held by it . . . My face also seems to gain significance by its removal." Mary, who had always been suspicious of Pamela's color choice, must have been relieved: "blue can be so *ugly* don't you think?" she had complained to their mother when Pamela had first announced her sartorial intentions.

Uncharacteristically, Madeline was causing trouble. At the Ribblesdales', Sargent had been adamant that "Mrs. Adeane in particular" needed to be changed, requiring a further week of sittings. The year before, Charlie Adeane's patience with "that blessed picture" had worn thin when Madeline had caught influenza while sitting for it. Now, with Madeline still recovering from her infant son's death, Charlie Adeane, as protective as he was devoted, might prove the spanner in the works. "I hope you will use your influence if Charlie is against it," Pamela implored her father; "it seems a pity if it is so near it shouldn't be managed." Madeline Wyndham, who could never refuse anything to her "Benjamina," as she called her youngest daughter, replied, "I think it would amuse her—& I should trust it was *warmer* in Sargent's Studio than it is in large drawing room at 44 this time of year without hot water or hot air which I am sure Sargent's studio has . . . *you* ought write to Madeline & beg her to go up for a week she can be snug as a bug in my bedroom and she & Charlie can be there."

In art, as in life, Mary was proving difficult to pin down. Marooned among the rugs, tapestries and antiques that formed the paraphernalia of an artist's studio, as Sargent, muttering unintelligibly under his breath, charged to and from the easel (placed, as always, next to his sitters so that when he stood back he might view portrait and person in the same light), Pamela had to exercise all her diplomatic skill when asked what she thought of Sargent's depiction of Mary. "I *could* say honestly I liked it," she told her parents, "but I did not think it 'contemplative' enough in expression for her." And "no sooner than I had said the word 'contemplative' than he caught at it. 'Dreamy—I must make it a *little* more dreamy!' " All it needed, apparently, was a touch to Mary's hooded eyelids, which Pamela agreed were "a most characteristic feature of her face"; but "of course he will not do it till she sits to him," she concluded, with not a little exasperation.

Astonishingly Mary—nicknamed "Napoleon" by her friends for her tendency to make monumental plans that rarely came to pass, and who seemed, in the view of her dear friend, the politician Arthur Balfour (himself tipped to be the next Conservative Prime Minister when his uncle the Marquess of Salisbury retired the post), "to combine into one disastrous whole all that there is of fatiguing in the occupations of mother, a woman of fashion, and a sick nurse"—got herself to London, and to Tite Street, in time for the painting to be completed so that it could be displayed at the Academy's Summer Exhibition that year.

The Wyndham Sisters, to the gratification of all (and doubtless Pamela in particular) was heralded as Sargent's masterpiece. This depiction of aristocratic beauty dazzled the hordes that streamed past it, no less the critics. *The Times* of London declared it simply "the greatest picture which has appeared for many years on the walls of the Royal Academy." Bertie, the elderly Prince of Wales, who had honed his eye for beauty over many years, dubbed the portrait "The Three Graces." The Wyndham sisters were already well known within Society. Now their faces were familiar to a far larger audience, in the most flattering of lights.

At a time when the upper classes felt that their traditional hegemony was being eroded by a myriad of diverse forces—the plutocratic fortunes that dwarfed their own; agricultural crisis that threatened their estates; the extension of the franchise that created a working-class majority electorate and challenged their paternalistic rule (to say nothing of the nascent Labour Party, founded that very year as the Labour Representation Committee)—the painting represented a distinct salvo on behalf of the beleagured aristocracy. It was, crowed the *Saturday Review,* "one of those truces in the fight where beauty has unquestionably slipped in." Though we now think of Sargent as the Annie Leibovitz of his day—intently flattering at all costs—at that time people did not see it in quite the same way. "In all the history of painting," commented the critic D. S. MacColl in the *Saturday Review* in 1898, "hostile observation has never been pushed so far as by Mr. Sargent. I do not mean stupid deforming spite, humorous caricature, or diabolic possession . . . rather a cold accusing eye bent on the world." MacColl likened Sargent to "the prosecuting lawyer or denouncing critics." His work made the viewer "first repelled by its contempt, then fascinated by its life." "I chronicle," declared Sargent, "I do not judge." The dazzling results seduced the aristocracy, but they commissioned him with trepidation. "It is positively dangerous to sit to Sargent," declared one apprehensive society matron; "it's taking your face in your hands."

One oft-repeated criticism, that Sargent did no more than replicate his sitters' glamour, is perhaps a misunderstanding of the emptiness that his brush was so often revealing. To defeat any accusation that *The Wyndham Sisters* is simply a pretty picture, one needs only to look at the sisters' hands. Pamela's fingers imperiously flick outwards as she lounges back on the sofa, in the most obviously central position as always, unblinkingly staring the viewer down; Mary's thin hands worry at each other as she perches on the edge of the sofa and gazes "dreamily" off into the distance showing all her "delicate intellectual beauty." Then there is Madeline, who uses her left hand to support herself against the sofa, while her right hand, quelled by sorrow, lies in her lap, patiently facing upwards, cupped to receive the blessings that fate, in recent months, had so conspicuously denied her. Underneath the serenity is the wildness of the Wyndhams, the foreign strain from their mother's French-Irish blood, that their contemporaries remarked on time and time again.

Before the sittings began, before the composition had been decided upon, Madeline and Percy Wyndham had arranged a dinner at Belgrave Square for Sargent to meet his sitters properly. Watching the family in the splendor of their home, Sargent had caught on immediately. Rather than paint these women in his studio, as was the norm, he set them in the drawing room of their parents' house. As one's eye becomes accustomed to the cool gloom behind the seated figures swathed in layers of white organza, taffeta, tulle, one can make out in the background the portrait of their mother that hung in that room: George Frederic Watts's portrait of Madeline Wyndham, resplendent in a sunflower-splashed gown, that had caused such a stir at the Grosvenor Gallery a quarter of a century before. Through the darkness, behind Mary, Madeline and Pamela, gleams Madeline Wyndham. So in art, as in life. Sargent had not missed a thing.

ONE

"*Worse Than 100 Boys*"

The eldest daughter of the portrait, Mary Constance Wyndham, was born to Percy and Madeline in London in summer's dog days on 3 August 1862 and privileged from birth. Percy, called "the Hon'ble P" by his friends, was the favored younger son of the vastly wealthy Lord Leconfield of Petworth House in Sussex, a county some fifty miles southwest of London. Percy's occupation was holding down a family parliamentary seat in the north of England as the Conservative Member for West Cumberland. He had a kind heart and the family traits of an uncontrollable temper and an inability to dissemble. It was true of him, as was said of his father, that he had "no power of disguising his feelings, if he liked one person more than another it was simply written on his Countenance."

Percy's Irish wife, Madeline, was different. Known in infancy as "the Sunny Baby," she was renowned for her expansive warmth. "She is an Angel . . . She has the master-key of life—love—which unlocks everything for her and makes one feel her immortal," said Georgiana Burne-Jones, who, like her husband, Edward, was among Madeline's closest friends. Yet in courtship Percy had spoken much of Madeline's reserve—"you sweet mystery," he called her, one of very few to recognize that her personality seemed to be shut up in different boxes, to some of which only she held the key. Madeline, rumored to be descended from French royalty, had a romantic, disreputable ancestry: breeding, but no money. She and Percy had married for love. The substantial dowry Madeline had brought to the marriage was provided for her by her doting father-in-law, Lord Leconfield.

At the time of Mary's birth, Percy and Madeline were twenty-seven years old, two years married, and lived an elegant, leisured life befitting the son and daughter-in-law of one of England's richest men. They divided their time between stately Petworth, Cockermouth Castle—a grandly named but ramshackle family property in Percy's constituency given to them by his father for their use—and fashionable Belgrave Square, at no. 44, where Mary was born. Madeline's mother, Pamela, Lady Campbell, came over from Ireland for the birth, and during Madeline's labor sat anxiously with Percy in a little room off her daughter's bedroom. The labor was short—barely four and a half hours—and difficult. Lady Campbell had threatened to call her own daughter "Rhinocera" when she was born because of her incredible size. Mary, at birth, weighed an eyewatering eleven pounds. "The size and hardness of the baby's head (for which I am afraid I am to blame)," Percy told his sister Fanny with apologetic pride, had required the use of forceps to bring the child into the world. "Of course we should have liked a boy but I am very grateful to God that matters have gone so well," Percy concluded.

Percy and Madeline's daughter held within her person the blood of Ireland and England—a physical embodiment of the vexed union between the kingdoms. Ireland was not, officially, a colony: it had shared a crown with England since King Henry VIII's time. Yet since 1800, when its Parliament was abolished and its MPs sent, outnumbered, to England's Westminster Parliament (a result of the abortive 1798 Irish Rebellion, in which Madeline's grandfather Lord Edward Fitzgerald had died a nationalist hero and martyr), Ireland had been little more than an English satellite. In 1844 Parliament debated the motion "Ireland is occupied, not governed." Benjamin Disraeli, writer and ambitious fledgling MP, described "a starving population, an absentee aristocracy . . . an alien church, and . . . the weakest executive in the world." The novelist was exercising some artistic license—by 1873 only 20 percent of Ireland's aristocracy were technically absentee—but fundamentally his depiction was and remained true. By the time Mary was a child, the republican Fenian Brotherhood was conducting a terrorist campaign in London. Instinctively iconoclastic, raised on stories of her rebellious great-grandfather and his French Catholic wife (known as "la Belle Pamela" for her beauty, and widely recognized as the illegitimate daughter of the royal revolutionary Duc d'Orléans and his fiercely intelligent mistress Madame de Genlis, a disciple of Rousseau's), Mary's childhood sympathies were with the oppressed and not the oppressors. She and her younger brother George—so she said later—were "the Fenians of the family."

The harum-scarum hoyden was—like the age that bred her—hopeful, endlessly curious, entranced by novelty and change. At the time of Mary's birth, Britain's explorers were expanding the boundaries of the known world, their imperialists extending Britain's governance over it. In Africa, Richard Burton and John Hanning Speke discovered the Nile's source. The British Crown was declared official ruler of India by parliamentary Act, wresting control from the East India Trading Company, which had hitherto governed the continent. The British were a "race girdling the earth," trumpeted the radical, imperialist politician Charles Dilke in his best-selling *Greater Britain.* The British mission was civilizing and Christian. Yet the mid-Victorian era's unquestioning faith had been seriously shaken by Charles Darwin's *On the Origin of Species,* published in 1859. Evolutionary theory challenged everything an evangelical nation had been taught to believe. Mary, who as a child had fossils shown and explained to her by her father, was born into a world ebullient in its capacity for exploration and invention but, in post-Darwinian terms, questing and unsure.

As Mary progressed from infancy to childhood, the landscape of modern London formed about her: Joseph Bazalgette built the great river walks along the Thames known as the Victoria and Albert Embankments (their purpose: to cover the new sewage system that meant the Thames was no longer the city's chamber pot). The telephone and the first traffic light (short lived, it was installed outside the Houses of Parliament in 1868, only to explode in 1869, gravely wounding the policeman operating it) were inventions of her early youth. Inside that Parliament, however, little had changed. The presence of a band of "Radical" politicians seeking social change did not diminish the fact that the patriarchy was dominant. Stringent property qualifications meant that in the early 1860s, only one in five males could vote. The 1867 Reform Act, which extended the franchise to the wealthiest of the urban male working classes, was known popularly as "the Leap in the Dark." In fact it was fundamentally limited: but the nickname demonstrates how the political elite feared democracy as a gateway to mob rule. Women could not vote at all. Upper-class women could not even appear in public without a chaperone.

Mary was the child of a love match—on one side, at least. It had been a *coup de foudre* for shy, crotchety Percy when he met dark, voluptuous Madeline Campbell in Ireland as 1860 dawned. Madeline was sensuous, earthy, physical. "People in her presence feel like trees or birds at their best, singing or flourishing according to their own natures with an easy exuberance . . . she has a peculiar gift for making this world glorious to all who meet her in it," said her son George, who never shied away from the Oedipal undertones of his relationship with his mother.

Percy and Madeline were engaged in London in July, and married in Ireland in October. During a brief interim period of separation, as Madeline returned to Ireland, Percy gave voice to his infatuation in sheaves of letters, still breathtaking in their intensity, that daily swooped across the Irish Sea. "[D]ear Glory of my Life sweet darling, dear Cobra, dear gull with the changing eyes, most precious, rare rich Madeline sweet Madge of the soft cheeks," said Percy, pouring forth his love, longing and dreams for the future. With barely concealed lust he begged Madeline to describe her bedroom so he could imagine her preparing her "dear body" for bed, and recalled, with attempted lasciviousness charming in its naivety, their brief moments of physical contact—a kiss stolen on a balcony at a ball; a moment knocked against each other in a bumpy carriage ride. "[I]f these letters don't make you *know* how I love you, let there be no more pens, ink and paper in the world."

No corresponding letters from Madeline survive. Brief fragments of reported speech suggest she was more world-weary than her besotted swain. "Oh Percy, Percy, I don't think you know very much about me, but that's no matter," she told him. Some of her descendants think that there may have been a failed love affair in her past; if so, she successfully, and characteristically, erased all trace of it. Her reserve only strengthened Percy's attraction.

Madeline's soldier father, Sir Guy Campbell (who had a baronetcy, but no fortune), had died when she was just thirteen, leaving his widow to bring up twelve children on an army pension. Madeline would receive just fifty pounds a year on her mother's death. The infatuated Percy persuaded his forbidding father—who succumbed immediately to Mad-

Percy Wyndham, in his mid-thirties, painted by his friend Frederic Leighton. The marks of Percy's privileged but emotionally chilly upbringing are plain to see in the hauteur displayed in this portrait of the young aristocrat. The greatest physical affection Percy's forbidding father ever showed his favorite son was to shake him by the scruff of his neck to keep him warm. The effusively loving Madeline Campbell transformed Percy's life.

eline's charm on meeting her—to dower his bride. A month before the Wyndhams married, £35,727 16s. 5d. in government bonds (equivalent to around $4 million today) was transferred from Lord Leconfield's Bank of England account to the trustees of Percy and Madeline's marriage settlement. The trust was to provide for Madeline and any younger children of her marriage. From the capital's interest Madeline would receive annually a personal allowance, known as pin money, of around £300. A provision stipulated that if the marriage proved childless, the money would devolve back to the Leconfields. Otherwise there was no indication that Madeline had not brought this money herself to the marriage. A baronet's genteelly impoverished seventh daughter had been effectively transformed into an heiress of the first water.

The provision was never exercised. Percy and Madeline had five adored children over the course of a decade—the three girls, and the boys George and Guy. "Ever since your birth has my Heart & Soul loved you & laughed with you & wept with you . . . [illegible] to you, to dance, & sang to you to sleep—& anguished with you in all your sorrows . . ." wrote Madeline Wyndham to her youngest, Pamela. She might have made the comment to any of her children, all of whom Percy deemed "confidential," his highest form of praise. Madeline Wyndham had been raised in a Rousseauesque environment in which she and her sisters (with no governess—doubtless partly for financial reasons) were encouraged to educate themselves, reading whatever they chose, and exploring the natural world in the fields around Woodview, their rambling house in Stillorgan, then a small village outside Dublin. Percy, raised in frigid splendor by evangelical parents who banned everything from novels to waltzing, was entranced upon first visiting Stillorgan. He vowed that his children would be raised in a similarly warm, loving and natural milieu. It has been said by George's biographer that, despite an aristocratic lifestyle, the loving intensity of life among the Wyndhams was almost bourgeois.

That lifestyle was indisputably aristocractic. An audience of staff overlooked their every move: butler, housekeeper, footmen, housemaids, cook, kitchen maids, stable boys, gardeners and the "odd-man" who lit the house's lamps each evening as dusk fell. The family rarely went anywhere without its retinue: Madeline Wyndham's lady's maid Easton (known as "Eassy"), Percy's Irish valet Thompson ("Tommy"), the children's nanny (the magnificently named Horsenail), nursemaid Emma Drake and, when the children were a little older, governesses and tutors. The Wyndhams belonged, impeccably, to "Society"—a close-knit, interconnected group, known sometimes as "the upper 10,000": being the four hundred or so families that constituted Britain's ruling class.

To outsiders Society seemed an impenetrable, corporate mass with "a common freemasonry of blood, a common education, common pursuits, common ideas, a common dialect, a common religion, and—what more than anything else binds men together—a common prestige . . . growled at occasionally, but on the whole conceded, and even, it must be owned, secretly liked by the country at large," said the Radical Bernard Cracroft in 1867. Yet by the 1860s a sea change was taking place. Following the death of her beloved Prince Albert (aged just forty-one) in 1861, Queen Victoria retreated into deepest mourning for near on a decade. The monarchy's public face—by default—became Victoria's son Bertie, Prince of Wales, the polar opposite of his high-minded father. Sybaritic Bertie's fast-living, hard-gambling Marlborough House Set was soon caught up in a number of scandals. Percy and Madeline knew the Prince and his wife, Alix, often attending the same social events. But Bertie and his friends considered Percy and Madeline's set markedly bohemian since, in the words of the novelist and designer Alice Comyns Carr, they "took a certain pride in being the first members of Society to bring the

Percy Wyndham with his eldest son, George, circa late 1860s, when Percy was in his early thirties and George four or five years old. Their relaxed pose, so different to the stiff postures adopted in most such portraits, speaks volumes about the closeness—indeed devotion—of Percy and Madeline Wyndham to their children.

people of their own set into friendly contact with the distinguished folk of art and literature."

Madeline and her aristocratic friends dressed in flowing gowns, tied their hair back simply and draped themselves in scarves and bangles. Madeline was reputedly the first woman in England to smoke, with a habit of three Turkish cigarettes a day, one after each meal. They were disciples of the Pre-Raphaelites: their bibles were Malory's *Morte d'Arthur* and Tennyson's poem of the same title. Against the backdrop of their own family seats—Scottish castles and English stately homes—they posed in medieval dress for Julia Margaret Cameron's camera. Madeline's friend Georgie Sumner even dyed her hair red to resemble more closely "stunners" like Lizzie Siddal, muse and wife of Dante Gabriel Rossetti. In London's Kensington, where an artistic colony was blooming, they frequented Little Holland House, home of Cameron's sister, Sara Prinsep, where G. F. Watts was literally the artist in residence (he moved in during a period of illness, and never left); and Leighton House, the creation of Frederic Leighton, later President of the Royal Academy. They considered Burne-Jones, then not yet famous, a genius. Madeline herself was a talented amateur artist, with a near-perfect eye and a skill for decorative arts. In 1872 she helped to found the School of Art Needlework

Madeline Wyndham in the early 1860s, after her marriage to Percy. Madeline, here in her mid-twenties, was soon to throw off the stiff crinolines of the mid-Victorian era in favor of more relaxed flowing garb, denoting her artistic instincts and her bohemian friends.

with her friend Princess Christian, one of the Queen's many daughters. In later life, she studied enameling under that craft's master, Alexander Fisher. Madeline's artist friends thought she had a true artist's soul. Beauty could cause her "thoughts that fill my heart to bursting," she told Watts: the beauty that for the Pre-Raphaelites and their heirs was a necessity: a civilizing force and civic responsibility intended to arrest the physical and spiritual ugliness of an industrial age, of the factories and urban slums sprawling across much of England.

Cumberland (now renamed, and part of Cumbria), in the northwest of England on the Scottish border, had escaped the industrialization that had blighted the landscape of the Midlands. Remote, wild, mountainous and unspoiled, even after the Cockermouth to Penrith railway line opened in 1865 it was still a full day's train journey from the capital—some ten to eleven hours. Life in Cumberland, land of the Lake District, of William Wordsworth and Samuel Taylor Coleridge, was strangely removed from the Wyndhams' normal existence. As if in a Pre-Raphaelite painting brought to life, Madeline Wyndham took her children out among the heather to draw and paint, and read aloud to them Arthurian tales. At night she sang *berceuses,* French lullabies learned from her own mother, and left them to sleep, soothed by the sound of the Cocker's rushing waters and owls hooting in the dark. She had miniature suits of armor made for George and Guy. The children played at knights and damsels with Mary dressed in her mother's long flowing skirts.

A portrait of eight-year-old Mary in Cumberland by the Wyndhams' friend Val Prinsep, in the flat, chalky style characteristic of their artistic circle, shows a tall, round-eyed beautiful child. In wide straw hat and loose mustard-yellow dress, she gazes directly at the viewer, bundling in her skirts armfuls of flowers.

One of Mary's earliest childhood adventures was scrambling after her father through thick heather up Skiddaw, the mountain dominating the Cumbrian skyline, with a trail of dogs in search of grouse; then sleeping overnight in a little lodge perched on the mountainside. In adulthood, Mary wrote lyrically of "the club & stag, the moss, the oak & beech fern, bog myrtle, & grass of Parnassus—Skiddaw in his splendid majesty— covered with 'purple patches' (of heather) with deep greens & russet reds & swept by the shadows of the clouds—my heart leaps up—when I behold—*Skiddaw*—against the sky . . ." Mary believed her Cumberland

FROM LEFT TO RIGHT: Guy Wyndham, aged three or four; Mary Wyndham, aged six or seven; and George Wyndham, aged five or six; at Cockermouth Castle in the late 1860s. Mary is wearing what looks to be a long riding skirt belonging to her mother.

Eight-year-old Mary's stillness in this 1870 portrait of her by Valentine Prinsep is uncharacteristic of the hoyden ringleader of her brothers, who kept pet bats and rooks, rode like a demon and marshaled her peers and siblings into rambunctious games.

childhood had made her a lifelong "pagan," fearlessly finding freedom in wildness. She mourned "beloved Isel" (Isel Hall being the Elizabethan manor to which the family moved from Cockermouth Castle in 1870) when the Wyndhams finally gave it up in 1876. Ever after, Cumberland was a lost Arcadia to her.

Society operated on primogeniture, accepting that parents hoped for a son. When George was born in August 1863, Lady Campbell told Percy he "deserved a boy for having so graciously received the girl last year!" In 1865 the Wyndhams had another boy, Guy. With two brothers so close to her in age, Mary was practically a boy herself. She learned to ride on a donkey given to the children by Madeline when they were toddlers, was taught to hunt and hawk by her father's valet, Tommy, and was keeping up with the hounds at just nine years old, even if, on that first occasion, she told her mother ruefully, "I did not see the fox." She kept pet rooks, which she fed on live snails, and begged her mother for permission to be taken down a Cumberland coal mine by her brothers' tutor. Some summers, the Wyndhams visited Madeline's favorite sister, Emily Ellis, at her home in Hyères, the town at the westernmost point of France's Côte d'Azur, which was becoming increasingly popular with the British. There Mary scrambled willingly along the narrow tunnels of the Grotte des Fées into a cavern of stalagmites and stalactites. While the other members of her party sat and ate oranges, she caught "a dear dear little soft downy long eared bat," which, she informed her mother, in her father's absence she had installed in his dressing room: "all day he sleeps hung up to the ceiling by his two hind legs."

High-spirited to the point of being uncontrollable, the children exhausted a stream of governesses. At Deal Castle in Kent, which looked out across the Channel to France, home of the Wyndhams' friend Admiral Clanwilliam, Captain of the Cinque Ports, marine sergeants were deputed to drill the children on the ramparts to tire them out. In London, their arrival in Belgrave Square's communal garden, clad in fishermen's jerseys, whooping and hollering on being released from their lessons, prompted celebration among their peers and anxiety among their playmates' parents. At least one couple instructed their governess not to let her charges play with "those wild Wyndham children." In Mary's stout babyhood Percy had nicknamed her "Chang" after a popular sensation, an eight-foot-tall Chinese man who entertained visitors—for a fee—at Piccadilly's Egyptian Hall. Mary grew into a "strapping lass." "How well and strong I was, never tired," she said in later life, now thin and enervated, recalling wistfully her days as a rambunctious, lanky ringleader. "I was worse than 100 boys."

Mary never mentioned her fairy-tale childhood's darker side. Intensely spiritual and religious, Madeline Wyndham concealed beneath her calm, loving exterior a mind seething with dread and paranoia. The death of both her father and a beloved elder brother in her adolescent years, against a backdrop of the "Great Hunger," the famine that, by death and emigration, diminished Ireland's population by up to a quarter, had a formative effect upon her: "the memory of death gave to the passing hours their supreme value for her," said her friend Edith Olivier, who had once looked through Madeline's vellum-bound commonplace books to find them crammed with dark thoughts. "All strange and terrible things are welcome, but comforts we despise," reads one entry. "God to her is, I think, preeminently the 'King of Glory,'" said Madeline's son George in later years, but in Madeline's mind glory came as much from darkness as from light.

When, during the Wyndhams' courtship, Madeline had confessed to bleak moods, Percy denied them. He did not think she was permanently in "low spirits," he said, advising against articulating such thoughts lest "the hearer should think them . . . permanently there when in reality they are not." For Percy, anxieties that seemed all-consuming at the time dissipated within "half an hour," a day at most, like clouds puffed across the sky. In fact, Madeline's volatile moods and her sporadic nervous collapses suggest that a strain of manic depression ran through the family—what George called the "special neurotic phenomena of his family." The impact on her children was intense. She invested in them all her apocalyptic hopes, determined they should prove her family's merit, convinced the world conspired to bring them down. It is telling that, despite her undoubted love for her mother, Mary described Percy as "one of the people—if not the one that I loved best in the world—who was unfailingly tender & who loved me more than anyone did and without whose sympathy I have never imagined life."

In 1869 the Wyndhams had a fourth child, Madeline (known as "Mananai," from what was obviously a childish attempt to pronounce her name). The death, shortly afterwards, of Percy's father, Lord Leconfield, made the wealthy young couple even wealthier. Lord Leconfield should have left almost everything in his vast estate to his disliked eldest son and heir, Henry. In a calculated, devastating snub, Leconfield instead disinherited Henry as far as he was able, bequeathing in his will everything that was not tied up in an entail—a fortune—to Percy.

Percy and his family were made beneficiaries of a trust comprising: vast tracts of land in Sussex, Yorkshire and Cumberland; the £15,000 proceeds of Lord Leconfield's life insurance; and £16,000 worth of shares in turnpike roads and gas companies. Percy received outright the family's South Australian estates (bought by Percy's maverick paternal grandfather, the third Earl of Egremont, Turner's patron and three-time winner of the Derby, for his estranged wife) and everything else Leconfield could reasonably dispose of in his many family properties—from oil paintings to plate (gold and silver dinner services), even the first choice of five carriage horses. In an undoubted attempt to ease family tensions the Wyndhams left Cockermouth Castle, renting Isel Hall a few miles away. For a while, the Wyndhams continued to visit Henry and his wife, Constance, at Petworth, but soon enough the brothers had a spectacular row over the port after dinner. The resulting estrangement between the families lasted for almost a decade, despite all the attempts of their wives, still close friends, to heal it.

Shortly after Leconfield's death, while Percy was in India visiting his sister Blanche, whose husband, Lord Mayo, was Viceroy, Lady Campbell died after a short and unexpected illness in Ireland. Madeline Wyndham, who was with her mother when she died, was bereft. Almost precisely upon Madeline and Percy's reuniting, Madeline fell pregnant again. Pamela Genevieve Adelaide, the Wyndhams' last child, was born in January 1871, at Belgrave Square like all her siblings. Percy and Madeline, now both orphaned, immensely wealthy and with their family complete, set about their new life.

With some of their new fortune, Percy and Madeline commissioned the most popular and expensive artist of their circle, Leighton, and his architect George Aitchison to decorate Belgrave Square's entrance hall. *The Cymbalists* was a magnificent mural painted above the central staircase—five life-sized, classical figures in a dance against a gold background. Above that was Aitchison's delicate frieze of flowers, foliage and wild birds in pinks, greens, greys and powder blue. Even the most unobservant visitor could see this was an artistic house.

A floor above, in the vast drawing room that overlooked Belgrave Square, hung another newly commissioned piece: a portrait by Watts of Madeline which Percy commissioned in 1867 and which took three years to complete, partly because painter and sitter enjoyed their conversations so much they were reluctant for them to end. In a nod to classical portraiture the statuesque Madeline, in her early thirties, gazes down at the viewer from a balustraded terrace. A mass of laurel, signifying nobility and glory, flourishes behind her; in the foreground a vase of magnolias denotes magnificence. Her gown is loose and splashed with sunflowers, proclaiming her allegiance to the Pre-Raphaelite world; the gaze from hooded eyes under swooping dark brows is direct and forthright. When the portrait was publicly exhibited some years later at the opening of the Grosvenor Gallery, a private venture of the Wyndhams' friends Sir Coutts and Lady Lindsay on London's New Bond Street, it caught the eye of Henry James, who was reviewing the exhibition for the *Galaxy.* "It is what they call a 'sumptuous' picture . . . That is, the lady looks as if she had thirty thousand a year," said James, recognizing that the aristocrat effortlessly superseded the artist.

Percy engaged in his wife's artistic interests, developing a reputation as a patron himself. At heart, he remained a Tory squire of the oldest sort, never happier than when riding to hounds and believing in his God-given duty to rule wisely the tenantry on his estate and in that of his class to govern the country as a whole. The Tories were the party of the monarchy, the Church of England and the status quo. Fearing constantly the unruly demos, for Tories, authority was "like a somber fortress, holding down an unpredictable population that might, at any moment, lay siege to it."

To the political spectrum's left were William Gladstone's Liberals. This polyglot alliance, brought to power by the expanded electorate in its first General Election of 1868, combined Celtic and Northern religious nonconformists wanting to disestablish the Church, Radicals seeking social change and a powerful clique of grandees, known as "Whigs," whose ancestors had ruled eighteenth-century Britain. On coming to power, Gladstone, a redoubtable fire-and-brimstone orator, immediately announced his divinely ordained mission to "pacify Ireland" (provoked, in part, by the recent Fenian bombing of Clerkenwell Prison), disestablished the Irish Church, and dealt several blows to the hold of Britain's elite over its institutions with meritocracy-promoting measures such as competitive Civil Service exams; the abolition of army commissions allowing the purchase of senior posts; and the removal of the religious "test" which had limited university fellowships at Oxford, Cambridge and Durham to Anglicans. His actions confirmed the Tories' worst fears about the imminent destruction of their way of life.

For Percy, Gladstone's popular appeal exemplified the danger of mass enfranchisement that—as expressed in *The English Constitution* by the celebrated political theorist Walter Bagehot—"both our political parties will bid for the support of the working man" and a "set of poor ignorant people" would be corrupted by "two combinations of well-taught and rich men" competing for their favor and "defer[ring] to their decision." Percy's children, raised as instinctive, loyal Conservatives, thought, like him, that Gladstone was a hypocritical demagogue. They had no difficulty in combining their Irish sympathies with their father's conception of power.

Life at Belgrave Square was extravagantly luxurious. Despite Percy's caviling (he disliked excessive socializing, much preferring the company of a chosen few "confidentials"), Madeline Wyndham kept open table in the eighteenth-century style, with sometimes forty people unexpectedly sitting down to lunch. Generous with her affection and material goods alike, Madeline Wyndham never spoke of the sudden change in her fortunes brought about by marriage, only fondly recollecting an Irish childhood in a "nest of lovely sisters" visiting relations in pony and trap. Her vague, bohemian warmth concealed to most her acute awareness of social gradations, exemplified by her assiduous cultivation of the boring Princess Christian as a friend. "*You* and Papa are rather *stupid* about knowing who people are!!" she told Mary, only half jokingly, as she discussed the "belongings" of fellow house party guests—by which she meant their connections and titles. "She is a humbug," declared the middle-class Philip Burne-Jones (son of Edward and Georgiana), finding that Madeline's warmth towards him as a family friend cooled rapidly when he tried to court Mary, with whom he had been in love since childhood. Madeline Wyndham could not contemplate a middle-class husband for her daughter, no matter how artistic. Her ambitions for her family were tied up with her anxiety to prove that Percy's gamble in marrying her had paid off. When her daughters married, she was terrified that one might bear a child with some "defect." She clearly feared what might be latent in her blood.

In the early 1870s, Madeline had an affair with Percy's cousin and close friend Wilfrid Scawen Blunt, a handsome poet who had spent part of his childhood living in a cottage on the Petworth estate. Blunt and his wife, Lady Anne (a granddaughter of the poet Lord Byron), were Arabists and explorers. They traveled voraciously in the Middle East, spoke Arabic, and lived part of the year at Sheykh Obeyd, their Egyptian estate just outside Cairo. Both wore Bedouin dress—Blunt, even in England. At Crabbet Park, Blunt's Sussex estate, which lay not far from Petworth, they founded a successful stud farm breeding Arab horses—"everyone went to the Arab sale at Crabbet," wrote the journalist Katharine Tynan, recalling Janey Morris, John Ruskin and the Pattle sisters sweeping through the beautiful grounds.

Blunt was notorious in political circles as an iconoclastic anti-imperialist troublemaker. Socially he was equally mistrusted as a lothario capable of seducing any man's wife. Yet this inveterate womanizer's diaries, in which he recorded every conquest (albeit sometimes a little embroidered), show him as nothing so much as a perplexed cork buffeted on the waves of strong women's personalities. With each affair, Blunt made grand plans for a lifelong passion. Almost invariably, his paramours called it off, returning to their husbands enlivened by their brief dalliance.

Blunt had always found Madeline seductive—"a tall strong woman, such as are the fashion now," and while he presented their affair as a meeting of artistic minds, Madeline was equally physically attracted to

Madeline Wyndham with the toddler
Pamela on her lap at Hyères, France,
1873. On the reverse, Madeline has
scribbled a note to Wilfrid Blunt,
making clear the distress their affair
was causing to her husband, Percy.

him. The affair—a series of piecemeal dalliances ranging from romantic
visits to Watts's studio in London to trysts among the olive groves of
Hyères—seems to have been an escape for Madeline from her sometimes
"overpowering" domestic life: the demands of her children and an adoring but irascible husband whose interests did not always coincide with
hers. Blunt maintained that it never diminished Madeline's familial love:
"What she gave to me was not a plunder robbed from any other. Her
tenderness was no mere weakness of the heart, but its strength . . . proving its wealth . . ."

Wilfrid glossed over the pain this affair caused Percy—and indeed
Madeline. Among Wilfrid's papers is a photograph of Madeline with
Pamela upon her lap. Madeline is in mourning, presumably for her
brother-in-law the Viceroy, assassinated while in his post in 1872. She
wears an elaborate dark hat that shades her hooded eyes. Her features
have refined with age. She is leaner and finer than Watts's voluptuous
beauty of three years before, and almost sad. Tousle-haired Pamela sits
on her lap, eyes skyward as though trying to glimpse her mother's face
even as Madeline grasps her daughter firmly around her stout waist. On
the back of this photograph is a note in Madeline's handwriting: frag-
mentary, it appears to have been written in a hurry. Wilfrid must not

come to look for her until later. "I think [Percy] is not happy at finding me not alone he has not said it but I think it . . . my heart fails me . . . you *have* chosen the lowest oh it makes me so sad—I don't know why my heart is not up to it I have no courage . . ."

In 1873 the Wyndhams rented Château Saint-Pierre, a neo-Gothic pile near to Emily and Charley Ellis in Hyères. They settled their children there with nurse, governess and tutor, and left for several months' travel across France and Italy, sightseeing and buying art. This trip—undoubtedly intended as a second honeymoon—was the Wyndhams' longest absence, by far, from their children throughout their childhood. The following year, Percy took the lease of Wilbury Park in Newton Toney, some ten miles from Salisbury on the Wiltshire Downs. The area was beautiful, mythic (ancient Stonehenge lay not far away) and conveniently accessible from London by rail. Madeline could maintain her life among the city's aristocratic art crowd, while Percy could enjoy excellent hunting and shooting and reasonable trout fishing. In later life, no doubt inspired by personal experience, Madeline wrote her daughters impassioned warnings (scored with underlining and written in her trademark purple ink) about the dangers of drifting from their husbands. Wilbury was to arrest that drift.

The affair finally ended only in 1875, at Madeline's behest. "What is this prate of friendship?" wrote Wilfrid furiously in a sonnet. In his diary, sore-pawed, he attacked Madeline as "a pottery goddess" and neither "beautiful, or wise, or good. Her beauty is a little too refined, her wisdom too fantastic, her goodness too selfish . . ." Casting aside his fantasies of a life together with her, he tried to dismiss the affair: "it was all pleasure, of a high sensual kind . . . Its departure caused no unbearable sorrow . . . I did not grieve for her because I knew she did not grieve for me . . ."

A veil was drawn over the incident. But between Madeline and Wilfrid there remained some friction. Many years later Madeline advised Pamela that the power "not to fret over spilt milk is a great *faculty* it almost amounts to wisdom." Years of "*experience* & hard toil" had taught her to let go of the regret "that kills." Madeline did not say what that regret was. One can hazard a guess.

TWO

Wilbury

In the late 1870s, with relations once again on an even keel, the Blunts visited the Wyndhams at Wilbury. As Wilfrid left, he kissed Mary on the cheek: "in a cousinly way." Mary blushed. Afterwards, Madeline scolded her with unusual and uncharacteristic vehemence. The incident, notable enough for Mary to remember it twenty years later, suggests that the adolescent knew something of the affair just past. It is also a rare chink in the Wyndham armor, a moment when one of Percy's "remarkable quintette"—in his words—lets slip something suggesting their family life was not so perpetually sunlit as they maintained.

Percy and Madeline's devotion to their children and their disregard for convention generated intense familial closeness. George spoke of "the Wyndham-religion"; Mary's daughter Cynthia echoed him: "Family love was almost a religion with the Wyndhams." A legendary anecdote—familiar to almost all their contemporaries—concerned Percy impatiently shushing his collected dinner guests, hissing, "Hush. Hush! George is going to speak!" as his schoolboy son prepared to give the table his views. Ettie Desborough, close friends with Mary and George, an intimate of the royal family and herself one of the most glamorous women of the age, described this clan as being bred up with the pride of Plantagenets. Their loyalty was fearsome. They would never listen to criticism of their own, far less give it.

The poet and self-styled iconoclast Wilfrid Scawen Blunt in his youth. With looks like these, it is understandable why Percy Wyndham's favorite cousin and friend was such a prolific seducer of the women of his acquaintance, including Percy's wife.

At the time of Wilfrid's visit to Wilbury, Mary was in her mid-teens, awkward, lanky, childish for her age. She was devoted to her dog Crack, a thirteenth-birthday present, and her pet rat Snowy. She adored the caricatures of Dickens and the historical romances of Sir Walter Scott. She had inherited her mother's artistic talent, and spent hours making elaborate cards and teasing cartoon sketches for her younger sisters, to whom she was known by a host of nicknames, "Black Witch," "Sister Rat" and "Migs" (or "Mogs") being just a few. She was a devotee of "Spression"—a sort of pidgin English mixed with baby talk that she spoke with her closest friend, Margaret Burne-Jones, given somatic form by cartoons drawn by Edward Burne-Jones for them, endearingly shapeless animals that have been described as part pig, part dog, part wombat.

An insight into Mary's character comes from one of her most vivid childhood memories, probably from the summer of 1875, which she spent at Deal Castle—a place she thought "must be haunted by my girl spirit I was there so much"—while recovering from whooping cough. She remembered sitting by the moat and, in a "moment of cruel curiosity," feeding a live bluebottle fly to a "huge spider [with] shining eyes." As Mary recalled, she was immediately "seized with remorse and probably killed both in righteous wrath." It is not too tendentious to extrapo-

Bertha Schneider, or "Bun," in her early thirties, a few years into her tenure with the Wyndhams. In old age, Bun returned to her native Germany but never lost touch with her charges. She was rewarded for her lifetime's service to the family with a legacy (in the region of $13,500 today) in Percy's will.

late from this fundamental elements of her character. She had a delight for the gruesome (demonstrated by a zestful account to her mother of a bilious attack aged eighteen: "I brought up *basins* of the thickest, gluest [*sic*] phlegm, slime, burning excruciating yellow acid with little streaks of browny reddy stuff in it, sometimes great gollops of brown fluid . . . Lastly Tuesday morning, came green bile"), a curious mind and an adventurous spirit. She had an inclination to "choose to prefer the gratification of the present . . . to slide & glide because it was pleasant or amusing & exciting & to face & *bear* the consequences *when* they came." In adulthood, Wilfrid thought Mary sphinx-like in her inscrutability, speaking of her "unfathomable reserve . . . her secrets are close shut, impenetrably guarded, with a little laugh of unconcern baffling the curious." Wilfrid was all too frequently baffled by women, but Pamela described her sister in similar terms, speaking of a "deep nature" that only Mary's closest friends truly knew.

In adulthood, Mary became renowned as a member of the Souls, an "intellectual" set of the aristocracy. Her education gave her little grounding. "An air of Bohemian quasi-culture" prevailed among the Wyndhams, who were artistic rather than intellectual. George and Guy, as a matter of course, were educated at Eton College, England's most famous and elite educational establishment; like their father, they eschewed university in favor of Sandhurst, the officer-training military academy. Like most upper-class girls of her generation, Mary was educated, in somewhat lackluster fashion, by governesses and, for the most part, deliberately not too well, lest it scare off suitors. "A woman's only hope of self-expression in those days was through marriage," explained Mabell Airlie, a near contemporary. Marriage was the only career ever contemplated for Mary, whose life was untouched by the strides made in women's education in the 1870s. The establishment of academic girls' schools and the admission of women as undergraduates by some forward-thinking institutions such as London University primarily benefited middle-class daughters. Mary's governess, Bertha Schneider, or "Bun," was originally from Saxony and had been poached from the Belgrave Square family who forbade their children from playing with the Wyndhams. She joined the family when she was twenty-eight. A photograph of her some years later shows her to have a pleasant, somewhat clumsy-featured face, pince-nez spectacles and fashionably frizzled hair.

Her brothers' departure for boarding prep school (to prepare them for Eton) coincided with the Wyndhams' move to Wilbury and domesticated Mary. From roaming across Cumberland's hills with a pair of ragamuffin playmates, she found herself in a tamer Wiltshire landscape in the company of Bun and sisters of just three and five. At sixteen Mary's day consisted of breakfast at 8 a.m., lessons from 9 a.m. until 2 p.m., "déjeuner" (lunch), some time outside—collecting ferns, blackberry picking, long walks or games of the new sport of lawn tennis— lessons from 4 until 6, dinner at 7, and reading aloud with Fräulein until bed. This was supplemented, during "term times" (dictated by the boys' holidays), by fortnightly music lessons from a Mr. Farmer in London and art classes at the Kensington School of Art. Each autumn Bun took Mary and the little girls to a Felixstowe boardinghouse on the Suffolk coast for "sea air," where they rode donkeys, ate potted shrimps, paddled in the sea and read aloud, endlessly, to one another. By the time they left Eton in their late teens, George and Guy had a tolerable grounding in the basics of Latin, Greek, astronomy, history and public speaking. After the same number of years of education by Fräulein, Mary was relatively well read so long as the literature was popular; spoke good French and German (with a ripe vocabulary in the latter); could play the piano; and could draw proficiently, having taken exams in the subject at the Kensington School of Art. ("I forget what it was now," she said vaguely, when pressed by her mother on the subject of her exam. "It had some sort of foliage.") Mary spent much of her adult life wading gamely through heavy tomes on esoteric subjects. In effect, she was an autodidact. Her education was rigor-free, her brain almost totally untrained.

Twenty years after she left home, Mary read over her adolescent diaries, recalling fondly the "happy life . . . that we all spent at Wilbury": games of sardines and nights of ghost stories, hunting and hawking in the winter, summer cricket matches and a host of friends and neighbors nearby. Philip Burne-Jones remembered Wilbury—a Palladian jewel of a house set on 140 acres of land—as a kind of heaven, "with the sun pouring down upon the lawn . . . and all the magic of youth & impossible hopes in the air." With his sister Margaret he participated in the stage-struck family's ambitious amateur productions, for which Madeline Wyndham constructed elaborate sets and costumes and refused to take any role with more lines than could be pinned to the back of her fan. Before an audience of servants, groundsmen and stray visitors, Mary and Philip played the leads; Pamela and Mananai were pages and fairies. Bun gamely took on whatever her assigned role—excelling herself, in collective memory, with an enthusiastic Caliban so lovelorn that Tommy the valet thought the character was a woman, and married to Prospero.

In London Mary and Madeline Wyndham frequently visited the Burne-Jones family at The Grange, their house in Fulham, once a village on London's outskirts, now scooped up in the urban sprawl. Mary loved these visits where Burne-Jones amused the children by playing wheelbarrows in the garden with Georgiana, holding her ankles while she walked on her hands, and told them fireside stories of his youth with William Morris, Dante Gabriel Rossetti and Lizzie Siddal in Bloomsbury's Red Lion Square. On occasion, Mary stayed overnight, sharing a bed with Margaret Burne-Jones, waking up in the morning to breakfast in bed and to chat "yards of nonsense" in "Spression."

Percy—a squire without a domain—had always intended to look for a suitable estate of his own. In 1876, the Wyndhams found the enchantingly named Clouds, a parcel of four thousand acres of land at East Knoyle, a village a little west of Salisbury. Percy sold Much Cowarne, the similarly sized Herefordshire estate he had inherited at the age of twenty-one (which he used purely for income, possibly never even visiting), and bought Clouds for just over £100,000. He immediately commissioned

Philip Webb, the visionary architect of William Morris's Red House, to design and build what was intended "to be the house of the family for generations to come."

Percy was building a family seat while his contemporaries questioned how they could maintain theirs. He could do so only because his fortune had the ungentlemanlike foundation of stocks and Australian estates. British land, for centuries the backbone of elite wealth, was ceasing to provide. Free trade was a fundamental political tenet for this commercial nation. But from the 1870s, domestic producers struggled to compete with New World imports (grain from the American prairies, refrigerated and canned goods from the Antipodes). Average wheat prices fell from fifty-five shillings to twenty-eight shillings a quarter between 1870 and 1890. Agricultural rents dipped. "Land has ceased to be either a profit or a pleasure. It gives one a position, and prevents one from keeping it up," declared Lady Bracknell in Oscar Wilde's *The Importance of Being Earnest*, written in 1895. Percy had no such concerns. He played with Home Farm, carved out of the Clouds estate for his own management, like a small boy with an entrancing toy. "He has made £184:10s by the sale of all his sheep and £146:15s by sale of wool and now has 190 lambs. His corn is in, 11 ricks of wheat, 5 of barley, 6 of oats," Mary told her diary in 1878.

Percy's parliamentary career had stalled on the backbenches, where MPs who do not hold government office sit. This may have been due partly to Percy's independent spirit: in an age of fast-growing party machinery designed to make MPs toe the party line, Percy (one of the few men in politics to advocate the heresy of protectionism rather than free trade) maintained the free-thinking approach of an older age. He "held his own principles and opinions unswervingly; and they were not always those of his party," his son Guy later wrote. Another probable cause was Percy's ungovernable temper, all too familiar to his children, nor ever properly concealed from his contemporaries, and which it has been suggested prompted his party's leader, Disraeli, from ever summoning Percy to higher office.

Disraeli, half genius, half charlatan, had returned the Conservatives from six years in the wilderness in 1874. "We have been borne down in a torrent of gin and beer," mourned Gladstone, blaming the unpopularity of the liquor-licensing limits promoted by his party's temperate nonconformists. Disraeli further wooed the voting classes (rendered still more independent by introduction of the Secret Ballot in 1872) and his Queen with an aggressively populist imperialist foreign policy. His breathtakingly audacious actions were underpinned by the principle that no action was too morally bankrupt so long as the imperial lodestone, India, was safe. Securing a loan from his friend, the banking tycoon Lord Rothschild, and without consulting Parliament, Disraeli bought the controlling interest in the Suez Canal Company from Egypt's bankrupt ruler, the Khedive, on the nation's behalf. The man-made waterway cutting through from the Mediterranean to the Red Sea was Britain's main route to India. Under some pressure from Victoria, he turned the Queen into the Empress of India, an act Gladstone denounced as "theatrical folly and bombast." He stood by the Ottoman Turks, notorious for the "Bulgarian Atrocities" committed when crushing rebellion in the Balkans, since the Ottomans were a bulwark against Russian expansion that might threaten the Raj. When Russia invaded the Balkans, Britain sent warships to the Dardanelles and mobilized Indian troops to Malta, and its music halls rang to the popular refrain "We don't want to fight, but, by Jingo if we do, / We've got the ships; we've got the men; we've got the money too!" The Conservatives were the party of patriotism, monarchy and empire; "jingoism" was in the ascendant.

Percy's attentions during these years were focused on designing and building Clouds. It took until 1881 to agree on drawings and find an acceptable tender from builders. Work was not finished until 1885. The ascetic Webb asked just £4,000 for his decade of labor. It is a mark of Percy and Webb's instinctive affinity that the two difficult men never fell out during the long process, beyond one protracted dispute over the buff color of the glazed bricks used in the stables. Webb became a familiar figure at Wilbury. When Mary's pet rat Snowy died, Webb provided an epitaph for the gravestone.

In the early summer of 1878, Madeline Wyndham took Mary, still not quite sixteen, to Cologne, in Germany, to be "finished." Mary retained fond memories of her months there, spent cramming in as many operas as possible and visiting cultural attractions like the Goethe House and the Jewish Quarter. Their return to Wilbury several weeks later was welcomed. "I am so glad glad glad glad glad that you are coming home . . ." wrote Mananai. Pamela, who swore that she could not sleep when her mother was away, maintained her usual signing off: "I love you and I've got you and I won't let you GO." A few months of Wagner was not enough to rub off the rough edges acquired over a lifetime of boisterousness: "Mary has upset the milk over her forock [*sic*]," Pamela informed her parents a few weeks after Mary's return, "but not the same one she tore yesterday."

That autumn, Mary sat entranced at the dinner table as Percy and Webb discussed the latest cause célèbre: the painter James McNeill Whistler's libel case against John Ruskin, the most famous critic of the day. The case had arisen out of the Grosvenor Gallery's opening the year before. A privately funded enterprise of the Wyndhams' friends Sir Coutts and Blanche Lindsay, the gallery, which, as advertised in *The Times*, was open daily to the public for a shilling was intended to champion the avant garde (in particular, Burne-Jones, who had not exhibited publicly for over a decade) and challenge the conservative Royal Academy. Many of the opening exhibition's pictures came from their friends' collections, and the gallery itself—all velvet sofas and potted palms— looked like a very expensive private house. The Wyndhams loaned two: *Nocturne: Grey and Gold—Westminster Bridge,* a Whistler that Percy had bought some two years before on a whim when passing Piccadilly's Dudley Gallery; and the magnificent Watts of Madeline. They attended the gallery's opening night, both Lady Lindsay's "magnificent banquet" for the inner circle, including the Prince of Wales and three of his siblings, and the larger reception in the silk-damasked, marble-columned galleries upstairs, to which critics and lesser personages were invited.

That opening made Burne-Jones famous and brought to notoriety the undergraduate Oscar Wilde, who caused a sensation in a velvet coat embroidered to look like a cello. Wilde was soon to earn his own fame as a magazine columnist (instructing *House Beautiful*'s readership on aesthetic living) and a lecturer (touring America in velvet breeches with a green carnation buttonhole). The public, adopting the fashions that Madeline and her friends had cultivated for over a decade, flocked to Liberty's department store on London's Regent Street for murky silks and sludgy velvets. Madeline's School of Art Needlework ("Royal" since securing Queen Victoria's patronage in 1875), which had long been producing Burne-Jones designs, moved to larger premises to accommodate demand. Sunflowers, peacocks and blue and white china, aestheticism's motifs, appeared everywhere. George du Maurier in the satirical weekly

Punch and the librettist and composer duo Gilbert and Sullivan joyfully let loose on the pretensions of the "greenery-yallery Grosvenor Gallery" and its devotees.

On that opening night, however, the great critic Ruskin was mostly struck by Whistler's effrontery in exhibiting work with so little apparent finish. "I have seen, and heard, much of Cockney impudence before now but never expected to hear a coxcomb ask two hundred guineas for flinging a pot of paint in the public's face," he wrote in *Fors Clavigera*, a series of pamphlets intended to morally and socially educate the British workingman. Whistler sued for libel, claiming *inter alia* that since Ruskin's review he had not been able to achieve a price comparable to that which Percy paid for his *Nocturne*. Mary, like the art world, was agog: "so funny," she wrote in her diary, "the jury going to Westminster Palace Hotel to examine the pictures, and hearing Mr. Burne-Jones, Whistler, W. M. Rossetti and all of them in the *witness* box."

Six months later, Madeline Wyndham took Mary and George, home for the holidays, to Leighton House for one of Leighton's famed chamber-music afternoons that introduced rising musical stars—Halle, Piatti, Joachim—to Society. Among the guests was Arthur Balfour, in his early thirties, Conservative Member for Hertford.

Balfour, who once said, "Nothing matters very much, and most things don't matter at all," was not one who thought politics should govern life. He maintained a keen interest in philosophy—the best known of his works, *Foundations of Belief*, was published in 1895—and held musical concerts at his own house, 4 Carlton Gardens, for which he had recently commissioned Burne-Jones to create a series of murals. Despite six years in the Commons and impeccable political connections as the favorite nephew of the Marquess of Salisbury (tipped to succeed the elderly Disraeli when the time came), Balfour was not to make his political name until the next ministry, as part of a maverick quartet known as the Fourth Party, who devoted their time to harassing in equal measure the Liberal Government and their own ineffectual Leader in the Commons, Sir Stafford Northcote.

Notwithstanding his limited political success, Balfour's impeccable pedigree and wealth (he had inherited from his dead father a nabob fortune—the term used to describe those whose riches came from working for the East India Company in the Indian subcontinent—and the prosperous Whittingehame estate in Scotland) made him a prime target for ambitious Society matrons with marriagable daughters. Above all, tall, dark-haired, humorous Balfour was charming: "He has but to smile and men and women fall prone at his feet," said Mary Gladstone, who had been besotted with him for years and whose father, William, considered him a protégé, despite their opposing political stances. Fifty years later, the Liberal journalist Harold Begbie commented caustically on Balfour's undimmed charm: "I have seen many [people] retire from shaking his hand with a flush of pride on their faces as though Royalty had stooped to inquire after the measles of their youngest child." Some years later, when Mary Wyndham was newly married, a friend would comment worriedly on her attitude towards Arthur: "He fascinates her—her attitude is that of looking up in wonder . . . Thinks him good . . ." Both Mary and George were fascinated that day. Their lives would ever after be entwined with his. And an elderly Balfour, attempting an autobiography, would put down his pen at precisely the moment he met the seventeen-year-old Mary Wyndham among the chattering crowds at Leighton House.

THREE

"The Little Hunter"

At three o'clock on an early-summer afternoon in 1880, Madeline Wyndham presented Mary at the Royal Drawing Room in Buckingham Palace. This was Mary's "passport to Society": her formal entry to her parents' world. Each spring, aristocratic households decamped, children, staff and all, to London for the Season. One year at Wilbury, Mary counted thirty-six boxes of luggage stacked up in the hall. The Drawing Rooms, ostensibly the most important element of the Season, required attendees, in stifling formal dress, to spend hours waiting to gain entry to the Palace. Crammed into ornate carriages attended by bewigged coachmen and liveried footmen, they sat in nose-to-tail traffic on the Mall that sometimes snaked back through St. James's Park, while the crowds thronging to the spectacle passed bawdy, affectionate comment.

The pageant along the Mall was a glorious affirmation of the social order, proving Henry James's observation that "nowhere so much as in England was it fortunate to be fortunate." As so often, the interplay between pageantry and power was more subtle. Over the course of a century, the traditions surrounding Britain's monarchy had become more elaborate as the reality of its sovereign power decreased. Similarly, as the century progressed, the patricians felt their hegemony being undermined and even overtly attacked.

After six years of Disraeli, Gladstone stormed back to power in 1880 on the back of his Midlothian Campaign. Then, as now, a Prime Minister is not directly elected. Ballot is by constituency, and the "first past the post" with the most votes becomes that constituency's Member of Parliament. By convention, the monarch invites the MP leading the party with the most parliamentary seats to become Prime Minister. Gladstone's campaign in Midlothian was ostensibly for a constituency. In reality, it was a national platform to inveigh against the moral iniquities of "Beaconsfieldism," for Victoria had rewarded Disraeli for her imperial crown with an earl's coronet making him Earl of Beaconsfield.

Gladstone's campaign was one of the first truly modern political campaigns although this whistle-stop railway tour of the North was more like a religious revival as the master orator lamented Britain's failure to act as the watchdog of weaker nations. People fainted in the crush of thousands and were handed out over the heads of those around them. Reports of Gladstone's latest address rattled across the wires to Fleet Street and were blazoned across the press. Gladstone's enemies deplored his demagogic approach. But the "GOM" ("Grand Old Man"), as he was now known, was the nation's moral compass, his party triumphant. Queen Victoria, mourning the loss of her favorite Disraeli, was in despair. Following an abortive attempt to buck convention by inviting the aristocratic Whig Lord Hartington to form a government (Hartington refused), the Queen was forced to accept the inevitable and invite this "half-mad firebrand" (in her words) to be her Prime Minister a second time.

Throughout Britain, tensions were inflamed. Far from pacifying Ireland, Gladstone had enraged it with halfhearted measures of reform. In addition to a raging Land War, waged by the peasantry against their absentee landlords and masterminded by the shadowy Land League, Gladstone now had to contend with the increasingly powerful Irish Parliamentary Party, which demanded Home Rule: a measure—as yet unspecified—of self-governance for Ireland. That the head of the league and the party was the same man, the half-American Protestant landowner Charles Stewart Parnell, exemplified how land and politics intertwined. Britain as a whole was on the verge of a violent, nationwide economic depression as real wages, which had risen steadily throughout the 1870s, began to slump and arable farming continued year on year in greater distress. Calls for electoral reform were growing in volume. Socialism was taking its first tottering steps into the political consciousness of the intelligentsia and the English working class. In 1883 Lord Salisbury, Eeyore-like in his perpetual gloom, published "Disintegration," an essay predicting the breakdown of the social and political order as a result of mass enfranchisement.

For the aristocratic dowagers who, gorgon-like, lined the ballroom walls of Mary's world, the more present threat came from capitalism: plutocratic fortunes from industry and finance trying to force entry into their hallowed drawing rooms and their children's beds. The Season was a marriage market for the children of the elite, although matches were "facilitated" by careful parents rather than expressly arranged. Access to that market thus needed to be strictly regulated. Throughout the 1880s the cry went up from within Society that the ruling class was losing its exclusivity. The percentage of women from the titled and landed classes presented at court fell from 90 percent in 1841 to 68 percent in 1871, to under 50 percent in 1891. Meanwhile the number of presentations was steadily increasing. In 1880, the year of Mary's debut, a fourth drawing room was added to the social calendar, in 1895 a fifth. "Society, in the old sense of the term, may be said, I think, to have come to an end in the 'eighties' of the last century," said Lady Dorothy Nevill in 1910. The anxiety this caused was immense. "Let any person who knows London society look through the lists of debutantes and ladies attending drawing rooms and I wager that not half the names will be known to him or her," thundered one dowager in 1891, inveighing against the advent of "social scum and nouveaux riches."

In fact, the English elite's permeability is a key reason for its continued survival. Its education system—Eton and Oxbridge—could soon enough turn the son of "social scum" into a gentleman indistinguishable from one of hallowed bloodline. It required thick skin though. Mary's friends Laura and Margot Tennant, the daughters of the Scottish industrialist Sir Charles Tennant, great-great-granddaughters of a crofter, found that even after securing presentation at court, most doors were still closed to them. For Margot, social entrée came only when she managed to engage the Prince of Wales in conversation in the Royal Enclosure at Ascot. "I felt my spirits rise, as, walking slowly across the crowded lawn in grilling sunshine, I observed everyone making way for us with lifted hats and low curtsies," she recalled. Even after the Tennant girls' entry into Society their father was always known, in barely concealed mockery of the nouveaux riches, as "the Bart"—a reference to the baronetcy of which he was so obviously proud.

Aristocratic if bohemian Mary had access everywhere and could ruffle feathers with aplomb. Writing her own memoir in later life, she remembered an incident with a young Oxford undergraduate, George Curzon, where the dancing couple:

> received the full impact of handsome Lady Bective's train, formed of masses and masses and layers and layers of black tulle wired and strapped, about as heavy and powerful as a whale's tail. It caught us broadside with immense force and we were swept off our feet and [hurled] to the ground and fell at my mother's feet, our heads almost under the small hard gold chair on which she was patiently sitting as chaperone.

In old age, validated by decades of social success, Mary could look back on such youthful exuberance with pride. For her contemporaneous feelings we must turn elsewhere. Not to her diary: the journal that Mary kept religiously from the age of sixteen until her death was an object of record, not of confidence, and her entries were generally masterpieces of pragmatism. That for 8 October 1884, by no means untypical, reads: "Put on orange frock, went down to tea, sat in draft, rested, black." It is far better to look to her sketches. On scraps of paper she drew top-hatted men about town carrying silver canes and strolling ladies in bustles and magnificent hats by day, drooping elegantly over their fans in ball gowns by night. She drew herself in balldress, shivering with cold in the early hours of the morning; bundled up against the spring cold in an umbrella and a muff; and on horseback, elegant in her riding habit, brandishing her riding crop under dripping trees in Hyde Park's Rotten Row. On the back of an embossed thick card inviting "The Hon Percy & Mrs. Wyndham & Miss Wyndham" to one of Buckingham Palace's two Court Balls each season is a caricature of herself entitled "Miss Parrot at the Ball"; she teased her little sisters with sketches depicting "Pretty Mary and her plain sisters."

These sketches show the curious eye of an eager young woman getting to grips with the rules of a new, sophisticated world. Around this time Mary visited Dr. Lorenzo Niles Fowler, a fashionable American

Arthur Balfour in his early thirties, circa late 1870s at around the time he met Mary. Balfour had inherited a fortune, including the Whittingehame estate, at the age of eight when his father died. He and his seven siblings were raised by their redoubtable mother, Lady Blanche, a daughter of the 2nd Marquess of Salisbury, through whom they were related to the politically influential Cecil clan. Lady Blanche's brother and Arthur's uncle Robert, the 3rd Marquess Salisbury, was Britain's Prime Minister as the century turned. The Balfour clan excelled in the sciences: Arthur's brother Francis became a professor at Cambridge University and his sister Eleanor principal of one of its first all-women colleges. Arthur himself had hoped to become a philosopher but was dissuaded by his mother, who told him that within a few years he would have run out of things to say.

phrenologist, in his Piccadilly offices. Phrenology, the art of analyzing character by skull shape, is now discredited, not least for its unsavory associations with eugenics. In the 1880s, it was Society's latest craze. Dr. Fowler must have been perceptive, since his report is curiously accurate. It describes an unself-conscious young woman, young for her years, and happy to let others—particularly her mother—take the lead; combative, but quick to forgive; loyal; easily interested in other people. Dr. Fowler also identified a normally well-hidden element of Mary's personality. "You are remarkable for your ambition in one form or another," he said, commenting on her desire "to appear well in society, to attract attention, & to be admired." This was undoubtedly true, albeit something Mary herself would always disavow. She visited Dr. Fowler at least twice more, taking her future husband with her too. Even given her love of novelty—Mary was always enthusiastic about the latest craze—it suggests she found some merit in his analysis.

The conventional expectation of a debutante was to marry as soon as possible, preferably in her first Season. Too long a delay, and, in the words of Mabell Airlie, "there remained nothing but India as a last resort before the specter of the Old Maid became a reality." Mary's parents were not so conventional, thinking eighteen too young to take on the responsibility of a husband and household, and reluctant to lose their daughter so soon. Yet while Mary later declared that "many wanted me to wife!" she did not become engaged until her fourth Season, in 1883. This delay was longer than Madeline Wyndham—responsible for guiding her daughter towards a suitable match, determined to prove her family's worth by securing a splendid one—had hoped.

In the autumn of 1880 Balfour invited Mary and her parents to Strathconan, his hunting lodge in the Scottish Highlands. The visit was not a success. Mary was tongue-tied with awkwardness: in her own words, "a shy Miss Mog . . . feeling very stiff & studying Green's history & strumming Bach most conscientiously listening with silent awe to the flashing repartee, the witticisms & above all the startling aplomb of 'grown-up conversation.' " It may have been this muteness that gave rise to the story that some of Mary's circle had initially thought her a little backward.

In London, Madeline and Mary invited Balfour to the Lyceum to see Ellen Terry in *Much Ado About Nothing.* Forever after the play would fill Mary with "a peculiar kind of sadness." Twenty years on she remembered the evening with startling clarity: "We sat in a box and when the audience tittered at the wrong part you said savagely 'I would gladly wring their necks' and I remember the sense of vague dissatisfaction when it was all over—the evening—one of my little efforts," she recalled to Balfour. Balfour subsequently declined Madeline Wyndham's invitations to visit the family at Wilbury. By the code of the times, it was an overt rebuff, rejecting the opportunity to spend time with Mary away from the prying eyes of all but a few fellow guests. By the end of Mary's second Season it was clear that the affair had come to nothing.

Looking back over the abortive courtship many years later, Mary blamed her shyness and Balfour's cowardice: "Mama wanted you to marry me [but] you got some silly notion in your head because . . . circumstances accidentally kept us apart—you were the only man I wanted for my husband and it's a great compliment to you! . . . but you wouldn't give me a chance of showing you nicely and you never came to Wilbury and you were afraid, afraid, afraid!" she teased him.

Many biographers have examined in some detail why Balfour never married. It has been suggested that the "Pretty Fanny" of press caricatures was gay, even a hermaphrodite. His devoted niece Blanche Dugdale suggested that he was nursing a lifelong broken heart after the death from typhoid in 1875 of his close friend May Lyttelton. Mary's analysis seems to hint at the most probable answer: Balfour was lazy, and emotion frightened him. Studiedly detached, in Begbie's memorable phrase, the world, with all its conventional enthusiasms, was never allowed to penetrate beyond Balfour's lodge gates. A decade into their acquaintance, Mary pressed Balfour to express some kind of affection in his letters. He recoiled. "Such things are impossible to me: and they would if said *to* me give such exquisite pain, that I could never bring myself to say them to others—even at their desire," he explained.

In December 1880, Mary, chaperoned by her mother's maid Eassy, made her first social visit without her parents. Stately Wilton, home of the Wyndhams' long-standing friends, the Earl and Countess of Pembroke, was a suitably "safe" first foray since Wilton was just fifteen miles by carriage from Wilbury. The house party included two men whom Mary knew only a little, but liked—Alfred Lyttelton (brother of May), "that nice youngest one" of the large Lyttelton clan, and Hugo Charteris, eldest surviving son of Lord and Lady Elcho, heir to the earldom of Wemyss. To Mary's delight, the house party was rehearsing Christmas theatricals in a delightfully shambolic fashion. "We all turn our backs on the audience, we don't speak up, we laugh, we hesitate and we gabble," she told her mother. "Hugo talks in a very funny voice." Acerbic, witty, balding Hugo, a talented amateur actor, was far more attractive to women than his average looks suggested. He was also a complicated soul, with a morose streak, a gambling problem and a tricky relationship with his parents. His father, whose own high-minded preoccupation—army reform—earned him the sobriquet "the Brigadier," thought him feckless. His mother simply disliked him. Hugo's two elder brothers had died in their early twenties (one an accident, the other a suspected suicide). Lady Elcho, a daunting figure even in the context of mid-Victorian evangelism, never troubled to conceal her feeling that the wrong sons had died. "Mums called Keems [Hugo] darling & patted him on the leg . . . neither of which has she done for years," Hugo noted with delight (referring to himself in the third person, something he often did in correspondence with his wife) when he was almost thirty years old.

Madeline Wyndham had known the Elchos socially for many years. In February 1881 she invited Hugo to Wilbury. Hugo accepted—but when Madeline tried to make her daughter commit to a date, Mary professed an utter lack of interest. "As to Hugoman, his is an indefinite arrangement. I suppose you will write to him before the time comes . . ." she wrote laconically in a letter otherwise devoted to plans for rearranging balls so that a friend might attend. Madeline persisted nonetheless. Six months later, Hugo was posted to Constantinople, capital of the Ottoman Empire, as part of a short-lived stint in the Foreign Office. His acquaintance with Mary was now better established. On the eve of his departure Mary wrote to him recounting her recent nineteenth-birthday celebrations at Wilbury, where she had been crowned with a wreath of roses and spent the evening celebrating with songs and dancing. She had decided, she told him, that "the [cat]"—and here she drew a little cartoon of a cat—"believes the [hog]"—a drawing of a pig—"to be most sage, large-minded and kind."

Meritocracy had not reached the Foreign Office. It was believed that only those with breeding could properly uphold British prestige abroad. Lord Robert Cecil famously commented that all a junior attaché

Wilbury Park in Wiltshire, where Mary lived with her family from her early teens until her marriage. "Wilbury," as it was known to the family, was rented by Percy and Madeline for the long years it took to build their dream house Clouds, which lay around twenty-five miles to the west and was completed in 1885. Mananai and Pamela were in their mid-teens when the family moved to the new house. Mary, who never visited Clouds except as a married woman, always saw Wilbury as her childhood home.

needed was fluent French and the ability "to dangle about at parties and balls." Several months later, bored and lonely in Constantinople, Hugo received a letter from his brother Evan, updating him on London gossip, including a nugget concerning a putative rival, David Ogilvy, heir to the earldom of Airlie:

> Apparently he [Ogilvy] came over here in the summer intending to stay for a year and a half but went back after two months as Miss *Wyndham* was too much for him. He never proposed to her but was afraid he would do so, so he retired. I suppose you keep up constant correspondence with her I daresay she has told you more about Ogilvy than I can . . .

On that mischievous note, Evan swore Hugo to secrecy.

Mary most certainly had not gossiped. Hugo only discovered the truth of the matter several years later. "I think that Mumsie [Madeline Wyndham] proposing to Ogles for you & being refused is very funni [*sic*]," Hugo told Mary gleefully upon discovering the real sequence of events in 1887. Mary, like her husband employing the third person, blusteringly denied all responsibility: "It had nothing *to do with Migs,* it was entirely the old huntress's transaction . . . I didn't care a *hang* about Ogles & knew he didn't care a rap for me . . . Mumsie wanted Migs to be *clear* of Ogles (or engaged to him!!!) to 'go in' for Wash [Hugo himself] with a clean nose!" It is quite possible that Ogles was the unnamed beau who allegedly abandoned his interest in Mary with the explanation that she was "a very nice filly, but she's read too many books for me."

Later in life, Mary was outspoken in claiming that her mother had pushed her into marrying Hugo. In 1887 she told him, rather acidly, that of all her suitors "*personally* Mum preferred you . . . was indeed rather in love with you." Mary prided herself on being enigmatic: "I don't think poor Mum could ever make out the Mig—she really couldn't fathom Migs," describing herself proudly as "the little hunter (who always hunted on her own hook & followed her own trail)." It is most likely that she still secretly had her heart set on Balfour. And if not him, no one at all.

Hugo returned to England in the spring of 1882, bearing bangles "for Miss Mary" and determined to start a new career in politics as a member of the Conservative Opposition. Mary was in Paris, flirting with

Frenchmen and having "a high old time." Madeline Wyndham "hunted" her annoyed daughter back to Wilbury and dismissed her wheedling attempts to secure an invitation for a handsome "Musha de Deautand," whom she had met in Hyères some weeks previously, with the excuse that there was no room. "There would be no harm done just a fortnight in the *country* . . . the house is elastic you could shove somebody some-where," pleaded Mary, to no avail. In the same letter of 1887 in which she told Hugo of Madeline Wyndham's preference for him, she explained what her mother's plans had been: Mary was to "go in" for Hugo and marriage "in the summer (together with reading & music!) that makes me laugh! Hunt the arts to keep one's hand in!"

That summer was one of the bloodiest politically for some time. Ire-land was in full-blown chaos. Parnell and others of his party had been imprisoned in Kilmainham Jail for "treasonable practices" in fomenting opposition to Gladstone's 1881 Land Act, which gave Ireland the "3 Fs" of fair rents, fixity of tenure and free sale of landholdings but which Parnell considered did not go far enough. Their incarceration triggered guerrilla-like reprisals in Ireland: a national rent strike by day, while by night the mysterious "Captain Moonlight" burned farms, mutilated cattle and terrorized landlords. In May 1882, the Kilmainham Treaty released the political prisoners in return for Parnell's using his influence to end the rent strike. W. E. Forster, the Irish Chief Secretary (the government min-ister who while nominally subordinate to the monarch's representative, the Lord Lieutenant, in reality governed Ireland) resigned in fury, con-sidering Gladstone to be negotiating with terrorists. His replacement, Lord Frederick Cavendish, and his Under-Secretary Thomas Burke had barely set foot on Irish soil when they were murdered in Dublin's Phoe-nix Park by a gang calling itself the Invincibles. In London, men poured hatless out of their clubs to disseminate the appalling news. Arriving at the House of Commons the following day, Wilfrid Blunt was told that Parnell and his fellow Irish parliamentarian John Dillon were the "con-spirators." Stoutly, Blunt refused to give credence to the rumors: "They looked very much like gentlemen among the cads of the lobby."

Blunt was preoccupied with another devastating blow to nationalism: the British occupation of Egypt, shoring up the corrupt Khedive's unsta-ble rule in the face of revolt by Colonel Ahmed Orabi, popularly known as the Arabi Pasha. This cold-blooded economic act—designed to protect the interests of the "bondholders" (those numerous Britons with investments in Egypt) and British access to India—was entirely contrary to Midlothian principles of self-government. Yet so firmly did the British believe that Suez must be protected that just nineteen members of the House of Commons voted against the occupation. Percy Wyndham was the only Tory to do so, vigorously opposed to what he believed to be Britain's illegal and oppressive behavior. He later made one of his increasingly rare Commons speeches on Blunt's behalf, for Blunt's fierce advocacy of the Arabi's cause—even to the extent of paying for his legal defense when the Arabi was court-martialed (the trial was abandoned, and the Arabi exiled instead)—earned Blunt exile himself, banned from reentering Egypt by order of Egypt's Consul General.

In January 1883, Hugo's grandfather died. His father, now the 10th Earl of Wemyss, was elevated to the Lords. Hugo inherited first his father's courtesy title of Lord Elcho and then, at a by-election a month later, the Suffolk seat his father had held since 1847. Seamlessly, a Lord Elcho once more sat for Haddington. At Wilbury, Mary, Mananai and Pamela decorated Mary's dog Crack with yellow ribbons to celebrate— the color of the Primrose League. The league, named after the favorite flower of Disraeli (who died in 1881), was founded by prominent Tories to promote working- and middle-class support, promising aristocratic proximity through jamborees and summer fêtes.

Throughout that year Hugo sent Mary bouquets which she unpicked and made into buttonholes for him to wear; they played lawn tennis, went to the theater, had tea and walked in the park, all under Madeline Wyndham's encouraging eye. Finally, on a July night in 1883, with "buttonhole no. 171" in his lapel, Hugo proposed and Mary said yes. The next day, Hugo went to Belgrave Square to seek formally the Wyndhams' blessing. Percy gave it to him "from my heart of hearts . . . Mary is a *great* treasure, and as I believe you know it I am very glad you have made her love you."

Mary had never properly met Hugo's parents. They were introduced the next day at tea at their Mayfair house, 23 St. James's Street. Annie Wemyss took to Mary "immensely," deeming her "so natural, so true, so good, & so free from affectation, fastness." "[This] is such a good thing," wrote a mutual acquaintance to Percy, "for as we know, she [Annie Wemyss] does not take always spontaneously to people. I confess

I felt rather nervous about it . . ." Madeline Wyndham was delighted. "She will bring you all nearer together," she told Hugo, as though her daughter were a sort of familial Band-Aid.

Mary's precipitation from the Wyndhams' loving bosom into the Wemysses' chilly embrace concerned the Wyndhams' closer friends. "Condolences" upon the loss of a daughter to marriage were conventional enough, as were the "icy congratulations" that Mary received from Hugo's desultory rivals. But many of the letters of congratulations sent to Belgrave Square could not conceal a certain bemusement at the match. Rediscovering them in middle age, Mary thought it obvious that most of her relations had thought Hugo was not quite good enough.

Mary did not particularly enjoy her engagement: "six weeks of racket" consisting of all the things she most disliked—endless trips "drudging around the shops" after her mother, and being prodded and poked by crowds of people "swarming about the house about bothering clothes." Hugo teased Mary about the new skills she was acquiring in preparation for life as a matron running a household: "I wonder what you are doing . . . learning how many apples go to a Pie, or what butter costs at ¾ a pound . . . or perhaps you have been philosophizing over the degeneracy of modern linen . . . & regretting the halcyon days of muslins."

Both lovers expressed the sentiments expected of them. The day after their engagement, Mary told Hugo she had passed a sleepless night, contemplating the great change before her. In the following days she professed herself "*completely* happy!" with her "darling Hoggolindo . . . angel-Hoggie." "My bounty is as boundless as the sea," she told "his Lordship Hogge the Good," quoting her favorite lines from *Romeo and Juliet.* Hugo had become the very model of young Victorian manhood, swearing to "to pray, pray with your photo before me . . . to become more deserving of my happiness, to be drawn out of my stupid narrow self to something higher, better, nearer what you are." But, all too soon, Hugo was back to his old habits, and doubts had surfaced in Mary's mind.

Barely a fortnight into her engagement, Mary had to intervene with the Wemysses on Hugo's behalf. Hugo had found his gambling poison, the Stock Exchange, and on his first flurry lost £700, the equivalent of over £33,000 today. In what would become a wearily familiar exchange, Mary persuaded the Wemysses not to tie up Hugo's inheritance in a trust, but she was worried about their future before they had even embarked on it. Nor did Hugo appear to think his engagement required him to stop his constant flirting. "I don't care how much 'nonsense' you talk to everybody or *any*body at the Fisheries tonight for I do feel that you love me truly as I do you from the bottom of my heart," Mary told Hugo in mid-July, but her stout avowals ring hollow.

Around this time—perhaps precipitated by the gambling incident—Mary tried to call off the engagement. Her formal, stilted letter to "Lord Elcho" reads like that of a slightly less tactful Elizabeth Bennet who has accidently accepted Mr. Collins. She was at home in Belgrave Square, dinner was ready downstairs and doubtless her father was growing increasingly impatient, but, she declared,

> I must write this at once . . . speak straight out & tell you that I have hour by hour become more forcibly, painfully & unmistakeably [*sic*] convinced that when I accepted you a fortnight ago I did *not* rightly understand my own mind . . . [I am] perfectly certain [that] I do *not* love & respect you as I feel I should . . . I feel it my duty my positive & absolute duty to break off our proposed marriage.

As soon as Mary had forced those words out, her relief is palpable: her tone becomes free and easy and her pen dashes across the page in her usual untidy manner:

> I hope you will not mind much! Tho' yr pride may be shocked at first—I feel assured that you will so feel it to be all for the best for both of us & I trust you will think of me *kindly* as your *true* friend MW p.s. Please excuse my untidiness! I feel our marriage would lead to endless misery to both of us as it is. N.B. I am sure we shall always be very good friends. I know you will not take it to heart.

The engagement was not broken. By the next day, Mary was writing to Hugo as though they were reconciled, but her tone remains sober and the pet names are nowhere to be seen. Whether it was an attempt to shock Hugo into good behavior or whether it was cold feet (thirty years later George Wyndham reminded Mary how all the siblings had "palpitated" over their marriages—although George and his wife would also prove incompatible), it was far too late for that. The broken engagement would have caused a scandal unthinkable for Madeline Wyndham, and while Percy gave his children a degree of independence, he held them consequently responsible for their actions.

Arrangements proceeded as normal: the wedding presents arrived at Belgrave Square and, as customary, were displayed for inspection by family, friends and household (although some, such as Stanway, the Gloucestershire manor house given by Lord Wemyss to the newlyweds, were not capable of display). Mary began work on hundreds of thank-you letters: "I have written 8 already and August is not even two hours old!" she complained to Hugo. Last-minute adjustments were made to Mananai's and Pamela's bridesmaid dresses. Mary's trousseau was packed in tissue paper in preparation for her honeymoon. Early on the morning of their wedding day, 10 August 1883, Hugo wrote to Mary anticipating their meeting in St. Peter's Church in Eaton Square later that day: "Darling God give you strength to go through it all—& make me a good Hogs worthy of the little angel Mogs . . ." He sketched for Mary a cartoon: a small round Mary (not entirely representative, it must be said, since Mary was tall and slender) with a tall thin bridegroom by her side shouting "hurrah!" Several hours later, as reported by *The Times,* Mary, dressed in white and decked with orange blossoms, walked down the aisle of St. Peter's, past relations, friends and royalty in the form of Princess Christian, towards "Lord Elcho M.P.," and became his wife.

As the assembled masses waited in the cool church for Mary to make her entrance on Percy's arm, it was Madeline Wyndham's nerves that were most frayed. "It *was* an awful bit that in the Church before *you came*—it felt *so long*," Madeline told Mary later, heady with relief that all had gone as planned. "The organ played *such a tune* . . . I could *have screamed* to the man, to *stop* his twiddles . . . & then, like hot & cold or magic music, as you drew near he played louder & louder!" Normally such a thing would have given Mary and her mother the giggles: this time it only gave Madeline a feeling of "teeth on edge."

The service was followed by a short reception at Belgrave Square. At a quarter past four, the bride and groom departed: first for Easton Lodge in Essex, lent to them by Lord and Lady Brooke, and then to Gober, in the Scottish Highlands, where Hugo was to go stalking. The Wynd-hams settled in for a quiet evening at Belgrave Square. Madeline and her sisters, Julia and Lucy Campbell, alternately laughed and cried over the events of the day. Then George and Guy Wyndham went to a play.

The rest of the family dined with Fräulein. After dinner, as Mananai sat and pulled apart Mary's bouquet in order to make nosegays for Mary's friends as keepsakes, her mother was reminded of her eldest daughter: "sitting there with a melancholy face picking and pulling at all the lovely flowers!" The comparison did not bode well given that all Mary's bouquets and buttonholes had been to do with Hugo.

FOUR

Honeymoon

Three years later, when the sheen of marriage had long started to fade, Mary reproved Hugo for spending their honeymoon deer stalking, a favored pursuit of the British aristocracy that requires hours of stealthy pursuit on foot against the heather-covered Scottish hillside. At the time, she had seemed happy enough to yomp across the moors after Hugo, and she reveled in a sense of recklessness as the Elchos drank champagne and played piquet by night. The Wyndham family was by now summering in Hyères, and Madeline Wyndham was missing her eldest daughter desperately ("I cannot get *reconciled* to being without you," she told Mary some two years after her marriage), but Mary's letters to her family glowed with delight in her marital state. One evening, she told Guy conspiratorially, the Elchos had got so "drunk" on champagne "to cheer our spirits" after Hugo failed to bag a stag that Hugo fell over. At this liminal honeymoon stage Mary had been freed from childhood's bonds without yet assuming matronly cares.

The little cartoons the Elchos sent each other in their marriage's early years, and coy references to "lonely little cots" when they were apart, suggest that sexually the union was a success. Not for the Elchos the horror stories of the Ruskins, whose marriage was never consummated, or of the young scientist Marie Stopes, who only realized her abusive husband was impotent after six months of study in the British Library. Madeline and her daughters were extremely frank with one another about all health matters, microscopically and enthusiastically recounting any oddities in relation to "Lady Betsey," their term for their menstrual cycle. It seems likely that Madeline gave all her daughters some kind of warning about what a wedding night entailed. What Mary told her mother after the event must remain a mystery. Madeline redacted Mary's first letter to her following her wedding. It tells us only that Mary had "a headache," before the next three lines are scrubbed out vigorously with black pen.

Romance was in the air at Gober. As Mary and Hugo ate their dinner by firelight, backstage in the little hut Hugo's valet Williams seduced Mary's maid Faivre. Prophylactics, not uncommon in the city, were hardly readily available in the Highland wilds; perhaps Faivre was also one of many unversed women who did not know how babies were made. Faivre consequently found herself unmarried and pregnant—"ruined," as Mary put it. It was a highly unfortunate position for any young woman, an untenable one for a lady's maid.

In most cases, Faivre would have found herself immediately dismissed without a reference. When the Elchos' friend George Curzon found out that a housemaid in his employ had been seduced by a footman, he "threw the little slut out onto the street" without a qualm. His contemporaries considered his attitude unremarkable. Mary responded quite differently. With the help of Madeline and Percy she helped Faivre find lodging with a tolerant North London landlady; assisted her financially from her own pin money (Hugo's valet had long since scarpered); and visited Faivre once the child, a little boy, was born in the spring of 1884. Most of Mary's friends thought her admirably liberal attitude towards staff overly indulgent. Servant troubles became a constant footnote to her daily life. Her anxiety never to hurt anyone's feelings did not serve her well as an employer.

On 14 August 1883, a few days after the Elchos had arrived at Gober, Hugo wrote a private letter to Percy concerning Mary's dowry. Hugo claimed that he had proposed "with no idea what Mary was to have or whether she was to have any[thing] at all," as unconvincing a statement as the rest of his letter was disingenuous. Mary's marriage settlement had been negotiated in the weeks between the engagement and the marriage by Percy and Hugo's solicitor, Mr. Jamieson, as was the convention. Mary received £15,000 (roughly $1,650,000 today), the interest on which would produce an annual income of £500 (around $55,000 today). Hugo had thought that £100 or more of this £500 would be given to him for his own use. Now conversations with Mr. Jamieson had made it clear that Percy intended the whole for Mary's use as pin money.

Hugo's frantic letter to Percy argued that Mary should not have an allowance disproportionate to the Elchos' income, lest she learn bad spending habits. His reasoning, while in line with contemporary attitudes, was patronizing and misleading. His concern was not that Mary's spending habits should be curbed but that his own should be supported. Mary was innately frugal. She spent almost no money on clothes (far too little, her friends complained). Her eldest daughter never remembered her buying even a trinket or a bottle of scent for herself. She invariably traveled third-class. Hugo traveled in first, and liked expensive cigars, but his greatest extravagance was his improvident gambling on the London Stock Exchange: "As far as his children could make out all he wanted money for was to have plenty of it to lose!" wrote his eldest daughter, Cynthia.

Hugo's haste to have this issue determined while on honeymoon suggests he was in yet another financial scrape. From his sheepish tone, even he realized that his behavior was grasping. Percy agreed that Mary should have only £350 to £400 a year as pin money, with the remainder going to the Elchos' common expenses. From the occasional sly comment over the years it is clear that Percy knew full well why Hugo was so keen to reduce Mary's pin money. Mary knew nothing of this until stumbling across this letter years later. "Typical," she scrawled across it in irritation, that on their honeymoon Hugo should have written to her father "not on love but Money!" adding, correctly, that Hugo's master was "Mammon."

From Gober the Elchos traveled to Gosford, just outside Edinburgh. Gosford, where each successive Earl of Wemyss lived, was the largest and grandest of all the Wemyss family estates. Mary hated Gosford on sight. A chill east wind whipped around the property, which looked out to the glassy grey Firth of Forth. Seagulls wheeled overhead in a "complaining chorus." The house itself, a daunting grey block built by Robert Adams, the greatest architect of eighteenth-century Britain, was under construction as Lord Wemyss, fulfilling a long-held dream, was adding on two vast wings. During the course of the works, Mary persuaded the builders to let her go up in the crane used for the building. She drew a picture for her mother to illustrate it: a tiny figure swinging high over a bare landscape.

In later life Mary described the rebuilt house as "like a large & gilded, dead & empty Cage." Her daughter Cynthia echoed her: "a great block of stone that seems to me very still-born. It has no living atmosphere." Sir Edwin Lutyens, who was to twentieth-century architecture what Robert Adams was to the eighteenth, likened it to a rendition of "God Save the King" sung flat. Newlywed Mary already dreaded the time

Gosford's marble hall, photographed here by *Country Life* (1911), was built by Mary's father-in-law, Francis, the 10th Earl of Wemyss, as part of the fulfillment of a childhood dream: the completion of Gosford's abandoned eighteenth-century Robert Adam–built "New House," with two vast wings to the south and north. The 10th Earl set to work in 1883, following the death of his own father, the 9th Earl (known as "the Hunting Earl" for his love of the sport). The building works, which were well under way at the time of Mary and Hugo's marriage in 1884, cost around £70,000 (around $8.5 million in today's money) and were completed in 1890. The centrally heated marble hall in its south wing was designed to be the family's principal living space. Over its fireplace is carved MDCCCXCI (1891), marking the date—give or take a week, since it was actually Christmas 1890—that the 10th Earl and his family finally moved in.

when Hugo would succeed to the Wemyss title, requiring her to relocate to the North.

Just days after they arrived, Hugo went rabbit shooting, leaving his new wife alone in the bosom of his family. He had accepted the invitation before his engagement, and claimed he could not in good conscience cancel. It was an early indication of his ability to costume selfishness as honor. In Hugo's absence, Mary attended Aberlady Church with the family, went for long solitary walks and wrote endless letters to her husband. Evan Charteris, on finding her at her writing desk once again, marveled teasingly that she had anything further to say. Annie Wemyss visited her in her bedroom before dinner and in her own stiff way "thimpashized" with her doleful daughter-in-law. Nonetheless Mary felt marooned in a strange place. "You *must* come back soon . . . the very first instant you can . . . it is too horrid—& . . . dreary & dismal . . . everything is rainy & black & miserable & Mogs feels very sad," she told Hugo. Hugo was sympathetic and unmoved.

At dinner the Wemysses lectured Mary upon the dangers of marital separation. Annie Wemyss noted proudly that she and Lord Wemyss had barely spent a day apart. Already, the Elchos seemed to have exceeded their tally, and Mary's solitude forced her into contemplation. "I think *now* that Hugo & I shall always love being together by ourselves better than anything else . . . [but] the habit of living together as one cannot be acquired in a minute any more than any other habit . . . the wedding day is but the *beginning* of the marriage not the 'fait accompli,'" she told her mother. She had taken as her mantra "I bide my time." With that she could "*remove Mountains!*" But Mary's brave words rang hollow. She was beginning to realize that molding Hugo into the husband she wanted might be even more difficult than she had anticipated.

A few weeks later the Elchos returned to London. Hugo had taken a small house in Hans Place in Chelsea, an artistic area close to but significantly cheaper than Belgravia. The Elchos stayed at Belgrave Square while waiting for work to be completed. Both their mothers warned Mary about the dangers of city life, full of distractions to drive an emotional wedge between a young husband and wife. Once installed in Hans Place, the Elchos made a good fist at domesticity. Sometimes they dined alone. Over champagne, Hugo practiced the speeches he intended to make the next day in the House of Commons, speeches they both hoped would gain the attention of the party leadership and raise him out of the backbenches. On other evenings Hugo read poetry to Mary as they sat by the fire.

Far more frequently Mary's diary recorded evenings spent in the company of others. In her journal the companions of her youth, cousins and Wiltshire neighbors, fall away. She adopted the pursuits of a fashionable, politically engaged woman of the day with pretensions to intellectualism. With Hugo's sisters Evelyn de Vesci and Hilda Brodrick she watched the debates from behind the metal grilles of the Ladies' Gallery in the Commons (an improvement on the old building, which required women to watch proceedings from a ventilation shaft), or spent evenings at the "New Club" (the New University Club on St. James's Street, founded only in 1864 and marginally less stuffy than its counterparts) drinking champagne and "getting lively" with Arthur Balfour, Hugo and Evan Charteris as they debated that day's point of interest with dazzling lightness and speed. When the prospect of a gentleman's club, those bastions of male privilege, did not appeal, they went to one anothers' houses instead. With Hugo, Laura Tennant and Alfred Lyttelton, Mary passed evenings at the bachelor lodgings of Godfrey Webb, where the company reclined in armchairs, played the piano and indulged in "nice long talk." "Webber," as he was known to the group, was a clerk in the House of Lords, and was somewhat older than the rest—he had originally been a friend of Percy and Madeline's. A celebrated raconteur and wit, he was described by some as their "court jester." This group, of which Arthur was the undisputed king, began to refer to itself as "the Gang." In a few years they would become "the Souls."

Mary would become notorious for her socializing. After a spat about flirtations in 1887, Hugo told Mary that "me almost wishes as a punishment—though not quite! That you were now playing the part of Lady Airlie [David Ogilvy had since become Earl of Airlie]—in some provincial garrison town—jealously guarded by Othello Ogles—no Migs—no Barkin [Arthur Balfour]—NO Tommie [Ribblesdale]—NO Stanywan [Stanway]—only Ernests [babies]—soldiers wives—& tea parties of 10th Hussar Sols—with Othello Ogles pouring out the tea." In that suggestion, Hugo imagined with great accuracy the existence of Ogilvy's actual wife, Mabell Airlie. Yet a comment by Mary in those early days suggests that Hugo's behavior, not her own, provoked her frenetic socializing. Two years into their marriage, Mary counted to Hugo the number of occasions that the Elchos had been "*quite* alone" in the countryside, without an array of hangers-on to keep Hugo amused. It was just twice: the time in Gober, "when you were stalking all day & one week at Whitsuntide at Stanway when I felt very ill—& yet you pretend to believe we are a domestic couple . . ."

In the spring of 1884, before the Elchos moved into Hans Place, Mary had a miscarriage. She was put to bed at Belgrave Square and a doctor summoned. Miscarriage, risking infections and hemorrhaging, was considered more dangerous than childbirth, but Dr. Cumberbatch said Mary's condition gave him no cause for concern. "I suppose I have gone about it methodically in an easy going manner . . . I am as jolly as a sandgirl, or rather matron, or *would be* matron!" Mary reassured her mother, who had stayed in London for as long as she could, until the stream of telegrams from Percy at Wilbury, left with a houseful of guests, grew too irate to ignore. In a quiet room, cared for by a nurse, Mary rested on a chaise longue and knitted, whiling away the days. Hugo drifted in and out between stints at the Commons. Friends and her sisters-in-law visited and recounted their own experiences of childbearing. Eventually the shows of blood decreased. "Betsey . . . from [her] kind of light out of door attire is about to put on tippet and depart," Mary told her mother, and she was allowed to reenter the world.

As Mary did so, she was unclear whether she was pregnant or not. Dr. Cumberbatch, perplexed by the nonappearance of "a 3 months ovum," confessed he could not tell what exactly had happened. Perhaps Mary had had a phantom pregnancy; perhaps she was still pregnant; perhaps the fetus would come away at Mary's next monthly period. If her period did not appear, "I shan't know whether I have picked up old threads or started afresh! It's very funny," said Mary, resolutely bright-faced, affecting nonchalance. Madeline Wyndham was terrified that Mary might produce a child with some kind of "omission": a living judgment upon the Wyndham blood and breeding. Such haziness about childbirth matters was far from uncommon. Twenty years later Mananai recounted to Madeline the story of an unfortunate girl who was told that she was to give birth in July and found herself still pregnant in September. In Mary's case, "Betsey" did not reappear. She began to feel sick and "squeamish." She supposed that she was either still pregnant or pregnant again.

That summer, Mary made her first visit to Stanway, the Gloucestershire house in southwest England among the beautiful Cotswold hills that was her wedding present from Lord Wemyss. The Elchos arrived on

31 July 1884, met at the station by a coachman, pony chaise and black horse all seemingly as ancient as one another. They emerged from the leafy lanes to find Stanway glowing in the evening sun, with the bells of the tiny church next door pealing in celebration. "[A] sort of heavenly feeling comes over one and laps one about," Mary told her mother of this arrival, the moment that she fell in love with the house that would be her home for the rest of her life. That evening the Elchos walked up to the Pyramid, a monument at the top of a gentle hill overlooking the house that was to become the site of many a tryst and midnight escapade. Half a century later Mary could still remember the sickeningly stuffy smell of the brand-new blankets and the next day's breakfast of trout fried in oatmeal made by the housekeeper.

Stanway, where the family still lives, is a magical place—a ramshackle sixteenth-century house of honey-colored stone shouldering onto a churchyard hidden away along an alley of pleached trees. The air seems thicker and stiller there: part of the house was originally a monastery, and a sense of this seclusion remains. When the Elchos arrived, the house had lain near-abandoned for half a century, peopled by a skeleton staff of ancient retainers and used by the family only as a shooting lodge on rare forays south. Drafts whistled through cracks in the walls and cold flooded in through the latticed windowpanes. Armies of rats and cockroaches scuttled across bare floorboards, and as dusk fell bats swooped through shadowy rooms. Mary was undaunted by the state of the house and, despite her pregnancy, was full of enthusiasm for transforming it. On pieces of rough paper she sketched out floor plans for her family, explaining the house's peculiar layout. Stanway had almost no corridors: most of the rooms led on from one another and it could only sleep sixteen at a pinch—remarkably small in the context of most houses the Wyndhams visited. Mary would continually struggle with this as a hostess.

Mary's first guests—Percy, Fräulein, Mananai and Pamela—arrived on 3 August to celebrate her twenty-second birthday. Fräulein had made "a cake with big raisins in it," and Mary had bought crackers, eagerly anticipating "a feast & revel" with her family. Madeline Wyndham, George and Guy arrived a few days later, and work began on transforming the house. As gooseberries gently ripened in the overgrown gardens, Madeline and her daughters picked their way through dusty attics hunting for treasures. They found Chippendale chairs which they brought down to replace the early Victorian plush-and-gilt furniture already *in situ;* and they patched together lengths of embroidered materials so that they could be hung as curtains in Mary's sitting room at the end of the house that looked up to the monument. Great pieces of furniture were trundled from room to room, old rugs laid out across floorboards.

A month later, while staying at the Wemysses' gloomy town house in Edinburgh, with the tick-tock of the grandfather clock echoing through the rooms, Mary reported to Madeline Wyndham that " 'Earnest' is alive and kicking!" Despite a riot of ailments ("rheumatic pains in back & tummy . . . flatulence, ript livers," insomnia and indigestion), she finally relaxed. Madeline was hundreds of miles away at Wilbury, where George was waxing and waning yellow from an attack of jaundice. She seized a moment to write to her daughter before dashing into the village to "beg borrow or steal" a hollyhock so that Val Prinsep, seized by the urge, could paint it. She sent Mary strict instructions not to travel unless she felt up to it, for "sometimes indigestion gets such possession of one during the last months that one is only fit *for home* [where] . . . you can give yourself up to a tea gown & your sofa."

Mary did not listen. Already she carried everywhere her "nest egg"—a wicker handbasket of unanswered letters, always full to overflowing, despite several hours spent each morning trying to reduce the Sisyphean pile. In December 1884, when she was almost to term, she hosted her first house party for "the Gang" at Stanway, their number including Arthur Balfour, Alfred Lyttelton, Godfrey Webb, St. John and Hilda Brodrick and Laura Tennant. It was a roaring success. Laura Tennant wrote, "It's such fun here . . . we quarrel about everything—we talk up to the top of our bent—we grow hyper-sentimental and blow blue bubbles into the stars & Hugo Ld Elcho comes down upon them with jeers & in pumps & a smoking suit. We play games & the piano—we none of us open a book or write a letter—we scribble & scrawl & invent words & reasonless rhymes." The guests "departed on the verge of tears!" Mary told Percy with pride. Her diary came alive. "Talk talk the whole time," she recorded, scribbling down in detail all the games they played. Six months later the Elchos hosted another party. "Remember darling you are staying with very nice people. Please be careful and do not do anything to shock or annoy them," Charty Ribblesdale warned her younger sister,

Margot Tennant. "At that moment," Mary recalled, "Margot was walking on the church wall, pursuing Willie Grenfell with a large sponge—and astounding Hugo by her habit of talking in the passage or in her friends' bedrooms till all hours of the night or morning." It was, in the collective memory, the first house party of the Souls. Mary at Stanway, in her delight, had found her métier.

FIVE

The Gang

A heavily pregnant Mary spent Christmas 1884 at Wilbury. She had planned to give birth in January, in London, but Hugo Richard Francis Charteris (later known as "Ego" from his childish attempts to pronounce his name) appeared early, and was born at Wilbury on 28 December. Thirteen-year-old Pamela was enthralled at having a "real live baby in the house," Madeline Wyndham almost sick with relief that the child was healthy. Hugo sat by Mary's side in her old bedroom as she recovered, allowing her to dictate her letters and diary to him until she was strong enough to wield a pencil herself.

Ego was born one day before Gladstone's seventy-fifth birthday and in the throes of another foreign policy crisis, this time in the Sudan, an Egyptian satellite gripped by rebellion led by the Mahdi, a mysterious fanatic. For almost a year, the Mahdi had been besieging General Gordon's British troops trapped at Khartoum. Small, fearsome Gordon, easily as zealous a Christian as the Mahdi was Muslim, had become a popular hero among the British public for his resistance. In fact, it was entirely Gordon's fault that he was besieged. Arriving in Khartoum in late 1883, he immediately disregarded his government's directions to effect a British withdrawal, dug in his heels and announced his intention to "smash up the Mahdi." The danger of having an uncontrollable "man on the spot" was one of many problems Britain's imperial government faced. In the autumn of 1884, caving to intolerable public pressure (and to an angry Queen at Windsor), Gladstone authorized the dispatch of relief troops to the Sudan. Almost every young officer longed to rescue Gordon. To his intense disappointment, George Wyndham, who had joined the Coldstream Guards on leaving Eton, narrowly missed out. Wilfrid Blunt also tried to become involved, publicly proposing at a meeting of the International Arbitration and Peace Association to lead a "friendly mission" intervening with the Mahdi on Gordon's behalf. From his home at Hawarden in Wales, a weary Gladstone acknowledged the offer, and promised to discuss the matter with Earl Granville, the Liberal Party's Leader in the Lords. Blunt's offer was quietly let drop.

Tucked up in bed at Wilbury, just days into motherhood, Mary must have barely registered these matters. Her diary records only an uncharacteristic interest in food: "pheasant and baked apples for luncheon," she noted. By convention, new mothers spent a month "lying in" after the birth, also known as accouchement, before, under nurse's instructions, they gradually made "all the steps back into Life! Such as walking, [putting on] stays [corsets] & sitting on the Commode!" as Mary explained. After that, they were "churched" with a religious blessing and reentered Society.

Mary was bored by lying in and frustrated by her difficulty in breast-feeding Ego, a fractious infant. As soon as she could, she threw herself back into the social whirl. Madeline Wyndham chided her daughter for "racketing around" at the expense of her health and her child. "The *rule* is that one cannot possibly live in the same way for 2 or even 3 months after '*The Crisis*' as one did before." But Mary did not listen. Before long her health gave out. In February 1885, Madeline Wyndham and Annie Wemyss joined forces, compelling a "pale and wasting" Mary to Gosford for "a nice quiet bit by the sea" with nothing to amuse her except long walks and her child—"who is a most important *personage*," Madeline reminded her.

Mary never really liked being by herself: "When I'm alone my spirits go down! Down!" she said, and she found Gosford as depressing as always. "I am very low but that's not strange!" she told her mother. In fact she was miserable, bursting into tears every time she heard Ego cry. On the advice of her maternity nurse, Mrs. Sayers, she began bottle-feeding him. Madeline Wyndham, fiercely opposed to the novel practice, immediately besieged her with prophecies of doom: too much milk, she said, might "fly to *ones head* & make one vy odd for a time! Go to one's leg & lay one up with what is called a milk *leg*." In her anxiety Madeline became vitriolic, and, though her anger was mostly reserved for the "wicked" Mrs. Sayers, Mary feared she was a bad mother and that her son was not developing as he should. Hugo had remained in London. What news he did deliver was dismal: Starway's housekeeper had dropped dead from diabetes. Mary's initial shock and sympathy were swiftly replaced by exhaustion and alarm as she worried about finding a suitable replacement.

The news in the wider world was just as poor. The relief troops arrived at Khartoum in January 1885 days too late to find the city fallen and Gordon's head impaled upon a stick under a sky as blazing as his own eyes. When the news reached Britain, the press renamed the GOM of the Midlothian Campaign the MOG: "Murderer of Gordon." In February it was announced that a further dispatch of troops would effect the original evacuation plan. Among these troops were Hugo's jubilant brother Alan and George Wyndham, "in the 7th Heaven of delight" at the prospect of a good old rout. "It's like a death in our hearts," said Madeline as she broke the news to Mary, convinced, as she reiterated in letter after anguished letter, that George was departing to his death. Percy was scarcely more optimistic, assuring his son that, notwithstanding his opposition to the British presence in Egypt and the Sudan, he did not think "*for a moment* your most *precious* life is thrown away" if his son should die in combat. At Gosford, Mary suffered a violent bilious attack. Madeline thought it was a direct response to her "grief" at the news.

As the troops prepared to leave, the Wemysses traveled south, and the Wyndhams congregated first at Wilbury and then in London. Only Mary was absent. Forbidden by both families from making the long journey while she was still frail, she remained with Mrs. Sayers and Ego, reliant upon her family's letters for updates. They were not encouraging. "Tonight is the *awful* night when we say goodbye I never felt such a horrible feeling as it is—Poor darling Rat [Madeline Wyndham] looks so unhappy but she bares [*sic*] it wonderfully," Mananai told Mary on the eve of George's departure after a day spent watching the inspection of the troops at Wellington Barracks. The next day they were among the cheering crowds waving the troops off from the barracks in the glittering sunshine of an early spring day, determined—said Madeline—to show George "no signs . . . of our sorrow but rejoice in his joy."

After a brief visit to Gosford—intended to raise her own spirits as much as her daughter's, but which seems rather to have made them confidantes in each other's misery—Madeline returned to Wilbury "with a distracted mind & a sad heart & eyes that have gone blind with much crying these last weeks." The house was in upheaval. Final preparations were being made for the move to Clouds, which was to take place while the Wyndhams were in London for the Season. "The packing that is going on here is terrific. 3 immense waggons came here the other day and were loaded I don't know how high & then trudged off at six o'clock in the morning," Pamela reported to Mary. On finding that her pet white sparrows had been left unfed and allowed to die in the chaos, Madeline saw another augury of George's fate. It was not long before her mind would find another avenue along which to race.

In April 1885 the Gang rejoiced at the engagement of Alfred Lyttelton to Laura Tennant, two of the most beloved of their group. All who knew Laura praised her to the point of hyperbole. Intensely spiritual, very flirtatious and extremely frank, Laura was possessed of "an extra dose of life, which caused a kind of electricity to flash about her . . . lighting up all with whom she came into contact," said Adolphus ("Doll") Liddell, one of the many men in love with her. In old age, Mary recalled the debut of Laura and her equally irrepressible sister Margot as causing "a stir indeed—one may almost call it a Revolution." She likened their effect to "[the] splash . . . of a bright pebble being thrown from an immense height into a quiet pool . . ." Unchaperoned by their mother, the Tennant sisters were "of totally unconventional manners with no code of behavior except their own good hearts," as the wife of Arthur's brother Eustace, Lady Frances Balfour, put it. At Glen House, the family home in the Scottish Borders known as "the Glen," they entertained male guests in their nightgowns in their bedroom, known as the "Doo-Cot" (Dovecot) in ironic reference to the heated debates on philosophy, spirituality, politics and psychology that took place there, lasting late into the night. In London—and in qualification of Mary's recollection—it took them some time to achieve entrée. Laura met Lady Wemyss—who lived not thirty miles from the Glen at Gosford—only when she married Alfred. Alfred's brother Spencer described the Tennants to his cousin Mary Gladstone as a family of "brilliant young ladies and vulgar parents."

Mary, who had been captivated from the first, considered Laura to be her closest friend. The two concocted grand plans for a literary salon.

Shortly after Laura's engagement the Elchos jaunted to Paris with Arthur Balfour, Godfrey Webb and Alfred Lyttelton to visit Laura, who was with Margot and Lady Tennant shopping for her trousseau. "We form a fine representative party of Englishmen, a married couple, an engaged couple, 'doux garcons' as Webber wd call it in his fine English accent . . . & Margot does well for a sporting 'mees,'" Mary told Percy.

Mary recounted this week in Paris to her parents in exhaustive, delighted detail. She told them about afternoons dozing on the sofa while Laura played the piano in their little shared sitting room; about their proficiency at lawn tennis that had roused the natives to applause; about their conversation, "as animated as the most spirited of Frogs." Mary complained to Percy about the stolid Lady Tennant: "Someone always has to lag & try to talk to her & she talks not at all! Except in the most commonplace manner." She told them about drives in the Bois de Boulogne, delicious déjeuners and dinners at the Lion d'Or. They went to Théâtre du Palais-Royal and then, Mary added in strangely bathetic phrase, they "walked home afterwards." She did not tell her parents that the person with whom she had walked arm in arm, deep in conversation, on the winding route home was not Hugo but Arthur. On their return to London Arthur dined with the Elchos. Mary was wearing a low-cut gown which startled her guest into an unexpected compliment. "You have a jolly throat," he told her, such an effusive comment for the reserved Arthur that Mary openly blushed.

One of the Gang's defining characteristics, stemming directly from the Doo-Cot's nighttime debates, was their belief that men and women could be intellectual equals capable of intimate friendship on the mental plane. They chided the earthy suspicions of scurrilous-minded outsiders, unaccustomed to seeing one man's wife deep in conversation with another woman's husband. Privately they conceded a little. Mary described herself to Hugo as a "little flirt . . . !" while maintaining this flirtation was innocent. Throughout the early years of their marriage, the Elchos conducted a satisfying and harmless double romance with the Ribblesdales. The couples holidayed together in the seaside Suffolk town of Felixstowe and the clement New Forest in Hampshire, splitting off into contented pairs: Hugo and Charty, Mary and Tommy. There was never a breath of scandal. As Mary explained, "Migs in practice (flirtation practice) dwells on the ambiguity of implications the possibility of a backdoor or loophole that Tommy considers the word to contain. Migs thinks it doesn't matter *what* she says in her letters to men conks [admirers], provided she only *implies* it . . . for if brought to book she can say that they have misunderstood her—and nice men conks never take one to task." In essence, it was courtly love, updated: men pursued, women teased, both remained beyond reproach.

Mary and Arthur's obvious mutual attraction, however, was not beclouded by the bavardage of "flirtation practice." "She reverences him," said Laura, and worryingly, when Laura broached the issue with Arthur, he seemed not "as indifferent heart-wards to her as I at first thought—he said several things about it that gave me qualms." This was dangerous: "the eyesight of the world [by which she meant Society] . . . is vastly farsighted & sees things in embryo," Laura warned Mary. The gossips of the New Club, seeing Mary and Laura dining with Arthur alone, could cause havoc.

Laura was not the only person concerned. Shortly after the Elchos had returned from Paris, Madeline Wyndham visited Stanway and had several lengthy private talks with Mary, undoubtedly about Arthur. Afterwards, Mary wrote to thank her: "I can't say what it was having you here & what it is to have you at all. You are the best influence in my life & stronger than myself . . . as noble healthy & cleansing as a gust of . . . mountain air removing cobwebs from one['s] moral mirror." Despite these protestations, her behavior did not alter at all.

Mary had boasted that in her debutante years, her mother had never quite been able to "fathom" her. Now it seemed no one could. Laura concluded that Mary was simultaneously paralyzed and driven by her infatuation with Balfour and ambition for her husband: "Her affection for Hugo is strangely mixed up with her affection for the man she knows can, will & does help Hugo more than anyone else does." Laura thought only her firm hand might prevent Mary from sleepwalking into disaster. "I never allow for a minute when I am with Mary that she is in love with A . . . were I to say 'you are in love' she would believe me and poking the fire is productive of flame; & at present the conflagration is chiefly smoke," she told Frances Balfour, privately criticizing Arthur, as one she thought capable of controlling his feelings, for failing to put a stop to things.

A letter written by Mary to her mother that summer suggests otherwise. Madeline Wyndham's anxiety had been exacerbated, rather than eased, by her visit to Stanway. Shortly after leaving Mary, and while

Twenty-three-year-old Mary holds her infant first son, Ego (wearing what appears to be an amber teething necklace around his neck), a poodle to her left and Hugo to her right at Stanway circa 1885. Despite the Elchos' air of domestic calm, Mary's increasing fascination for Arthur Balfour was causing concern to those around them.

visiting her friend Georgie Sumner, she sent Mary a frantic letter. She did not directly mention the subject. Instead, over numerous pages of increasingly illegible scrawl she dwelt long on the cautionary tale of Georgie, estranged from her husband, suffering "deadly remorse," feeling she had "sinned against God & Man . . . and would die . . . sooner than act again as she did . . . ." "I thought perhaps you might send me a wopper," Mary replied, treating her mother to a tortuous, abstract discourse on the nature of wrongdoing. In short, she divided the world into wrongdoers too stupid or wicked to know they did wrong; and those who knew, but did it anyway, preferring to face the consequences later. Mary classed herself in the latter camp. The only remedy she saw was to "pray . . . to set one's heart & to keep it fixed in the right direction & day by day the effort will become less . . . the backsliding & driftings less frequent—to be able to make one's will want to do the right thing." Taken out of the abstract it is a startling admission. Mary's heart was not fixed in the right direction. She wanted to be with Arthur.

The following year, the Elchos and Arthur went on a walking tour of North Berwick, near Gosford in Scotland. Printed backwards in tiny letters in Mary's sketchbook from the trip are these words: "How I wish I could, but you know that would be impossible." It has been suggested that the "impossible" thing was divorce, although it might have been sex or something more innocent. It is startling to think that Mary could ever truly have contemplated divorce—which would have made her a social pariah, given Hugo custody of her children and destroyed Arthur's political career. More likely, Mary simply chose not to think of the consequences at all. She ceased to confide in her mother. She seems almost to have stopped communicating at all.

Desperate and panicked, Madeline Wyndham grew relentless. From Hyères, as Mary's birthday approached, she exhorted the Elchos in frenzied underlinings to "*Cling* on to doing things together . . . don't get separated in *your lives.*" On the Elchos' wedding anniversary, invoking the memory of the "*good Dear good* single-minded Child" Mary had been two years before, she demanded that "Hugo . . . keep you from all *pitch* . . . I know he first loved you for *all that* & Married You to have a Wife different from all the world. I'm sick of some of the Wives I see . . . I love you. I believe in you. I worship you." Mary broke her silence with cheerful obfuscation and a generous approach to the truth. "Hugo read . . . the birthday exhortation & wondered whether you thought I didn't care for him any more!" she said. ". . . I told him yr words were as warnings not as remedies . . . I don't think two people could easily be more united than we are & will always strive to be . . . I would rather kill myself than make you miserable & disappointed in me."

Mary fell pregnant shortly afterwards (her second son, Guy Lawrence, was born on 23 May 1886). That pregnancy was not enough to calm a "wretched" Annie Wemyss, who had also heard the rumors and recruited Laura to keep Mary and Arthur apart. Laura enlisted the redoubtable and pragmatic Frances Balfour. The two conspired to prevent Arthur from going to Stanway in December for the house party which was fast becoming an annual tradition, ditching it themselves in order to keep him away: "v [sic] good of us I think!" said Laura, who used her own six-months' pregnancy as an excuse. In the early months of the new year Laura trailed Mary like a shadow: almost every engagement with Arthur set down by Mary in her diary, whether visiting Sir John Millais's new gallery or drinking hot chocolate at Charbonnel et Walker in the West End, records Laura gently, inexorably, interposing herself between the two, trying with all her might to reduce their relationship to innocent friendship.

SIX

Clouds

As soon as the Stanway party ended, Mary left to join her family for their first Christmas at Clouds. The Wyndhams had finally moved in, in September 1885. Throughout the autumn her excited younger sisters had bombarded her with letters giving her every detail of their "scrumtious [*sic*]" new domain. If Mary was disappointed by Arthur's previous absence, she showed no signs of this to her family. She arrived at Clouds, loaded down with "millions of packages," Ego, his nurse Wilkes (known as "Wilkie"), her poodle Stella and a cageful of canaries, and was rushed around the house by her sisters demanding to know if it was exactly as she had imagined. All Mary could manage was "delightful."

The house was enormous. Built of green sandstone with a red-brick top floor, it looked like a storybook house that, like Alice, had found a cake saying "eat me" and mushroomed to a hundred times its normal size. "I . . . keep discovering new rooms inside and windows outside," marveled Georgie Burne-Jones on her first visit in November. Half a century later, an estate agent's particulars listed five principal reception rooms, a billiard room, thirteen principal bedrooms and dressing rooms, a nursery suite of two bedrooms, twelve other bedrooms, a separate wing of domestic offices including thirteen staff bedrooms, stabling for twenty-three horses, garaging for four cars (presumably carved out of the stabling facilities) and a model laundry. At a time when the traditional landed elite were retrenching, fearful of how they would maintain their estates, Clouds trumpeted to the world that the Wyndhams were founding a dynasty that would operate at the very heart of power.

In an age of country-house politics Clouds, built for entertaining, became famous as a "palace of weekending" where deals were brokered in luxurious privacy, far away from the hub of Westminster. An invitation to Clouds was a prize indeed. The press focused on the fact that, from the late 1880s, Clouds was where Arthur Balfour spent each Easter, passing his days playing golf on the private links built by Percy, engaging in brilliant "general conversation" at dinner, of which he was always the star.

The nerve center of the house was a spacious skylit central hall, two stories high. Opening off it at ground-floor level were Percy's suite of rooms—bedroom, bathroom, dressing room, study—and the reception rooms—billiard room, waiting room, smoking room, dining room, adjacent dining service room, and the long south-facing drawing room and music room, connected by double doors, where floor-to-ceiling French windows revealed a wide grass terrace melding gently into the misty Downs beyond. Magnolia trees clustered up against those walls, with a border of roses, myrtles and rosemary beneath. Spiraling stone staircases in the hall's corners led up to a vaulted, cloistered gallery overlooking the hall, off which were the family's bedrooms, and up again to the nurseries and housemaids' rooms on the top floor. The lower ground floor was the masculine domestic sphere. There the underbutler slept, guarding the gun room, wine cellars and butler's pantry, where the family silver and other valuables were locked in the plate closet. There too were the butler's sitting room, odd-man's room, lamp room, gun room and brushing room, dedicated entirely to brushing dirt off woolen clothes.

The servants' offices, where the majority of Clouds' thirty-odd indoor staff slept, were connected to the main house on the ground floor through the dining service room and on the lower-ground floor by a web of subterranean passages. The offices were a long, low wing designed by Philip Webb to look like a series of cottages, with uncottagelike proportions. The beamed servant's hall was nearly forty feet long, the housekeeper Mrs. Vine's bedroom and sitting room two-thirds as large. The housekeeper's ground-floor rooms led directly to the china closet, the table linen room, the still room, store rooms, larder, game larder and bakehouse: all her responsibility and domain. Forbes the butler slept on the first floor, next to the footmen's rooms, where he could keep an eye on them. Footmen, chosen specifically for their height, good looks and turn of calf, were apt to be troublesome. Further rooms for visiting valets were beyond. At the far end of the offices was the gardener's cottage of Harry Brown, who had come with the Wyndhams from Wilbury; beyond that stood the stables with their controversial bricks.

The vast kitchen was modeled on a medieval abbot's kitchen at Glastonbury. Huge joints of meat roasted on a spit over the fire, kept turning by a hot-air engine. The dripping, caught in a vat beneath, was sold to East Knoyle's villagers for a penny. Next door the scullery maids scrubbed stacks of dishes and dirty pans. In a separate laundry building containing washing house, ironing room and drying room, four local girls washed and rinsed muslins, linens, cottons and woolens three days a week, mangling, starching and ironing for another two. A house like Clouds might go through on average a thousand napkins a week; soap and soda were delivered annually by the ton and half ton.

The imaginative gardens, designed for tête-à-têtes, were a collaboration between Madeline Wyndham and Harry Brown. Madeline's bedroom on the main house's east side overlooked a series of gardens, walled on one side by the offices (which were covered in vines and fig trees). The gardens were "a succession of lovely surprises," said Harry Brown, with rose gardens, yew hedges clipped to resemble peacocks' tails, a chalk-walled spring garden blooming annually with tulips, narcissus and cyclamens, and a pergola garden. The garden to the house's northwest, with its winding "river walk," was wilder. Cedar trees towered in the distance. The walk itself was planted with bluebells, primroses, Japanese iris, azaleas, bamboos, magnolias and rhododendrons.

When the Wyndhams moved in, the house was not quite complete. The hall's chandeliers had yet to arrive; the drawing room's intricate plasterwork was not finished until 1886. The plumbing was so full of glitches that Percy complained it required the assistance of the house carpenter and an engineer for "a common warm bath." The house had to be unpacked, and decorated. "Lately the floors have been strewn with scraps of carpet and we have stood with our heads on one side . . ." said a perplexed Mananai.

When finished, the house had a distinctive scent of cedar wood, beeswax and magnolias and was decorated with near-monastic simplicity. Percy's bedroom was papered in Morris print. Otherwise all the ground-floor rooms were painted white, their woodwork unpolished oak. Against the hall's stone walls hung two large tapestries: "Greenery," commissioned from Morris & Co., and a Flemish hunting scene. Over the vast fireplace was a large painting, believed to be by the Italian Renaissance painter Alesso Baldovinetti, of *The Virgin Adoring the Christ Child with the Infant St. John the Baptist and Angels in a Forest,* bought by Percy at auction. A Morris carpet, pale pink, green, blue and white, covered the floor. The hall had little furniture: a broadwood piano, four black-lacquer cabinets, and chairs upholstered in Morris's "Honeysuckle" design.

The light-flooded drawing room, filled with comfortable sofas and chairs, was piled high with periodicals and books rebound by Madeline Wyndham in her favored vellum. There was no library, and books were everywhere in the house, with a trolley for trundling them about. At the drawing room's far end stood Madeline's "scrattle table"—at which she sketched, and wrote, hands constantly moving even as "her mind was free, moving among her guests." The furniture was eighteenth-century Hepplewhite or Chippendale. On the walls—finally displayed to perfection—was the Wyndhams' collection of many years: works by

Clouds House from the south, where the drawing room windows overlooked a tamer fenced garden before the soft wildness of the Downs took over.

the Pre-Raphaelites, the Etruscan School, and Old Italian Masters. Over the main staircase hung Burne-Jones's cartoon of the Ascension, depicting in glowing raw umber and gilt "the figure of Christ blessing those on Earth from above surrounded by the Arch-Angels." This might well have been the house depicted by Henry James in *The Spoils of Poynton*: "the record of a life . . . written in great syllables of color and form, the tongues of other countries and the hands of rare artists . . . all France and Italy, with their ages composed to rest. For England you looked out of old windows—it was England that was the wide embrace."

In every room cushioned baskets awaited Madeline's pampered fleet of fox terriers; over thirty peacocks and peahens strutted through the gardens. The south terrace beyond the drawing room rang to the "wild satanic laughter" of a pair of African jackasses; fifty to sixty doves, which were fed in the walnut tree court, flew freely about the rooms. Three times a day, Madeline scattered birdfeed outside to attract wild birds. A packing box used originally for Mananai's possessions was turned into a squirrel house, still bearing the faded legend "Miss Wyndham's bedroom." The house teemed with life.

The Wyndhams' arrival at Clouds coincided with George's return from the Sudan with tales of some "hot" engagements and a souvenir in the form of a three-foot-long Crusader sword liberated from a Sudanese prisoner of war. Madeline was "simply *brimming over* with thankfulness" at entering the house with her family safe and well. The villagers of East Knoyle and Milton greeted the rising up of a great house in their midst with feudal-like enthusiasm. They twice turned out to cheer the family's arrival, East Knoyle's church bells pealing in celebration: when Percy, Guy, Mananai, Pamela and Fräulein arrived on the afternoon of 23 September 1885, and when George and Madeline, delayed by George's regimental inspection, followed the next day. The handsome, eccentric family was a source of fascination: village children whispered that drawling, impeccably dressed Percy had his valet wash the coins jingling in his pocket, so bleached clean did he seem (in fact, such a practice was quite common and the rumor probably accurate). By contrast Madeline "never seemed like an ordinary rich person . . . she . . . was the easiest and most sympathetic person to talk to that I have ever met," remembered Violet Milford, one of the daughters of the canon of East Knoyle Church.

The family were diligent and generous squires. When a bad spate of influenza struck East Knoyle, Madeline Wyndham took Mananai and Pamela with her to visit the sick "nearly everyday," and shortly afterwards employed a London-trained nurse permanently to attend the parish's sick. Each day's lunch leftovers were delivered by the little girls and Fräulein to the cottages of the poor—piled up, as was customary, in one pungent mess. The village's children remembered Punch & Judy shows in the hall at Christmas; charity bazaars where the female Wyndhams manned the stalls; vast feasts held to celebrate the marriages of each of the Wyndham children where all the toys in the nurseries were turned out onto the lawns—a very heaven.

From that first Christmas, the family established traditions. Madeline provided each of East Knoyle's 190 or so schoolchildren with a new, warm jumper. Semley Station's employees were invited to toast and ale on Boxing Day. On New Year's Eve the family threw a staff ball with dancing from 10 p.m. to 3 a.m.; an orchestra was bussed in from Salisbury, chairs laid out along the passages for sitting out, rooms provisioned with card tables for those who preferred gin rummy to waltzing,

The peaceful white-painted drawing room at Clouds with its rich Morris carpets, delicate eighteenth-century furniture and glowing works of art. On the left-hand wall, Ellis Roberts's large portrait of an eighteen-year-old Pamela Wyndham is just visible. In an era of heavy furniture, flock wallpaper and overstuffed upholstery, Madeline Wyndham's decorating style was refreshing, bold and unusual.

and a music show held in which footmen and kitchen maids displayed their talents. George reinforced his hero status by rescuing a village child who had fallen through the bathing pond's ice—although, the ongoing plumbing problems meant no hot bath to follow. "There is something refreshing in the idea of patrician and plebean [*sic*] after their common danger being relegated to the humble copper kettle of daily use but that is not what I am paying for," wrote Percy to his architect Philip Webb, unable to resist a good-natured dig.

Percy, like all his family, was delighted with their new house, which they thought embodied their exceptionalism. And though the Wyndhams' friend Godfrey Webb thought, privately, the house "the largest and ugliest in England," for the most part the Wyndhams were flooded in praise. "Influential people (or donkeys as you would call them) are putting it about that this is the house of the age. I believe they are right," Percy wrote to his architect, as he surveyed his new domain.

This was a house of esoteric delights, overseen by a consummate hostess. Regular guests found hand-bound copies of their favorite books at their bedsides (a favorite family anecdote concerned a tiny bound copy of the Lord's Prayer containing a slip bearing "the Author's Compliments"). In the evenings, Madeline plied her visitors with blankets while they listened to music recitals in the hall. Masseuses were on hand to give "Swedish rubbing," gymnastics classes were conducted in the garden, and invariably in a darkened room somewhere in the house a spiritualist was conducting a bout of table-turning for the Wyndhams' guests. Madeline had been a convert to spiritualism since inviting her first medium to Wilbury in 1884, and at Clouds the Wyndhams hosted the most prominent theorists of the day. Walburga, Lady Paget, an eccentric vegetarian, thought Clouds perfection in all its entertainments, except for the adders that slithered through the Downs, preventing her from walking barefoot through the morning dew.

In microcosm, the mix of guests at Clouds reflected "the oncoming of a great new tide of human life over the Western World"—a post-Darwinian, post-Industrial Revolution experimentalism, seeking to find meaning in and improve the new age. Spiritualism epitomized this trend. Born, for many, out of a loss of religious faith, it attracted serious, reputable minds to the cause. Arthur Balfour, Sigmund Freud and William Gladstone were all members of the Society for Psychical Research (the SPR), founded in 1882 by a group of Cambridge scientists (among

The Wyndhams' tradition of elaborate theatrical productions began at Wilbury and continued on their move to Clouds. For Christmas 1887 a cast composed of the family, including Madeline Wyndham's orphaned niece and nephew Dorothy and Guy Carleton, and the Milfords, the family of the Canon of East Knoyle Church, performed Shakespeare's comedy *Love's Labours Lost* over three nights. The cast list reveals: sixteen-year-old Pamela had the central role of the high-spirited, witty "Princess of France" and eighteen-year-old Mananai (doubtless happily) played the background part of a lord in waiting. Hugo Elcho, a keen actor, was Longaville, one of the three noble companions of the King of Navarre, and Fräulein Schneider gamely took on the part of "fantastical Spaniard." Mary bowed out of the performance entirely, choosing to act instead as "prompter."

them two of Balfour's brothers-in-law) "for the purpose of inquiring into a mass of obscure phenomena which lie at present on the outskirts of our organized knowledge." Frederic Myers, one of the SPR's founders whose faith had been destroyed by Darwinism, spoke for many when admitting his desire to "re-enter . . . by the scullery . . . the heavenly mansion out of which I had been kicked through the front door."

Madeline Wyndham, who designed beautiful prie-dieus for her children, and illustrated biblical tracts to hang above their beds, had no difficulty in reconciling her powerful religious faith with a belief in "sproits and spiris [*sic*]." Pamela, the child who most enthusiastically adopted her mother's creed, explained her teachings in later life: "I learned that death is an incident in life . . . that communication with those we call the dead, under certain conditions is possible . . . never was I led for a moment to think that [spiritualism] should stand in the place of religion . . . Spiritualism supports rather than conflicts with [the] narratives of the life of Christ."

Percy, though more skeptical, was nonetheless superstitious. In the spring of 1885, as builders were putting the finishing touches to Clouds, a tall woman dressed in black appeared, asking to see the house. She was shown inside—such requests were not uncommon. She stood in the dusty hall, the walls rearing up around her. "This house will be burnt down and in less than three years," she announced, before disappearing as mysteriously as she had arrived. When later that year Percy arranged with Webb for the insurance of the house and its outbuildings, he expressed particular concern about the provision for loss by fire.

Clouds' magical luxury depended on a silent army of staff. Its occupants woke to fires crackling in the grate, laid soundlessly by a housemaid who had risen long before dawn, then scurried downstairs to clear away the previous evening's detritus: wine-stained glasses, full ashtrays in the smoking room; pieces of paper from a game, torn up and carelessly thrown aside. While the family and guests breakfasted, staff flung open windows to air bedrooms, whipped off still-warm sheets to perfectly remake beds and emptied full chamber pots. They dusted, swept, polished and mended linen before preparing the bedrooms again for their occupants to dress for dinner (men attended by their valets, women by their ladies' maids), and again while the house dined: drawing curtains, lighting candles, turning down beds. Rarely did they throw their exhausted bodies onto their own mattresses before eleven or twelve at night.

Sarah, "the pretty 2nd housemaid" at Clouds, was probably glad to leave service when she married Pearson the coachman and moved into his rooms above the coachhouse. She was fortunate in being able to live with her husband. Married footmen, valets or butlers generally lived separately from their wives, setting them up in a nearby cottage and visiting them on their days off. The wife of William Icke, Clouds' butler from 1892, was housekeeper to two spinster ladies in East Knoyle. Her loyalty was rewarded when they left her their house in their will. Housekeepers and cooks, who bore the courtesy title of "Mrs.," could actually be married—the Wyndham children's nanny of Cumberland days, Horsenail, had in fact married Forbes the butler, graduating to housekeeper in the days before Mrs. Vine. Otherwise, a female servant who married would immediately leave her employ.

In 1891 there were over one and a half million domestic servants in the United Kingdom—almost 16 percent of the workforce. Service was an honorable profession with loyalty and affection on both sides. Eassy and Bertha Devon, a tall, tranquil housemaid who first joined the family in Cumberland, both stayed with the Wyndhams until retirement, the former then moving to a cottage in East Knoyle. Nonetheless, in 1898 the average length of stay by a servant in a household was less than eighteen

months. The turnover at Clouds, from the names on the ten-yearly cen-
suses, was not notably different. The reasons were numerous: marriage, a
promotion elsewhere or abandonment of domestic service entirely. Periodicals like the *Lady* complained of young men and women with "ideas
above their station," thinking themselves too good for service. As the
century wore on many took that view, rejecting the snobbish hierarchy
of the servants' hall for the greater freedom and excitement available in
other jobs. All Madeline's daughters bemoaned the impossibility of finding good staff.

In 1885, domestic calm was rocked by a young woman's distress: "Poor
Lucy the housemaid in London I'm afraid she has gone mad—she went
for a holiday & came back *quite off her head.*" The situation, relayed by
Mrs. Vine to Madeline, was grave, if comical. Lucy, whose head Madeline thought had been "turned" by the marriage of her fellow housemaid
Mary Brown, veered between lucidity and moments of "wild" behavior.
Following a composed conversation with Dr. Gibbons, the doctor summoned to examine her, Lucy "came down and said to Bertha 'if I take
any one I think *I'll take Dr. Gibbons!*'"

While amused by Mrs. Vine's decorous alarm, Madeline nonetheless
took the matter seriously. She reported to Mary:

> It is quite too awfully sad . . . she is *full of* delusions thinks people
> are coming to take her *away* & that something dreadful will happen
> because Mary Brown had to sign some cheques for her that they will
> f[i]nd out she could not wright [*sic*] and a lot more I told her that she
> must not let her self give way . . . but . . . she is so miserable she would
> break her heart Bertha & Charlotte had to sit up with her & hold her
> down in bed. *Don't* talk about this with anyone but is it not horrid?

History does not relate what happened to Lucy. She does not appear
in the 1891 census either for Clouds or for Belgrave Square. Presumably
she was dispatched back to her family: it is likely that Madeline took care
to make sure someone would look after her.

Reportage of such untoward incidents was part of the traffic of communication between Madeline and her daughters: their own children
picked up snippets and came to Clouds wide-eyed, alert to a servant to
whom such gossip had lent an air of celebrity. Lizzie Beaver, the stillroom
maid (in charge of cakes, jam and preserves, so a good person for hungry

children to befriend), nearly died when, returning from the village to Clouds early in the morning of 31 December 1886, she got lost in snow and fog, and was only found at midday on New Year's Day, frozen half to death. Howard "the married stable-man" slipped over when carrying a heavy sack and injured his back badly enough to be confined to lying "quite still" for a lengthy period of time. The daughter of Wareham the undercoachman suffered from paralyzed legs, "the awful result, it was thought, of sitting on a cold stone when she was very hot." Eassy raised the alarm in 1888 with fears about her own heart, although Dr. Collins pronounced her as suffering only from "nervous shock"—most likely a panic attack, for reasons unknown. In 1892, Enfield, who had replaced Forbes as butler in 1888, was struck by a sudden "chill" and "rheumatic pains" one Friday night that left him "unable to wait at dinner," followed swiftly by "inflammation of the brain . . . he died in convulsions at 2:30 o'clock." Enfield's wife, who had gone to London "to be confined," was left to give birth to a fatherless child.

In her youth Madeline Wyndham had compiled a photograph album of "all the dear Servants at Petworth," with handwritten commentary beneath, identifying each. Yet she, like most, thought nothing of loaning her daughters a spare footman when they had large house parties "in the same way the poor borrow a frying pan, or a rub of soap," said an ex-butler, Eric Horne, scornfully in a best-selling memoir published in 1923. Percy rewarded his favorite, William Mallett, the clerk of works responsible for all maintenance on the house and estate, with a house that was two cottages knocked into one. It allowed Mallett—who had worked his way up from house carpenter—a comparatively palatial four bedrooms for his family of eleven. But Percy's attitude towards his staff was aristocratic, to say the least. Hyde, Clouds' head keeper, lost a finger when Percy swung round carelessly and pulled the trigger of his gun. That might have been sheer absentmindedness. The occasion on which Percy shot a beater called Fletcher in the foot for picking up the wrong pheasant most certainly was not.

SEVEN

The Birth of the Souls

The Wyndhams had barely moved into Clouds before Percy's time at Westminster was brought to an end by further franchise reform. Almost twenty years after the 1867 Reform Act lowered the property threshold for urban males, Gladstone's 1884 Franchise Act gave the same rights to their rural counterparts, adding a further 1.7 million men to the electorate. The following year's more radical Redistribution Act took electoral seats from the overrepresented rural constituencies to give to the underrepresented towns, eliminating in the process Percy's West Cumberland seat. The General Election that took place over three weeks in November and December 1885 brought these reforms into effect.

Percy was not particularly sad to leave Westminster. At fifty, he was content to rule over his fiefdom of East Knoyle, where he had far more power than he ever wielded as a backbencher in Parliament, and to otherwise be an armchair politician, fulminating about what he perceived to be the imminent end of aristocratic rule. There was plenty of material for him: as the last of the electoral returns were counted in December 1885, the political world reeled at the "Hawarden Kite," a carefully worded letter from Gladstone's son Herbert to *The Times* indicating that his father now supported Home Rule. The political bombshell was an intentional leak designed to gauge public and political appetite for the measure. But Pandora's box once opened could not be closed. When the election results were posted, 63 Irish Home Rule MPs held the balance of power between 237 Conservatives and 352 Liberals. Ireland was the fulcrum on which day-to-day politics would balance.

In January 1886, Parliament reconvened under Lord Salisbury's minority government. Gladstone moved an amendment to the Address (that is, the Queen's speech made at Parliament's State Opening which sets out the government's agenda for the coming session). Supported by the Irish, he brought the government down, and himself to power for a third time.

The news was greeted with gloom at Clouds. "What *do* you think of the Govt being out?!!!! Worst fears realized, says Papa," Mary told Hugo. The next day, still enraged, she wrote Hugo an impassioned letter sitting in bed after breakfast: "The irish [*sic*] party can turn *any* Government out or in, me thinks! . . . besides which its [*sic*] infamous that the old scoundrel should have had the joy of getting in again . . . I'm sure he is singing in his tub lustily of mornings & Mrs. G must be much elated & foreign politics will go to the devil again . . ." A true Conservative, Mary thought Home Rule must lead to imperial disintegration. But neither Mary nor Percy had fully read the runes of the vote. Twenty Whigs, led by Lord Hartington, had voted with the Conservatives against the amendment and against their leader, Gladstone. The more imminent disintegration was the Liberal Party's.

A week later, Mary, now some six months pregnant, visited London to buy furniture for the Elchos' new house in Chelsea, 62 Cadogan Square, which Hugo had bought to replace Hans Crescent, of which the Elchos had never been fond. Mary's political fervor was superseded by thoughts of interior design, as she plotted how to achieve Morris-inspired style on the Elchos' comparatively limited budget. She was staying with her parents-in-law in Mayfair, and had left Ego with her parents at Clouds; after a series of visits to friends throughout January, she felt as though she had barely seen her son for weeks. She told her mother she felt "quite shy" of seeing him again.

It was an exceptionally cold winter, amplifying the distress caused by prolonged economic depression. In early February riots broke out—literally on Mary's doorstep—when socialist marchers, up to ten thousand of them, were provoked by servants of the gentlemen's clubs along Pall Mall. Windows throughout the length of Clubland were smashed, shops on Piccadilly looted, "nobs" pulled from their carriages and stripped of their valuables. For several days London looked like "a city under siege." As a thick black fog blanketed the city, wild rumors spread of a further march of fifty thousand unemployed. Mary was strangely oblivious: "There was a demonstration of the unemployed today & they broke all the windows in St. James's," she told her mother in an offhand postscript to a letter about beds. Thereafter, her letters resumed their exclusivity of subject: furniture. "I think about *nothing* else."

This was not quite true. A week after the riots, around St. Valentine's Day, Mary went privately to visit Arthur Balfour at 4 Carlton Gardens, which had been at the heart of the affray. Twenty years later, she wrote to him preparing to re-create the incident: "I must settle to pay my first visit to yr house . . . and be received by you alone and step over the threshold and I shall remember a certain day exactly 20 yrs ago. f-rst k-ss." Shortly afterwards, Mary wrote to Hugo from St. James's Place in a particularly affectionate manner. "Me feels xceeding [*sic*] full of tremendous love for Wash," she told him. It would set a pattern.

At Easter, Mary and Hugo went to Stanway. They had not been alone in the country "for a 'minit' hardly since we married," said Mary, explaining to her mother why they would not spend the holiday at Clouds. Their days at "Stangewange" were a success. "You can't imagine how delicious it is here & we're having the nicest Time, I think since we married," Mary told Laura Lyttelton. Laura immediately passed the news to Arthur verbatim, adding, with masterful tact: "Knowing you a little I think [this] will please you . . . I am v. happy about this . . . and you must be too, dear old friend." Was wily Laura double-bluffing: did she know of the scene at Carlton Gardens a few weeks past? Possibly— for years later, Margot Tennant, to whom Laura was as close as a twin, allowed to Wilfrid Blunt that Arthur might once have kissed Mary, although adamantly denying the possibility of anything more.

In London a few weeks later Laura gave birth to a healthy boy. At Stanway, Mary, now entertaining a party including the Brodricks and Godfrey Webb, rejoiced. But Laura's apparent good health began to fade. On 24 April 1886, with an ashen Alfred and Margot by her bedside, she died, her last words "I think God has forgotten me." She was twenty-three. Tommy Ribblesdale telegraphed Stanway with the news: "all over between 9 & 10 this morning." "She was not able to struggle through after all, poor thing," Mary wrote in her diary that night as thunderstorms raged outside and light flooded through the oriel window into the hall. "It makes one utterly miserable."

Laura's death left Mary bereft. She wrote bleakly to her mother:

We had so counted on living . . . our lives together . . . at least I feel how much I had counted on it . . . & bringing up our babies & helping one another . . . all the future was mixed up with her; for she twined into everyone's joys & sorrows . . . it seems beastly being allowed to live when other people . . . the best & most needed people are not.

All Laura's friends felt the same. Margot's statement that "Laura made & left a deeper impression on the world in her short life than anyone I have ever known" was, for once, without embellishment.

In her will Laura left Mary a Chippendale cradle, and a crescent necklace that was a wedding present from Arthur to Laura. "She must wear it because 2 of her dear friends are in it, as it were," Laura directed. It was presumably a public benediction intended to scour out any remaining hint of scandal. In fact, Laura's death—or perhaps her final letter to Arthur—temporarily drove a wedge between the two. The day after Laura's funeral Arthur visited Mary at the Elchos' new house. Alone in the half-finished drawing room he attacked her for being "hard" and failing to give him the "comfort" he sought. He did not explain what that "comfort" was. Probably Balfour, unmoored by Laura's death, did not know himself. Mary, as so often in moments of extreme emotional turmoil, was tongue-tied. After Arthur had left, she spent a sleepless night poring over her feelings and the next day wrote apologizing for her inability to lessen the "awful blank" left by Laura's death. "If you could really know my thoughts 'hard' would be the very very last word you could apply . . . I would do anything for you . . . you must forgive me."

The Gang all later believed their particular closeness had been fostered by this intense period in the somber late spring of 1886 when they withdrew from Society to mourn Laura. In the summer, Margot and the Ribblesdales joined the Elchos quietly at Felixstowe, and later visited Stanway with George Curzon, Evan Charteris and Arthur. In October, the Elchos were at the Tennants' Glen with Arthur, the Ribblesdales, Godfrey Webb and George Curzon. In November, they entertained at Stanway those same people, minus Webb, but plus Violet Manners, wife of John Manners, the future Duke of Rutland; Lucy Graham Smith (another Tennant sister); and Doll Liddell and Earl and Countess de Grey. Ten days later they were at Ashridge in Hertfordshire, home of Lord and Lady Brownlow, with the Brownlows' nephew and heir Harry Cust, the Brodricks, the Pembrokes and Arthur. In December, they were at Clouds, with George Wyndham, the Ribblesdales, Arthur, the Pembrokes and Margot; in January, at Wilton with Sir Jack and Lady Horner (the latter, Frances Graham, was Mary's childhood friend) and Harry Cust. Returning to Society's "dreary ocean," the Gang had found how much they preferred their company to that of anyone else.

Society frowned upon cliquishness as somehow improper. More unusual that autumn was that a group containing Liberals and Conservatives was meeting at all. Gladstone's determination to press on with Home Rule had torn his party and Society apart. In June, his Home Rule Bill was defeated by the Conservatives allied with ninety erstwhile Liberals, an uneasy combination of Radicals led by Joseph Chamberlain, the charismatic, opportunistic ex-Mayor of Birmingham, and Lord Hartington's Whig grandees. The defectors became known as Liberal Unionists, the allied forces as Unionists. As Oscar Wilde had Lady Bracknell explain in *The Importance of Being Earnest,* Liberal Unionists now "count as Tories. They dine with us. Or come in the evening, at any rate."

The addition of the Whig peers rendered the Unionists the party of the aristocracy, with an unimpeachable majority in the Lords. In the surviving rump of the Liberal party, the Radical element formerly tempered by the Whigs, now flourished. From this split came the ability of the Unionist Lords to veto legislation passed by a Liberal House of Commons, claiming disingenuously as justification that the Upper House's role was to prevent "hasty and foolish" legislation by a hotheaded Commons. In the short term, it split Society—even families. By the autumn Unionists and Liberals no longer met.

Only the Gang refused "to sacrifice private friendship to public politics." In Margot's grand recollections, "at our house . . . and those of the Souls, everyone met. Randolph Churchill, Gladstone, Asquith, Morley, Chamberlain, Balfour, Rosebery, Salisbury, Hartington, Harcourt and, I might add, jockeys, actors, the Prince of Wales and every ambassador in London," resulting, in Margot's estimation, in a place where "men of different tempers and opposite beliefs" could discuss their differences "without heat and without reporters."

Politics was the warp and weft of the Souls' daily lives: Margot recounted an afternoon spent by Souls women discussing which of George Curzon, George Wyndham or Harry Cust would become Prime Minister. But this "fascinating, aristocratic, intellectual coterie" possessed "special charm" beyond the political. Some thought their pretensions to intellectualism hollow ("They read the Bible & they read the Morte d'Arthur in the same spirit," said Wilfrid Blunt), but the less cerebral members of the aristocracy were impressed: "I think they sent us all back to reading more than we otherwise would have done, and this was an excellent thing for us," said Daisy, Countess of Warwick, flibbertigibbet mistress of the Prince of Wales.

In November 1886, Mary sat for a chalk and crayon portrait by Edward Poynter. Hugo, for unknown reasons, had resisted the idea, and Mary found the sittings a "nuisance." In the portrait, Mary leans back on a chaise, gazing into the distance. She is surrounded by aestheticism's accoutrements: a japonaiserie screen; blue and white ceramic vases. Her hair is fashionably shirred; her waist, in her plain mustard-yellow gown, tiny (the envy of her friends, she said proudly). One hand loosely holds a sketchbook, another book lies unopened before her. She looks deep in thought: a beauty with greater things on her mind. The features of a child are still there in her face, but her languid ease suggests someone increasingly comfortable with her place in the world.

Poynter captured many elements of a typical Souls woman in this portrait. He reflected her style of clothing—Souls women did not, by and large, indulge in feathers and furs but dressed "with a kind of aesthetic smartness all their own," said Susan, Lady Tweedsmuir, wife of the author John Buchan. Arthur was quite alarmed when Mary proposed having a gown made by Worth, the grand Parisian couturier, commenting that he did not expect to recognize her in such finery. Poynter also alluded to her intellectual, artistic bent (as a corollary, the tables of Souls hostesses were comparatively frugal by the standards of their time and class. Conversation, rather than rich food, sustained their guests, and Souls women were, in general, notably slim).

Yet Poynter, himself not renowned for his sense of humor, failed to capture the essence of Mary, and the group to which she was integral. Her family thought the solemn portrait captured neither the "dancing gaiety" of her eyes, nor the swallow-like quickness of her movement. In the flesh the Souls were "more pagan than soulful," said Daisy Warwick. While publicly advocating chastity, they were impossibly flirta-

Mary, aged twenty-four, a mother of two, by Sir Edward Poynter, just a few months after the death of her beloved friend Laura Tennant and while her relationship with Arthur Balfour was growing ever deeper. Mary's family later criticized this portrait as far too solemn. Yet perhaps in Mary's forlorn expression Poynter had seen some of the turmoil in which Mary found herself at this stage of her life.

tious with one another, to the extent that Lady Tweedsmuir described them as "a little suspect as not conforming to the rules of the social game." Irreverent, they termed the group's elder statesmen (the Cowpers, Brownlows and Pembrokes) "the Aunts"; and Balfour, their lodestar, "the adored Gazelle." With quick, inconsequential wit and a ready turn of phrase, they spent hours playing games: "Clumps," requiring participants to guess by questions abstractions like "the last straw," "the eleventh hour" or even "the last ball Mr. Balfour drove into the [golf] bunker before lunch"; "Styles," parodying well-known authors in prose or verse; "Epigrams," inventing new ones; and "Character Sketches," describing someone present in terms of something else, such as a vegetable, building or color.

The name bestowed upon them during the 1888 Season reflected some of this mockery. In the spring, Mary attended a dinner party at Lord and Lady Brownlow's house. The Gang engaged in their usual heated debate. "You all sit and talk about each other's souls. I shall call you 'the Souls,'" said Lord Charles Beresford, an outsider, a courtier. Mary was sure that the quip—which no one thought very funny—was a well-rehearsed line, trundled out several times that season. Nonetheless, it stuck. The Souls always professed to hate it, denying being a clique at all.

Such denials were unconvincing. In London, they were constantly in and out of one another's houses. Outsiders finding themselves at a country house party of Souls often made their excuses and left: "Either . . . they were bored with us or . . . they saw that we were bored with them," Arthur said to Mary of uptight Field Marshal Viscount Wolseley and his family, who left Wilton fully two days earlier than planned. Conversely, at a house party held by the non-Soul Baron Ferdinand de Rothschild at his magnificent Buckinghamshire château Waddesdon Manor, it was Mary and Charty Ribblesdale who retreated to Mary's room, "exhausted" by the talk of their (non-Souls) fellow guests. They were soon joined by Hugo and his sister Hilda Brodrick, whereupon the intention that Charty should read Shelley aloud was abandoned in favor of an afternoon of vivacious "chaffing" of Hugo. Three weeks later, Mary, Daisy White, George Curzon and Hugo whiled away the train journey from London to the Pembrokes' Wilton House in Wiltshire learning poetry by heart; the following Sunday at the Cowpers' Panshanger in Hertfordshire, a large number of the party, Mary included, decided to forgo church in favor of a morning in which "we sat out on the grass talking [about] . . . Dickens etc . . ." The Souls, notwithstanding their name, did not share the previous generation's religious fervor.

Rarely apart, they developed a "ganglanguage" incomprehensible to the outsider: "dentist," a private meeting; "floater," an embarrassing situation; "stodge," the company of women; "flash" or "sparkle," the company of men. The vocabulary is revealing. A Souls gathering was quite different from the traditional, gender-stratified house party where shooting was the order of the day and the two sexes united only briefly to eat (the women joined the "guns" at damp outdoor lunches, at tea in the drawing room and again at dinner, following which the women left the men to their port, smoking and billiards). The young niece of Lord Wenlock, whose wife, Constance, was a Soul, was startled when, visiting the Wenlocks' Escrick Park in Yorkshire she found that certain men including Harry Cust, Evan Charteris and Doll Liddell declined to shoot, seeming instead "to prefer the society of ladies and stayed at home on stormy or doubtful days, reading aloud to my aunt and her friends while they painted or modelled—or sometimes just talking, whimsically, wittily (as I know now, if I didn't then) all day long."

Lady Violet Bonham Carter, daughter of Henry Asquith, and a child of the next generation, thought the Souls had a "liberating and civilising" impact on Society, and she appreciated that "much of our fun and freedom was a direct heritage from them." In old age even the Souls themselves struggled to describe their evanescent charm, which was of the bon mot; behavior that startled, but amused; a delightful but fundamentally unthreatening disregard for convention. Their benign rebellion pushed the boundaries. It did not breach them. The best illustration comes from one who was not a Soul. Intellectual, acerbic Lady Frances Balfour did not always approve of the Souls. Her daughter Blanche Dugdale recorded her fury on returning from church at Whittingehame (Arthur's East Lothian home) to find nine-year-old Blanche playing backgammon for half-crown stakes with Hugo. On visiting Mells, Somerset home of the Horners, Frances described the scene at dinner to her sister-in-law Lady Betty:

> Lady Ribblesdale talking of a Peacock said it was a voluptuous bird, at which old Mrs. Graham [Frances Horner's mother] took exception and said "that word beginning with a 'V' ought not to be mentioned" I stood up for it and said it was what we all would be if we knew how, on which the old lady nearly fainted, and Lady Ribblesdale screamed with laughing, and asked the dear old soul if she would like to be if she knew how, and then there was a rapid proposal that a class should be formed and a Professor found (Lady Ribblesdale proposing Swinburne) to teach us the way wherein to walk. Wild nonsense but so refreshing I felt inclined to walk all round the room on my head.

Notwithstanding her fundamental disapproval, Frances recognized the group's merit: "There is no doubt that with a hostess who understands how to manage them and with a real personality there is something very interesting in the 'gang' . . . All these people have lived together through some of the great experiences and feelings of life, they know each other to the very core, and the absolute freedom and ease are delightful . . ."

At heart, this was a group of very good, fiercely competitive friends, whether in romance, politics or friendship. Only the Souls would read

Ettie Grenfell (later Lady Desborough), one of Mary's closest friends and rivals. An heiress who was orphaned before she was three years old and whose only sibling, a brother, died before she was ten, Ettie's defining characteristics were her stubborn will to joy and her refusal to yield to self-pity. These traits were admired by her friends, but her children found this inability to acknowledge reality challenging, along with the host of younger male admirers whom she cultivated in later life.

out "Collinses," the effusive letters of thanks sent after each house party, from guests recently departed to "roars of mirth & groans of contempt" from those remaining, as Mary, Ettie, Harry Cust and Harry White did one November day at Stanway in 1890. "We acted like traitors that afternoon!" said Mary to Ettie, with a "crushing sense" that her own letter was even at that moment being read out "as a sample of idiocy!" Slender, fascinating Ettie Fane, the Cowpers' niece, was drawn into the circle after her marriage to Willie Grenfell in 1887. "I feel really that *you* & *I* (& Laura [Lyttelton] who left so swiftly so long ago) . . . *were* really— the *soul*! & center in a way of the elusive set," Mary wrote to Ettie in old age. Privately, to Arthur, Mary called Ettie "Delilah," crowing when Ettie, the least intellectually able (or interested) of the group, failed to grasp some point of debate. Margot once challenged Balfour with not minding if Mary, Ettie and she all died. "I should mind if you all died on the same day" was Balfour's laconic response.

At twenty-three, George Wyndham, who had moved into the Gang's orbit through Mary, scored a palpable hit when he secured the hand of the widowed, exceptionally beautiful Sibell, Countess Grosvenor, over a reported eighty rivals, including George Curzon. Sibell was eight years older than George, a mother of three, and renowned for her indis-

Lady Sibell Lumley, the daughter of the 9th Earl of Scarborough, was just nineteen when she first married Victor, Earl Grosvenor, heir to the 1st Duke of Westminster, himself reputedly the richest man in Britain. Ten years later, Victor died at the age of thirty, leaving twenty-nine-year-old Sibell with three small children, of which the eldest was Hugh, nicknamed Bend'Or after his grandfather's winning racehorse. Bend'Or was to inherit the 1st Duke's great wealth and title. Sibell's beauty, soft charm, wealth and impeccable connections made the young widow irresistible to a host of suitors, including George Wyndham.

criminate warmth and sweetness. When she clasped someone's hand in her own soft one, said the Anglo-Irish hostess Elizabeth Fingall, it was never quite clear whether she knew whose hand it was. Sibell had been charmed by George's exuberant volubility and intense romanticism—the poet "riding to hounds across his prose, looking with wonder upon the world as upon a fairyland," as T. S. Eliot described him—and his dark, "French" looks, which were those of a troubadour according to Elizabeth Fingall, who added that George lived "every minute of his life at high pitch." In maturity, George earned the tired sobriquet of "the handsomest man in England." But it required Madeline Wyndham to plead George's case with her old friend the Duke of Westminster, Sibell's father-in-law, before the Duke reluctantly agreed to Sibell's marrying the bumptious young man. He stipulated that Sibell maintain her title after marriage. It was unthinkable that the mother of his heir, Bend'Or, should be plain Mrs. George Wyndham.

George's unmistakably oedipal choice was regarded with misgivings by many who knew him. Alfred Lyttelton expressed concern about the effect on a "smart youth . . . very keen about his profession and about intellectual things . . . from a family where there is throughout an air of Bohemian quasi-culture" of being "plunged into deadalike decorous ducal circles coldly hostile to him and all that produced his unstupid but ill-ballasted personality." George survived—but Sibell was no match intellectually for him. Soon enough he took up with Gay, Lady Plymouth, and conducted a contented lifelong affair.

EIGHT

The Summer of 1887

I n January 1887, while staying at Clouds, Mary realized to her horror that she was pregnant again. With her younger son Guy barely
six months old, she chided "*Naughty* Wash" for "pinting [*sic*] too
soon after Betsey at Panshanger," breaking the news in a carrot-and-stick
manner: "if ou comes veggy early! Migs will receive ou in cot & no more
precautions needed, for Migs is quite certainly in the family way," she
told him. Hugo was several days overdue. Suspecting, with good reason,
that Hugo had been delayed by another woman's charms, Mary promised sex to entice him back.

Mary disliked being pregnant. It made her feel fat, dull and unable
to compete socially among her friends. The mid-Victorian days of ten
or twelve children were past. Souls women, appreciating their figures,
their health and their consuming social lives, did not have many children. Carefully coded advertisements in women's periodicals recommended purges of pennyroyal and compounds of aloe and iron to restore
a young lady to good "health." It seems that at least some of Mary's
friends employed these, but Mary decided on this occasion that she
"daren't send for Zach's stuff its [*sic*] too naughty," and resigned herself
to the inevitable: "Me looks forward to it [the pregnancy] with disgust
& loathing . . . my season with Mad knocked on the head" (for Mananai
was due to be presented that spring and Mary had been looking forward

to showing her younger sister the ropes in her first Season). "Migs propose Pints dispose," Mary mourned.

Mary was still in her first trimester when she attended George and Sibell's quiet marriage in the private chapel of the Westminsters' Cheshire house, Eaton Hall. The service was attended only by immediate family, although conducted by the Archbishop of Canterbury, the Church of England's premier prelate. In what must have been a significant blow to George's ego, *The Times* reported that the Countess Grosvenor had married *Guy* Wyndham of the 16th (Queen's) Lancers, with George acting as best man. The Wyndhams celebrated the occasion more lavishly on their return to Clouds with a vast tea for Milton's and East Knoyle's inhabitants. A band played from the terrace, a cricket match was held for the adults and a bag of sweets and a bun given to each child. On the newlyweds first visiting, the villagers followed the still fairly widespread tradition of intercepting their carriage and replacing their horses with eighty men who pulled them up the driveway to Clouds themselves.

While on honeymoon at the Italian Lakes, George received a telegram from Arthur Balfour. Sir Michael Hicks Beach, Ireland's Chief Secretary, had resigned, citing cataracts that had left him nearly blind (his resignation evoked a predecessor's, Sir George Trevelyan, whose hair went snow-white within twelve months and who resigned within twenty-four, pleading for release from a post that he described as "not a human life at all"). In a shock appointment, Salisbury had chosen his favorite nephew to replace Hicks Beach. The decision—so startling that it has prompted the suggestion (probably incorrect) that this was the source of the popular phrase "Bob's your uncle"—provoked incomprehension at Westminster and jubilation in Dublin. "We have killed Cavendish, blinded Beach and smashed up Trevelyan. What shall we do with this weakling?" boasted the Irish crowds. Now Arthur asked George to join him as his private secretary. Citing the Wyndham tradition of public service, George cut short his honeymoon and hotfooted it back to "throw my lot in the political boat."

George's new post was a triumph for the Wyndhams, establishing in the Souls' fiercely competitive world how close the family was to the "adored Gazelle." But both offices were dangerous. Cavendish's and Burke's murders were still fresh in people's minds. Arthur, the tenth Chief Secretary in as many years, pointed out with typical detachment that Ireland was a place where people tended to lose their reputations, their lives or possibly both. Shortly before Arthur's departure, Mary visited him at Carlton Gardens. It was a Wednesday afternoon, fast becoming their ritual meeting time when in London, for on Wednesdays the House of Commons rose early. Perhaps it was the urgency lent by anxiety that provoked what Mary described as a "small very private and personal incident (gear changing!)" in the same downstairs sitting room where they had first kissed a year before. Mary gave no further clues to what the incident might have been, beyond teasing Arthur that it would not appear in his memoirs.

Some years later, Mary explained to Wilfrid Blunt the exact nature of sexual relations among the Souls. "Nearly all the group were married women with husbands whom they loved & by whom they had children, but each had her friend who was a friend only." Those friends' relationship was "a little more than friendship, a little less than love," which Wilfrid translated as everything but "the conjugal act"; or, from the male perspective, "Every woman shall have her man, but no man shall have his woman." Later correspondence indicates that Mary and Arthur developed a sexual relationship involving role play and mild sadomasochism (Arthur's fondness for vigorous spankings lends disappointing force to the accusations frequently leveled at public-school-educated Englishmen). Quite possibly this "incident" was the first time that Mary—then almost three months pregnant—and Arthur engaged in such activities.

Arthur left a few days later, leaving with Frances Balfour a pouch to be opened only in the event of his death. "Accidents have occurred to a Chief Secretary for Ireland and (although I think it improbable) they may occur again. If the worst (as people euphemistically say!) should happen," said Balfour, Frances was to cut open the pouch with her penknife and "read the scrawl inside. It relates to a matter with which only you can deal."

Arthur did not need to elaborate on these instructions, or on his request that in such an event Frances check through his papers for any incriminating correspondence (Arthur's preparations for his departure included burning a multitude of letters, many, presumably, from Mary). Fifty years later, an elderly Frances and Mary sat down together to open the pouch. "My dear Frances," wrote Balfour:

> I write this in a great hurry, but as you will only have to read it in the event of my death you will forgive my handwriting. I think you and all

whom I love will be sorry that I am not any longer with you. But you will be able to talk it freely over with each other and all whom such an event may concern. There is however one who will not be in this position. I want you to give her as from yourself this little brooch which you will find herewith: and to tell her that, at the end, if I was able to think at all, I thought of her. If I was the means of introducing any unhappiness into her life I hope God will forgive me. I know she will.

The year 1887 marked Queen Victoria's Golden Jubilee celebrating fifty years of her reign. The Queen was reluctantly persuaded out of purdah for a Season glittering with magnificent balls, processions and banquets. Mary spent it more quietly in intellectual self-improvement. She was a keen attendee of weekly ethics classes organized by her sister-in-law Hilda Brodrick, who hired a graduate from Girton (Cambridge's first women's college) as tutor. The day chosen was Wednesday, so male Souls could join. The small group that gathered each week included Mary, Betty Balfour, Charty Ribblesdale, Lady Pembroke and Ettie Grenfell. The sessions, on themes including "Conscience self love etc" and "Kant," were a qualified success. "Miss Anderson gave us a lecture which as none of us (except Betty) knew anything about the subject or had read anything was rather above our heads," Mary told her diary, noting that week's essay title: "Is it necessary for ethical reasoning, to assume or establish an ultimate end to rational action?" Attendance diminished as the Season wore on. Mary was just one of three participants at the final class in early July, although their numbers had been boosted when Willie Grenfell and Tommy Ribblesdale joined after the House rose. The triumphant ethicists went out for a "farewell ethical luncheon" that continued into the early hours of the morning: "We argued about the word implied & implicit till 1 o'clock & then couldn't sleep from excitement," Mary recorded.

A brief respite followed, as Mary, Hugo, the Ribblesdales and their eldest son, Thomas, went for a few days to Lyndhurst in the New Forest, staying in the Crown Hotel. The weather was baking, and the forest even more lovely than Mary had expected. "We have been out all today laying [*sic*] on our backs looking up at the trees [while] Charty read aloud," Mary told her mother. Later in the day Hugo, Tommy and little Tommy raced around, hot, flustered and excited, trying to catch butterflies in nets. That night the adults dined with Sir William Harcourt, who had served in Gladstone's most recent Cabinet as Chancellor, and Harcourt's wife, Elizabeth, and then took a moonlit drive back to their hotel. The trip was a "great success" for the two flirtatious couples.

Shortly afterwards, Mary went to Clouds for the summer, while Hugo made it clear that he preferred to stay in London for the Season's final weeks. Mary had her misgivings. She knew her husband's inclination for flirting with other women—"pairing off with a conk & having long tête-à-tête & purely (or impurely) personal conversations"—and feared he was neglecting his Commons duties. "You see too much of Violet [Manners] & [I] am getting uneasy," she told him in early August: for Mary suspected rightly that beautiful, artistic Violet did not subscribe to the group's morality in the way Mary and her other friends did. A few weeks later, under pretext of recounting a heated lunchtime debate with Hilda Brodrick and Betty Balfour on the philosopher John Stuart Mill's *Utilitarianism,* Mary wrote Hugo a lengthy letter about "systematic self-ishness" and the necessity of quelling one's hedonistic will. The subtext was not hard to see.

By late August, Mary, Hilda and Betty had finished Mill and were planning two days of Butler's sermons and dissertations before taking the "plunge into Sorley's Ethics of Naturalism, which I *hope & trust* to have finished before practical Physics in the shape of giving birth to an infant puts a temporary stop to my Ethics," Mary said. The other goings-on of the house impinged little upon her. "Mr. Adeane's here (Marie's brother) rather a muff I think," she told Hugo.

Twenty-three-year-old Charles Adeane, whose sister Marie was a maid of honor to the Queen, had been courting Mananai since her debut that spring. Of all the sisters, Mananai came closest to replicating their mother's "sweetness and social charm," without the underlying steel. Few were likely to exclaim, as Mananai did, how "lovely" February was as a month, and mean it. Her solemn interest in clothes and titles prompted Percy to nickname her "Madeline the Mondaine." Like Guy Wyndham, she was a lesser star in the family constellation, and as a child she had had a tendency to "twitch! & wink! Terribly." Despite being older by two years, her development had always noticeably lagged behind the precocious Pamela's, but she was passionately supportive of her siblings, championing their achievements and mourning their defeats with utter sincerity.

Mananai found the Souls' intellectual jousting daunting. Harry

Cust earned her lasting affection by confessing to her that he was just as bashful as she: a lie, but a comforting one. She felt far more at ease with Charlie Adeane, a good-hearted, rather ponderous Cambridgeshire landowner, apt to pontificate about the problems besetting agriculture, and from a more stolid family of courtiers (although not entirely without spark: Charlie's jovial uncle Alick, a groom in waiting, had provoked one of the Queen's most famous comments when he recounted a risqué joke at a state dinner. "We are not amused," she replied).

None of the Wyndhams was particularly impressed by Charlie. Mary and Pamela found the "lon-

Portrait of Miss Madeline Wyndham, Aged Sixteen: sweet-natured Mananai on the brink of adulthood, by Edward Burne-Jones.

gueurs" in his conversation a little trying. With glee Mary told Hugo that the hapless suitor had tried sounding out Fräulein in confidence about his prospects—a confidence not kept. After leaving Clouds, Charlie tried to send Mananai a bracelet as a gift. Madeline Wyndham refused. In a friendly but reserved letter, she explained that the Wyndhams thought Mananai too young to marry and did not approve of the age gap between the lovers. Her response was without a shadow of the affection shown to Hugo when he was courting Mary—who was also five years older than his intended bride. Displaying the tolerant good humor that he almost always managed to employ with the Wyndhams, Charlie agreed to make no declaration to Mananai just yet. He asked whether he might send the bracelet to Madeline Wyndham, who could then give it to her daughter: "May I say, with my love? . . . Certainly being in love is not cheerful," he added, assuring Madeline that he had read over her letter "about fifty times."

Madeline Wyndham's excuses were a pretext. As Souls, it did not matter that Charlie was a Liberal. What mattered was that Charlie's income, from the estate he had inherited upon his alcoholic father's death, was just £3,000 to £4,000 a year (around $400,000 in today's terms). He could not hope for any more. Given the parlous state of eastern England's arable estates, he might end up receiving markedly less. As Percy commented, Charlie and any wife of his would not be "*poor*" but they would not be "at all rich" either. Madeline Wyndham thought her charming daughter could do better.

The last weekend of August found the Wyndhams at Clouds with Percy's niece Sibyl Queensberry and her two youngest children, Alfred and Edith Douglas, known respectively as "Bosie" and "Wommy" (the nicknames themselves abbreviations of "Boysie" and "Little Woman"), and with Wilfrid Blunt and his teenage daughter Judith. Sibyl and her children frequently visited Clouds, all the more since Sibyl's acrimonious divorce from the abusive Marquess of Queensberry that year. On Saturday, Arthur Balfour, George Wyndham and Henry James were due to arrive.

In the months since his arrival in Ireland Balfour had shown the Irish—and Westminster—that they had underestimated him. The Unionist policy was to kill Home Rule with kindness, but conciliation went hand in hand with coercion. Balfour made good on his promise to "be as relentless as Cromwell in enforcing obedience to the law." Anyone inciting tenants in the rent strike, known as the Plan of Campaign, was immediately imprisoned. Prisoners' complaints about the putrid conditions in their cells were met with short shrift: the connection between diseased lungs and Irish patriotism was interesting, said Balfour drily. By late August, the political world was alight with the news that the Government was putting the Irish MP John Dillon on trial for his part in the Plan of Campaign.

George, erstwhile "Fenian," proud descendant of the Patriot Lord Edward, was now an instrument of one of the most brutally effective periods of repression since the British had crushed the 1798 Rebellion. Yet the Wyndhams managed to reconcile the two. George wanted to save "darling Ireland," as Mary called it, and to gain "high office." Quelling agitators could, just about, be interpreted as helping the country reclaim calm. And the Wyndhams were ambitious. They ignored any contradiction, including Madeline Wyndham, who while visiting George in Ireland trawled through antique shops, collecting commemorative buttons of the heroes of '98 to distribute to her children and grandchildren, and requested all family members making the trip to do the same. Wilfrid Blunt was resolutely of the opposing view. Ireland was his latest anti-imperialist hobby horse, and he recently had published in the *Pall Mall Gazette* (under the editorship of the sensationalist journalist W. T. Stead) a series of trenchant firsthand accounts decrying the barbarity of the evictions. He intended to return to Ireland in October to join the fray. He was keenly looking forward to confronting Balfour at Clouds. By the time Balfour arrived, Blunt was feeling still more combative since Blunt had decided that he was in love with Mary: "the cleverest best & most beautiful woman in the world with just that touch of human sympathy which brings her to the level of our sins," he wrote in his diary.

All the political world knew by this point of Mary and Balfour's closeness, and Wilfrid seized upon the opportunity to examine at first hand the relationship that was the subject of whispered conjecture. He found himself little the wiser. "Balfour is here under particularly favourable [circumstances] as he is in love with Mary Elcho, to whom he makes himself of course charming, but, possibly for the same reason, I do not like him much . . . He has a grand passion for Mary—that is quite clear—and it is equally clear that she has a tendresse for him," said Wilfrid as he watched the two, heads bent in conversation, drift off on long walks. "But what their exact relations may be I cannot determine. Perhaps it is better not to be too wise, and as all the house accepts the position as the most natural in the world, there let us leave it."

Still, it made Blunt bad-tempered. No one—except Mary—escaped criticism in his diary. James, "always a little behindhand" in conversation, was disappointing—"For a man who writes so lightly and well it is amazing how dull-witted he is." Judith was unacceptably mute at dinner while Pamela and Bosie played boisterous rhyming games. Blunt's pen was most acidic about Balfour: "As a young man he must have been charming and still has some of the ways of a tame cat."

On the tennis court, a red-faced and ferocious Blunt triumphed over a nonchalant Arthur. That night at dinner (in one of those confidences that Clouds seemed to breed) Balfour admitted, to Blunt's astonishment, that Home Rule was inevitable: that his party's coercion was merely stalling. "When it comes I shall not be sorry," Arthur told the assembled party. "Only let us have separation as well as Home Rule; England cannot afford to go on with Irishmen in her Parliament. She must govern herself too."

The next day Arthur and George left Clouds for Ireland. Mary, always feeling a little guilty after spending time with Arthur, wrote a particularly affectionate letter to Hugo, professing herself to have been "mad with *low* spirits" in his absence. "You are such a deeer [*sic*] companion to Migs," she added, looking forward to a honeymoon planned by the Elchos after the birth of the child "as a caged bird to freedom." Two weeks later Blunt mounted the hustings at a public meeting. "Men of Galway," he declared, and was promptly pulled down by English troops and arrested. "We are trying to put yr cousin in jail. I have not heard whether we have succeeded," Balfour wrote to Mary as Blunt awaited trial, imagining that Blunt would be "horribly disappointed" if he were set free. On 27 September, at Clouds, Mary gave birth to her third child, a girl named Cynthia ("Cincie") after the goddess of the moon, in tribute to Clouds. A month later, one of Madeline Wyndham's sisters, Mary Carleton, died. "The poor mad sister," as the Wyndham children knew her, had been the least fortunate of Madeline's sisters. Widowed young, with no money, she had been a frequent guest at Clouds, although not always a welcome one in Percy's view. Clouds now received two new inhabitants, her orphaned children, Dorothy and Guy, who came to live with the Wyndhams as their wards. Madeline Wyndham went into mourning for her sister, leaving Percy to chaperone Mananai on the round of country-house visits that autumn. Percy was "splendid," Mananai loyally reported, but he had no experience in the art of marrying off a daughter and no inclination to develop the requisite skills now.

All that autumn, Home Rulers massed in London's Trafalgar Square, their numbers swelled by socialist agitators and members of the unemployed. In Ireland, police shot down rioters at Mitchelstown, and Balfour stood by them. In London, in November, a nonviolent protest demanding the release of William O'Brien—imprisoned again for his part in the Plan of Campaign—turned into "Bloody Sunday" when police set upon the socialist marchers, whose numbers included the prominent figures William Morris, Annie Besant and George Bernard Shaw. In the resultant fighting, which spilled all the way along Shaftesbury Avenue, three died (including two policemen) and a further two hundred were injured. It was to prove the last great outing of the London crowd. In the Commons, Irish MPs compared Balfour to Heliogabalus, a Roman emperor who revived himself by bathing in children's blood. At Christmas, Arthur wrote to Mary in red ink: "Greetings from Bl[oo]dy B[a]lf[ou]r, I write to you in the hue appropriate to my sanguinary character," using the name by which he was now most commonly known in Ireland and to the world at large. Six months later, when buying a copy of the popular periodical *Funny Folk* to while away a train journey from Stanway to Clouds, Pamela was diverted by a cartoon she found therein depicting Balfour as Dr. Jekyll and Mr. Hyde in reference to R. L. Stevenson's recent smash-hit novel. Better still, Pamela told Mary, "the 'ill-starred advisors' were you & Mamma!!!"

The Wyndhams had, very publicly, made it clear where their allegiances lay. In January 1888, Blunt was sentenced to two months' hard labor in Kilmainham Jail. He secured maximum publicity, first refusing to swap his greatcoat for the standard prison-issue one that barely covered his knees, and then bringing a case against Balfour for assault. The more liberal-minded of the Wyndhams' friends—the Morrises and the Burne-Joneses—staunchly supported Blunt. Janey Morris thought it a "splendid commotion." The Wyndhams believed, as George said, that "Wilfrid is temporarily out of his senses." They left him to his latest hobby horse. On the very day that Wilfrid was returned to his cell after his failed appeal, Percy, Madeline Wyndham and Mary arrived at the Chief Secretary's Lodge to hold "high revel," in Wilfrid's own phrase. He passed a sleepless night in his cell composing anagrams of his rival's name on a slate. The Right Honourable Arthur James Balfour of Whittingehame became "How! Am I not Arthur B. a huge thief, the brutal jailer of Irishmen?"

NINE

Mananai

T hat spring, the Wyndhams broke with their fast-establishing tradition of Easters at Clouds. On Good Friday, Pamela wrote to Mary from Madeline Wyndham's darkened bedroom at Belgrave Square. Their mother had been given "a fresh brain tonic" by Dr. Cumberbatch and "is going on capitally." She was "quite quiet," and either Pamela, Mananai or Percy was constantly at her bedside. "Darling Mary it is such a relief that she is better isn't it?"

From the tone of Pamela's letter this was not the first such episode, although it may have been more serious than most. Certainly it was closely concealed. Visiting the Poynters around this time, Percy was horrified when Agnes Poynter said something to suggest that "she knew *how* Mamma had been unwell. I hope it was my fancy but I fear not," Percy reported to Mary, questioning her closely as to whether she had "by any chance" told Georgie Burne-Jones (Agnes's sister) "that Mamma was muddled, or had a temporary loss of consciousness, or in short anything of that kind?" Whatever reply Mary sent is missing from the letter books Madeline Wyndham compiled when in better health.

The catalyst, most likely, was the combined pressure of Mary Carleton's death, the responsibility of her new charges and no doubt Charlie Adeane's inexorable progress—for he and Mananai became engaged in May. "Thank goodness there has been no 'scratching up of dirt'! but everything has been as 'serene as oil!'" Mananai exclaimed to Mary. The Wyndhams invited Charlie's mother, Lady Elizabeth, and her second husband, Michael Biddulph, a Liberal Unionist banker, to a slightly stolid engagement dinner at Belgrave Square, which wanted, Percy said, for "our two brightest stars"—Mary and George—to liven it up. A recovered Madeline Wyndham swallowed her misgivings and embraced Charlie with the warmth that she had Hugo. Charlie began addressing her as "M.M.," short for "Mother Madeline," and soon proved an infinitely better son-in-law in every way. "I like what I know of Charlie, I like him very much, the more I see of him the more I like him," Percy told Mary stoutly.

Six weeks later, on a Monday afternoon in late July, Mananai and Charlie were married, as Mary had been, at St. Peter's Church in Eaton Square. The nineteen-year-old bride, reported *Modern Society*, wore a white satin dress embroidered with silver, ruched with crêpe lisse, onto which was pinned orange blossoms, as was traditional, signifying fertility and good fortune. A diamond-encrusted sun (an Adeane family heirloom) pinned her tulle veil to her hair. Mary's toddler sons Ego and Guy were page boys in blue satin and rather alarming-sounding "fanciful hats and feathers"; the bridesmaids, among them Pamela and Dorothy Carleton, wore white crêpe dresses and bolero jackets, white tulle hats, pink stockings and heart-shaped enamel brooches with a double heart picked out in pearls and diamonds—a gift from the triumphant, not entirely indigent bridegroom.

The newlyweds spent the first part of their honeymoon at elegant Panshanger House in Hertfordshire, which (as was frequent practice) the Earl and Countess Cowper had loaned to them for a few days as a wedding gift. It poured with rain every day, but, holed up reading aloud to each other in Lady Cowper's boudoir, Madeline and Charlie were "much too happy to care for the elements." *"Tout va bien,"* Charlie assured his "beloved M.M." in a letter marked "private," so not to be read out at the breakfast table. "Madeline is *quite well* . . . & perfectly comfortable." Charlie's coded message was scarcely needed. Madeline Adeane's ecstatic letters expressed delight at every aspect of "this delicious new life." "I . . . wonder if you felt and thought the same as I do," she asked Mary, longing for a "confidential chat." She could hardly wait to show her family "how truly, and *blissfully* happy I am—letters are very nice but not quite satisfactory. I don't think that I shall have to tell you because I think that when you see us you will *see* how happy we are," she enthused to her mother. "She is so beloved your & my Madeline," Charlie told his mother-in-law, "& *so good.* No words of mine can express my love & adoration for her—she is *a perfect woman*—& that article which is rare is certainly the most wonderful & most beautiful of all God's works—much love to you my dearest—to whom she owes her existence, to whom I owe my love."

The Adeanes snatched a brief visit to Stanway, where the Wyndhams were staying with Mary. Mananai and Pamela experienced the novelty of walking alone outside for the first time in their lives. As a married woman, Madeline Adeane could now chaperone her sister. The Adeanes then headed for London's Victoria Station and the boat train that would carry them (Madeline Adeane dressed in her new "most comfortable" traveling clothes: a grey suit with hat and veil to match), Charlie's valet, Madeline's lady's maid Alice and a vast amount of luggage to the Continent.

"Fancy me in Paris!" said Mananai the next day as she lay on her bed in the Hôtel Meurice, gazing out of the window at the Tuileries baking in the August heat, reveling in the sounds of bells ringing, horses' hooves clattering and whips cracking outside. "Charlie knows Paris very well," she informed her mother, recounting drives up the Champs-Élysées and through the Bois de Boulogne; an "excellent" band in the Jardins d'Acclimation; and visits to the Invalides and the Louvre. Shortly afterwards, defeated by the heat, they retreated to Chantilly, a short distance outside Paris, to stay with "dear Baronne de St. Didier," one of many in Lady Elizabeth's large network of friends eager to fête the newlyweds. Everything was a source of wonderment to Mananai, from the tremendous amount that French grandees seemed to eat and drink to the turquoise-studded gold butterfly that awaited her on her dressing table at Chantilly: so clever, it could be either a brooch or a hairpin.

"Fancy me in *Switzerland*!!!" exclaimed an incredulous Mananai two weeks later, snatching a moment before "déjeuner" to write to George from the Hôtel National on Lake Geneva, while Charlie peered out of the window, examining through opera glasses the boats on the lake. They had attended a breakfast "for 16!!!" held by the Baronesse de Rothschild ("quite the ugliest lady I think I have ever seen but most kind"), at which guests entered as if to dinner, in pairs, and were quite outnumbered by footmen. From Switzerland they headed onwards to Italy. "Florence is the most perfect Paradise of the sightseer," George advised Mananai: "You have everything packed in the space of Belgrave Square, and can walk in and out of scores of historical Treasure-houses of Beauty with all the ease of a turn in the East garden and round by the green river at Clouds . . ." The Adeanes read diligently in anticipation. "We have just read *The Makers of Florence,* Charlie is now finishing *The Makers of Venice* & I am going to begin *Lives of Italian Painters* by Jameson," Mananai reported to George. They kept a joint diary, and Mananai filled a "birthday book" (that is, an autograph album) with the signatures of all the people they met along the way.

Travel worn, weary and still blissfully happy, the Adeanes returned to England in September. They went directly to Clouds, where they were

Babraham Hall. The estate came into the Adeane family in the eighteenth century when Colonel James Whorwood Adeane married Anne Jones, the only daughter of a wealthy landowner who had made his fortune in India. The "neat small seat" that existed at that time was rebuilt in red-brick Jacobean style by Charlie's grandfather Henry in the 1830s, with mullioned and transomed windows, gables and a large square tower. At the same time, the two-hundred-acre park surrounding the house was landscaped. Babraham was enlarged and remodeled again in 1864 by Henry's son (Charlie's father), another Henry, who added the Italianate colonnade and a formal garden, by which time the money had run out. On Henry's death in 1870, the house was shut up and his widow, Lady Elizabeth, moved to the Continent with her children, where they could live more comfortably and cheaply than in England, while still maintaining appearances.

Still a teenager when she married, Mananai took to the responsibilities of matronhood far more easily than either of her sisters despite their being older when they assumed this role (Mary was twenty-one and Pamela twenty-four, each comparatively mature by the standards of the time). Doubtless this was a combination of Mananai's easygoing temperament, her long experience of nurturing her siblings and, not least, her genuinely happy relationship with her husband.

crowned with wreaths made by Fräulein and slept in a bed decorated by Madeline Wyndham with handmade angel wings. From there they went to Babraham to open the house, shut up since the death of Charlie's father nineteen years before. Charlie's old nurse accompanied them. She was so overwhelmed by the occasion that she broke down and wept when they arrived.

Babraham Hall near Cambridge was a rambling red-brick Victorian-Jacobean mishmash possessing, thanks to Charlie's profligate father, a disproportionately large ballroom and a somewhat incongruous Italianate colonnade. Mananai was undaunted. An exploratory drive around the estate revealed "belts of trees and banks of firs" that she thought somewhat reminiscent of the Wiltshire Downs. She took out a subscription to her mother's favorite periodical, the *Garden,* and began devising plans for wild flower beds like those of Clouds—perhaps even a small golf course like the one that Percy had recently built. Cautious Charlie may have caviled at the cost of the latter, but he gave his new wife free rein inside the house. She painted the upstairs rooms white and papered the downstairs reception rooms with Morris patterns. She poked about in the attics hoping to find treasures as Mary had done (there were sadly few), covered bulky, old-fashioned cabinets with curtains and swathed tables in lengths of silk sent to her by Madeline Wyndham for that purpose. "All I do is a feeble imitation of you," she told her mother cheerfully.

Mananai threw herself with relish into the life of a county squire's wife. She made friends with the local gentry, visited the poor of the estate and the nearby villages, entertained the tenant farmers and had their families to tea. "Our life is that of an ordinary English house," Charlie said, by which he meant ordinary for the landed gentry, since most English households did not portion their time between "1 day's partridge shooting to 2 days' croquet (new) tennis—walking, talking, reading." Perhaps the only hint of the bohemian roots of young Mrs. Adeane was the pet fawn that followed her, like a puppy, everywhere she went.

TEN

Conflagration

M adeline Adeane's precipitate departure from schoolroom to matronhood grieved Pamela intensely. She bickered with Fräulein and snapped at Dorothy, itching to enter the adult world. The Wyndhams had a tradition of taking each daughter to Ireland for their first "grown-up" visit. In September 1888 it was Pamela's turn. She was bewitched by this first trip to the country of her ancestors: "It is like an enchanted land," she rhapsodized to Mary from Killarney in County Kerry, looking out from her bedroom window onto lush green fields, a lake "twinkling and sparkling in the sunlight like beautiful Lohengrin's armor" and shadowy mountains in the distance, shifting color from smoky grey to "hearts ease purple." She and her parents visited George and Sibell, the de Vescis at Abbeyleix and, briefly, the Vice Regal Lodge in Phoenix Park, where the Viceroy lived when not residing in state at Dublin Castle. "It is *great* fun visiting and it . . . doesn't feel like me; I feel very 'grown-up' going down to dinner in long reach-elbow gloves," she told Mary, drawing for her sister "word pictures" of her fellow guests.

Pamela returned to a Clouds echoing with Mananai's absence, counting down the months until her own debut. The sisters were briefly reunited when the Adeanes spent Christmas at Clouds. But by the new year the party was just Percy, Madeline Wyndham, Pamela, Dorothy

Carleton, Fräulein, Mary, now pregnant for a fourth time, and her three children. George and Sibell were in Ireland, Guy in India with his regiment, Hugo off shooting. Mary was planning to leave for Stanway the following day. The Charteris trunks stood packed and ready. That night, Mary sat up score-keeping for her mother and Fräulein in an animated game of piquet, going to bed rather later than planned.

When the clanging of a bell woke her from a deep sleep Mary presumed it to be the bell that rang around the house at eight o'clock every morning to rouse its inhabitants for breakfast. She "got out of bed, put on dressing gown, picked up a few things almost leisurely," when her bedroom door was flung open by Bertha Devon, now head housemaid, with five-year-old Ego in her arms, crying, "Oh Miss Mary, you must leave the house the house is on fire." Mary rushed onto the landing, "saw the ruddy glare & heard the low sharp snapping." At that moment, Percy dashed past. He told her that Guy and Cincie had been carried to safety by their nursemaid Mrs. Fry. "I was wild to see the children at once & rushed down to find them."

The passages down which she raced were already filling with dense, scorching smoke. Once safely outside in the freezing January night she found most of her family, a nightgown-clad Madeline Wyndham desperately bruised from hoisting the giant oil painting by Baldovinetti off the hall's wall and toppling off the chair on which she stood under its weight (the bruises were so deep that they did not fade for weeks), but only one of her children: a small scared Ego in his red dressing gown still being held in Bertha Devon's arms. "Mama and I were in despair," said Mary, "helpless distracted anguish . . . we could see Guy & Cynthia *nowhere* & . . . the roaring crackling flames & the showering sparks & smoke spreading everywhere made one wild with fear . . ."

"Don't Mamma, don't," screamed Pamela as Madeline Wyndham and Mary tried to force their way back into the burning building. "Where's Fraulein, has anyone awakened Fraulein?" Percy shouted above the din, having forgotten in his panic that he had awakened her himself. "Then," said Mary, "through the panic and the terror came the cry of 'they're here, they're safe'": Fräulein and Mrs. Fry carrying Cincie and Guy. In the time it had taken to wrap the small children in blankets to protect them, the smoke had made the passage down which Bertha had fled carrying Ego impassable. Only Clouds' warren of entrances, exits and passageways had allowed them to find another route.

The horse-drawn fire engines sent from nearby Mere, Wilton and Salisbury were horribly delayed by the perilous conditions. Wilton's horses fell down three times on the icy roads in the eighteen miles between the two houses, and were ultimately too injured to continue, requiring fresh horses to be borrowed from nearby farms. Villagers, who had rushed up the hill in wagons from East Knoyle and Milton, helped the house carpenters form a human chain that saved most of the Wyndhams' treasures from the ground floor: books were piled high in dog baskets on the lawn; paintings, furniture and even the huge Morris carpet from the drawing room were saved. Someone (presumably a plucky housemaid) flung out of the window the contents of Mary's trunks (not the trunks themselves, Mary hastened to add), which were caught by Mary and Fräulein standing underneath. The firemen reached Clouds too late to do more than contain the fire and save the offices from becoming part of the conflagration. As the great chandelier in the hall crashed down in a shower of glass and sparks they aimed their hoses at the flames now dancing from the roof of Clouds, but "the flames seemed rather to like the water," and, fueled by the draft provided by the hall, roared more fiercely still. It was so bitterly cold that the captain of Wilton's fire brigade froze solid to the side of his ladder. The villagers retreated to their wagonettes, munching on egg sandwiches and "hugely enjoying themselves," said Mary, likening them, without rancor, to the crowd at the races in William Powell Frith's *Derby Day*.

On the slippery terrace, with the trees laced with hoarfrost silhouetted behind them, the family stood "& . . . watched the dear house burn." Unknown hands covered them in a scarecrow assortment of warmer garb: over Mary's orange dressing gown she sported several shawls and an ulster, and on her head a bowler hat. "Oh, my Bible, and oh, my canaries!" cried Pamela, wringing her hands beside her. Madeline Wyndham, standing a little apart with a rapt look on her face, was silent. She wore "a rough homespun coat" over her nightgown, remembered one neighbor, "and the lace frills escaped beneath the tweed sleeves and fell over her hands which were flung out in an unconscious gesture of wonder at the sight. She was entranced by its beauty and terror."

The cause of the fire, it was later discovered, was a lighted candle left by a sleepy housemaid in a linen cupboard. A moment of carelessness—borne, doubtless, of exhaustion—resulted in a conflagration that gutted the house, leaving only its shell standing. It took three days for the

Dating back to the Jacobean era and completed, like the rest of the house, shortly before England's Civil War in the mid-seventeenth century, Stanway's great oriel window (a form of bay window) contains more than a thousand panes of glass that flood the hall with light.

smoldering ashes to cool enough for it to be safe to approach the ruins; the cellar was still hot for a week after the fire. Treasures had been lost: Burne-Jones's cartoon of the Ascension up in flames, along with many items on the first floor and everything on the second floor. "All the childrens [*sic*] lovely wardrobe toys silver cups birds etc & all the nurses clothes & money *gone*," mourned Mary. She parceled out her own clothes among all the females in the household. "Mrs. Fry looks very nice in my red lawn tennis jersey & skirt," she told Frances Balfour of the Charteris children's nurse.

Two weeks later, back at Stanway, Mary was hosting Doll Liddell, Gladys de Grey, Emmie and Eddy Bourke, the Pembrokes, Harry and Daisy White, George Curzon, Alan Charteris and D. D. Balfour. D.D., who later married Alfred Lyttelton, was no relation to Arthur Balfour. A London businessman's daughter, she was drawn into the Souls by merit of her brilliant talk and engaging intellect. Curzon, meeting her for the first time, was drawn by her considerable personal charms and tried to grope her when they were momentarily alone in the dining room at breakfast. The Whites, the only non-British Souls, were Americans who had been in England since 1884 by reason of diplomat Harry White's position as First Secretary to the US Legation. Daisy White, a close friend of Edith Wharton's since childhood, was well admired, pretty, ambitious and a keen player among the rivalrous female Souls. That evening, the party dressed as Cavaliers and Puritans, and sat on the stairs, moonlight streaming over them as D.D. and Emmie sang. "Most of us looked quite picturesque and we all felt very sentimental. I wish you had been there and then it might have been perfect for me; or as perfect as anything can be," Mary told Arthur.

In fact, and unusually for Mary, she had counted the days until the party ended. The fire had left her "physically abattu . . . as if everything had been wiped out of my brain with a clean sponge or *burnt* away." Each morning was devoted to writing "Fire letters," replying to the scores of condolences she received—many asking if it was true that Clouds really had been razed to the ground. "I've done 25 today & yest & spent whole mornings in bed, writing and blotting self & sheets," she recounted to Arthur some two weeks after the fire itself.

In the fire's aftermath, the family "knew nothing except how much we all loved each other & how close together we were drawn." "How tightly we are bound . . . how we all stand and fall together," George Wyndham said to his mother. Volatile Pamela was "very brave and behaved splendidly" despite the loss of everything she owned, but she had nightmares about the fire for years. To doubtless intense relief, Madeline Wyndham's nerves held up under the strain: perhaps the destruction of her jewel-like house confirmed her belief that the forces of light and darkness walked hand in hand. At least, she often said, death had never entered into the house. Yet the utter destruction of Clouds—what Georgie Burne-Jones called "that beautiful monument of loving and successful labor"—was, said Frances Balfour, a "heart-breaking event." Philip Burne-Jones cited the calamity to Gerald Balfour as philosophical proof of the existence of evil. The most romantic of the Wyndhams' children echoed this view. "Who the gods love die young," said Pamela, describing Clouds as "too ideal to live." From Ireland, George vowed to "begin at once defeating evil Fortune and making it lovely again." Both he and Pamela regarded the fire, the first calamity they had faced, as an indication that the world must have been corrupted. Their self-conscious bravery is a reminder of how distinct remained Disraeli's "two nations" of rich and poor, described in his 1845 novel *Sibyl,* which examined the conditions of the English working classes. Their reaction displayed the arrogance of the Wyndhams' "Plantagenet" strain. Of all the Wyndhams' children only Mary put the loss in perspective, not railing against fate, only pitying her parents. "I've aches and aches for them and I have not suffered half enough it's too hard; all their love and labor lost, when one *did* so want them to enjoy the well-earned fruits of all their pains," she wrote to Arthur.

The conflagration in *The Spoils of Poynton* destroys, forever, the work of a lifetime. The Wyndhams defied this. Webb's estimate for rebuilding was £26,741 17s. To Percy's relief, the insurers of the house and its contents paid in full, £28,345 12s. from the Sun Insurance Company and £27,000 from the Royal Insurance Company, enabling him to rebuild Clouds identically—except with fireproof flooring, additional tin-lined water pipes to avoid further troublesome plumbing and a new boot cupboard for Percy in his dressing room—and to refurnish it, replacing treasures lost in the fire. Percy calculated that he was only £3,000 out of pocket. The Wyndhams moved into the offices for the duration of the rebuilding, operating a reduced staff and having only close friends to stay. "It is a good thing that our architect was a socialist because we find ourselves just as comfortable in the servants' quarters as we were in our own," commented Madeline Wyndham cheerfully. They reentered the "Beautiful Phoenix," as they termed it, two and a half years later on 29 August 1891.

ELEVEN

The Season of 1889

I n Society's collective memory, the 1889 Season was a good one, enlivened by the Shah of Persia's visit and the bursting into the public consciousness of the Souls after a dinner held by George Curzon for his thirty or so closest friends at the Bachelors' Club in Piccadilly. It was also the Season in which George Wyndham entered Parliament as the Conservative Member for Dover after a by-election in July 1889 ("Isn't it *delightful* George being an M.P.? & for Dover too such a nice place," said Mananai); and the eighteen-year-old Pamela Wyndham finally made her debut.

"The Babe," as Pamela was known to her family and their friends, appeared to have been granted all the blessings that accrue, fairy tale–like, to the youngest child. With her delicate features and refined air, she was considered the most beautiful of the sisters, second only to George in terms of Wyndham looks and, like him, "literary and clever," as Mary remarked admiringly. Her mother's friend Edith Olivier said that Pamela "seemed to pour ideas into one's mind like an empty glass." Like George, galloping across the Downs at sunrise and quoting the sixteenth-century French poet Ronsard, Pamela rejected crude reality in favor of an idealized past. From a young age she collected folk ballads, and noted picturesque examples of village dialect. She read avidly, and kept a tally:

seventy books for 1889. She adored the Brontës' tales of wild moors and love against the odds ("I can always read anything by them," she told Mary), the romances of Scott and the diaries of her Fitzgerald ancestors. George addressed Pamela as "Pamela III" in homage to Lady Edward (their grandmother, Lady Campbell, being "Pamela II"); and there was certainly something regal in the way she comported herself. She disparaged "the tyranny of the red blotting pad" over Mary, which meant that her sister spent her time writing letters rather than reading books: Mary's never diminishing "nest egg" of unanswered letters "is too much of a time-sucker with you!" said Pamela.

On seeing Pamela at this age, Wilfrid Blunt was struck by her similarity to Mary, but Mary disclaimed the resemblance: "Imagination I may have but wit *never*! & I was so silent." In fact they were very little alike. Pamela was born demanding attention: she was passionately jealous of those she loved. From little more than toddlerhood she sobbed if a sibling received a letter or present from their parents and she did not. At Clouds, as cherished youngest daughter of the squire, she was queen. Villagers and guests alike were well accustomed to recitals from Pamela, singing folk ballads while accompanying herself on her ribbon-bedecked guitar, a Lacôte—the Stradivarius of guitar makers—which she received for her eighteenth birthday.

Pamela had a constant sense of expectation, of greatness imminent; a sharp tongue; a facility for damning with faint praise; and her mother's love of birds: "They would fly to her finger when she called, which she thought was marvelous," remembered Sir Stephen Runciman, a neighbor and contemporary of Pamela's children. The comment might be a metaphor for Pamela's relationship with people. When she entered Society, people flocked to her, attracted, no doubt, by her air of lofty unconcern. She did "not allow her partners much time for talking or nonsense but kept them going," said Percy approvingly of her tendency to whisk her partners efficiently around the dance floor. At almost a decade younger than most of the Souls, she was still too newly arrived in Society to be a guest at Curzon's farewell dinner on 10 July 1889. Curzon had been diagnosed with lung trouble. He intended to summer in the healthful Alps, then travel across Central Asia to Persia, the buffer between India and Russia and fulcrum of Anglo-Russian rivalry. Renowned even at twenty-eight for his imperious manner and a self-confidence so fervent that people thought it must be hubristic, he was doggedly pursuing his long-held ambition to be India's Viceroy. Comprehensive knowledge of Persia seemed to Curzon a good place to start.

The club itself, barely eight years old, was a novel social experiment: only bachelors were admitted as members and those members who subsequently married had to pay a fine of twenty-five guineas to be readmitted as honorary members. Unlike many gentlemen's clubs which viewed female company with horror, the Bachelors' Club welcomed women, allowing them to dine with their male friends with perfect respectability. Nothing could have been more conducive to the ethos of the Souls.

The guests, most of whom were very familiar with the club, arrived to find a long, well-dressed table lit by candles, covered in blue glass and silver, and decorated with crystal bowls of flowers. Behind each chair, instead of footmen, stood club servants. On each chair was a lengthy piece of doggerel by Curzon listing and eulogizing each member of the Gang, both present and absent. Margot Tennant, always mindful of posterity, swiped her copy and recorded the work fifty years later in her memoirs. The verse on Mary and Hugo, with its sly reference to Hugo's infidelity, exemplified Curzon's tone:

> *From kindred essay*
> *LADY MARY today*
> *Should have beamed on a world that adores her.*
> *Of her spouse debonair*
> *No woman has e'er*
> *Been able to say that he bores her . . .*

Curzon's recital of his poem raised his already ebullient guests to exuberant spirits. Raucous singing and dancing followed. Even the normally reserved Balfour was capering as if possessed amid fun "so loud it was impossible to hear anyone speak." Eventually the party adjourned to the Tennants' house in Grosvenor Square, where they danced until the early hours. The survivors, including Lady Brownlow, made their way home via the old flower market in Covent Garden, weaving through sleepy streets hazy with the morning sun, their arms full of flowers.

The dinner of these beautiful, insouciant aristocrats made the Souls famous. By 1890 the popular periodical *World* was devoting articles to "this highest and most aristocratic cult . . . as liberal in its views as it is

exclusive in its composition . . . Certain intellectual qualities are prominent among the Souls and a limited acquaintance with Greek philosophy is a *sine qua non.*" Three years later Henry Labouchere's self-funded
radical *Truth,* a weekly that pronounced itself devoted to exposing fraud
and injustice (which subjects often permitted interesting tangents into
prurient gossip), got its hands on an "Expression Exam paper," a quiz set
by female Souls to while away a rainy afternoon, and printed it in full:

1. Explain the following: The dull box. A greenhouse. A gorge riser.
   Gilletmongering. Atrophasia. Stinche. A Lou-good. Jephson.
   Whippingham. A felbrig. A float-face. Barloon.
2. Describe accurately the Block including the duties of the Mopper
   and the chief blockites, and explain in a few lines: a Stodgite, a
   groffality, blue face and horns, a John Stone, a Molly Corker, poivre
   aux pieds, manchettes, Eternity soup, six cloisters, type drawers.
3. Analyze the following phrases: This is distinctly Sir Giles. She almost
   pecked him. He has got a touch of egg. I have got three dentists
   today. Je suis mariée, vous n'êtes pas. He's got a cruet.

The Souls professed themselves appalled by the disclosure, presuming
that an enterprising servant must have filched the crumpled-up paper
from a wastepaper basket. The rest of Society was fascinated, envious
and derisive in equal measure. Not long afterwards, Alfred Lyttelton and
his second wife D.D. (Edith) found they received a frosty reception on
a trip to Cairo when their fellow holiday makers realized who they were.
"There is a 'set' in this hotel who hate & abuse our 'set' they call us 'the
Souls' . . . & say we are always laughing & that we read Herodotus &
those sorts of crimes," reported D.D.

"Lady Mary," who always hated missing out, was herself doubtless
furious at being unable to attend. Frustrated and bored, she was in bed
at Cadogan Square, recuperating from the birth of the Elchos' fourth
child, a boy, christened Colin, some six weeks prior. The story went
about among Mary's friends that when asked the sex of the child, Hugo
said he did not know: "the usual hardy annual," he presumed. Mary
was not hardy. More or less annual childbirth had weakened her to the
extent that, a month after Colin's birth, despite for the first time following to the letter her lying-in's requirements, her condition was so far
from improved that she was returned to bed. Dr. Collins warned her that

she would risk her life if she had any further children. By Mary's own account it appears to be at this point that sexual relations between the Elchos ceased entirely for a period of some six years.

The rude health of Mary's childhood was long gone. Her family and friends attributed it to her frenetic socializing. She rushed around, forgot to eat, slept little, never sat still and worried constantly. A light schedule consisted of "only one, or perhaps two! Operas a week." Mananai thought Mary should be forced to stay in bed one day in seven simply to regain the energy she expended. Instead Mary, who was prone to illness and on occasion thought herself the victim of arsenic poisoning and diphtheria, relied upon purported "miracle cures." In the spring of 1891 after a particularly fierce bout of influenza, she took the Atkins-style approach of the "Salisbury system: lots of hot water, which really does suit me & meat, no farinaceous food & very little vegetable." "Sounds odd, doesn't it? but its [sic] really easier to digest & for the pains gives more nutriment & doesn't create fermentation acidity etc," she explained to her sister-in-law Evelyn de Vesci, adding that her mother "told me I looked 5 years younger!" She became dependent on her annual spa trips to the Continent, taken at each Season's end, to recoup the reserves of health and energy she had plundered during the rest of the year.

As transport to the Continent became cheaper and faster, spa tourism became a feature of the English social calendar. Each mineral spring—Kissingen, Baden-Baden, Ems, Schwalbach and Carlsbad to name just a few—had different medicinal properties. A multitude of guidebooks (most in convenient pocket editions) explained to the eager health tourist which resort would best suit their ailment: which of the alkaline, saline, sulfurous and ferruginous waters were aperient and which suited those prone to diarrhea; which were best for gout, for skin diseases, for anemia, for chlorosis and for "female diseases" (these covered everything from hysteria to failure to conceive); and (for the socially ambitious hoping to make contacts abroad which might be more difficult to effect at home) which grandees might also be found taking the waters at each. Bad Kissingen in Bavaria, the first spa Mary visited, in August 1890, was her favorite. By the turn of the century she rarely ventured anywhere else, making the journey each August, third-class by rail, after several weeks' worried consultation of Bradshaw's railway timetable. She detailed with relish in her letters home all the elements of her "kur" and her body's response, dutifully swallowing the three revolting glasses of water required daily that were mixed with whey to mitigate their horrible taste. At the giant *Kurhaus* that lay in the center of each town she was subjected to inhalations, to lengthy baths and to "douches" in which the bloomer-clad patient stood inside a cage and was pummeled by jets of water from all angles. The only respite came when she was menstruating, for then the treatment temporarily ceased: "[I] am rather longing for Bets[ey] so's to give me a Kleine Pause," Mary informed Hugo wearily from Kissingen in 1900.

Throughout the Season, Mary had received reports of Pamela's excellent progress through the social scene. Pamela nonetheless maintained an amused distance from "worldly" Society's preoccupations. She thought a Saturday-to-Monday at the Earl and Countess Brownlow's stately Ashridge in Hertfordshire quite the nicest of the summer—principally, so she told Mary, for an "Elysian conversation" about books and poetry with a fellow guest, which proved so different from the commonplace small talk concerning dance partners and grandees: "After the ordinary 'partner shah twaddle' it was doubly delightful." Pamela's dance card was always full, but she avowed her preference for intellectual engagements. While dinners with the Burne-Joneses and Henry James were "really delightful," she described balls and parties with a wry, self-mocking tone, amused at her own frivolity, clear that, unlike most, she could see the emperor's new clothes for exactly what they were.

At a ball held by the Rothschilds towards the end of July, Pamela was inundated with compliments on her gown: a simple white tulle dress, its bodice trimmed with "a tiny wreath of forget-me-nots." It was a "dream-dress," she told her admirers. The inspiration had appeared to her in her sleep the night before. On waking she had headed straight to Woollands' department store and trimmed the dress herself. "It was *such* fun & really it looked very pretty & *every* one admired it!!!" she boasted to Mary, proving by her own effort the prophetic power of dreams—a concept in which she wholeheartedly believed.

Pamela's Season ended in a flurry. She danced until 4 a.m. on consecutive nights (at Mrs. Hope's and at the Dudley House Ball). The next day she lunched with her parents at the gentlemen's club White's to watch the Royal Procession. The oldest and most exclusive club in London, White's guarded its male-only status jealously, normally refusing to allow females across its threshold, but it had been opened to women specifically for that occasion. "It was like another Jubilee all the poor women kept fainting all round in the crowd, they kept handing glasses of water and salts to them from where we were." In the evening, they attended the opera, *Otello* at the Lyceum, just off the Strand, where only the fact that Desdemona was "very ugly & rather fat" made the harrowing last scene bearable. The next day Pamela wrote to Mary as London emptied out and the Wyndhams prepared to visit the Leconfields at Petworth. "It seems incredible that *my* first Season should be over . . . I am not at all sorry it is over but filled with a sort of placid triumph at having managed to have had such a *delightful* time on this to most people unsatisfactory Earth!"

Mary was delighted to receive Pamela's "capital" letter. She had packed off children and servants to Stanway, and on doctor's orders was spending a blissful fortnight on the Suffolk coast at Felixstowe's Bath Hotel, doing nothing but lying on a wicker chair, basking in the sunshine, reading intermittently and looking out to sea. Much as Mary missed her children "it really *is* a great rest being *without* them for a time," she admitted to Evelyn de Vesci. She received regular updates from Mrs. Fry, and by return of post sent to her children paper "jumping donkeys & cats & clowns" that she made to amuse them. "I shall hardly know [Colin] when I see him," she added. "Babies alter *so much* at first."

In September 1889, the Wyndhams gained another grandchild when Mananai gave birth to a girl at the Adeanes' London house, 65 Cadogan Place, a new build just doors down from the Elchos in Chelsea. The Adeanes had been hoping their firstborn would be a son to inherit the estate, and Mananai had decorated Babraham's nurseries accordingly: the day nursery papered with a Morris trellis of birds and roses, the two night nurseries painted pale yellow and pale blue. They bore the disappointment of the sex bravely. "Having a little baby does make me love you more . . . if that is possible," Mananai told her mother, who came up to London with Percy and Pamela after the birth. Mary "loaned" her the use of Wilkes as a nurse. Charlie, who spent most of his wife's lying-in at her bedside eating muffins, gave her a small enameled locket studded with diamonds intended to hold the baby's first "fluff." Pamela was godmother, but she felt nonetheless "left behind & wretched" with "Mamma, you & worst of all Madeline . . . all three away from me on a shelf of experience I knew nothing about," she later recollected to Mary.

Because the child was a girl she was christened with little fuss, a month later, after Mananai had been churched. The Wyndhams and

Pamela were again in Ireland so Georgie Burne-Jones was Pamela's proxy at the font. Mananai wore a white "nun's veiling dress" that had been part of her trousseau and a white felt hat with a large bow. The infant, who made "just enough cry to be lucky," was named Pamela Marie after her maternal and paternal aunts, who stood as godmothers—and "of course because of Lady Edward FitzGerald," said Queen Victoria knowledgeably when she inquired of her maid of honor the child's name; she recalled meeting the famous beauty when she was a small child and Lady Edward's looks had long gone. "Is it not wonderful she should have such a memory and take such an interest in all one's belongings? It sounds trivial but these are the little things that make one love the Queen," said Marie Adeane.

TWELVE

The Mad and Their Keepers

In 1891, after two years of traveling, George Curzon returned to England. The Souls celebrated with another Bachelors' Club dinner. Yet snobbish Curzon was appalled by developments in his absence. As the Souls gained in prominence, they had invited into their midst the talented and amusing, regardless of social background. For Curzon, the "degradation" wrought upon "our circle" was epitomized by "the Cosquiths," a shorthand he used to describe Herbert Henry Asquith, the middle-class barrister shortly to leapfrog directly from Liberal backbencher to Home Secretary under Gladstone; and Oscar Wilde, lecture-giving aesthete, whose notoriety had taken a darker turn with the publication of his first novel, *The Picture of Dorian Gray,* in installments in the popular *Lippincott's Monthly Magazine* (it was deemed so scandalous that the newsagent W. H. Smith refused to sell those editions of *Lippincott's* at its stalls).

"Gone forever is the old Gang and a few magnificent souls [*sic*] like you and Harry [Cust], [Doll] Liddell, Mary Elcho and myself remain. The rest are whirling after new Gods and baring their heads in the temple of twopenny Rimmons," Curzon told Harry White, sadly and grandly, upon hearing that Ettie Grenfell had invited Oscar and Constance Wilde, Henry Asquith and his wife, Helen, and the actor-manager Herbert Beerbohm Tree and his wife (also called Helen) to Taplow Court, the Grenfells' house in Berkshire. Curzon urged White to capsize the interlopers' punt while on the river. In fact, Mary had turned traitor too. In the previous six months alone, she had gone to the theatre *"a quatre"* with Wilde, Arthur and Ettie, and had had Wilde to dine at Cadogan Square, where he kept his end of the table "alive with paradox" and her guests, including Arthur, George and Sibell, and Edward Burne-Jones, stayed until well after midnight: "So I suppose they weren't bored," she said with relief. With her consuming interest in people, and her expansive warmth, Mary was to become renowned for introducing new people into the Souls.

That same summer, Curzon forced an uncomfortable confrontation between himself and Wilde at the meeting of the Crabbet Club, an all-male club that met annually at Wilfrid Blunt's Sussex estate. The Crabbet's stated purpose was "to discourage serious views of life." Its annual meeting consisted of a poetry competition and a night of Bacchanalian excess. Its membership, recruited by Wilfrid and George Wyndham in collaboration, was primarily male Souls. By convention each new member was subjected to "jibes"—a grilling on his life and work. The two new members that summer were Curzon and Wilde. Curzon demanded that he be the one to grill Wilde.

As recorded by Blunt in his diary, Curzon was ruthless: attacking Wilde for his treatment of sodomy in *Dorian Gray* and suggesting that Wilde engaged in such practices himself. The fleshy Wilde at first smiled helplessly, but eventually gave "an amusing and excellent speech." The debate continued until dawn, when some of the Club, including Curzon and George Wyndham, went to swim in the river, followed by a game of lawn tennis—"just as they were, stark naked, the future rulers of England," said Wilde, perhaps the only one to be aware of the irony of this homoerotic display following so quickly on the heels of Curzon's attack of him on related grounds. Shortly afterwards, Wilde met the Wyndhams' cousin Bosie Douglas, and their destructive mutual infatuation began. Bosie later joined the Crabbet, but Wilde never attended another meeting—an indication, probably, of his distaste for it.

The following year, the poetry competition's theme was "Marriage." Harry Cust's offering brimmed with ironic self-knowledge:

Various vigorous virgins may have panted
Wailing widows wilted in the dust

To no female has the great God granted
Grace sufficient to be Mrs. Cust

Contemporary paeans to Harry's heavenly blond appearance must be measured against the adolescent Judith Blunt's cool estimation: "fat podgy and coarse, his hair and eyes too light for his red complexion." Indisputably, "Cust bulged with sex." His quicksilver charm could, and did—quite literally—lay all before him. His "harem" included his long-term mistress, Violet Granby (as Violet Manners had become when her husband succeeded as Marquess), and Lucy Graham Smith. Harry did not adhere to the Souls' morality. He conceived sexual improvidence as an aristocratic right; moral restraint was mealy-mouthed and middle class. "What if all had been forbidden *but* the apple? Imagine polygamy advanced by God and man, and at this moment all the upper classes would have been dwelling in the joys of illicit constancy and despising the cowardly unenterprising middle classes who were forced to content themselves with profligacy," he mused to Mary in 1887. Violet had little truck with Souls morality either. By 1892, she was pregnant with Harry's child.

By the summer of 1892, Pamela was the only one of the Wyndhams' children yet to be settled. In May, Guy had married Edwina Brooke (nicknamed "Minnie"), a widow with two children who was five years older than he. Both Madeline Wyndham's sons had sought out maternal figures, but this marriage was to prove very happy. Shortly afterwards Harry Cust joined the Wyndhams for a performance of Wagner's *Tannhäuser* at London's Covent Garden Opera House, part of a sell-out season of German opera conducted by Gustav Mahler. In retrospect, the choice was ominous. *Tannhäuser* skated on the edge of respectability, examining the choice between sacred and profane love. Wilde used it in *Dorian Gray* to reflect the darkness of his hero's own soul.

As Mary sat in the Wyndhams' box and saw Harry's exaggerated flirting with Pamela, leaning low over her to point out some detail in the program, whispering in her ear, she was filled with foreboding. Harry, although a close friend, was a dangerous proposition, capable of severely damaging Pamela's reputation. To test if Harry was serious, Mary invited him to Stanway when Pamela was there. By unspoken convention, if he accepted, it would mean that he planned to court her in earnest. Harry turned down the invitation. Mary and Madeline Wyndham, nipping

Harry Cust, the golden boy, drawn by his lover, Violet Manners. Violet gave birth to their daughter Diana (later Lady Diana Cooper) in 1893. Rumor has it that by this time Harry had fathered at least one other small girl, called Beatrice, the daughter of Cust and a pretty housemaid named Phoebe Stephenson who worked at the seventeenth-century Belton House in Grantham, Lincolnshire, home of Cust's uncle and aunt the Earl and Countess Brownlow. Almost thirty years later, Beatrice married Alfred Roberts, a Grantham grocer. Their daughter, Margaret Roberts, a bright and ambitious child with piercing blue eyes, is more commonly known by her married name of Thatcher and as Britain's first female Prime Minister.

things in the bud before any further harm was done, forbade both parties from seeing each other. A month passed in this way, causing Pamela intense anxiety as she scanned crowded ballrooms for his tall blond figure, playing out in her mind what would happen if he "accidentally" appeared.

Harry's eventual appearance was every bit as dramatic as Pamela might have hoped. On 15 August 1892, a fortnight before Violet Granby gave birth to his daughter, Harry pitched up unannounced in Belgrave Square's drawing room before a startled Madeline and a delighted Pamela. The incident, as recounted by Pamela to Mary, had aspects of a drawing-room farce. Barely had Harry managed to explain that he had turned down the Stanway invitation because "he does not want to make love to me (only less crudely expressed by him!)" than the butler Icke precipitated into the drawing room a young "Mr. Allhuisen" who was intending, most likely, to pay court to Pamela. Harry was hustled off into the front drawing room by Madeline Wyndham, Pamela left to sit and drink tea with the hapless "Mr. A" while trying to eavesdrop on the muffled conversation behind the double doors.

Behind those doors, Madeline Wyndham laid down the law in somewhat unsatisfactory fashion. She told Harry he could see Pamela only if he promised to stop his "coarse flirting." If and when he was willing to seek her hand in earnest, then he could. Harry promised. Pamela was delighted, although she protested that Harry had never been flirting. "His manner which has grown upon him misleads people . . . he says 'How do you do' as if it was 'you are the Soul of my Life' but he is unaware of this, I really believe like people who clear their throats continually," she explained to Mary.

Osbert Sitwell, meeting Pamela in middle age, recognized the discordance between her image and her reality: "Far from being a rather remote, reasonable woman, under which guise she saw herself, presented herself, and was accepted . . . [she was] . . . violently and enchantingly prejudiced in a thousand directions." Her sitting room was filled with photographs "of the most astonishing rakes and rips" whom Pamela would "unflaggingly, and with the greatest display of ingenuity defend" or, where defense was impossible, "ignore." Pamela declared that she would not be "deceived by outside views!!!" but she was more than capable of deceiving herself by her own tortuous logic.

Now Pamela persuaded herself that the best way to get over Harry was to see him as much as possible so that she should harbor no illusions about him. "If I in any way let my friendship with him spoil my life it would be voluntary foolishness on my part" she told Mary. Mary worried that Pamela was motivated merely by pique. When she heard that her youngest sister—who as Madeline Wyndham's "Benjamina," a biblical allusion to Jacob's beloved youngest son, could twist her mother around her little finger—had persuaded Madeline to invite Harry to Clouds, Mary was horrified. She immediately wrote to Madeline warning against this course of action. It was too late.

Harry joined the tail end of a house party to find Pamela distracted by the company of a young man called Arthur Paget. It was idyllic late-summer weather. The party had spent a "delicious" week making excursions to Stonehenge and taking long walks across the Downs. Pamela confessed to Mary privately that she thought more "highly of [Paget than] any man before . . . delightfully clever, original & nice—good & kind & honest (what a funny lot of adjectives strung together!)." Harry sulked, moped and glowered until finally (as no doubt he designed) Pamela confronted him on the Sunday afternoon in the empty hall, whereupon he told her "all that he meant *not* to say (so he says) but *I* think, it was all that he *did not expect to feel.*"

Pamela wrote the conversation out in full for Mary. The exchange is worthy of a cheap melodrama, with Harry the mustache-twirling villain. Harry declared his love, explained (without explaining why) that he was not free, and asked Pamela—supposing that, in two years or so, he could make himself free—whether she would agree to be his wife. To Pamela's surprise, as she stood incredulously by the fireplace with hands like ice, she found herself saying that she was not sure:

> "In the Summer I was afraid I let you think more than I was prepared actually to *do*—I think that I have changed."
> And he put his head against the mantelpiece, & looked very miserable, & said: "Perhaps you are right"
> "But I cannot believe it—it seems so odd if you could, would you ask me to be your wife?"
> "I would"
> "And if in this next year I was to marry somebody would you mind?"
> "I would mind *awfully*"
> & then we were quiet for a long time.

Harry then broke out into a rage of self-recrimination, berating himself for having broken his word to Madeline Wyndham, blaming his intolerable, uncontrollable jealousy, his feeling that to lose Pamela would be to miss "a most perfect good":

> & again & again, I kept saying "I do not think you mean it—are you serious—do you really love me or do you think you do?"

The great two-story central hall at Clouds was divided into three bays by two arches supported on piers, each bay lit by a roof lantern. The gallery around the top of the hall (which led onto family and guest bedrooms) was glazed to prevent eavesdropping on conversations below: useful in this instance for Pamela and Harry as they exchanged confidences by the large hooded fireplace that contained a freestanding inglenook stove.

"I love you, & you only, & you always"
Mary, would even the most self-blinded flirt say that? Surely he would have kept to the suggested vaguenesses that he has hitherto spoken in—not compromised himself unless he meant it?

Harry's final words were a masterpiece of manipulation: "I want to try & get as right as I can—and in the mean time no words of mine are to tie you in the very *least*—think of nothing I have said—when you are tired of me . . . you are to throw me away like a sucked orange, & marry the best man you can—though I shall be *furious* if you do—but that will be nothing to you."

On hearing of this "episode," Mary was furious: "Just like him I feel inclined to say & think he has shown great want of self-control *his great vice*. Why not now if he really means it?" she asked her baffled mother. Mary's fingers were crossed for the "nice-sounding" Arthur Paget, but she knew the "horribly clever" Harry and her own sister too well for that. Mary was right. By Christmas Arthur Paget and another young suitor had been dispatched, the Wyndhams' friends were beginning to gossip that the unorthodox parenting methods practiced at Clouds were coming home to roost, and Percy was concerned enough to write to Mary about the matter at what was, for him, some length.

As a rule Percy concerned himself little with his children's marriages. His personal experience made him sympathetic to the pull of "magnetisme, attraction." He thought parents pushing their children into loveless, wealthy marriages were simply "wrong." But he believed that relying upon mere attraction was far worse and he balked at the "apparently insane" justification of "love conquers all" woven by his youngest daughter and Harry Cust. When he tried to enumerate the risks of marrying a man like Cust, he had to put his pen down, overwhelmed by the multitude that presented themselves. Eventually, he adopted a light-hearted tone, dividing the world into two camps: the "mad" and the sane, who were their "keepers." "Myself, Mamma and Pamela are undoubtedly mad, Mananai I am *sure* is a keeper." Mary seemed to veer between the two. Percy was clear where Harry stood. "N.B. He, Cust, is sane," he wrote in a tiny postscript that revealed the root of his misgivings: for, spiderlike, Cust seemed to be playing with Pamela, trapped like a fly in his web.

THIRTEEN

Crisis

As Christmas approached, the atmosphere at Clouds was tense. Percy's doubts about Cust were growing, as were his fears for his wife's state of mind. His irascibility was enhanced by the presence of all four of Mary's children in the nurseries. Mary frequently left her children at Clouds for extended periods of time. It saved the Elchos the expense of running Stanway in their absence; and Mary disliked taking her children to Gosford, believing the journey too long. Cynthia Charteris visited Gosford for the first time that she could remember when she was six years old.

Three and a half years of no physical relations had shown what a binding force sex had been for the Elchos. They bickered like children. In January 1891, Mary sent Evelyn de Vesci a long apology for their recent confused departure from Abbeyleix. The morning they were due to leave, Hugo refused: "Said he had a boil on his nose & sat on his bed & would not dress." Mary stormed off to the railway station, servants and luggage in tow, before her rage quelled. She returned and played the "ma[r]tyr." Eventually they took the later train that Hugo had wanted. In the process, Mary accidentally made off with John de Vesci's latest copy of the periodical *Nineteenth Century*. She told Evelyn that she had left it with the railway porter. "I hope he will get [it]." Evelyn was wearily familiar with contretemps like these.

Lady Hermione Duncombe, a daughter of the 1st Earl of Feversham, was married to Gerald Fitzgerald in January 1884, then Lord Kildare and heir to the Dukedom of Leinster. The young couple moved to a Fitzgerald property, Kilkea Castle in County Kildare, but the marriage was not a success, prompting the bored and unhappy Hermione to write the lines "Kilkea Castle and Lord Kildare / Are more than any woman can bear." Hermione's beauty, said her friend Elizabeth, Countess of Fingall, "has not in any way been exaggerated," but the vivid contrast of Hermione's translucent skin and the flush of color in her cheeks and lips was the beauty bestowed by tuberculosis.

Mary's letters, which had once mixed admonitions with caresses in "Spression," were now primarily couched in plain English: asking Hugo where he was, when he was coming back, and why he did not reply. By the turn of the decade Hugo was more often at Carton, the Irish home of his mistress, the renowned beauty Hermione, Duchess of Leinster. Hermione was a distant kinswoman by marriage of Mary's. If, as he sat at dinner underneath Lord and Lady Edward Fitzgerald's portraits, joking with Hermione's friends, he felt any pangs of guilt he did not show it. Mary represented the humdrum minutiae of married life. Hermione, who told Hugo that his love for her was "the one happiness of her unhappy life," allowed the errant son and disappointing husband to be the perfect lover.

Mary was widely regarded as a saint for putting up with Hugo. Her perceived forbearance regarding Arthur Balfour was considered, even by the most morally exacting of her contemporaries, to be "wonderful." Arthur had returned from Ireland in 1891 to take up the post of Leader of the House of Commons and First Lord of the Treasury (a position now always held by the Prime Minister) and was now Salisbury's undisputed heir to the leadership of the Conservative Party. The 1892 election, which delivered Gladstone to power for a fourth time, afforded Arthur, no longer part of government but now in opposition, greater free time. Yet, "I *cannot* make it out," remarked Ettie Grenfell, wondering at the fact that neither Mary nor Arthur capitalized on this situation—"she [Mary] seems never to see him [Arthur] alone, positively to avoid it." Ettie put this down to Mary's "prudence . . . I do admire her courage intensely." "Lady Elcho is an angel: of all the women I know, an angel," said another friend.

These onlookers, however, were not behind the closed drawing-room doors when Mary visited Arthur alone each Wednesday afternoon when they were in London. And privately, among Mary, Hugo and Arthur there remained, in Mary's phrase, an "unstable equilibrium!" As she drily pointed out to Arthur, on the increasingly rare occasions when Hugo was with only his family, "he has more time for observation." On a summer's evening in 1890 when all three were visiting the Adeanes at Babraham, Hugo materialized in Mary's room before dinner and tormented her with questions. Had Arthur ever openly expressed his fondness for her? What exactly had he said? Such questions "screw up my entrails! And make me feel quite quivering," Mary told Arthur the next day, apologizing for her silence all evening. "Chilld to the bone" and feeling "particularly helpless and nervous," she had been unable to talk to him normally. Sitting after dinner in the Italian colonnade, she had only been able to hope, impotently, that Arthur would ask her to watch the moon rise on the other side of the house, allowing her to escape Hugo's sardonic gaze. Arthur didn't. Mary was anguished. She perpetually feared that Arthur would abandon her for a younger, prettier woman who could offer him more by way of sex than she. Arthur, capable of cattishness, did not always dispel those fears. In a particularly low blow he even once eulogized Hermione and her artistic skill. "No woman, wife or mother is ever quite her own master," said Mary. Hugo's and Arthur's behavior often forcibly reminded her of that.

By the time Mary arrived at Clouds on 21 December 1892, she had not seen her children for over a month. Her primary concern was for Ego, still overly nervy after a bout of scarlet fever he had contracted in the autumn, but she put it down to Christmas excitement. A shoot planned for 28 December had kept the Adeanes and their girls at Babraham; George and Sibell were at Eaton in Cheshire with the Westminsters; Guy and Minnie were in India. It being a high day and holiday, Hugo was present too.

On Christmas morning the children's stockings were crammed with toys. As the family walked to East Knoyle church, three-year-old Colin delighted every passerby with a prattling "Merry Christmas." Just a few hours later he was struck by scarlet fever; Hugo and the other children fell sick the next day. Five-year-old Cynthia remembered "a timeless blur of bewildered suffering. Burning heat, raging thirst, tossing and turning in sheets that seemed on fire." In a journal that recorded her children's infancies and early youths, Mary recalled that she had been ordered by the doctor not to go to her children in case she caught the fever herself. But she had already had scarlet fever in her late teens and would have been immune. In fact, as Mary recorded to George in a letter just a few days later, she had disregarded the doctor's advice and stayed by Colin's side until Hugo "begged me to go with tears in his eyes" for "the others' [children's] sake." Half an hour after Mary left him, Colin died. Heartbreakingly, Mary was told that Colin had been conscious and had asked for her.

"I think there must be *no* heartache like that of losing a child," said Pamela as she watched over Mary, lying "very still" in her quiet darkened room. "I am sure she is brave & *wonderful*," wrote Mananai impotently to her mother as the news reached the Adeanes at Babraham; "kiss her from me." Colin was buried on a sunny bank under a laburnum tree in the East Knoyle churchyard. By convention Mary did not attend to see the small white coffin decked with flowers go into the earth. A notice in the *Evening Times* alerted the world. Letters of condolence flooded in, offering varying degrees of comfort. Almost all spoke of how close Mary had been to her son, how much she had loved him, how happy his life had been.

Around 14 percent of infants born in England and Wales between 1860 and 1900 never reached their first birthday. Disease was the most common cause of death, and scarlet fever, gastroenteritis, dysentery, measles, smallpox and tuberculosis among the most prevalent diseases. Upperclass children had a better rate of survival: approximately 8 percent of infants died in their first year, and 5 percent between the ages of one and five. The old assumption that parents of this era were somehow immune to infant death has been discredited. Parents cared deeply, particularly when, like Mary, they had no strong religious faith to console them.

Outwardly and for the sake of her children she put on a "resolute, almost jaunty brightness." Cincie, who tiptoed out of the nursery to find her mother sitting on the stairs "weeping as if her heart must break," knew differently. Mary was plagued by the fear that Colin had died in pain, alone, thinking his mother had abandoned him. She asked Arthur whether life could be checked without great suffering. But all Arthur's philosophical detachment could not help her, even as he reminded Mary that between herself and her son "there never was anything in your relations . . . which now you need desire to be unsaid or undone. How rarely can a mother say this of any child?"

Mary and her children, accompanied by a nurse and Cincie's governess Miss Jourdain, left Clouds only in March, joining Madeline and Percy in Hyères, where they had developed the habit of wintering. Hugo was to make sporadic visits from London.

The departure was bleak. Guy, whose enduring fragility had kept them at Clouds until then, was sewn up in an eiderdown to protect him from the cold; Cincie wept all the way. Mary had been set on cramming her entire family into one sleeping car, and only with great difficulty was dissuaded from sleeping top-to-toe in a bunk with Cincie, an instinct that seems driven by vulnerability rather than frugality. A party of friends and relatives saw them onto the boat train in London; another met them at Hyères, where they settled into a tiny doll's house of a place called the Villa Marguerite.

Anyone who has grieved will be drearily familiar with the path that Mary trod that "long and un-ending" spring, as the exaltation of grief gives way to the dull realization that what seems an experiment in loss is actually a new reality. Without a strong faith—throughout her life, her letters spoke little of God—or her mother's spiritualist beliefs, Mary found little to console her. "I do *not* feel as if he were near! . . . but then I should hate & could not bear to feel that he was hanging about, missing the spring and wanting to live," she said to her mother. Not knowing what to think, she had only unanswerable questions and a deep sense of guilt. Watching her children grow stronger and play among the same olive groves she had run through as a child, she felt some relief, but "spring intensifies everything." She was "horrid," she told her mother, and nothing could help her.

Mary and her children left Hyères in mid-May and went straight to Felixstowe. In deep mourning, Mary eschewed the Season entirely, only stopping briefly in London to see Madeline Adeane, who had given birth to a third girl, called Madeline after herself. She then left to summer in

Sweden, where a Dr. Widegren had promised to restore her to health. With a distracted mother, the Charteris children ran wild and unruly. They did not return to Stanway until October 1893, almost a year since they had first left it. Colin's death drove his parents still further apart. Hugo's absence is notable in the records of this period. Reading Mary's bald account of her son's death in *Family Record,* it is hard not to escape the conclusion that she blamed Hugo for her absence from Colin at his death—even, perhaps, for his death. That, even as Mary mourned, in Hermione Leinster's nurseries was a six-month-old son, a child that was undoubtedly Hugo's, cannot have failed to intensify Mary's deep-seated grief and rage.

In mid-August Arthur attended a Saturday-to-Monday with the Earl and Countess Brownlow at Ashridge. Harry Cust, the Brownlows' heir, Violet Granby and her young cousin Nina Welby were among the party. A drawing of Nina by Violet shows a dark, slim, pretty girl with a distinctly doleful air. Nina was utterly in Violet's thrall, and well known to be besotted with Harry. Arthur described to Mary an uneventful weekend. He had unsuccessfully tried to evade the clutches of Adelaide Brownlow and been "carried off" by her for a long walk before dinner: "She nearly makes me cry with boredom." He had written a little more of *Foundations of Belief,* which he had begun in 1892 (it was his second book, following on from *A Defense of Philosophic Doubt,* published in 1879), played some lawn tennis and had a nice talk on art with a young female guest. "H.C. seemed to me rather to neglect his harem—those who were there—but was pleasant enough to the outside world."

Shortly afterwards, Harry went west to Clouds. His behavior seemed promising. "He does not flirt in the coarse way he did but is deferential & attentive & vy. pleasant to evry [sic] one. He & George have endless arguments on Poetry," Madeline Wyndham told Mary. Percy thought Pamela looked prettier, happier and more hopeful every day, though he maintained some misgivings. "I *hope* it may all turn out well," he told Mary. "I wish I had better grounds for *thinking* it would." It seems likely that at this point Harry and Pamela became secretly engaged. George Wyndham subsequently told Wilfrid Blunt that only the thought that Lucy Graham Smith might "make trouble in the matter" had prevented an announcement before Lucy had been duly mollified.

As Harry left Clouds, the state of affairs was "like an extremely delicate weather glass," said Pamela. She knew the dangers of marriage to Harry, but it offered the chance to do more than "just live and be passive." "I feel I could without any hesitation jump into a chasm for someone . . . or cut off a finger—or anything *real*," she told Mary. Her letters were filled with rhetorical flourishes: she was a lone warrior going out to meet an army; a sailor refusing to turn back at the sight of stormy seas. She discussed the conflict between her "hill self"—the self of thoughts, ideas and inspiration, found in church and at Bayreuth (the Bavarian town famous for its annual Wagner festival)—and her "earth self"—"the one who talks, sleeps and comes down to breakfast"—in a convoluted discourse that would have done justice to George pirouetting in the House of Commons. She explained to Mary:

> One thing I have learned in my life & I am glad I have learned it so young, is that to look for peace & happiness in perfect *entirety* is a wild goose chase in this world . . . in the end the *chances* of happiness are more equally balanced than one thinks, what may seem "wreckage" viewed in one way—may not be more "wreckage" than lives outwardly perfectly matched.

It was doubtful logic.

In September, Madeline Wyndham took to her bed. Her guests were told she was suffering from rheumatism and a bad cold. It is likely that her nerves were succumbing under the strain. Pamela took pleasure in the ill-concealed surprise of their eminent guests—mostly male Souls—at finding her and Mananai, who was visiting, hosting with not one of the Souls hostesses, like Mary, Ettie or Margot, in attendance. She took equal pleasure in defeating their attempts to make her change her mind about Harry. On a sunset walk Richard Haldane, a Scottish Liberal Imperialist barrister who was gradually being drawn within the Souls' ambit (and whom Walburga, Lady Paget, a fellow guest that week, thought conversed "in epigrams and aphorisms"), told Pamela that Harry was a man she could better help as friend than as wife, and that he "should not regret it" if she "postponed a decision." The following week Asquith, now Home Secretary, and courting Margot Tennant, talked urgently of silk purses and sows' ears. Later that day it was Arthur's turn. From Sweden Mary had begged him to make Pamela see sense, but Arthur was "on a pedestal of perfection as always" and could not bring himself to come down off his plinth to talk about Cust, "so we reached home again having discussed civilization!" said Pamela mischievously, particularly delighted to have outwitted Arthur, whose understated intelligence always made her own pretensions seem florid, and whose loyalty to Mary made her feel scorned. Pamela liked having primacy in people's affections.

For almost a decade, the Souls had prided themselves upon being the intellectual, thoughtful and moral face of the aristocracy. This was blown out of the water by what ensued. Unbeknown to everyone except Violet, Harry and Nina Welby had been conducting an affair for the previous year, aided and abetted by Violet, who pushed forward Nina, her acolyte, as her candidate for Harry's wife, knowing that that way she could maintain her hold over her lover. At Ashridge, as a "leave-taking" Harry and Nina spent "some nights together . . . with the result that she had become or thought herself with child," wrote a fascinated Wilfrid Blunt in his diary some months later, agog at the scandal that threatened to undo the Souls.

In the aftermath of the affair, the Souls shunned Violet, the Machiavellian Circe who had sacrificed the virginal Nina to her own sexual ends. Such outrage over premarital sex was to a degree dissimulation. It happened among the elite. It is suggested that Lord and Lady Randolph Churchill had used Lady Randolph's unwed pregnancy (the child was Winston Churchill) to secure their families' approval of their match. Even among the Souls, Margot Tennant used Wilfrid Blunt to relieve her of her virginity—if his diary can be believed. But it was not common, and a scandal like this was unthinkable. In September, Nina wrote to Harry to tell him that she was pregnant; Harry either did not reply, or replied "with great brutality." In desperation, Nina sought Violet's help. Violet, in Nina's words, took "the matter out of my hands" and bruited the affair about the Souls, imploring the Brownlows, Balfour, Asquith and Curzon to help save Harry from "worldly disgrace" and make him marry Nina.

The resultant chaos is reflected in the tangle of papers in the Whittingehame archives, with the instruction "Mr. Balfour says burn eventually" scribbled across the front. By unspoken agreement, Arthur, as "High Priest" of the Souls, was to resolve the crisis. His inclination to destroy this evidence is unsurprising. "I am coming to you on a matter of life and death" reads an undated scrap of paper from Nina; "Oh! I feel more fiendish than anyone can ever have felt before" reads a letter from Violet. A letter from Lady Welby-Gregory, imploring Arthur to use his influence to make Harry marry her daughter, is followed by outraged missives from Adelaide Brownlow deploring her nephew's behavior and telegrams from George Wyndham and George Curzon, Balfour's lieutenants, "tearing about the country on one sad errand after another" trying to settle the matter and keep it hidden from the outside world.

The matter was so heavily hushed up at the time that even those within the Souls were not sure of exactly what was happening. To this day, accounts differ. "Believe nothing that you hear," George told Ettie Grenfell. "No one whom you will meet knows the whole truth & those who know a part spend their time in perverting it." "I am so anxious so anxious," said Pamela, bombarding Sibell with questions and God with her prayers. By this time, George had broken the news of Nina's pregnancy to his family, and Madeline Wyndham, collapsing along with the whole house of cards, had been hustled off to Bournemouth in an invalid's carriage (that is, a railway carriage fitted out with a brass bed and sprung mattress so that she could lie flat all the way).

There was only one way this matter could be resolved. Harry must marry Nina, although Balfour had to threaten Cust with social ostracism and political exile before he complied. On 3 October 1893 Harry stood once again before Pamela by the hearthstone in Clouds' hall. With George lurking quietly in the background he revealed to Pamela the full extent of events and his impending forced marriage. "Whatever I did, sad, mad and bad I always said to myself, 'I have got Pamela, *like a star in a cupboard* to come back to,'" said Harry. Pamela did not castigate Harry then, or ever. She had already cast him as a Christlike figure and reserved her anger for the world that had sacrificed him on the altar of conventional morality. Harry described Pamela as "a little heroine thro'out & a little saint as well." He immortalized their mutual sacrifice in the poem "Non Nobis," which presented Pamela as that saint and himself as a flawed mortal purged by suffering.

It was inevitable, perhaps, that the Wyndhams should send Pamela abroad to escape the scandal. The Adeanes had been planning a trip to India. Percy paid for them to take Pamela with them: no expense was spared. A passage was booked on the *Ganges* in November (fortunately not on the same ship as Lucy Graham Smith, who was also dispatched to India by her family to recover from Cust). In the intervening weeks, Pamela was sent to Saighton Grange, one of the Westminsters' houses in Cheshire, to stay with George and Sibell.

Many years later Osbert Sitwell commented to Pamela on her apparently unlimited reserves of social grace. In response Pamela showed him her scarred palms: to maintain composure when enraged she clenched her fists so tightly that her fingernails cut into the skin. She remembered this time as a blur of pain and suffering: shaking and sobbing in Saighton's chapel while clasped in Sibell's arms. But in front of the other guests she tried to maintain her composure. She sang old sea ballads and read Blunt some of her poetry. He thought her "delightful, with wit and sense and feeling," her poetry "really excellent, original and good, far beyond what is usual with young ladies," and was so taken with his young cousin that he was moved to compose one of his acrostics, a favored seductive tool, using her name—Pamela Genevieve Adelaide Wyndham—to praise her to the skies as a woman capable of inspiring a knight to valorous battle, for whom "empires bend and break" and "kingdoms crumble down."

Such was Society's understanding of a common code that when, on his return to Crabbet a few days later, Wilfrid read the bald announcement in *The Times* "that Harry Cust has been 'recently married' to Miss Welby," and that the newlyweds had departed England for the Continent—without the customary engagement announcement—he immediately knew something was up. As George Curzon made his way to the Carlton Club, the Conservatives' gentlemen's club in Pall Mall, he was "inundated with enquiries" from intrigued acquaintances who had also seen the suspicious notice. London was pricking up its ears for a scandal. The Souls closed ranks. "Since H.C. has, though tardily done the right thing I am sure you will agree that we should now try to save both of them from the consequences of this foolish delay," Curzon proposed in a note dashed off to Arthur as soon as he was safely inside. He suggested they cobble together a story that "will impose upon none of the innermost circle: but if industriously circulated may shut the mouths of the public." The approved version, neatly typed and sent *inter alia* to the Tennants at the Souls stronghold of the Glen and to the intractable Brownlows, explains a long attachment, familial opposition on both sides (due to Harry's "entanglements with married women": a positively safe vice now in light of recent events), and a decision to marry "at all hazards nonetheless." The story contained enough truth to be almost plausible, although as Nina's elder brother Charles said ruefully, "It's a thin veil at best."

"Flirtation practice" had brought the Souls to the edge of public scandal and they recoiled. "To a good many pretty tough and experienced men and women of the world this has been a positively startling revelation of the things that can happen amongst people presumably refined and well-meaning," said Lord Pembroke. Eight months later, Wilfrid Blunt lunched with Margaret Talbot, not herself a Soul, to find she had given up all vanity, in part "thanks to the hideous scandals connected with Harry Cust, they have frightened her, as they have many others." Violet was shunned. Harry's own status within the group never quite recovered. By the spring of 1894 he was out of politics, his editorship of the *Pall Mall Gazette* his sole occupation, and to the next generation a tired, somewhat seedy figure with only the faint glow of someone of whom greatness had once been predicted. The Cust affair showed how determinedly the Souls, despite steps towards gender parity, were of their time. Violet was deemed the ultimately culpable sorceress; Harry, albeit deceitful, the mortal man unable to control his impulses. When it became apparent shortly after the marriage that Nina was no longer pregnant—the inescapable conclusion being that Nina, forced by Harry, had had an abortion—D. D. Lyttelton thought that Nina should die of shame. "I don't want her to, though I generally feel it to be the only solution," she added charitably.

FOURTEEN

India

S everal weeks later, on a grey November's day, Pamela stared out of the window of the boat train taking her from London Victoria to Southhampton, sick with misery. The most prosaic details of ordinary life that flashed past—"even the milk-cans & the papers at the station"—were "each a separate little agony" reminding her of a world that she was leaving behind.

The weeks between Harry's marriage and Pamela's departure for India had not been easy for any of the Wyndhams. Madeline Wyndham remained in the throes of a breakdown in Bournemouth, under the care of a nurse until early December. Percy stayed at his wife's side. Pamela was kept at Saighton, out of Percy's way. Father-daughter relations, already at breaking point, deteriorated still further when Percy found out in late October that a stream of letters and keepsakes were still passing between Harry at Fontainebleau and Pamela at Saighton. *"How long is the writing to continue,"* he demanded of Mary as he realized Sibell's limitations as a chaperone: "In my judgment the things [*sic*] seems *very far from over* with the chains, rings and copies of Browning poems! . . . I feel that they are all so sunk in fatuity that no words can save them." Enraged by his daughter's "freaks" and tears, astonished by her lack of sense, Percy banned all communication between Pamela and Harry: to little effect, since the lovers continued to communicate through Sibell.

"Except by English law I am not one bit married, save to Pamela only," Harry told Sibell in a rather belated conversion to chastity. Pamela, "the one pure perfect love" of Harry's life (so he said), received each message with joy. She seems to have thought of Nina not at all.

As Pamela prepared to depart for India she saw nothing but pain ahead "for the next 10 years." Her gloom did not lift once on board the *Ganges*. Minna, Pamela and Mananai's shared maid began unpacking their travel trunks. Mananai and Charlie set off to explore the ship and peruse the captain's list of their fellow travelers. Pamela sat in her cabin "very mis[erable] very alone," clutching a bundle of Harry's letters and a prayer book that he had sent her, waiting for the clock's hands to reach midnight, the hour appointed for the *Ganges* to steam out. "It hardly seems real," she wrote in the first of many lengthy letters to her confessor Sibell. Desperate for the smallest details about Harry, Pamela implored Sibell to write the moment she saw him with "long minute descriptions: color of clothes etc or even if his dog was with him."

The passage, and passengers, to India were familiar to an imperial nation. Ships carrying brave soldiers (returning from leave to garrison the Jewel in the Crown of the Empire, as India was known) and "the Fishing Fleet" (unfortunate young ladies who had failed to secure a husband in England now trying their luck abroad) passed Gibraltar, made their way through the Suez Canal and across the Gulf of Aden to Bombay. Pamela was surprised to find how accurate the caricatures that she had seen in the popular press were: "The people on the steamer are beyond *words*—typical—& more like the young ladies in 'shirts' & skirts in the *D[aily] Graphic* than I ever expected," she told Sibell. Mananai was more optimistic about the caliber of passengers. "There are very many nice people on board, especially men," she told her mother, scrolling off a list of names as proof. She was particularly taken by one Lieutenant Baker-Carr of the Rifle Brigade, a "delightful & very good looking man" who reminded her of her brother Guy. Robert Baker-Carr was a seasoned veteran of India, about to take up a post as the Viceroy Lord Elgin's aide-de-camp. To Mananai's delight, he was the son of an acquaintance of Madeline Wyndham from her Irish youth. "I am trying to describe the people to amuse Papa," said Mananai, but she was doing her best to sell the dashing infantry officer to her parents, and to Pamela as well.

Pamela was not openly dismissive of Mananai's plans, but she did not leap to embrace new prospects either. Shipboard life was busy: games of deck quoits, shipboard croquet and nightly concerts. Pamela had brought her guitar with her, but she sang her folk ballads rarely and socialized less. She preferred to be out on deck watching the blue horizon flash unchangeably past: marveling at the "wonderful Opal days . . . such sunsets . . . *such* Waves & Sea." At dinner she escaped from the chatter of the captain's table as soon as was polite and stood in the darkness on the ship's prow, watching it plow "a great white *path* up the Waters," with "the flying fish, & the funny porpoises, & the lovely phosphor" lighting up its way. The greatness of the ocean, its space and darkness, gave Pamela a momentary sense of perspective and escape. Surrounded by "something Unimaginable . . . it was all perfect, & beautiful, & *great*,—& wiped away the dreadfulness of those 3 months."

The *Ganges* docked in Bombay, and the party, accompanied by Baker-Carr, headed north for game hunting near Peshawar, the town that lay at the mouth of the Khyber Pass on the Afghan border. All their Kipling, all the tales of India they had heard and their distillation in exhibitions visited had not prepared Pamela and the Adeanes for the country's assault on their senses. The dusty windows of the rackety train revealed "a new world—new Birds, new grasses, new animals, *everything* new." The rushing air was hot and filled with alien smells and sounds. They stretched their legs at stations "swarming with natives in *brilliant* clothes," and as the train puffed and hissed at the siding drank soup quickly boiled up for them in the waiting room. Once they had reached their destination they traveled in "touges," little dogcarts pulled by small sturdy ponies— "too delightful," said Mananai—while bullock carts bearing their piles of luggage brought up the rear. They jolted past Buddhist rock temples and past Muslims at prayer in the mosque: "[They] touch the ground again & again with their foreheads . . . some pray out loud—calling on Allah in high mettalic [*sic*] tones," Mananai reported.

The northwest border, from where the Khyber Pass—Kipling's "narrow swordcut in the hills"—led to Afghanistan, was tribal land, bandit country. Through the pass wound the "kafilas" of traders heading for Peshawar. The cries of the tribesmen, the clattering of iron pots over hazy campfires, the musty exotic smells of camels, carpets and musk: Rudyard Kipling's *Plain Tales from the Hills,* published some five years prior, had imprinted all these images into the minds of the British public. They were accustomed to press reports touting imperial derring-do in the frequent skirmishes between the British and the guerrilla forces of the bandits. The slash-and-burn tactics employed by imperial forces to stabilize the region were quietly overlooked. Soldiers who burned down villages, slaughtered livestock and destroyed food stores sat at odds with the propaganda of a noble, civilizing Empire.

At Peshawar the party camped out in the wild and trekked over rocky terrain. By day vultures and eagles swooped overhead through sparkling blue skies; on nighttime drives through the arid country they heard the terrifying howl of jackals in the dark. "This *is* the land of the Bible," said Pamela; "it is *very* enchanted . . . & sometimes I am living in an Arabian Nights Tale—& sometimes in the old Scriptures & often—very often—in Fairytales. For there are Blue-birds here—the real Fairy-bird . . . and Night shuts down like a great Curtain on the day—& the stars quiver instead of shine."

They parted ways with Baker-Carr, promising to meet him again in Calcutta, and traveled on to princely Rajasthan, where on a swaying howdah they made their way through the forest to the sixteenth-century fort of Chittor. As they passed through the monumental entrance gate, "the Native Guard played God Save the Queen . . . it is wonderful the way the Natives Salaam & bow down to white people," said Mananai. They made their return at dusk, and as their elephants waded across a river the howdah began to pitch and slide. The mahout barked instructions at his passengers to shift their weight: "We all clung on to each other . . . there was *really* no fear & we were roaring with laughter all the time but it was anything but comfortable," Mananai told her mother.

They visited acquaintances made on the *Ganges,* dined with them at mess and reviewed the soldiers on parade, dazzled by the contrast between the dark skin of the Sikh soldiers and their vibrant red tunics and turbans. At Udaipur they toured the white stone palaces of maharajas. The British Empire professed to civilize, but its roots lay in commerce and Mananai was appalled to find these eastern palaces furnished with pieces "all from Birmingham cut glass beds & chairs & tables . . . too dreadful." She thrived on the rough and ready nature of traveling— "one goes to bed *regularly* & can wash & dress quite well" on trains— and was dazed by the sheer amount she saw: "To me it['s] extraordinary to think that your little 'Em-Wem' [Pamela] & 'Jessie Rat' [Mananai] are seeing & doing all this—we can never be glad enough," she wrote, before remembering the reason that had brought them there and hastily amending the line to read: "shall have *such* things to look back on & remember & tell you about shan't we."

Mananai reported proudly to her parents every conquest her little sister made, from elderly misty-eyed Englishmen on ferries, made nostalgic for "Home" by Pamela's singing, to those rather younger, attracted by her vibrancy. At Calcutta they met up with Baker-Carr and Eddy Tennant, the eldest son of the Tennant clan, who was in India checking on his sister Lucy Graham Smith. On paper, responsible, good-natured Eddy was immensely eligible: vastly wealthy, tall and good-looking. His fundamental shortcoming was pithily summed up by his younger sister. "Eddie lacks *drive*," said Margot of her favorite brother. More brutally, one of Eddy's children, who had inherited his aunt's acidic streak, later declared that his father was so boring that he couldn't even remember what he looked like. That Pamela and Lucy were in India for the same reason did not appear to disconcert anyone. Diffidently, Eddy made his interest in Pamela plain. There was an uncomfortable afternoon when both he and Baker-Carr accompanied Mananai and Pamela to the Eden Gardens cricket ground. The group got caught in a thunderstorm and retreated to the Adeanes' rooms to sit it out, where a drenched Eddy and Baker-Carr cast dark looks across the sitting room at each other.

Pamela did not mention these suitors in letters home, but told her friends that she was "much happier—happy even." Arthur, having been shown one such missive by George, thought Pamela in "tearing spirits." "I put her at the head of all the letter writers I know at least for certain qualities . . . the vividness of the presentation and the life and color . . . glowing in every line were extraordinary," he told Mary. Pamela was not so buoyant as Arthur supposed or hoped. She confided to Mary and Sibell that misery still frequently leapt upon her: upon receipt of a postbag empty of letters from Harry; upon glimpsing others in love, as when the party met up with Guy and Minnie Wyndham at Lucknow, who seemed to exist in "a *nimbus* of pure happiness."

Pamela, no enemy of misery, once proposed, in some seriousness, the instigation of a national holiday of grief: an annual two-day "regular out of door . . . celebration of being really, thoroughly, impossibly, cruelly unhappy." Time did not diminish her emotional self-indulgence. " 'Life' is one damned thing after another . . . hardly has one pulled one's bleeding roots from under one severing blow, than one has to trail them before another hatchet, & have yet another length hacked away . . . I wonder why—then—we are all sent into the world with such a longing for joy: for happiness as one's birthright," she wrote to Mary in middle age.

The seeds of this trait are plainly evident in her letters of this time, but the unhappiness of a heartbroken twenty-two-year-old is very real, her isolation in stifling rooms, bemused and angry at the jabbering hordes around her who seemed to have happiness so easily in their grasp. At those times "all the strength & philosophy" that she tried to practice "goes for very little . . . one flattens ones [*sic*] nose against the glass window, at the hot sausages inside," she told Sibell. In Lucknow's steamy heat, with green parakeets chattering about her, Pamela's heart and mind were back in rainy England with Harry.

Pamela felt as though a curtain had been drawn across her past as soon as she stepped on board the *Ganges*. The letters she received from home were evasive about Harry: "I feel so far away & wonder sometimes if anybody but myself remembers anything about that time," she told Sibell. Their party set sail from Bombay on 20 March 1894, on the *Peninsular*—"one of the *best* ships & we have the best cabins on board," reported Mananai to her parents. There were a few disappointments: Charlie had not bagged himself a tiger, and time constraints had forced them to drop items from their itinerary: "One can't do everything." Most important, Pamela finally seemed better. Mananai had been as encouraging as she could to Baker-Carr, on Pamela's behalf. They left with the lieutenant promising to write, and to visit when next in England. As Pamela and the Adeanes lay out on deck at night, looking up at the moon and stars and tousled by warm night winds, their previous crossing's misery seemed a world away.

The travelers docked at a misty Southampton in April, with Pamela's guitar intact and a parrot that Mananai had brought back home for a pet. In the summer that followed, Pamela's family spoke with relief of her buoyant spirit, how pretty and well she was looking, and enthused about her hordes of admirers and innumerable engagements. "How much *better* she is again," said Mananai, hoping that finally her sister's fortunes would improve.

FIFTEEN

Rumor

The travelers returned to a political landscape irrevocably altered by Gladstone's retirement from politics little over a month before their return. Few had thought that the octogenarian's fourth ministry, which began in 1892, would be anything but short-lived, although the young Welsh Radical David Lloyd George was one of many in the Commons who marveled at how, in moments, the shrunken figure huddled on the front bench could become "an erect athletic gladiator, fit for the contest of any arena." But Gladstone was broken when his second Home Rule Bill, after battling its way through the Commons—in a sense literally, for a fistfight broke out on the benches between Unionists and Home Rulers at its final reading—was rejected by the House of Lords. In an incandescent final speech in the Commons, Gladstone asked his fellow Members how long "a deliberative assembly, elected by the votes of more than six million people," could continue to be defied by the inherited wealth and privilege of the Lords. As he left the House for the final time that evening, making his way to Windsor Castle, the monarch's Berkshire residence just outside London, to offer the Queen his resignation, he was applauded to the rafters by MPs, all aware, even then, that an era was at an end.

Since 1886 and the defection of the most aristocratic elements of the Liberal Party, Unionists had dominated the Lords. Their leader Lord

Salisbury's "referendal theory," as it was known, stated, in a nutshell, that
if a government elected by the people put forward controversial legislation, the people ought to be given a chance to decide specifically on that
legislation. On that basis, it was not only justifiable, but necessary, for
a Unionist-dominated House of Lords to defeat legislation of a Liberal
government passed by the House of Commons so that the issue could be
referred back to the electorate. The Lords claimed to know better the
vacillating public's wishes than their directly elected representatives. It
was an intellectually hollow argument, and constitutionally dangerous—
but it appeared to be vindicated when the Unionists triumphed at the
polls in 1895.

Gladstone's successor came from within the Wyndhams' extended
circle: Lord Rosebery, formerly Foreign Secretary, was Constance Leconfield's brother. He had been chosen personally by the Queen, who could
not bring herself to invite the more obvious candidate, Gladstone's
Chancellor, Sir William Harcourt, since, despite being an aristocrat,
Harcourt had introduced in his most recent Budget the devastating salvo
against the landed classes of death duties of 8 percent on all estates worth
over £1 million.

Rosebery was not a good choice. Acutely shy and prone to deep depression since being widowed in 1890, he was undermined by the thwarted
Harcourt and his son Lewis (or "Loulou"), who were both renowned for
their capacity for manipulative intrigue. The two were instrumental in
further spreading rumors already doing the rounds that Rosebery was
having a homosexual affair with his own secretary. That secretary was
still more closely linked to the Wyndhams, being the "excellent, amiable"
and "instantly loveable" Francis, Viscount Drumlanrig ("Drummy"),
eldest son of Sibyl Queensberry, and the Wyndhams' cousin. Whether
or not the rumors were true (and Drummy's extraordinary elevation to
the peerage after just one year of service and his appointment as lord in
waiting to the Queen did little to dispel them), Drummy's father had
believed them enough to pursue Rosebery to the German spa town of
Bad Homburg in August 1893, threatening to thrash him to the bone.
Only the intervention of several other spa-goers, including the Prince
of Wales, the Chief Commissioner of Police and the Society lawyer Sir
George Lewis, drove Queensberry out, restoring peace to the town.

When Drummy began to court Pamela on her return to England
in 1894, the Wyndhams did not put a stop to it, but they were uneasy.

Their reserve was in marked contrast to the enthusiasm of Drummy's immediate family, in particular his doting maternal grandfather, Alfred Montgomery. From later elliptical references to the "opinion of the world," it is clear Pamela had heard the rumors and knew her family were unenthusiastic about the match. At the end of the summer, Pamela told Drummy she could not marry him, being unable to love him as she had Harry Cust, "simply & honestly—& without knowing why." A few weeks later, Drummy became engaged to someone else.

Throughout the summer and autumn of 1894, Pamela's misery had been growing. The anniversary of the break with Harry loomed. The past year, she said, "makes one afraid of living. The waking every morning—the needle of pain coming through sleep." She was suffocated by her feelings, unable to "make Mamma the receptacle" but terrified of "getting shramped [sic] up instead of opening out." She scribbled out her "bursting feelings" to Sibell in lengthy letters, but felt keenly that she should keep them from her immediate family. In October, she and her parents visited Mary at Gosford. Pamela let slip some of her misery to her sister, and, despite a sympathetic response, was immediately mortified at "even letting you [Mary] think I had anything but the easiest surroundings . . . [or that] I'm always like that." As soon as she left, she wrote to Mary to apologize, blaming "Betsey" for making her overemotional: "There is nothing about me that isn't really to make life easier & happier for me . . . I was a coward to let you say there was! It is entirely in my own hands—and is my own fault if I'm unhappy, or ill."

By then Pamela had been provided with an opportunity to express her feelings. The Wyndhams' stay at Gosford had been cut short by devastating news. Drummy, attending a shooting party in Somerset given by his fiancée's family, had been found dead in a hedge, his collar and head "very much sprinkled" with blood from a gunshot wound through the mouth. The coroner made a finding of accidental death: another sad example of a loaded gun going off as its owner climbed a stile. The fact that Drummy's body had been found nowhere near a stile and that the postmortem suggested that his mouth had been wide open when the shot was fired was carefully overlooked.

The Wyndhams immediately returned south, meeting Drummy's shattered family in London, before taking them to Clouds. "Cousin Sib" seemed shrunken inside her mourning garb; Bosie was thoughtful and gentle. During their brief stay in London, Pamela accompanied

A photographic portrait of Pamela, aged around twenty-three, in the mid-1890s in uncharacteristically stiff, dark clothes. The likelihood is that this was mourning dress for her cousin Drummy, who died in October 1894. As a general rule, Pamela wore white.

Wommy to a dreadful interview with Alfred Montgomery, who seemed more interested in talking to Pamela than to his own granddaughter. She described it to Mary: "He kept saying 'he was so fond of you—he loved you so—how fond he was of you—let me look at you—ah my dear'—& then breaking down—and all the time I felt like *swords* inside me the 'one-moment-too-lateness' of Life." Now, at Clouds, Wommy seemed simply dazed, "but I am afraid she [Wommy] feels it terribly at night when she is alone," Pamela told Mary, kept awake by the sound of sobbing echoing down the corridors.

Pamela plunged into a frenzy of self-recrimination, castigating herself as "blind and afraid," unworthy of Drummy's love. It is clear she knew that Drummy had killed himself, suspected that it was related to the rumors about Drummy and Lord Rosebery, and thought she could have saved him by marrying him. She crucified herself accordingly, enduring the limpet-like affections of Wommy, who, having always hero-worshipped her cousin, now refused to leave her side, insisting on sharing her bed and watching her as she slept. Bosie did not stay long at Clouds before disappearing to be comforted by Oscar Wilde.

Pamela plummeted from a rhapsody of grief into a deep depression. Plans had been made for the Wyndhams, Sibyl Queensberry and

Wommy to travel abroad in the new year, escaping scandal once again with a flight to the Continent. In the meantime Pamela was sent to Babraham to recuperate, although with limited opportunities to do so, since Wommy came too. A worried Mananai plotted ways to restore her younger sister to health and spirits. Still hopeful for Baker-Carr, she wrote to her mother proposing to effect a meeting between the two when Baker-Carr returned on leave. Madeline Wyndham's reply does not survive, but it is evident from Mananai's reluctantly parroting response that her mother poured cold water on the plan: "I *quite* agree if she [Pamela] is not *very* much in love not to *help* her marry a man not rich enough for the comfort of Life . . . let her *wait* now that she can . . . & help her to meet [a] nice man with money enough." Pamela barely noticed, consumed by the feeling that she had let down her family and herself. "Ever since I was grown-up I wanted to be worthy of all the rest of you. Of Mamma, & you, & all," she told Mary. With Harry gone, Drummy dead, scandal in the air and her mother on tenterhooks, Pamela felt only that she had failed. "I don't mind the mills of God grinding small if only they wouldn't grind *so* slowly:—I think I have had an *eternity* in the last 3 years."

SIXTEEN

Egypt

In 1894 a new play was put upon the London stage. *The Case of Rebellious Susan,* by Henry Arthur Jones, considered the plight of aristocratic Lady Susan, who wanted revenge on her philandering husband. Lady Susan leaves her husband and travels to Cairo, where she has a brief romance and falls in love. But, mindful of convention and of her place in Society, she returns to England and her cheating husband and they are reconciled. In a final display of rebellion she refuses to reveal the details of the affair to him unless he will do the same regarding his.

At the insistence of the actor-manager Sir Charles Wyndham (no relation to the Wyndhams) and his leading lady Mary Moore, the version that made it onto the stage at Wyndham's Theatre on Charing Cross Road was deliberately ambiguous about whether Lady Susan had actually been unfaithful. Chastity was "that one indispensable quality in respect for womanhood," Sir Charles told Jones, asking how he could expect "married men to bring their wives to a theatre to learn the lesson that their wives can descend to such nastiness, as giving themselves up for one evening of adulterous pleasure and then return safely to their husband's arms, provided they are clever enough, low enough and dishonest enough to avoid being found out"? Reluctantly Jones agreed, but his published preface to the play maintained what he believed to be the moral of the piece: "That as women cannot retaliate openly, they may retaliate secretly—and *lie!*"

The revised play, a roaring success, was part of a wave of productions considering "the marriage question," which began in 1889 with the first English performance of Ibsen's *A Doll's House,* but is better exemplified by Wilde's smash hits in the early 1890s. In *An Ideal Husband, Lady Windermere's Fan* and *A Woman of No Importance* the pure unyielding wife is pitted against the "fallen woman," while an ostensibly upright husband has a dark past. Love, secrecy, scandal and convention all play off against one another. The overwhelming impression is that in Society the truth is something to be dispensed carefully and in very small doses.

In 1892, Wilde had suggested Mary take a walk-on part in *Lady Windermere's Fan.* Mary asked Wilfrid Blunt's advice, but he dismissed the idea out of hand as unsuitable for a woman of her class. By 1894, Mary was fair placed to play the wronged wife in any of those dramas. That summer, the Elchos' marriage had reached a critical point. Hermione Leinster, suffering from incurable tuberculosis, had gone to live out her final months in a more temperate climate. She packed off her sons to relations and left with her mother and sister for the south of France. Over the course of the summer the Elchos came to an agreement. Hugo would go to Hermione until the end came. When it did, Hugo and Mary would reconcile and have another child to seal their marriage. In the intervening period Hugo's sister Evelyn de Vesci was to act as go-between for the Elchos. It seems that even the long-suffering Mary balked at maintaining anything more than cursory contact with her husband during this time.

In August 1894 Wilfrid Blunt and Bosie Douglas made a pilgrimage to Shakespeare's birthplace of Stratford-upon-Avon in Warwickshire, stopping at Stanway en route. They arrived unannounced to find a house party typical among the Souls: the Adeanes, George Wyndham, Arthur Balfour and Mary playing cricket while a band of brightly dressed Neapolitan musicians serenaded them from the sidelines. Hugo was in the Engadine in Switzerland on a cure, Mary about to depart for her own spa treatment at Bad Ems in Germany. The following days were filled with Stanway's standard amusements: croquet in the rain, a golfing trip to Cleve Hill, the highest point in Gloucestershire commanding a glorious view over the surrounding countryside, evening games of battledore (an early form of badminton) played across a string rigged up in the hall.

Normally Hugo's absence gave Mary a chance to spend time with Arthur without challenge. But this time, while Arthur played golf, Mary was not on the links but sitting with Wilfrid in an inn garden nearby while he read poetry to her.

In the years since Blunt had first discovered his fascination for Mary a friendly, cousinly relationship had sprung up. In 1887, he had been allowed back into Egypt, and his small family were now accustomed to spend half their year at Sheykh Obeyd. Over a decade after the British occupation had started, Egypt was the fashionable holiday location of choice for upper-class Englishmen and -women. Large elegant hotels sprang up in Cairo and Alexandria catering to linen-clad panama-hatted tourists eager to visit the Pyramids and cruise down the Nile. "Someday I must take my children there!" Mary had told Blunt on receipt of his latest tales of desert life in 1893. Blunt insisted to himself that he had built El Kheysheh, the little pink guest house in Sheykh Obeyd's grounds, expressly with Mary in mind.

On Blunt's last night at Stanway he found himself momentarily alone with Mary and "by a sudden inspiration kissed her." "She turned pale, said nothing, and went away to Arthur," Blunt told his diary, but the seed had been planted. The next morning Blunt and Bosie left to continue their journey. Mary got up early to say goodbye and went for a short walk with Blunt in the churchyard that lay adjacent to the house. In the churchyard, in the rain, Mary agreed to go to Sheykh Obeyd that winter. A few weeks later, lest Mary should waver, Wilfrid sent the keen horsewoman one of his finest Arab horses from the Crabbet stud—"the most delicious hack I have ever been on—it's like riding a swallow," said Mary blissfully.

In October 1894, Hugo left for France and Hermione. Mary was quite alone at Gosford. The news of Drummy's death had just broken, and her family had hastened back to Clouds. The Wemysses were spending October in the spa town of Malvern in Worcestershire, oblivious even to their son's departure since, fearing their reaction, Hugo had decided not to tell his parents anything at all.

That departure was the provocation for Mary's own trip to Egypt and the bargaining tool that enabled her to go. Ignoring the warnings of her friends, she booked her passage on the *Bengal* at exactly the time that Hugo left. In late December, in the middle of the worst winter that anyone could remember, Mary, ten-year-old Ego, eight-year-old Guy and seven-year-old Cincie, Cincie's governess Miss Jourdain and Mary's latest maid crossed to Cairo in terrible seas (Mary, teased Arthur, seemed always to attract the stormiest of crossings). They arrived at Sheykh Obeyd, dusty and footsore, in the freezing early hours of 5 January 1895. Mary woke later that morning to sparkling blue skies and "paradise." She embraced everything about her new surroundings: the Bedouin clothes that Wilfrid had left out for her, the heat, the silence and flickering shade in the garden as the leaves of the *gemeyseh* tree rustled in the wind and sunlight sharpened off the white stone dome of Sheykh Obeyd's tomb. The children were terribly happy "grubbing in a little Bedouin tent a few yards from this house," she reported to Evelyn in the first of many anodyne letters; their party had made a trip into the desert, with Mary, Wilfrid and Anne Blunt on Arab horses and the children and Miss J on donkeys. Photographs of this excursion show Mary still in a Western riding coat and top boots, white blanket draped over her head to protect her from the dust, a green-and-white umbrella in her hand. Behind her a black-clad Miss J looks hot and uneasy on her donkey; the children are so small one can scarcely make out their faces.

All Mary's friends had warned her before she left that Wilfrid would try to seduce her. They reiterated these warnings in every letter they sent. She kept her letters home cheerful and bland, proffering sanitized tales of picnics of dates and fresh camel milk in Bedouin tents. "The little bits we get of *real* Eastern life are very interesting," she told Evelyn in a letter headed "Desert, Cairo." "We might be living in the time of Joseph (this is just about where Potiphar's garden might have been)." Staying with the Blunts was delightful: "so *much* nicer than being in an hotel." The true story of what happened lies in Wilfrid's own account, and in Mary's later correspondence with him: for of all her diaries that remain, the only volume missing is for 1895. The inference that it was destroyed either by Mary or by a diligent descendant is inescapable.

Four days after Mary arrived she appeared at the main house alone, dressed in Bedouin clothes and asking Wilfrid to show her Sheykh Obeyd's tomb. When they were by the tomb Wilfrid kissed her once again and in the flickering shade of the *gemeyseh* tree the cousins sat and talked. Mary confessed her childhood crush on Blunt, and on gentle pressing revealed something of her relationship with Arthur on which others had speculated for so long. "To him she is pledged far more than to Hugo," Wilfrid duly noted in his diary. "She loves and honours and respects him, and he is constant to her, and she has always been constant to him, and she is bound to him by a thousand promises never to give herself to another. On this understanding he has been content that their love should be within certain limits—a little more than friendship a little less than love."

Mary's explanation to Wilfrid is the clearest indication we have that her relationship with Balfour, while undoubtedly sexual, had not been consummated. That night she wrote to Arthur confessing that Wilfrid had "made a little love": confessing and needling simultaneously. Arthur replied almost immediately from a fog-ridden London, where he was battling "the important trifling of politics" and influenza: "All the things I really want to say are unsayable so that if you wish to know them you must imagine them for yourself. Think of what you would like best to hear and have faith that that is what I should like to speak. I do not think you will be far wrong."

It is as close as Arthur would ever come to a declaration, but hardly a satisfactory one. It was also too late. A few days earlier, Mary had sent the children and Miss J into Cairo, to see the ancient Egyptian treasures in the museum, while she stayed in bed, recovering from a bad cold. In the late morning, as she dozed in her cool darkened room, she was woken by a soft knock on the door. It was Wilfrid, who found, as he had hoped, Mary alone. One thing led to another. "My extremest hopes were achieved," Wilfrid wrote in his diary that evening, jubilant at having seduced the cousin he had been pursuing for so long. It was almost certainly the first time that Mary had had sex with anyone other than Hugo. Wilfrid did not think that she had "intended quite all that happened," and Mary later agreed. "We might have been lifelong friends but *you* excluded it with yr eyes open," she said, explaining that she before "had only had to do with *different* men"—the men of the Souls who flirted, cajoled, kissed, fondled (and possibly spanked) but never (at least not in Mary's experience) crossed over into "the conjugal act." Later still, when nostalgia had cast a rosy glow upon everything to do with her time in Egypt, she would tease the "unscrupulous" Wilfrid for having taken advantage of her.

In early February, the party set out on what Blunt called their "desert honeymoon." As intended, Anne and Judith accompanied them only on their first day, after which they turned back, leaving Blunt and Mary, albeit "chaperoned" by the children and Miss Jourdain and numerous servants, on their own. Each night, in the wadis where they pitched their camp, Mary secretly left the tents set up for the women and children and went to Blunt, under the canopy of his traveling carpet a little way away. The clandestine visits did not go unnoticed by all the members of the party. "I think the Arabs with us knew that we were lovers," confided Wilfrid to his diary: "Indeed they must have known it, for there were Mary's naked tell-tale footsteps each morning in the sand . . . Mary is now my true Bedouin wife."

Far from being intimidated by the desolate, unforgiving landscape, Mary felt free for the first time since her Cumberland childhood. "I was made for the desert," she told Wilfrid proudly. "I *knew* how to live in a tent (have 'blackened cooking pots!') & to rise high on a camel with streamers flying in the . . . wind! It all came to me by instinct." Years later, even a kettle's singing in an Edinburgh convalescent home recalled to her the sound of Wilfrid's servant, Mubarak, playing to the company on his flute, as they reclined under tents made of rugs set among the sandhills, and conjured up the memory of "lying in a tent in the hot clean sand & making foot prints in it": the telltale signs left of the lovers' nighttime wanderings.

On their return from the desert, the affair continued. Judith, who was in her early twenties, dropped by El Kheysheh one evening, to find "H.F. ["Head of the Family," Judith's nickname for her father] sitting on Mary's bed . . . They looked horribly confused but I suppose it means nothing," she recorded in her diary. Cynthia's biographer believes that both the little girl and her governess had some idea of what was going on. It would seem impossible that Anne Blunt had not noticed as well. But Mary buried thoughts of Anne, of Arthur, of the fact that she had taken her mother's lover as her own. "I am & *always* shall be sorry for wounding the feelings of anyone I care for but otherwise its [*sic*] difficult to wholly regret days of beauty & romance," she assured Wilfrid later. "I am quite happy living in the present," she told Evelyn innocently in early February, just after her return to Sheykh Obeyd.

The ramifications of the past and thoughts of the future could not be held at bay forever. The next day—Valentine's Day—Mary broke the news to Blunt that "it being the 36th day . . . she is certainly with child." Blunt received the news with sheer delight—"For me it is a pure gift from heaven." Throughout the affair, Mary had alluded with concern to possible "consequences." Her period came like clockwork, and a rough-

and-ready calculation with the dates suggests she fell pregnant almost the first time she slept with Wilfrid. Perhaps this knowledge informed her recklessness: since she was damned she might as well embrace it. Yet from Blunt's bald report now that Mary was "a little troubled and anxious" one can sense a world of apprehension and confusion for her. "She will not, if she can help it, give up her husband, or her children, or her friend," he told his diary. Nor can Mary have forgotten that six years before her doctor had warned her that another pregnancy would risk her life—the reason why Hugo had not had sex with her in all that time, and why she could not now hope to pass off the child as his, even if she wanted to. Almost magically, a solution to the latter problem appeared to present itself: the next day, they received a letter from Hugo announcing his imminent arrival—and, hot on its heels, the author himself appeared, bowler hat plonked firmly on his head and Cymru, Hermione's fluffy chow, on a chain.

Hugo had made the decision to go to Egypt long before he notified his wife. Settled in Menton, the quieter town down the coast to which he and Hermione had moved from Monte Carlo, he had become uneasy. Insidious rumors about the state of the Elchos' marriage had already begun to trickle back to London: the *World* had reported mischievously that it was *Lady Elcho* nursing the Duchess of Leinster in the south of France, and he was equally worried by rumors of Mary's activities. "She is leading an odd sort of life & I fear people may be talking [about] them," he explained to Evelyn. "I think I ought to go . . . to let it be known I have been in Egypt. I know that she [Mary] is wildly happy . . . & not really wanting me. But this does not make any difference." Hermione became agitated at the very thought of Hugo leaving her, and several times she had made pitiful attempts at suicide with an overdose of chloral pills, a crude sleeping aid. Now, despite her state, Hugo deemed it necessary for him to make a brief visit to Egypt, informing Mary of his imminent arrival only when he was already on his way.

On Hugo's arrival Wilfrid seethed silently at the sight of his rival enjoying himself in the Egyptian sunshine, with apparently no inkling of what was going on. He was anguished at the sight of Mary dressed once again in Western clothes, as the party, which now included Frederick Harrison, a hearty diplomatic acquaintance of Blunt's, visited the Cairo museum. He cheered darkly when Hugo went out in a boat on the lake to shoot duck and capsized. But he was enraged when he found Hugo's

"Christian hat" left in the Bedouin tent in the grounds: evidence that "she who was my Bedouin wife" had brought a stranger into his tent. "When I get her once more into the desert I shall cut off her head," he vowed.

Wilfrid's revenge was more subtle than that. An overnight expedition to Goshen was planned, to give Hugo and Harrison a brief taste of the desert, camping on the supposed site of the house of Potiphar, to whom Joseph of the fabled many-colored coat was sold as a slave. The party were not all so accustomed to such expeditions: "D'you remember how *funny* F Harrison looked in his grey dittoes [*sic*] & white puggery [*sic*] & miss J *on donkey* with a Margate Sands straw hat!" Mary reminded Wilfrid. Later, Harrison published in his memoirs letters to his family describing this desert expedition: the women of the party in "long flowing white burnouses [hooded capes] and Oriental head-dresses worn over embroidered satin, looking like Roxana and Fatima," Blunt biblical in his white robes, his hawk-like face craggy and sunburnt. He wrote of being woken by a "thin moon like a scimitar" shining through a cranny in his canvas tent, of watching, in the cool early morning, the sun "rise out of Mount Sinai," and dawn feasts of tea, coffee, fruit, dates, chicken, lamb and tongue. Only when Harrison, a keen mountaineer, begins to liken the sand on the dunes down which they slid to Alpine snow is one brought back to earth with a bump.

If the desert could inspire even the plump, prosaic Harrison to lyricism, then the expedition should have been an ideal time for a reconciliation that would enable Mary to pass off the child as Hugo's. Blunt put paid to that. "I would not allow Mary to share her tent with Hugo as that would not have been proper. Suleyman and all the Arabs know that she is my Bedouin wife," Wilfrid told his diary primly. And so Mary and Judith slept in one tent, Hugo and Harrison in the other, with Blunt rolled up in his blue-and-white carpet set up under a bush "a little apart" so that Mary could come to him "as in the night of our honeymoon."

It seems unlikely that Mary was quite so reckless, but nor did she go to Hugo that night or any other. A few days later Hugo left. From the Grand Hotel Abbat in Alexandria, waiting for his passage back to France, he wrote Mary an awkward letter in which he could only sidle up to intimacy in the third person. He hoped that his "Wigs" understood that he had not been able to say all he wanted. "Perhaps I made her feel how I loved her . . . have loved her all the time more than she knew

& more than even perhaps I knew—perhaps it is not too late to shew her even now—though I don't deserve that she should care for me . . . please take care of yourself little Wigs & let us be together again soon & stay together . . ."

Hugo was frozen, and Mary unable to make a move herself, too guilty to deceive him, or preferring, almost literally, to bury her head in the sand. With foolhardiness doubtless partly provoked by fear, she plunged back into the desert one final time. This time the expedition planned was lengthy and dangerous: just Mary, Wilfrid and Anne on a camelback pilgrimage to St. Anthony's monastery, lying in the heart of the Eastern Desert between the Kalala Mountains and the Gulf of Suez, one of the oldest monasteries in the world and a place that no European woman had visited for fifteen hundred years.

"I am wretchedly, I suppose stupidly anxious about Mary," Hugo confessed to Evelyn, having tried without success to dissuade Mary from going. The journey, as recorded by Wilfrid in his diary, is a jumble of images: of Mary carrying apples and biscuits in her pocket like a schoolboy; Mary in a white robe up to her waist in water in the Red Sea "like Andromeda clinging to the rocks"; Mary collecting shells near their camp, an oasis of palms a few yards from the sea hemmed in by high precipices of brown stone; Mary's black hair tangled in the canvas after a fierce hot wind had blown down her tent in the night, a tent where Wilfrid had been only shortly before—for every night, despite the presence of Anne so close by, the footsteps in the sand made their way from Wilfrid to Mary.

And then over time danger crept in, as Mary grew tired and provisions grew short; vultures ringed their camp at night, watching and waiting in the dark. When finally at the monastery, Blunt lit three candles to Sheykh Obeyd and left them burning as they made the long journey back. They returned exhausted, travel-weary but still high on the excitement of the desert. "There is no doubt now of her pregnancy, & she suffered not a little from the lack of substantial food," Wilfrid wrote in his diary upon their return. "Still no harm has been done & her courage has carried her through—only we are glad that she can rest. It has been a delicious time for it is not often given to lovers to lead thus a wholly married life for 15 days." Mary herself never regretted a moment. "I was made for the desert & so I do not forget those few days of life spent there—the night by the sea & the dome palaces & many other things . . . we were sons & daughters of the desert & the desert loved us & we it," she wrote to Wilfrid a few years later. They returned to find "much changed." The old Khedive had died and been buried in Egypt; George Curzon was engaged to the American heiress Mary Leiter. And it was not long before Mary received a telegram from Hugo that finally spelled an end to her time in Egypt.

Hugo returned to Menton from Egypt to find Hermione with "death written on her face." On an early-spring afternoon in March, in her bedroom at the Hôtel des Îles Britanniques, she slowly but inexorably slipped from life. When it was over, Hugo sat by her still, throughout the long afternoon, "and it seemed just as it often has when she has been tired & sleepy, only she smiled all the time," he told Evelyn. That night he dined, as always, in the adjacent sitting room with the connecting door ajar "as she liked to have it . . . & I have gone backwards & forwards—& it has been the same as other nights excepting that she has not coughed—nor sent for me when she woke up." That night he telegraphed Mary. "Am unhappy. Shall go Grand Hotel Rome," where by arrangement Mary was to meet him. Hugo left Menton the next morning with Cymru the chow, too miserable to write or even speak.

Understanding immediately the meaning of this cryptic telegram, Mary went to bed early and wept—or so she said. "I cannot bear to think of it—I did *love* her . . . and if I feel it what must you feel?" she asked Hugo in a lengthy letter she wrote a few days later. When Mary was truly overcome by emotion, she lost her tongue. Here, the words positively dripped off her pen: the letter is suffused with praise for Hugo's loyalty, almost gushing as she writes of her own "love" for Hermione. She promises to be a "help and comfort" to Hugo, prays "that you will love me & that we may help each other to live our life as we ought to live it." Doubtless Hermione's sad death did touch Mary's heart. But her overblown tone—more characteristic of her friend Ettie than of herself—spoke of only one thing. As Mary prepared to tell Hugo of her pregnancy she was doing everything in her power to remind him of their bond, to stress her generosity so that he might exercise his.

Mary and her party sailed from Alexandria on Tuesday, 26 March. They met Hugo in Rome on Friday, took a train via Milan to Basle, then another overnight train to Calais, and crossed the Channel on Sunday. They were at Cadogan Square by 5 p.m. Arthur Balfour "turned up" shortly afterwards to see Mary; Mary, tired out, went to bed before dinner. The next morning she rose early to see her lawyer Mr. Jamieson, had tea with Evelyn de Vesci, dined with George and Sibell, and just two days later was at Stanway, where, she informed her mother, for the foreseeable future she intended to stay.

Mary's precipitate and uncharacteristic haste to leave London and the prying eyes of her friends was for a good reason. She was "bent on keeping . . . dark" the "beautiful secret" of her pregnancy for as long as she possibly could; "*nobody* need ever suspect anything," she told Wilfrid, assuming that no one but a few curious Souls would ever trouble to compare dates. "All that society resents is a scandal and so long as Hugo is mute & shields her with his marital countenance, Mary's woman friends will only think she has been quite right to enjoy herself, and that they wd have done precisely the same if they had had the opportunity," said Wilfrid.

SEVENTEEN

The Florentine Drama

On 14 February 1895, the day that Mary told Wilfrid Blunt of her pregnancy in Egypt, Oscar Wilde's *The Importance of Being Earnest* premiered at St. James's Theatre in London. Critics hailed it as an almost perfect comedy; audiences loved it. But the opening-night atmosphere was uneasy for insiders. After Drummy's death, his father had focused his vitriolic attentions upon the relationship of his youngest son, and Queensberry had made known his intention of throwing a bouquet of rotting vegetables onto the stage at *Earnest*'s opening night. Forced by police presence to abandon this plan, he left a note for Wilde at his club instead. Later, much would turn upon whether the near-illegible scrawl, handed unsealed to a club servant, was addressed to "Oscar Wilde, ponce and somdomite [*sic*]" or "Oscar Wilde, posing as a somdomite [*sic*]." In any event the message, discreetly placed in an envelope by the embarrassed club porter, was a terrible insult. Urged on by Bosie, disregarding the warnings of the more worldly-wise, Wilde sued for libel. The trial opened on 3 April 1895.

"How dreadful this libel suit is . . . poor darling Cousin Sib there seems no end to all she has to bear," Mananai wrote from Dresden, where the Adeanes were enjoying a season of German opera, and marveling at the disproportionate pomp of the Saxon state's miniature court. Cousin Sib was with Wommy and the Wyndhams in Florence waiting for the spring, which even there seemed slow to arrive after the worst winter that anyone could recall.

The reports were dreadful. Queensberry's ruthless counsel Edward Carson QC (signifying Queen's Counsel, the most senior form of barrister), stopped at nothing to prove the truth of Queensberry's statement: Wilde was either a sodomite or he had posed as one. He put rent boys on the stand. He all but destroyed Wilde under cross-examination. The flippancy that served the playwright so well in the theater scandalized when uttered in the forbidding Royal Courts of Justice. As Wilde denied kissing a youth on the grounds that he was too ugly, and as detail after sordid detail was revealed, it became daily more apparent that Wilde could not hope to escape criminal prosecution for what were, after all, illegal acts.

Wilde refused the advice of his friends to flee to the Continent. He lost his libel case. On 26 April he appeared in the dock charged with offenses under section 11 of the Criminal Law Amendment Act, known as the "Labouchere Amendment" after its instigator, Henry Labouchere (the virulently homophobic editor of *Truth*), which provided for a term of imprisonment not exceeding two years for any man found guilty of "gross indecency" with another male (a catch-all, ill-defined phrase that was understood to stop short of actual sodomy). The Wyndhams, like most of Society, thought that Wilde had brought this upon himself. Their concern was for Bosie. With Percy abroad, George took on the responsibility of paterfamilias. A truculent, defiant Bosie told him that nothing on earth would induce him to leave London or Wilde until the trial was over. "You may be sure that nothing will . . . he is quite insane on the subject," George told Percy. "Were 'W.' to be released . . . Bosie would do anything he asked, & no entreaty from you or his mother could weigh with him." But Arthur Balfour, who had been "told the case" and its most sensitive details by the prosecution, had reported to George in confidence that "W. is certain to be condemned." The evidence of the "systematic ruin of a number of young men" that was to be put before the court was too serious not to require a scapegoat; the strength of "public feeling" against Wilde was "fiercely hostile . . . among all classes." George now secured from Bosie the promise that, if "W." were imprisoned, "he will do what I ask."

George further gave Bosie advice, although "when I call it advice I should call it an offer." If Bosie agreed to leave the country George would see to it that he received an allowance, and that "we [meaning the Establishment] would all fight his battle." The Wyndhams' cousin Algy Bourke had even offered to ensure that Bosie was not expelled from their club, White's. Sibyl's hopeful suggestion that Bosie should join the party in Florence was nipped in the bud: "For Bosie's own sake & ultimate chance of shaking off all this nonsensical view, he must break fresh ground," said George, proposing the colonial backwaters of Ceylon or Australia, "which would enable his friends to say that he was going to prove himself a man." The unreliable Trelawny Backhouse, famous in his day as an oriental scholar, and posthumously for his scurrilous memoirs, claimed in those memoirs that Wilde's prosecution was the tit for tat offered by the Establishment to prevent Queensberry going after Rosebery once more. These conspiracy theories seem likely to remain unproven.

Thanks to the Wilde affair, Percy and George were to-ing and fro-ing from London. In late March Arthur passed on to Mary in Egypt gossip delivered to him by Margot at a London dinner party, "telling me that Eddy Tennant is going out to Florence with the Hon'ble P and that she and Charty want him to propose to Pamela!" "He is an excellent fellow," added Arthur, wishing him "every luck" but obviously amused, for placid, affable Eddy was no match for his inexorable sisters.

The putative Florentine romance was a slow-moving affair. Eddy seemed "very much in earnest," but the matter was "too long and important to go into in letters," Percy insisted to Mananai when she asked for an update. In the end the Wyndhams' friend Walburga, Lady Paget, brought matters to a head. Lady Paget (whose daughter Gay had inherited her mother's artistic spirit and devoted vegetarianism, and would soon begin a long-running affair with George Wyndham) was an inveterate matchmaker. Thirty years before, she had helped bring about the engagement of the Prince and Princess of Wales. In early May she invited Pamela to stay for a few days at her villa in the hills above Florence. While Pamela was there, she asked Eddy to dinner, and after dinner suggested they both walk with her on the moonlit terrace looking out over the distant city lights. At this point, Lady Paget told her diary, she gave an elaborate shiver and withdrew, leaving the tentative lovers alone. On taking his leave that evening Eddy bowed low and kissed his hostess's hand. "I knew then that the balance had dropped on his side," Lady Paget wrote.

Eddy Tennant in 1913, still displaying at fifty-four the somewhat glassy-eyed good looks of his youth. A combination of a gentle temperament and an unhappy childhood in which he had been beaten by his tutor and bullied by his overbearing father gave Eddy a lifelong fear of confrontation. Heir to the Tennants' business empire, Eddy was nonetheless a reluctant capitalist. Left to himself, he would happily have been a forester, chopping and planting trees in the thousands of acres that surrounded his childhood home, Glen.

Legend has it that while they were in Florence Pamela told Eddy that she could never forget Harry Cust. The conversation probably took place that night. In any event, Eddy had proposed, but Pamela had not accepted. By agreement Eddy returned to Glen, leaving Pamela to mull things over with her family—including George, who arrived shortly afterwards, feeling that with Wilde now a fortnight into his prison sentence and Bosie safely abroad he had earned his holiday.

Despite the Tennant sisters' conquering of Society, there remained residual suspicion of the men of their family. "Lots of people love *Laura* and me and Lucy or Charty," Margot had explained to George Curzon in 1890, but those people also looked down on "boys parents place hills," as being "not common," by which she meant "unusual," but which might be read more straightforwardly as nouveau riche, more vulgar and less charming. As much is evident in E. F. Benson's wildly popular novel *Dodo—A Detail of the Day,* published in 1893. The eponymous heroine, child of an industrial tycoon who slays all before her as she becomes the hit of London Society, was widely rumored to be based on Margot. Dodo's family, the Vanes, have not the same success: "Somehow none of Dodo's glory got reflected onto them." A decade later, St. John Brodrick complained of a visit by the Tennant brothers to Gosford, where they had been "distressingly familiar . . . you cannot make gentlemen."

Eddy's looks, wealth and kindness could not dispel the feeling that something in him did not quite "fit."

Were Pamela not twenty-four, had the Harry Cust debacle not occurred, it is quite possible that the Wyndhams—certainly Madeline Wyndham—would have resisted Pamela's marriage into the Tennant clan. In the end, Eddy clinched it with a letter. He was an excellent letter writer, of quiet humor and with an air of comforting gravitas. Whatever he said, it worked. Pamela wrote an acceptance in reply and walked with George through the sun-baked streets of Florence to the post office, where she also telegraphed Mananai the news: "Engaged E.T. still private." Eddy, who swiftly returned to Florence, was more fulsome when breaking the news to Charty: "A little letter to tell you great things, if my hand will not shake. The uncertainty is at an end and Pamela accompanies me through the world to the end . . ."

"You can imagine my surprise! I think they have all been in such a whirl . . . they have forgotten about everything! & kept us all in the dark!" Mananai exclaimed to Mary. She swallowed her disappointment for Baker-Carr—"*poor* man . . . he has known now for some time it was practically impossible"—and embraced this new prospect. "To think that such a nice person should . . . come forward—and at last no obstacles . . . one can only be deeply thankful." "Waiting and waiting would never have done for Darling Pamela," Mary agreed, now back at Stanway from Egypt, amused, if a little irritated, that she had to wait several more days before her "*extraordinary* sister" sent her a telegram of her own.

Eddy arrived in Florence to jubilation: "I seem to be holding some one in my arms all day long in congratulations and even the old concierge woman looks disappointed that I have no embrace for her." Yet none of Pamela's family pretended that Eddy would be other than a "very nice husband," and provide Pamela with the means to make a happy home. Wilfrid Blunt thought privately it was "no great marriage" for Pamela, thinking of "the somewhat coarse fiber in [Eddy]," but George spoke to outsiders with generous condescension of a "nice simple letter" he had received from his future brother-in-law. Mary, reminding her parents of the "many 'fan breaking' times & sick monkey faces we have passed thro," thought the calm prospect offered by marriage to Eddy, "so sensible, so reposeful, so himself," was enough. Pamela would appreciate "the change, the peace of mind, the . . . clearing . . . away of

Pamela, aged twenty-four, in 1895, around the time that she became engaged to Eddy Tennant. The portrait is by Violet Manners, the woman who the year before had (at least in Pamela's mind) thwarted Pamela's hopes of marrying Harry Cust, the dashing and womanizing member of the Souls whom Pamela swore never to forget. This may partly explain the somewhat challenging look in Pamela's eyes.

doubts & emptiness & vain regrets." Implicit in all the family's comments was that Pamela would have to provide any spark in the marriage with her "splendid natural spirits . . . & capacity for enjoyment." As for the power balance in the match—that was evident even to six-year-old Cincie Charteris, for "when I announced Pam's marriage to Cincie, she merely said 'Did Auntie Pansie arx him to marry her, or did the man arx her?'" Mary reported to Arthur.

The Wyndhams returned to England, but not before one final upheaval. On their last night in Florence Percy was in the palazzo's drawing room when his peace was interrupted by a bone-shaking roar. His manservant Giovanni knew the sound's significance. "Saying 'il est mieux de s'asseoir' he sank into the largest armchair in the room," Percy told Guy. "Oh god god god," shrieked Madeline Wyndham, who was with Pamela, Eddy, Dorothy and Fräulein in the ballroom as the force of the earthquake cracked walls around them and tumbled bricks down the chimney. The earthquake destroyed treasures in Florence's Duomo and caused a stampede at the opera house in which several were killed. The palazzo's inhabitants were thankfully unscathed. Dorothy displayed "her usual calm" and slept like a top until morning; to Percy's relief the more highly strung members of his party appeared no more unnerved. "Pamela has a faculty for sensational catastrophes which is really out of place, unless in a novel," said George upon hearing the latest installment of the "Florentine Drama."

Mary's greatest concern about Pamela's engagement was that the wedding and attendant festivities required her to see everyone she knew. All spring she had kept a low profile at Stanway. Even once in London, two days before Pamela's wedding she reproved her mother for letting slip the news to Lucy Graham Smith that Mary was pregnant: "Telling a female Tennant is like telling the Town-Crier, why did you tell her? Wicked Mum!" she wrote, despite admitting that Lucy would have guessed when seeing her at the wedding anyway.

Mary had let herself "slide & glide" and now had to face the consequences. Yet she is at her most cipher-like this summer. Her diary is missing, although this would probably not have revealed thoughts, only whereabouts and actions. To gauge her interior self we can only judge from that which she presented to others. Her letters to her family and friends that summer are masterfully normal. In August she even mentioned to Arthur "baddish nights" caused by pregnancy-related pains, moments of being "frightened and miserable in the watches of the night"—for Mary must have been afraid that she might not survive this pregnancy, which was against her doctor's orders.

Mary had confessed to Hugo about her pregnancy on returning to Stanway that spring. Hugo's reaction is reported secondhand—Wilfrid's report of a conversation he had with Mary later that summer. On that account, Hugo was silent for three days. Then he said, "If it had been Arthur I could have understood it, but I cannot understand it now . . . I shall forgive you, but I shall be nasty to you . . ." Mary also told Wilfrid, rather irritably, that Hugo's primary concern was that Hermione's family would think the Elchos had reconciled sexually while Hermione was dying.

The next occurrence, again recorded by Wilfrid, is his receipt of a furious letter from Hugo, blasting him for having "wrecked the life and destroyed the happiness of a woman whom a spark of chivalry would have made you protect." In Hugo's letter, Mary "was a happy woman when she went to Egypt, and her misery now would touch a heart of stone." Then came a letter from Mary, breaking off all contact: "You did try and wreck my life and the only thing that prevents my being utterly angry with you is that I believe you *did* care for me in a way," she wrote.

The letters' linguistic similarity, dwelling on the word "wreck," suggests that Hugo stood over Mary as she wrote it. It contrasts with another letter from Mary to Wilfrid written shortly afterwards which, although again a transcription, is recognizably Mary's voice. She was sorry that he was upset—"I know you are suffering"—but matter-of-fact. Wilfrid was to behave towards her mother and George—neither of whom knew anything yet—"just as usual." In time, she thought things would blow over. "These things must be done gradually," she told Wilfrid:

I can only be deeply grateful to [Hugo] for not making my life unbearable . . . It is a cruel thing to destroy a person's *ideal* . . . & make them feel one is something quite different from what they imagined—all one can do is to labor painfully to build up a new image & to deserve it, to earn it . . .

Wilfrid told George the following month on his return from Italy. George, the "largest-minded" of all men in such matters, seemed to understand: "[He] neither blames me nor finds it strange," Wilfrid noted in his diary. From Mary's reproof to Madeline Wyndham in July, it seems that she had still not told her mother the truth of the child's paternity by then.

Wilfrid found Mary's sangfroid baffling. In the days before the wedding he enlisted Judith, to whom he had intimated some and possibly all of the truth, as a makeshift spy and sent her to storm the fortress of Cadogan Square. She reported:

The door opened cautiously and revealed the end of Mary's nose and one eye through the crack . . . I was immediately let in and taken to the dining room where Miss Jourdain and Mrs. Guy Wyndham still sat at lunch. Mary is looking well and was extremely cheerful. She asked where you were . . . when lunch was over Mary took me upstairs and we talked about things in general and nothing in particular . . .

After that, Judith and Anne Blunt went to view Pamela and Eddy's wedding presents, laid out on display at George and Sibell's house, 35 Park Lane, since Belgrave Square was still let since the Wyndhams' Continental trip. "Old Madeline was most affectionate to us both, Percy was amiable, Pamela kissed me if I remember right four times in the course of 30 seconds . . . Sibell was most caressing and sat in a corner holding mother's hand when she was not holding someone else's . . . There is evidently not a shadow of anything between us and the Wyndhams," concluded Judith.

On 11 July 1895, Pamela and Eddy were married at Holy Trinity Church on Sloane Street, in London. Pamela's hopes for a wedding at Salisbury Cathedral had been dashed by the Tennants citing logistical difficulties. But there were nods to her fondness for rustic life. Her ten bridesmaids (including Wommy, Dorothy and little Cincie Charteris) resembled shepherdesses in white chiffon and large white straw hats trimmed with white roses—albeit wearing diamond-and-pearl lockets that were the bridegroom's gift. Pamela's low-cut satin bodice and full court train were embroidered with silver thread, the skirt trimmed with handmade Brussels lace and her fashionably large sleeves chiffon like her veil. She wore sprays of orange blossoms in her hair; a "circle of brilliants" pinned her veil in place. As she and Eddy made their way back down the aisle Pamela, her veil thrown back, diamonds glinting in the light and a "seraphic" expression on her face, seemed "like a thing inspired . . . I have never seen a bride so lovely," thought Lucy Graham Smith, erstwhile rival and now one of Pamela's many new sisters-in-law.

Wilfrid and Mary finally met in late August, clandestinely on the London-to-Brighton slow train, at Mary's direction. Wilfrid recorded their conversation almost verbatim in his diary. Heavily pregnant, dressed in a black dress with a white scarf and a pearl necklace, Mary was looking "well and strong and pretty" and cheerful. She gave every appearance of being happy to see him. Wilfrid had brought her a basket of peaches to remind her of the apples she carried in the desert, and as she munched her way through them she recounted how she had dealt with Hugo's interrogations and weathered the storm of the last few months. She had refused to be drawn on the "seduction" beyond the bare fact of its occurrence. "He asked me 'whether I intended to bring it up with his own children' and I said I supposed so and that was all . . . he will not take any notice of it [the baby], but nobody will remark that." Now, she said, the Elchos never talked of the matter: "Perhaps he [Hugo] does not think of it." She said that Arthur, though a little jealous of Wilfrid, suspected nothing either.

There is nothing to suggest, beyond Wilfrid's tendency to embroider, that this is not an accurate account of the conversation. As discussed on that journey, George was indeed made a godfather of the child, and Wilfrid did provide through him. Nonetheless certain statements leap out oddly. It cannot be, for example, that Mary was genuinely considering calling the child "Zobeyde" if it were a girl, as Wilfrid insists. And while it is probable that she was hoping the child would be a girl, so as to avoid "the dynastic question of the Wemyss inheritance," her alleged comment that "I know my own children will die as a punishment to me" jars, particularly since she had lost a beloved child only three years before. Hugo required Mary to play the victim in order to forgive her; Blunt could only accept Mary, pregnant with his child yet seamlessly maintaining her life as Lady Elcho, if she was wracked with secret remorse. Wilfrid departed the train, as agreed, a stop before Mary, at Preston Park, leaving Mary, still eating peaches, to travel on to Brighton alone, where she was to be greeted by a Campbell cousin, Edward Stanford.

Mary Pamela Madeline Sibell Charteris was born on 24 October 1895 ("a most delicious little baby girl, exactly what I wanted," Mary told Blunt disingenuously of the "family baby" who was named after one side of the family only). To the great relief of her family and friends Mary was unharmed by the birth, and recovered well. She was enraptured by the child, from the first the most beautiful of all her children: "She is absolutely round plump healthy and beautifully made, very dark with long soft brown hair—huge glittering eyes with long drooping lids and pencilled eyebrows, *lovely* hands bewitching mouth and *arched* feet . . . when she opens her eyes she looks you thro' and thro'—and she might be gazing fearlessly across the desert," she told Wilfrid, who met the child for the first time in a rendezvous at an inn near Cheltenham the following year. The engagement was deliberately planned in Hugo's absence, for Mary was acutely aware that "a meeting might be very terrible." Four years later, Blunt still sent letters to Mary via Belgrave Square, lest Hugo catch sight of his handwriting. "There's a letter to you from Wilfrid, Mary, extraordinary fellow that he is! Why doesn't he write to you at your own house?" Percy's bemused response demonstrates just how successfully the secret was kept.

In the years to come Mary would often be vexed by Wilfrid's reproachful urgings to see her and their daughter. But on other occasions she was willing to remind him of her time as "yr Bedouin wife"; to speak meaningfully of "footsteps in the sand!!"; even to revisit the romance. "I *am lost*—in a tent," she told him blissfully in 1901 after "stumbling" across him and his blue-and-white carpet while on a solitary early-morning walk through Clouds' grounds. Five years on, she gloated over a night-time visit to a convalescent Wilfrid in London, when her "somewhat unorthodox treatment" had managed "in a few seconds, [to] turn an invalide [*sic*] into a distinctly rampageous young man."

After each sexual encounter, Mary assured Wilfrid that it was the last, threatening to become the model of "professional cousinly" rectitude, "quiet and undisturbing." "I shall have on a quaker or salvation Army bonnet . . . or a nun's veil . . . or rather my soul will be draped in such-like garments . . . I shall be as dull as anything," she announced with relish after her nighttime visit in 1906. One of the strangest twists of this tale was that by this point Dorothy Carleton was living with Wilfrid, ostensibly as his nurse but actually as his lover. When Wilfrid recovered, he "adopted" Dorothy so that she could continue to live with him, which she did until his death in 1922. It caused the final breach between Wilfrid and Anne, and occasioned much bitterness from Judith Blunt and Dorothy's brother Guy. The Wyndhams accepted it without blinking an eyelid, and continued to be as close to Dorothy as they had ever been.

The real distress for Mary came when she revealed to Arthur the truth of her child's paternity, and genuinely did have to destroy an ideal. A cryptic letter from her in the spring of 1896 speaks of an unhappy after-noon spent at Arthur's house at 4 Carlton Gardens. "I hated having to distress you," she says. Mary was already five months pregnant with Yvo, the Elchos' true "reconciliation baby" born in 1896, who was the apple of Hugo's eye, so the revelation is unlikely to have been her pregnancy. But she did not lose Arthur. In fact, it reminded him—as it had Hugo—that Mary could be desirable to other men. And as one thinks of pregnant Mary, elegant in her black dress and pearls, dismounting at Brighton to be met by her cousin, with her hold on her husband, her "friend," her children and her social life intact, it is very hard to resist giving her a silent, heartfelt cheer.

EIGHTEEN

Glen

The Souls thought the marriage of the youngest Wyndham to the eldest Tennant would provide a new nexus of power. "I am so glad they have got anyone so delicious as Pamela to take over Glen!" Frances Horner enthused to D. D. Lyttelton. It did not take Pamela long to rectify these misapprehensions nor much time before a civil war had developed between her and her redoubtable sisters-in-law.

After a brief honeymoon, Eddy and Pamela made their way to Glen, where the entire Tennant clan had decamped for the summer. Wilfrid Blunt, on seeing Pamela briefly in London just before, thought her looking "very slight, and rather pale, and perfectly lovely," and also happy: "not rapturously . . . but perhaps sufficiently." Pamela assured her family that she was indeed happy, and thankful, she declared to George, of the decision she had made in Florence.

But Pamela's tone was muted, and there are clues which indicate that her honeymoon, such as it was, had been a shock to her. In 1918, the pioneering scientist Marie Stopes's best-selling sex manual *Married Love* confronted its fascinated readers with the necessity of the female orgasm, attributing many of the neuroses of modern women to unsatisfying marital relations. Pamela, when she was nearly fifty, told Stopes that "meeting with your book has given me a sense of fellow-feeling & comfort." She referred to a conversation in which "I have never spoken to anyone as I did to you." It is hard to escape the conclusion: sexually, Pamela and Eddy were a mismatch.

For both Pamela's sisters, the novel delight of sex had eased their transition into married life. Pamela was precipitated into a new world without that comfort. Glen compounded her loneliness. A mock-baronial monstrosity, windswept and cold, the house was "so *different* to what I have always lived among," she complained to George, shrinking into herself and longing for the light and air of Clouds—"it is as if Morris were not—nor had been." Meanwhile the fundamental differences between the Tennant and the Wyndham ways of life were daily becoming more apparent.

"I find Sir Charles very difficult to get on with," said Pamela, "a curious grown-up child—with whims & tantrums" and a line in selective deafness that drove her to distraction. She found the Bart overbearing, dictatorial and ridiculously sentimental: "Eddy says he can't read Prayers without wobbling," she told George exasperatedly, and at dinner, she explained, "the conversation trails like a winged bird, lower and lower till it gradually settles down among stocks and shares, or the indifferent among the poems of Burns . . . it's true . . . there is an awful leg to the table corner which takes all my thoughts;—it's the kind of leg to the table you can't forget, but still I think it's his fault rather."

By marriage to Eddy, Pamela was "grafted" onto the Souls, "a world of friends already so formed & complete" a good decade older than her. Dominant in her own social circle, she had no inclination now to assume a junior role, and was constantly enervated by her sister-in-laws' reminders of how much better they knew "dear Eddy" than she. Mary advised Pamela to remember that the Tennants were akin to the vultures in the Bible verse: wherever there was death and destruction, there they would be, teasing out pain and worrying away at weak spots.

Pamela agreed entirely. "The more I see of them," she wrote to Mary of her caustic, unsentimental sisters-in-law two years into her marriage, "the more I realize what *very* remarkable women they are [and] I don't mean it in a wholly complimentary sense . . . they have so many qualities that *equip* them almost unfairly for the fray of Life compared to most other women."

Pamela seized upon the opportunity provided by her first pregnancy to escape. Eddy had promised to take a house in Wiltshire, and paid over the odds to secure the rental of Stockton House, just a few miles from

The first page of a vellum-covered "Garden Book" given to Pamela by Madeline Wyndham while Pamela was staying with her parents at Clouds in May 1896. The original purpose of the book was soon subverted as Pamela used it to record press cuttings featuring herself and her family.

Clouds. While waiting for it to be made ready, Pamela retreated to her childhood home. Barely six months after her marriage, she was back at Clouds, embroidering hats with Wommy and knitting the intricate patterns at which she excelled for the baby due in July 1896. She wrote Eddy long letters about the minutiae of her days, her quick pen sketching out a scene in its quintessence: the obsequious waiter who had served her and Wommy with tea at Mere; the children round the maypole at Clouds; Charlie Adeane lecturing the assembled company at Clouds with his views on matters ranging from educational reform to poultry breeding.

Eddy visited Pamela when he could in between conducting family business in London and shooting and fishing at Glen. He diligently corresponded with her when he could not. Adoring and fearful of his beautiful wife, Eddy canvassed opinions among his sisters and sisters-in-law as to the best possible nursemaids and governesses; trailed around Glen's nurseries with Pamela's latest letter in hand checking that everything from skirting-board length to the new Morris wallpaper accorded with her instructions. He dealt with all Stockton's furnishing and staffing—by convention, Pamela's domain—even down to buying the glasses, linen and crockery for the servants' hall, and sourcing and interviewing staff. Notoriously parsimonious, Eddy had long been casting a critical eye over the extravagance of the Bart's practices at Glen, but, to Margot's rage, he encouraged his wife to buy whatever took her fancy for the new house. He gave each of Pamela's points his full attention, whether considering "Wommy's [newly trimmed] Hat" ("sounds fascinating") or the news that Pamela had dreamt on three successive occasions of flowers ("it is curious"). He scoured Glen from top to toe for a book of Scottish songs she was missing; he was enraptured when she wrote to him of a drawing she had done, and was "longing" to have it framed and hung up. He was thrilled when she told him that she was beginning to read about politics in the newspapers. And as Pamela's complaints about her first pregnancy steadily increased—a litany of aches and pains, neuralgia, indigestion, excessive "wriggling" from the baby and haunting dreams—Eddy provided all the sympathy for which Pamela could have hoped. By the end he was swearing never to leave her again.

"He is *A.1.*," said Madeline Wyndham delightedly, likening Eddy's stoicism to the way that they had tested the chandeliers in Clouds' hall, hanging on them many hundredweight more than they would ever bear: "I feel [that he] is like a Chain *tested* to bear so much weight that the *small* weight of every day life must hang light on it." Her remark was provoked by an incident in which Pamela, departing from Clouds with the mountains of luggage that accompanied her class's perambulations, had failed to see that boxes meant for London were marked accordingly. Half their things had disappeared, presumably Stockton-bound. Mary concurred with her mother's views: Eddy was "a very kind good unostentatiously upright & useful man . . . so wonderfully sweet & gentle & nice."

At Stockton Eddy and Pamela replaced footmen with housemaids (Margot thought it an affectation). Pamela declared herself Eddy's "loving Wyf [*sic*]," and he her "dearest husband," but her descendants believe that by the late 1890s she was already involved in several affairs—one with the ambitious young architect Detmar Blow, a romantic figure with dark curls and dashing manner; another with Ivor Guest, heir to a steel fortune. Nor, true to her words in Florence, did Pamela forget Harry Cust. They continued to see each other, although, as a scribbled note from Harry to Pamela at the turn of the century attests, they preferred such visits to be made when her husband and children were not around.

Pamela's main focus was her children. Clarissa Madeline Genevieve Adelaide, known as Clare, was born on 13 July 1896; Edward Wyndham

Tennant, or "Bim," on 1 July 1897; "Kit," Christopher Grey Tennant, on 14 June 1899; David on 22 May 1902 and Stephen on 21 April 1906. Pamela was enchanted by them—more accurately, by her boys. She quickly earned a reputation as a devoted—even too devoted—mother. But motherhood did not dispel her lurking unhappiness. All the Wyndham children found it hard to leave the cradle of their family. "I feel I have . . . transplanted *very* badly and am always lean & hungry for want of the soil I am accustomed to—*everywhere* except at home, I feel like a mangy fir tree with a bald top," Mary remarked to her mother, on leaving Clouds after a visit, some three years after her own marriage. Yet in those early years Pamela wept inconsolably every time she left Clouds. In later years, she recalled vividly a visit by Wilfrid Blunt to Stockton. "I was still so unhappy, and so strangely situated in my new life that I remember answering you almost in a dream when you said how you hoped everything was well with me."

In her enforced summers at Glen Pamela locked herself away in the library with a pile of books, emerging only to play with her children. At dinners, she sat aloof and silent. Charty taxed her with this. Pamela

The Glen, the Tennants' family seat, was built by Eddie's father, Charles, "the Bart," in the 1850s in a style known as "Scottish Baronial." The twenty-nine-bedroom fantasy of crenellations and turrets surrounded by 3,500 acres of rolling hills and forests was, for Eddy, nothing short of perfection. Pamela hated it.

recounted their conversation to Mary, triumphantly scornful of Charty's "pathetic" attempts to appeal to her vanity: "She said she wished I would take more *trouble* to make people *like* me! and . . . know how clever I *could* be . . . 'perhaps . . . you may meet a man at dinner & *never* see him again—and he may *never* know what a wonderful memory you have! How you can say pages by heart, how quick you are at understanding & what a lot of funny little stories & things *you know.*'" Pamela added, "I said I did not think anyone could recite at dinner & that if one was going to get to know a person I could not shell out *all* I had before fish."

With Pamela's most recent tearful departure from Clouds fresh in her mind, a worried Madeline Wyndham advised her daughter to "get [Philip] Webb or [Detmar] Blow to build you your large Family Cottage for your own that you may live in it & love it & the Babes also." George came up with another plan. He was fast earning a reputation as one of the most promising young backbenchers of Salisbury's ministry, a trenchant imperialist seeking a more aggressive foreign and colonial policy. His support of "Uitlander" rights in one of the Boer republics, Paul Kruger's Transvaal—"Uitlanders" being the foreign prospecters exploiting the Transvaal's gold rush—had earned him the nickname of "the Member for South Africa." George was part of a new breed of vocal and proactive imperialists. Their figurehead was the Colonial Secretary, Joe Chamberlain, who had secretly colluded in the Jameson Raid, a botched coup in 1895 by which the disenfranchised Uitlanders attempted to overthrow Kruger's Government. In 1897, Chamberlain pushed the appointment of Sir Alfred Milner as High Commissioner overseeing Britain's Southern African republics. Behind a judicious façade, Milner was a fanatical imperialist, determined to render British supremacy in South Africa complete.

The imperialist faction was buoyed by the glorious spectacle of the Queen's 1897 Diamond Jubilee. Almost half a million imperial troops and a panoply of native royalties processed through a London garlanded in bunting, past billboards advertising the very best imperial products, to pledge allegiance to their Empress at a service of thanks at St. Paul's Cathedral. Gladstone dismissed it as "the spirit of Jingoism under the name of Imperialism," while Salisbury privately deprecated its vulgarity, but the public was intoxicated by this visual reminder of the sheer reach of Britain's power. Gloomy political naysayers began almost immediately to look for the nadir that must follow this imperial zenith, referencing Edward Gibbon's *The History of the Decline and Fall of the Roman Empire,* the mammoth eighteenth-century work that attributed the fall of Rome to a lack of civic virtue.

Polymath George had been dabbling in journalism for a number of years, earning his reputation with a promising introduction to Thomas North's sixteenth-century translation of *Plutarch's Lives* (reprinted for the *Tudor Translations* in 1895) and translations of the poems of Pierre de Ronsard, the French poet of the same era. In the winter of 1897–98 he was in the process of launching *Outlook,* a periodical intended to combine in a weekly paper his favorite interests, politics and literature, with a strongly imperialist slant.

George thought Pamela would be the perfect contributor. Shortly after her engagement, Percy had teased her and Mananai with a newspaper cutting, claiming that they, with their Liberal husbands, were nonetheless "Tory by birth & conviction." Furthermore, both Charlie and Eddy fell to the far right of their party's spectrum as Liberal Imperialists, or "Liberal Imps," who privately harbored doubts about Home Rule and were reluctant to advocate disestablishment. One might call them Liberal by birth rather than by conviction. Pamela's early attempts to educate herself politically had quickly failed for lack of interest, but instinctively such views as she had corresponded with George's: romantic, nostalgic and imperialist. George thought her writing skill might even be better than his. "How I wish you would write something, anything!" he told her early in the new year of 1898. Urged on by her brother and her family, Pamela began.

For the first time in her life when faced with a blank sheet of paper, she balked. Since childhood she had shown an interest in letter writing unmatched by her sisters: crossing words out and replacing them with others more apposite, dwelling on form as well as substance. But now her mind, she admitted to George, felt like the five fingers of the hand, all spread out in different directions. She agonized that she couldn't possibly know enough to start; or that she had more to say than she could ever put down. "My dear when you have seen more, felt more and thought more than others, you have *always* too much to say," replied George. Whatever she wrote was sure to be interesting, "the point is to make it intelligible." Words were something to be wrestled with, stripped down to sinews and bones: "A *faculty* for writing is a pearl of contentment," George proclaimed, writing lyrically of days in

Pamela in the early 1900s by the renowned portraitist Lallie Charles, one of the most successful female photographers of the era. At the time this picture was taken, Pamela, in her early thirties, was carving out her own career as a writer. The delicacy of her clothes (doubtless carefully chosen) reflects the delicacy of the visions that she chose to put down in print.

his own turret writing room at Saighton, with its whitewashed, book-lined walls, oak writing desk and two armchairs in cozy conversation before the fire.

Once Pamela took "the plunge!" she scarcely looked back. Sheaves of letters whisked between brother and sister as they discussed everything from subject matter to Pamela's proposed pen name. Pamela agonized over editing; George discoursed on the art of prose writing and the importance of style, counseling brevity as he lectured at length. Pamela's Glen days were now full as she scribbled and crossed out, read, read more, and rewrote. At George's suggestion she began with a series of sketches, "painting in words" the world around her. He suggested that she look at an essay by a young Irish writer in the periodical *Nineteenth Century*. William Butler Yeats was doing "for Irish Faery lore just what you could do for Wiltshire . . . invent new names for your people and places and then reproduce their words exactly . . . giving the sensation which they aroused in you."

Pamela's resulting essays were serialized in *Outlook* under the pen name of "Clarissa." While comparisons with Yeats were fallacious, her keen ear for dialect and her ability to skewer an apposite and unexpected turn of phrase gave them a certain charm. "I love your imagination," said George; "sometimes I think of it as a horse turned out to grass: so happy and irresponsible and quaint."

For the same reasons that Pamela's writing so appealed to *Outlook's* readership, it has not stood the test of time. Pamela depicted a sunlit, semifeudal world in which peasants tugged their forelocks and uttered naïve wisdom; children were towheaded and rosy-cheeked, the aristocracy wise, benevolent and handsome. As imperial propaganda, it was magnificent. It was not a realistic portrait of the nation. When Heinemann published "Clarissa's" essays as *Village Notes* under Pamela's own name in 1900, braver critics hinted as much. "The modern cottager is a very wide-awake person, who reads penny novelettes and likes her clothes made 'in the fashion,'" pointed out the *World*. The *Glasgow Herald* took exception to Pamela's rendition of the Scottish dialect ("'Parn' is not the Scotch for pan, nor 'coof' for cough"). By and large the reviews were soft and deferential. It was "eminently soothing," said the *Pall Mall Gazette* (still under Harry Cust's editorship), just the kind of thing to read in a hammock; she had written it *con amore,* reported the *Globe,* in a typically breathless phrase. Pamela was not so foolish as to take these condescensions as compliments. "The harshest blow was 'pretty booklet,'" she commented wryly to Mary.

Yet Pamela did not wish to engage in the actuality that might take her work beyond "pretty" and "soothing." Like many great ladies, Pamela visited London's slums, Bim trailing behind her, clutching a tin of sweets for the "poor children." She did a considerable amount of charity work later in life, becoming involved in a home for working mothers in Westminster, offering those mothers an annual fortnight's holiday in her Wiltshire village. But that was not her reality. She stopped Bim's visits to the slums when he grew too disturbed by the squalor, physically removing him from the cause of distress. She similarly excised from her interior world unpalatable facts that might cause her that same distress, or even bring her to face mundane reality. Pamela's literary world was no mere fiction. It expressed how she willed her existence to be.

NINETEEN

The Portrait, War and Death

In December 1898 Percy received a letter from an American expatriate who had inherited Watts's mantle as the finest portrait painter of the day. "I am looking forward with the greatest of interest to painting your three daughters," Sargent told Percy. A price of £2,000 was agreed, and a preliminary meeting between painter and subjects at 44 Belgrave Square arranged to take place early in the new year. Percy had begun thinking of commissioning a portrait of his daughters in 1895, as soon as Pamela became engaged. His pencil sketch of stick figures from that time is fortunately made intelligible by a written explanation: "Mary at tea table with pot in right hand. Pamela guitar by her side (dog in lap?). Mananai first finger of right hand within leaves of a book, background of trees; tennis racquets and balls in foreground—all three looking out of the picture."

Three years later Percy made good on his plan. The Wyndhams were flourishing and finally seemed to be attaining the fame that Madeline Wyndham had always thought they deserved. Guy Wyndham had been stationed in South Africa, although his wife, Minnie (now mother of his three small children), Mananai and Madeline Wyndham mourned that he was not being promoted as quickly as he ought. George as always was achieving the lion's share of glory. On 10 October 1898 he took a long stride towards his goal of being "a Minister of Victoria" when he was appointed to a junior government position as Under-Secretary at the War Office: the youngest MP to sit in that office since the Whig leader Lord Hartington in 1865. George was jubilant at his promotion, which was widely considered as a stepping-stone to higher political office, largely "because it will please you & Papa," he told his mother. In strictest confidence he sent his parents Salisbury's letter offering him the post: "It belongs to us three for the present and to the archives at Clouds when we are all gone."

George's promotion was rightly taken by political observers to signify the strengthening of the jingoist faction of Salisbury's ministry. That September, fifteen years after General Gordon had been killed, Sir Herbert Kitchener's troops in the Sudan had finally avenged his death, defeating the Mahdi at the battle of Omdurman. The Wyndhams and East Knoyle's parishioners had been among the first to hear the news. The Wyndhams (possibly in an effort to bolster Guy Wyndham's career) were hosting a party of military houseguests at Clouds, including the illustrious general Lord Roberts, whose own glittering career had taken in positions of command in India, Abyssinia, Afghanistan and South Africa, and St. John Brodrick, whom George was shortly to succeed as Under-Secretary of War. On Sunday morning, as the party made their way to church, Brodrick received a telegram. He handed it to the rector to read out. As the news of victory at Omdurman boomed forth from the pulpit, as if by magic the guns of the camps on the Salisbury Plain echoed out their confirmation of the news.

The triumph at Omdurman, sealing Britain and Egypt's control of the Nile, thereby curtailing France's colonial ambitions for the region, was followed by the Fashoda incident, in which both countries laid claim to the strategically key southern Sudanese town and went to the brink of war. "George is in high spirits . . . he and the ultra-Jingo section of the party are all for war," Wilfrid Blunt commented in his diary. Charlie Adeane's sister Marie (now married to the civil servant Bernard Mallet) was one of many who thought George's aggressive stance the reason for Fashoda: "He is almost the best hated man in the House of Commons . . ." she commented to her diary.

George's sisters were meanwhile most anxious that their portrait grouping should not appear contrived. Mary's suggestions for a "reposeful" setting with all three studying a book or staged as "if the *Evening Post* had just come & one was reading a letter to the others" were resoundingly rejected. Their discussions grew more tense. Pamela announced her intention to dress in blue and Mananai was wearing pink chiffon. Mary, who had her own plans to wear "cream or white, with perhaps some fur," was concerned. "Don't you think Pink white & blue will look rather like a Neapolitan ice?" she asked her mother, appealing for her help to steer the obdurate Pamela from her choice.

Few managed ever to change Pamela's mind, and neither Madeline Wyndham nor Mary appears to have given it a serious try. Mary abandoned her plan to wear a dress she already owned and ordered a new white chiffon gown to match Mananai's pink: "Same sort of *shape* will look well I think." The sisters and their parents had a preliminary dinner with Sargent at Belgrave Square in February 1899. Even arranging a date which they could all attend proved almost impossible. Mary had spent the first weeks of the new year in an Edinburgh nursing home, recovering from an operation to correct a prolapsed uterus, the result, it is to be presumed, of her two recent pregnancies in quick succession. She reported the details of her "curating" to her mother in minute detail: morphia suppositories, chloroform-induced bilious attacks and "a pessary (*round*) . . . which I am told is a *perfect fit*!" Mary took her "Spring-Cleaning" and *"Furnishing"* in good humor. She reveled in the peace and quiet of the nursing home, free from the demands of servants and friends. A bored Hugo was being unexpectedly uxorious and visiting her daily, and she had managed to persuade the nurses to allow her to keep Cymru, the chow inherited from Hermione and now her most beloved pet, by her side despite a recent incident in which he nearly floored "an invalid lady bobbing round the corner from the bath room in the red dressing gown & curl papers." Nonetheless, four weeks of bed rest had left her "thin and pinched," and she looked, she told her mother, "exactly like Miss Havisham!"

The final composition was suggested by Sargent after that dinner—a brilliant choice that reveals their characters and nervous energy more clearly. None of the sisters seems to have felt there was anything pointed in Sargent choosing a pose of indolence. Once his initial sketching had outlined the group, each sister sat separately as the artist began work in earnest.

The experience of sitting to awkward, gruff Sargent was not reflective of Madeline Wyndham's enjoyable time with Watts. Additionally, London in February was inhospitable. On several occasions the sittings had to be curtailed when "smelly thick yellow fog" made it too dark to work. No number of fires seemed capable of truly warming Belgrave Square's vast drawing room. Pamela, pregnant with Kit, caught influenza and refused to leave her house; Mary, in the throes of "Betsey" and fearing that her face was still insufficiently plump to be painted, directed all her energies to getting Pamela to Belgrave Square without swallowing a mouthful of fog (her favored method involved a Shetland rug covering head and face). Mananai diligently made the lengthy journey from Babraham for each sitting without tardiness or absence and finally succumbed to the "demoniacal Influenza" while at Belgrave Square. The doctor ordered a period of total bed rest for several weeks, forbidding her to travel back to Babraham. "Sargeant [*sic*] must be fairly puzzled at the intricate health problems presented to him," said Mary.

At Easter, while the rest of the Wyndhams went to Clouds, Mananai was still tucked up in bed at Belgrave Square. She was in good spirits, snug in her room, a fire blazing in the grate, an amenable "little nurse" on hand, reading her mother's copies of Ruskin on the Pre-Raphaelites

The Adeane family at Babraham in 1897. From left, Mananai, four-year-old Madeline, seven-year-old Sibell, eight-year-old Pamela and Charlie. Twenty-eight-year-old Mananai, who looks a little under the weather, is likely to have been pregnant with the Adeanes' fourth daughter, Lettice, at the time, although her cinched-in waist suggests the pregnancy cannot yet have been far advanced.

and delighting in Madeline Wyndham's annotations to the text: "*What* wonderful people and *dear* B.J.'s name just mentioned with promise of *great* fame & the start of *Morris & Co*! I long to ask you *all* about it for you know it all—how *curious* Miss Siddal was."

Charlie Adeane was less content. His four daughters were well cared for in Babraham's nursery, but he was unaccustomed to being without his wife, and worried about her health. "It seems that when once you have fallen a victim a victim you remain . . ." he told his mother-in-law sternly, lamenting his wife's "sense of duty with regard to that blessed picture" that "overcame all caution." Charlie threatened no further sittings until the family decamped to London for the Season in May. "It was a very unfortunate time of year to choose for a picture to be painted. But I suppose these painters are tyrants. This one is a real drill-sergeant," Charlie added in a postscript, employing a rather good but almost certainly unintentional pun.

Charlie was tired of playing second fiddle to his wife's family. For months Mananai had been fretting over the welfare of Minnie Wyndham and her children while Guy was away. The political temperature was rising. A conference between Milner and Kruger at the Bloemfontein Conference in June 1899 over Uitlander rights ended in deadlock. "It is our country you want!" Kruger told Milner with tears in his eyes. In August, Guy Wyndham received a longed-for promotion: Deputy Assistant Adjutant General under Sir George White, the commander of the British forces in Natal. "I suppose it is a great honor but I do trust there won't be war," said Mananai. From the War Office, George assured his family that there would not. Mananai began to relax. She was past her first trimester, she felt preternaturally well and active. The baby was kicking strongly and, as she told her mother, "I always like it so much when they begin to be lively it is quite company! & a little 'individual' is'nt [*sic*] it."

Neither George nor the War Office thought Kruger's and Milner's elaborate schemes of bluff and double-bluff would come to a head. But the daily reports grew darker. On 4 October George wrote to his mother to tell her that "between you me and the gatepost we mobilize on Monday." A week later Kruger delivered an ultimatum to Milner. The British were to withdraw their troops from the border of the Transvaal and send back all the troops currently on their way out to South Africa or face war. Such a concession was unthinkable for the British. The ultimatum expired at 3 p.m. GMT on Wednesday, 11 October. "Well it has come," said George. Britain was at war.

The British public greeted the news with a great outpouring of truculent jingoism. Still drunk on the glory of the Diamond Jubilee, most people thought that it would be mere days—weeks at most—before Britain put a handful of backward Boer farmers firmly in their place. Bunting was strung up in London's Trafalgar Square; Rudyard Kipling and the alcoholic Algernon Charles Swinburne (once part of the Pre-Raphaelite circle and popularly considered to be one of England's greatest poets) composed verses for the occasion published in *The Times*. Theaters hastily revised their programs, putting on suitably imperialist productions: Wilfrid Blunt reluctantly accompanied George to Sir Herbert Beerbohm Tree's production of *King John* at Her Majesty's Theatre—full of "jingo tags and no popery talk," said George. Blunt was hoping the fracas would prove the Empire's downfall, but he did not really think that it would. The cream of the British Army was at that very moment being shipped out to Africa. And George heartily denied rumors that the War Office was ill prepared. "Don't pay the slightest attention to alarmist rumours, we are well enough ahead with our work," he assured his mother.

It soon became painfully apparent that this was not true. Poor communications and inadequate preparations paved the way for a series of disasters on the veldt hollered out by paperboys on every street corner at home. On 31 October 1899, when the war was almost three weeks old, Mananai was at Babraham. "We are all very well here," she reported to her mother, enjoying the crisp late-autumn day, "only almost sick with anxiety [about Guy Wyndham] . . . still the days are going by and each day brings the end of the War nearer." But the evening's headlines reported the disastrous battle of Ladysmith in Natal: twelve thousand British casualties and Sir George White's forces driven back to the besieged town by a torrent of Boers who now blockaded them in. Among those soldiers was Sir George White's Deputy Assistant Adjutant General.

Mananai slept fitfully that night with battle images storming around her head. At three o'clock in the morning she woke up "to find quite a '*show*' of . . . 'Betsy' . . . a bad threatening [*sic*] of a 'mis-carriage' I who had *never* had any symptom of such thing before," she told her mother. Charlie roused the coachman and head housemaid and sent for the doctor. For twenty-four hours Mananai lay "like a log," clinging on to the hope promised by each passing hour. "The little thing is *splendidly* lively," she assured her mother from her bed. "[Doctor] Wherry and Nurse consider me *out of the wood* & so do I now . . . Don't you worry about this Darling, I feel quite sure we have warded it off."

At nine o'clock on the evening of 2 November 1899 Mananai gave birth to a twenty-four-week-old child. "The premature baby was unfortunately a boy & lived 12 hours this has been a great aggravation of the blow . . . Madeline however is going on well and with her fund of sound sense is well & that is the only thing we care about you & I!" Charlie wrote to Madeline Wyndham, who on receipt of the letter left Clouds immediately for Babraham. Mananai's family were devastated by the tragedy, which they all believed had been brought upon her by reading of the horrific news of Ladysmith. Mary worried over might-have-beens: wishing that an incubator had been handy; dwelling on the peculiar fact that the child had managed to live so long, yet no longer. Madeline Wyndham tried to console herself with the fact that the child "might not have been realy [sic] *sufficiently developed* to be perfect or *strong* and might only have been a weakling." On receiving her mother's long, sad account of the scene at Babraham, of Charlie's "*gentleness & brightness,*" of Mananai's "*quietness & wonderful* resignation," Pamela was simply distraught.

"You must not grieve for Madeline," Madeline Wyndham told her youngest daughter sternly, "as those who have no hope & make *yourself* ill & thereby make *her* & all of us more unhappy & give us *more to bear* than we have already! Your duty now is to . . . write Madeline a cheerful letter for *outside things do interest her* & they take her mind off the sorrow . . ." Madeline Wyndham took comfort in the fact that, like herself, both Mary and Pamela had had "2 boys running . . . so let us *hope & pray for that for her* . . . don't think of anything emotional but pray pray pray because sometimes . . . dwelling on the horrors of the war . . . does *overmaster* one [and] makes one feel as if one must *die* of it & it would be *dreadful* if we all died of fright & Guy were to escape & come home & find us dead . . ."

In December 1899 came Black Week, a trinity of defeats that stupefied an already bewildered British public: "The bloody waste of Magersfontein, the shattering retreat from Stormberg . . . Colenso that blundering battle . . ." in the words of H. G. Wells. At Colenso, the cruel climax, Louis Botha's five-thousand-strong Boer force, concealed behind the

Tugela River's steep banks, mowed down Sir Redvers Buller's army of eighteen thousand men. In a few short hours, and assailed by an enfilade of bullets that came "in solid streaks like telegraph wires," Britain's strongest force in the field since the Crimea was decimated. "It is a weird and soul-shaking experience to advance over a sunlit and apparently a lonely countryside, with no slightest movement upon its broad face, while the path which you take is marked behind you by sobbing, gasping, writhing men, who can only guess by the position of their wounds whence the shots came which struck them down," wrote Arthur Conan Doyle, whose rose-tinted account of the conflict, *The Great Boer War*, falters when it comes to Black Week. "I never saw a Boer all day till the battle was over," said a dazed General Lyttelton, Alfred's brother.

Christmas at Clouds was bleak. A pale and anxious Minnie Wyndham could think of nothing but Guy, trapped at Ladysmith in an apparently never-ending siege. George arrived and went straight to bed, worn down by the flu and on the brink of nervous exhaustion. Madeline Wyndham prayed constantly in front of her prie-dieu, and urged her daughters to do the same. Percy was left to sit by the fire in his favorite armchair, fulminating impotently at the shortcomings of generals who had not even thought to send a reconnaissance force before them. "I wish the ferret [Pamela] had been at Colenzo [*sic*]," he told Mary. "I think she would have asked questions about the banks of the river."

TWENTY

Plucking Triumph from Disaster

Black Week shook Britain's confidence and forced a complete over-haul in the Government's conduct of the war. With the eyes of the world upon it, Britain was faltering. Its army had showed itself "mortal and human," its officers simply "the pleasant, rather incompetent men they had always been," the troops "neither splendid nor disgraceful . . . just ill-trained and fairly plucky and wonderfully good-tempered men—paying for it," said Wells. "The history of the future will have to summarize the causes of the decline and fall of the British Empire in three pregnant words—'suicide from imbecility,'" declared a trenchant commentator in the *Review of Reviews*, urging root-and-branch military reform.

General Lord Roberts—"Bobs," as he was known—was brought out of retirement to replace Sir Redvers Buller, and told, in the meeting in which he was appointed, that his only son was one of the Colenso dead. The change in command was not enough to protect the War Office from allegations of ineptitude from either Radical anti-war Liberals, led by Henry Labouchere ("Labby"), or Alfred Harmsworth's *Daily Mail,* just three years old. George was anticipating an attack when Parliament remet in February 1900. But "I think I have a pretty good case," he said. "Anyway I am keeping low like a Boer and shall not fire until they come into the open."

The Opposition came into the open at the Queen's Address, which declared, "We are not interested in the possibility of defeat: it does not exist." The Opposition moved for an amendment deploring "the want of knowledge, foresight and judgment of Her Majesty's Ministers in preparation for the war now proceeding." "Arthur was *most* foolish to speak at all," said Margot of Balfour's pitiful response. "Some want of passion in his nature" made him unable to give the "grand uplifted bugle . . . sort of speech" the situation required. Balfour's intellectual, measured oratory was completely out of step with a country thrown from jingoistic euphoria to the pit of despair in barely three months.

The role of standard-bearer fell to George. Fueled by incandescent patriotism, his speech was, by agreement of all who heard it, the making of his career. He spoke for an hour and thirty-four minutes, leaving out "about a quarter of the stuff" he had prepared. He admitted that blunders and miscalculations had been made. But soon there would be 150,000 British troops in South Africa. The question now was one of faith and courage. Long live the British Empire! said George. All Hail Her Majesty! When he sat down, "I thought they would never stop cheering," he told his mother.

"George has *covered* himself with glory . . . I have *never* heard anything better in my long experience of the House . . . is it not splendid! *all* the best and severest judges would agree my praise is not exaggerated," Arthur wrote to Mary, in tones more characteristic of his excitable protégé. Margot acknowledged that George "defended a very attacked office in a very critical moment & did it quite xtraordinarily [*sic*] well." "The speech has given him Cabinet rank," Percy claimed exultantly. Arthur agreed. George's rise seemed now "beyond the reach of fate."

The press hailed George as one of the "men who will lead Britain into the twentieth century." His very person seemed proof that Britain could still breed heroes. "From man of fashion to soldier, from politician to statesman, from speaker to orator, from dilettante to critic, he has never yet shown himself contented with the beginning or with the outside," commented one article that Pamela liked enough to cut out and keep. The "completely thoroughbred" George with his "aspiring and adventurous" temperament, "vivacious and lofty expression" and "richly sonorous voice" reassured the public that Britain could reach greatness once again.

As if by magic, or rather thanks to Bobs, British fortunes began to turn, with the relief of Cecil Rhodes, the founder of Rhodesia who was trapped at Kimberley, and victory at the battle of Paardeburg nearby. On 28 February Ladysmith was finally relieved. The Wyndhams rejoiced at the news that Guy Wyndham was safe and well, but "how *could* they have survived . . . ?" asked an appalled Mananai, reading press reports that the troops had subsisted on a daily diet of just 1½ biscuits, 30 ounces of meal and a Bovril-like soup called Chevril. The relief forces immediately sought out Guy, eager to tell him how George's speech had made them feel finally as though the country were behind them. The British public held their heads higher. Labby's determinedly "pro-Boer" stance in *Truth* made him, in the estimation of *The New York Times,* "the best-hated man in Britain." On St. Patrick's Day Mananai attended a concert at London's Albert Hall, where a new patriotic song to the tune of "The Wearing of the Green" raised the roof with uninterrupted cheering for over ten minutes.

Mananai followed each day's triumphs and reverses in the press with near-obsessive avidity. Her anxiety for the nation provided an outlet for, and distraction from, her personal grief. Pamela had sent her a copy of her latest work, a religious, mystical compilation of poetry and prose entitled *The Book of Peace.* "It is a good book, full and sharp, with the sweet-bitterness of Birth and Death," George told Pamela after first "incontinently" reading the work: "You have washed the Gates of life . . . from the insolent and vapid scribblings with which they have been defaced." In the first weeks after the baby's death the book barely left Mananai's side. Once she had convalesced she sought out those neighbors who had been bereaved in the war and devoted herself to charity work, volunteering at the Soldiers and Sailors Yeomanry Hospital, and collecting clothes for the troops abroad. Even the most minor of reverses could cast her into a deep gloom. "I sometimes despair of the end," she told her mother. Mananai herself would never make the link, but the analogy with her own grief is clear to see.

That grief is plainly evident in Sargent's portrait. Sittings began again in the spring of 1900. Of all the sisters, Sargent had been most keen to work on Mananai. Pamela had to beg her parents to exert all their influence on Charlie to make him allow Mananai to return for more sittings. The Wyndhams prevailed, and Charlie and Mananai made their way to London for a week of sittings at Sargent's studio (as Madeline Wyndham pointed out, much warmer than Belgrave Square at that time of year).

The air of patient sadness that Mananai gives off is palpable and at odds with the frippery of her white gown as she gazes off into the distance, apparently lost in thought.

Detained at Clouds by a host of responsibilities, Madeline Wyndham was unable to make more than one brief visit to Babraham around Easter time. Instead she deluged her daughter with gifts. During that spring hardly a week went by without some kind of package arriving at Babraham, whether it was a toy kitchen and modeling clay for the little girls, hundreds of flower bulbs for the garden, or curios such as the eighteenth-century Battersea enamelware boxes of the kind that Mananai collected. (Madeline Wyndham had begun to practice enameling under Alexander Fisher. With her own stove set up at Clouds, she was rapidly becoming a proficient amateur. However, on this occasion she was so keen to send Mananai a present that in her haste she melted it and so sent her instead a "Battersea Enamel Lemon, so beautifully made with little blisters like a lemon.") In May an "overwhelmed" Mananai opened a parcel containing a belt—"so 'out of the way' . . . & will give such 'cachet' when I wear it"—and a spangled black net dress—"*so* beautiful & yet *so* French & smart (such a horrid word but the only one to express one's meaning)." That same day came the "blessed" news that "Mafeking is well!"

At the news of Mafeking's relief after a 217-day siege, punctuated by plucky "Kaffirgrams" of the garrison commander, Colonel Baden-Powell ("All well. Four Hours bombardment. One dog killed" was a typical example), flag-waving hordes poured onto Britain's streets in such jubilation that "mafficking" was added to the *Oxford English Dictionary,* to denote indulgence in extravagant demonstrations of exultation. A fortnight or so later Bobs's troops entered Pretoria, the capital of the Boer Republic. In London, Sargent's portrait of the sisters was the hit of the Royal Academy's Summer Exhibition. "The greatest picture which has appeared for many years on the walls of the Royal Academy," said *The Times.* The Prince of Wales dubbed the sisters "the Three Graces." Pamela received particular attention for her spectacular looks. The portrait hung in the billiard room at Clouds as intended (a room now painted dark blue to complement the portrait) but was frequently sent off for public viewing. "What it has seen and heard if it could only speak!" said Madeline Wyndham in 1908 as the picture returned from the Franco-British Exhibition and the Exhibition of Fair Women at London's New Gallery; the Watts of Madeline also appeared at the latter.

That the subjects of the portrait were George Wyndham's sisters enhanced their celebrity. Six months after his Commons speech, George remained the hero of the hour. In August, Mary was delighted to find that every English paper she read in Kissingen spoke of George in glowing terms, and everyone she met was eager to congratulate her on her brilliant sibling. "He is no longer Lady E's brother but I am Wyndham's sister that's as it *should be*," she told Hugo proudly. On 1 September the British public's delight knew no bounds when their troops annexed the Transvaal. "The country is war-mad . . . blatantly and truculently out of their minds," George told Madeline Wyndham. He knew there would be a backlash eventually, "but while it lasts I make hay."

TWENTY-ONE

The 1900 Election

On receipt of Mary's proud missive about George, Hugo must have felt a little sour. Described by Balfour as "too self-indulgent to succeed and too clever to be content with failure," Hugo's own brief parliamentary career had been notable largely for his annual, impassioned attempt to give MPs six weeks' extra holiday by recommending that the House should rise before Derby Day (the Epsom Derby, the country's most important horse race, took place annually in early June), rather than waiting until the end of the Season, in late July. In an earlier age Hugo might well have made such a speech until he inherited his father's title and seat in the Lords. But now the electorate had a greater say in who represented them, and in 1895 Hugo was "chucked!" (in Mary's phrase) from his Suffolk parliamentary seat at Ipswich. Blunt thought this a misfortune for Mary, as Hugo "will have nothing to do being shut out of public affairs." So it proved. Since Hermione's death and his fortieth birthday in 1897 Hugo's outlook had become ever gloomier. "Time is advancing and we two with it," he told Mary dolefully on her thirty-eighth birthday in 1900. "Its [*sic*] rot to talk about *old age*," replied Mary staunchly, but her assurances that Hugo had never been so youthful "in being & in seeming" fell on deaf ears. The fundamental problem, as Mary said, was that "it's dreadful for you having nothing to do."

Vincent Brooks Day & Son Lith.

"Derby Day"

Lord Elcho

An 1892 caricature of Hugo in the popular weekly *Vanity Fair,* entitled "Derby Day" in mischievous reference to Hugo's inevitable annual speech on the subject in the House of Commons. This British publication ran from 1869 to 1914 as "A Weekly Show of Political, Social and Literary Ware" and was well known for its caricatures of notable parliamentarians of the day. The title was bought in 1913 by the visionary publisher Condé Nast, who relaunched it the following year as an American journal.

Hugo hung about with brittle, hard-living members of the Marlborough House Set, who frittered away time and money on the Continent yachting, gaming at Le Touquet, a popular and glamorous seaside resort in northern France favored by the British known for its sporting facilities and the laissez-faire morals of its visitors, and watching bullfighting in Spain. Mary berated him for "the 'Common' folk you herd with!!!" and the "bad ways & foolish tricks" they encouraged. "I wish you were a fox hunter & would live 6 months in one place or that you had a passion for agriculture!" she said, but she knew that Hugo was "not really keen about things & never [had] been," save gambling, for, in 1899, Hugo had gambled his way to his most spectacular loss on the stock market yet: around £80,000, roughly $1.07 million today. "At last the crash . . . has come and Hugo is undone!" Mary told Arthur from the Palace Hotel in St. Moritz in Switzerland, where she had met Hugo, post-cure, and been told the news. Furious and anguished, Lord Wemyss bailed Hugo out, but made good on his oft-repeated threat to tie up Hugo's inheritance. He set up a trust of £100,000 for the Elchos during their lifetime. Arthur was one of the trustees. It is hard not to see a punitive element therein.

A year later, in 1900, Mary was agog with excitement at the suggestion that Hugo might stand as Unionist candidate for Bristol South (one of the city's four constituencies since the redistribution of seats in 1885). All summer long from Kissingen, with a general election due to be held that autumn, Mary bombarded him with letters planning the campaign trail, "quite ready to be a thorn in yr side & to help in every way I can." The candidacy (and, ultimately, the seat itself) went to Sir Walter Long, a Unionist who had made himself a name on the Local Government Board and the Board of Agriculture. Mary was crushed, particularly since she only found out this news from Arthur: "You must have known it was most cruel not to tell me, you said you had been asked—I wired to you . . . I talk to you about it in every letter & you say nothing, so I quite believed it," she wrote to Hugo in a frenzy from Paris. "I suppose he [Arthur] couldn't squash Long," she added, unintentionally rubbing salt in the wound.

Arthur was often as baffled by Mary and Hugo's push-me, pull-you relationship as everyone else, and Mary's toleration of Hugo's continuing, flagrant infidelity. "I cannot conceive why you permitted yourself to be saddled with her," Arthur wrote, on hearing that Hugo had dumped his latest paramour, the celebrated actress Mrs. Patrick Campbell, on Mary at Stanway for three weeks in 1896, while "Mrs. P.C." recovered from a theatrical flop and conducted an affair with Hugo under Mary's nose: "Had you been in robust health, with no worries . . . of your own, I should still have thought that England might have been searched through before a less suitable recipient of three weeks' hospitality could have been found." An answer is found in a letter from Mary to Percy in 1899. Percy had written lamenting that Mary would not be able to enliven a sticky dinner with her presence. Delighted, Mary replied, claiming to have inherited from Percy her consuming interest in people from all walks of life: "If I thought about it at all I should probably find that I prided myself on being a sort of Nasesmith [*sic*] Hammer! Able to crack iron hazelnuts to cut thick or thin—and to sing (or talk) both high & low!" The Scottish engineer and inventor James Nasmyth's steam hammer, one of the Industrial Revolution's greatest inventions, could vary the force of its blow. In a famous demonstration the hammer was used to break an egg in a wineglass while the glass remained intact. Hugo, difficult, childish, stubbornly impervious to improvement, was the iron hazelnut Mary could not crack. He gambled; he rowed with tenants on the Stanway estate so that she and Smith, Stanway's agent, had to step in; as a "landlord and financier" and a "husband" Hugo was hopeless. "I wish Hugo would do himself justice," she told Arthur. "I wonder if it's my fault and if I could manage him differently and better. He makes one always hope and yet he so often disappoints hope, one can neither count on him nor give him up!"

As Mary made her way to Gosford that autumn, flustered and despondent, her sisters were preparing for their own stint on the campaign trail. Eddy Tennant and Charlie Adeane had been approved as the Liberal candidates for seats nearby to where they lived: Peebles in Scotland and Huntingdonshire in Cambridgeshire, respectively. The Boer War had provoked yet another rift in the fragmented Liberals between anti-war Radicals and pro-war Imperialists. Margot, who had her doubts about both men's convictions, delivered Eddy several lengthy lectures on corporate political loyalty: "What no man who thinks for himself like you & Adeane can grasp (tho I know you do) [is that] they don't come off these big things H[ome] Rule Disestablishment etc . . . they *don't* happen . . . Compromise & stick to yr regiment even if they are going to do a stupid thing." Margot was still more mistrustful of Pamela. As she revealed to Eddy tidbits of the party leadership struggles between Asquith, Henry Campbell-Bannerman, a Glaswegian merchant, and Lewis "Loulou" Harcourt she hoped, pointedly, that "Pamela will keep our party dirty linen to herself."

Pamela was not interested enough to be a double agent. Mary was astonished to find that she was even "*really* canvassing." "I am *indeed,*" Pamela triumphantly replied from the rented Peebles villa from which the Tennants were conducting their campaign, although "I don't know enough about politics to 'canvass' in the ordinary sense of the word . . . I just tell them how keen I am my husband should win—how long we've been here & how many children I have!" Pamela did not quite express Lord Salisbury's visceral loathing for the "nauseous mire of a general election," requiring "weeks of screwed-up smiles and . . . mock geniality . . . the chuckling reply . . . to the coarse joke . . . the wholesale deglutition of hypocritical pledges," but she intensely disliked the campaigning process: "long drives, of 18 miles home in pelting rain & wind after a whole days visiting & canvassing & putting up at little evil smelling whisky-drenched Inns and attending hot long meetings!" Unruffled by public singing, she hated public speaking. She gave a talk to the 150 members of the Women's Liberal Association of Innerleithen, learned by heart in advance, with "a dreadful stomachache from nervous excitement & terror." Her sisters-in-law were horrified by what they considered an insufficiently committed approach, particularly since the Bart was bankrolling Eddy's candidacy. When the Tennants visited Glen halfway through the campaign, Charty cornered Pamela at breakfast for a "tremendous talking to." Politics was "the *life* of the country, the history that is being formed around one," she said hectoringly over the marmalade, imploring Pamela to exercise "a mind that merited being *bent* upon wider issues," and praising "powers of *observation*" that warranted being turned to "*larger* matters." As always, Pamela gave Charty short shrift. "It was really all very good advice but I am perfectly certain [if] I read all Joe [Chamberlain]'s speeches I shouldn't be much the wiser for it! [and] if in going into cottages, I tried to speak about what I don't understand, I should make lamentable mistakes & failures."

Canvassing was more than ever a requirement of an expanded franchise. From the turn of the century there was a marked expectation that women would take a more involved political role. Charty and Pamela both accepted that, although Pamela dragged her heels. For Kate Courtney, activist sister of the Fabian Beatrice Webb, political involvement led her to suffragism: "I cannot understand the state of mind of a man who encourages women to canvass electors . . . organize meetings, speak at them, and even coax and bother electors to go to the poll by every art they possess, but draws the line at the simple act of voting themselves. It is nothing but stupendous egotism," she said in 1913. None of the Wyndham sisters expressed any particular position on female suffrage. In this they resembled most women of their class, feeling that the social and political influence they wielded was far in excess of that granted by a vote, and with corporate loyalty to class outweighing that to gender. The person in the family who felt most strongly was Eddy, a strident opponent, who later became President of the Scottish Anti-Suffrage League. (It is cheap but irresistible to suggest that Eddy had suffered from enough strong women in his life.)

Mananai was the only one of the three sisters truly to enjoy campaigning. The Adeanes were funding Charlie's campaign themselves, and they had thrown themselves into the contest with vigor. They had set up camp in a "snug pretty little house" lent to them by Lord Sandwich on his Hinchingbrooke Park estate and were planning, said Mananai, "to work as hard as we can & be on the spot for all the meetings." Mananai thrived on the excitement. Each day she met up with a band of local Liberal women: the wives of the local chemist, the Hinchingbrooke estate's land agent, and the leading local nonconformist—and canvassed every day from ten-thirty in the morning until six or seven each night, ticking off lists provided to them of "doubtfuls" and "Tories," snatching quick lunches, once in the carriage and once, to Mananai's rather doubtful delight, in a "pub." On one day in "a poor sort of street in Huntingdon" she visited seventy houses before lunch. Indefatigable in her charity work, she immediately saw an opportunity to do some good: "Some make me very sad . . . they are so ill & poor—as soon as the Election is over I shall be able perhaps to help them a little."

Across Britain philanthropic social reformers (often from nonconformist backgrounds, such as the industrialists Benjamin Seebohm Rowntree, whose family's firm was one of the country's largest confectioners, and Charles Booth) were addressing themselves to the plight of the poor, cast into the spotlight by the Boer War, and fed by anxiety about the future of the nation. Army recruiters had been appalled to find that the majority of volunteers were so malnourished that they did not reach the required minimum height of five feet three inches. "The building up of the nervous and muscular vitality of our race [is] the principal plank of any Imperial program of reform," said the Fabian Sidney Webb, husband of Beatrice. In the decade that followed, imperial interests were used to justify ostensibly "socialistic" reforms of New Liberalism such as the provision of child welfare measures and free school meals.

Notwithstanding these imperial concerns, Bobs's victories still cast a glow over the "khaki election," which was a Unionist landslide. Nonetheless, change was afoot with the return of two members of the Labour Representation Committee, the trade-union-sponsored association which became the Labour Party. "Things have touched the button now & I think we shall see very interesting Times in the next few years," Margot told Eddy, who, like Charlie, had been defeated. "Khaki was well worked by them . . . the tide is going too strong against us owing to that wretch Labby we are all branded as traitors and pro-Boers!" mourned

Mananai. At Glen, Pamela bit her tongue as Margot provided tips for the next campaign.

George was returned at Dover with a huge majority. In November, he was appointed Ireland's Chief Secretary. "I think it will be a very fine appointment . . . It will give George a great opportunity of xcercising [*sic*] his judgment & tho a very hard place I think his charm will attract them," said Margot. After a meteoric rise (although still without the Cabinet rank he yearned for) George had returned to his ancestral land. The prominent Irish writer Katharine Tynan, an ardent nationalist, was one who saw in him Ireland's hopes of salvation. But George's position was more ambiguous than that. For he appointed as his Under-Secretary the Irish Catholic Antony MacDonnell, a brilliant civil servant who was also rumored to be a Home Ruler. And, while avowing to Balfour that MacDonnell was "non-partisan," George also agreed with MacDonnell that his aide could offer in the post more than "mere secretarial criticism" and be "given adequate opportunities of influencing the action and policy of the Irish Government."

TWENTY-TWO

Growing Families

Sargent's portrait had caught the sisters like flies in amber, frozen forever in trinity. In reality, their worlds were moving ever further apart. Of all the siblings, Mary and Pamela saw each other the least. They were "widely unlike," and while Cincie Charteris diplomatically tried to attribute their prolonged absences from each other to "their very different ways of life"—Mary "was at everyone's beck and call" while Pamela "exercised a certain thrift in the spending of her time"—the fact was that Mary often found Pamela difficult and remote. With the perspective given by an age difference of a decade, she recognized her youngest sister's flaws better than the rest of her family, and was capable, on occasion, of a "heated . . . skirmish!" with her, something that faithful Mananai would never do. Publicly, Mary maintained her support of her difficult sister: "I know you'll forget any little hardnesses of speech about your Pamela. I could not bear you to think me stupid enough not to see her extra out-of-the-way cleverness," Margot wrote to Mary in 1900—a rare enough apology from Margot, suggesting that Mary must have defended Pamela quite forcefully. "It is the fashion to abuse Pamela," Mary remarked almost twenty years later to Lady Desborough (as Ettie Grenfell became after her husband Willie's elevation to the peerage), thanking her for understanding her sister as she did.

In 1902, however, Mary and Pamela were united by the common bond of pregnancy, giving birth just weeks apart in May. The children were born into a new era of peace—the Treaty of Vereeniging, which marked the end to the Boer War was signed on 31 May, the day that Mary's third daughter was born. They were Edwardians, not Victorians: Bertie, the Prince of Wales, who succeeded his mother upon her death on 22 January 1901, was crowned Edward VII in August 1902, after appendicitis had forced cancellation of the original ceremony in June.

The coronation and the peace promised the fresh and new. Pamela longed to call her son, born on 22 May, "David Pax! It sounds so short and manly," she told Mary. At Pamela's suggestion, Mary named her own child Irene Corona after the peace and the coronation, although she was known always as "Bibs." Both mothers were delighted with their new arrivals. "David Pax is such a squawler . . . you never heard such a voice—peppery & imperative," said Pamela. Mary thought Bibs was like spun wire, with a combination of fragility and toughness "that makes me *ache* for the little creature . . . her eyes shine like stars."

Both sisters knew how anxiously Mananai awaited the birth of her own child due that autumn. After the terrible loss of 1899, Mananai began to visit Schwalbach, a German spa providing the "iron cures" recommended for "women's problems." She also subscribed to the popular theory that a baby's sex might depend on the month in which it was "started": "I had a feeling I *must* begin the *same* day of the *same* month as last time (May) . . . I don't feel able to trust any other month," she told Madeline Wyndham, herself enthusiastic about the scheme. Her sisters felt a twinge of guilt at having so effortlessly succeeded where Mananai had failed. "You, at least, can feel you have not mopped up a possible son from darling Madeline!" Pamela told Mary when Bibs was born. To quiet disappointment, in October 1902, Mananai gave birth to a fifth girl, named Helena.

Helena Adeane was the only one of the newborn cousins whose paternity was not questioned. The Adeanes were devoted to each other, moving together between London and Babraham, where at the turn of the century Charlie built a large hall in the grounds, named the Madeline Hall after his wife. In January 1901, Charlie went to Egypt, while Mananai, run down after the election's excitement and her exertions during the "benevolent season," made a longed-for trip to Ireland to see George

and Sibell, followed by several weeks' convalescence in the gentle sunshine of Hyères. "It will be so strange being a 'grass widow,'" she said of
this rare separation.

It is unlikely that the angelically blond Bibs was, as some rumored,
actually Arthur Balfour's child. Bibs looked like her undoubtedly legiti-
mate brother Yvo, and Hugo doted upon her—in marked contrast to his
coldness towards Mary Charteris. More plausible is the suggestion that
David Tennant was the son of Edward Grey, a close friend of the Tennants, godfather to their second son, Christopher, a reluctantly prominent Liberal Imperialist and an obsessive birdwatcher and fly fisherman,
pursuits of which he wrote lyrically in a series of essays published under
the title *Recreation*.

Fishing was the foundation of the two Edwards' friendship, forged in
the mid-1890s. Their decades-long, quietly affectionate correspondence
is mostly blow-by-blow accounts of days thigh-deep in a rushing river,
with only occasional intrusions of finance or politics. Both quiet, unos-

By the turn of the twentieth century, Percy and Madeline Wyndham had
more than twenty grandchildren. They are pictured here, circa 1903, with
six of them—Guy's three: George, Dick and Olivia, and Pamela's three
eldest: Clare, Bim and Kit. From left to right (ages approximate): back row:
Bim (six), Kit (four); front row: Dick (seven), Percy (sixty-eight), Madeline
(sixty-eight), Clare (seven), George (ten); seated on floor, Olivia (six).

tentatious and honorable, they were politically as well as temperamentally aligned, occupying the far right of the Liberal Party.

Pamela's instinctive jealousy of Grey as a rival to her husband's attentions was quickly mollified by admiration of his character. By the turn of the century, she numbered Grey and his wife, Dorothy, among her closest friends: "two of the elect," she said, "each of them nearly the nicest person in the world." The connection between Pamela and Grey, however, was particularly intense. They had "nearly every taste and interest in common." The "peculiar sympathy" between their minds "eludes words, because it is so intimate!" said Grey.

The Greys divided their time between Fallodon in Northumberland, Grey's family seat in the north of England, and a small tin-roofed cottage in Itchen Abbas, a village in the New Forest within cycling distance of the Tennants in Wiltshire. It was common knowledge within political circles that the Greys' marriage was, at Dorothy's request, *un mariage blanc*—a sexless marriage—and most thought the courteous Grey celibate. But his fellow Liberal Lloyd George, the unabashedly philandering "Welsh Goat," maintained that Grey was a man of "sham honesty" in both public and private life. Certainly Grey's reputation as the most reluctant of politicians sits oddly with his part in the "Relugas Compact" of 1905, in which he, Asquith and fellow Liberal Imperialist Richard Haldane tried to weaken their leader, Campbell-Bannerman, in the Commons by forcing him upstairs to the House of Lords. As for his private dishonesty, Marie Belloc Lowndes—Pamela's close but indiscreet friend—recalled in her memoirs that after many years of marriage Dorothy Grey had suggested to her husband that they resume a physical relationship, but Grey refused. The implication was that Pamela had forbidden it, but the anecdote is inconclusive. Pamela would most likely have issued this edict even if she was not having sex with Grey. Pamela was very demanding with those she loved.

This approach extended to her children. Charlie Adeane spoke to Mary with "the greatest admiration" of the way in which Mananai "has obtained *complete* control over all her children by *love & influence*. Punishment & Reward can never obtain this. I think you all inherit this wonderful power—a very rare one—from your mother." This was true of the docile, loving and obedient Adeane girls. Pamela's was a hothouse love and her children were her acolytes. "What a child we could have," she once told her son David with reference to their striking good looks.

Visitors arriving at Glen were startled to find the family seated in greeting, in the hall, "in a sort of photographic pose": with Clare pouting gently, Stephen perched on her knee, and Pamela in the central role. As a young man, Stephen wrote a scrap of thinly veiled autobiography in which Pamela is the remote Lady Brandon, "whose charm and beauty had greeted her in the glass every morning for more years than she cared to remember [and] was greedily exacting as to the admiring allegiance of her family and immediate circle."

Pamela only reluctantly left her children, yearning for the days when they went no farther from her than Glen's village school each morning on their ponies, sobbing when delivering seven-year-old Bim to the train that was to take him to boarding school for the first time, making every excuse to keep her younger sons at home. Only Clare, whom she thought "spiritually short-sighted," did she willingly send to school. She was fiercely jealous of the children's nanny, Rebecca Trussler, a stout, middle-aged Cockney from London's East End who joined the family in 1906. When Stephen—whom she dressed, long after his infancy had passed, as the girl she wished he had been—was eight years old, she appeared on stage with him in a charity tableau at the Royal Albert Hall, the vast Kensington concert hall named by Queen Victoria after her beloved husband, cradling him in her arms as though he were an infant. She immortalized her children in two of her most successful books: *The Children and the Pictures,* in which the subjects of the Bart's Old Masters came alive and joined the Tennant children in midnight adventures, and *The Sayings of the Children,* which recorded their childish wisdom.

Pamela's approach to child-rearing was considered strange. "I never care for a woman draped in her children—let them go," said Margot. "I do NOT cart my children about like Pamela," Mary retorted hotly to Hugo when he charged her with having taken Bibs to Clouds to amuse herself, rather than leaving her at Stanway with her nanny, Cliffe: implicitly the latter was better parenting as providing stability and routine. Cliffe herself complained, as politely as she could, of the Liberty Hall atmosphere among the Tennants when visiting with Mary Charteris and Bibs in 1906, shocked that nine-year-old Clare, attending school in Salisbury each day, "as a rule dines with her mother, at 8, I feel that is much too late for *Mary* . . . they do not rest at all in the *day.*"

Cliffe sometimes struggled to impose a routine on her own rambunctious charges. In *A Family Record* Mary recorded a plea she received at

A 1900 photograph of twenty-nine-year-old Pamela and three-year-old Bim in rustic clothes, hinting at the bucolic life Pamela wished to lead. This portrait appeared in the weekly periodical the *Sphere* at the time that Pamela's first book, *Village Notes,* was published, alongside photographs of George Wyndham and his son Percy and their ancestor Lord Edward Fitzgerald, noting the family resemblance. Pamela cut out the article and pasted it across a double page in her "Garden Book." It was not to be the last time that Pamela's children and ancestry featured heavily in relation to her writing.

Gosford from Cliffe, with Yvo, Mary and Bibs at Stanway, asking "Our Dear Ladyship . . . to write certain things down for them *what they are not to do* . . . the chief things are, if I may name them, getting out on the roof, *or between* the *ceiling* and plaster, *climbing the garden wall* . . . after the fruit, or going down to the cellars where the furnaces are, or in the place where Mr. Fletcher keeps the chimney sweep brushes . . ." "Between the ceiling and the plaster!" marveled Mary, equally delighted and appalled by her children's ingenuity.

Mary's love for her children was laissez-faire, combining "with the maximum of fondness the minimum of possessiveness." She longed for her children's confidences but never demanded them, and her children, like her friends, had to compete for her attention with a host of daily trivialities: "Mary is generally a day behind the fair and will only hear of my death from the man behind the counter who is struggling to clinch her over a collar for her chow," said Margot. They took advantage of this to run wild. But from an early age they were brought into the orbit of their mother's guests, an ever more eclectic mix.

In 1902 Mary met the Fabians Beatrice and Sidney Webb at a dinner hosted by their fellow Fabian George Bernard Shaw, the celebrated playwright who combined comedy with a social conscience. The Fabian Society was the epicenter of Edwardian intellectualism. Its aim was to subtly indoctrinate the ruling classes with ideas of "practical Democracy and Socialism." Mary, a prime target, returned to Cadogan Square, shining-eyed, full of talk about how her new friends had promised to save her from being first against the wall when the revolution came. "I suppose you are going to ask the creatures to Stanway," Hugo remarked. By September, Beatrice was recording in her diary time spent with "Lady Elcho, a fascinating and kindly woman married to a card playing aristocrat, living in the most delightful old house." Through the Webbs, Mary met a fellow Fabian, the socialist author H. G. Wells, credited with being one of the fathers of science fiction. By 1903, the designer and craftsman C. R. Ashbee, who, influenced by the socialism of William Morris, set up cooperative Arts and Crafts workshops intended to promote and protect traditional craftsmen in Chipping Campden, near Stanway, was writing in his diary of visits from "Lady Elcho the wonderful the nonchalant the strangely fascinating," whirling over, often with Mrs. Patrick Campbell in tow, extravagant in crackling black glacé opera coat. "Tigrina," as Mary called her, had become a frequent visitor at Stanway, as had Harold Large, a charlatan psychic whom Mary nonetheless found amusing. She had become renowned for having "these outré people around her."

Her children called the more eccentric of these her "Freaks and Funnies." Stories that sound apocryphal were in fact true—for example, Mary's telegraphing Hugo from Taplow Court, where she was staying with Ettie Grenfell, with instructions to provide beds at Cadogan Square for three "spiritual" disciples of a Persian sage invited to London by the Gothic revivalist architect Sir Arthur Blomfield and his wife: "It's just a sort of neighbourly thing that does help people . . . they'll dash round to [the Blomfields'] flat before breakfast & return after dinner just to sleep . . ." she told him. She found that her guests provided her with all the friction needed to spark a house party into life. Beatrice Webb divided the world into two sorts: the "A's" ("Aristocrats, Anarchists and Artists") and the "B's" ("Bourgeois, Bureaucrats, and Benevolents"). Mary challenged her to define where she (Mary) stood. Beatrice characterized her as "the purveyor of the Bs to the As! A very rare thing requiring great sympathy and one [must] be able and willing to intellectually subordinate oneself, to be able to carry a hostile force to another."

"The Charteri,' as the Charteris clan were known, at Stanway circa 1903. From left, standing: Guy Charteris (aged around seventeen), Hugo, Ego Charteris (around nineteen); seated: Mary Charteris (around eight, hugging a chow), Mary with infant Bibs on her lap, Yvo (around seven) and Cincie (around sixteen).

Notwithstanding the barb therein, Mary was thrilled: "What she said is really what I mean . . ." "Don't you agree with me, Mr. Balfour, that the only excuse for a dinner party is that it should end in a committee?" Mrs. Webb challenged the Prime Minister across the dinner table at Stanway. In 1907 Mary triumphantly reported to Balfour that "le beau Norts"— her friend, the staunchly Tory Robert Norton—"has fallen head and crop over heels and become a collectivist," while Beatrice Webb had succumbed to two glasses of champagne on Saturday night and the following morning "actually gone to church . . . !"

Mary's house parties were becoming famous. In the first decade of the twentieth century, Stanway was a house where an ambitious young man could make his mark over "general conversation," as guests rallied across the table at dinner like a game of tennis as, in Cynthia's memory, Mary turned her head delightedly from side to side. Yet Mary was largely responsible for generating this conversation herself: her gift was to throw in "bones." "If for an instant it flagged over an entrée or a plover's egg she lifted it again and withdrew herself to listen. The result of course was that we all felt we were at our best and came away radiant with satisfaction," recalled C. R. Ashbee. She and Balfour were a well-practiced double act. Cincie Charteris drew a picture of long afternoons spent in the "boudoir," Mary's personal sitting room: curtains drawn across the two great mullioned windows to keep out the icy cold and the fire lit, vigorous debate among some guests while others nodded off gently in the corner, the reading aloud of treatises and poetry, chows underfoot and sleeping on cushions, books and pictures piled up around:

> whose voices and laughter I can hear again; while now with tempered heat they earnestly discuss some burning question of that day; now, like verbal ballet-dancers, glide, twist and pirouette in airiest fancies; now rollick in fantastic exuberant nonsense. I remember how the hours flew, and how much I used to dread the dispersing sound of "that tocsin of the soul—the dinner bell."

In 1905, the thirty-six-year-old Mananai fell pregnant for the seventh time. This pregnancy felt quite different from the others. "I have never felt so 'unjumpy' I think before," she reported to her mother. In October, the Adeanes went to London, sending their five daughters to Clouds. The wet nurse had been booked, Mananai's bedroom newly painted and papered, and the expectant mother was upbeat and enthusiastic: "Whenever 'Twinkie-Twankie' (this one's name!) chooses to appear . . . we shall all be prepared!" On 3 November, after seventeen years of marriage and, curiously, six years to the day after their first son (the "dear little Boy Baby") had died, Madeline and Charlie became the jubilant parents to a healthy son, Robert. "This wonderful gift is a mighty relief and a load off our backs . . . The anxiety has weighed on us for many years and just in a moment it was gone!" Charlie told Mary.

The whole family was "wild with delight." Mananai's always affectionate letters reached new heights of effusion. "I couldn't half thank you or at all thank you Angel for fresh proof in this Joy of the Worlds & Worlds or rather Heavens & Heavens of never failing LOVE you shower upon me & mine . . . Bless you," she wrote to her mother, when Madeline Wyndham sent little Robert a present. Mananai greeted each new ounce with wonder: "This week [he] has put on 14 . . . & nice firm flesh!

Isn't it a mercy?" she exclaimed to Mary as she completed her lying-in. Her great fortune made her "long . . . to give large pieces" of happiness "to the many who have none or so little[. . .] the feeling of Thankfulness is overwhelming . . . Baby is a splendid little fellow & we are so grateful for him."

Mary and George were godparents. As part of her duties, Mary warned her brother-in-law against indulging the child. Charlie acknowledged "the inclination . . . to spoil a Benvenuto" but assured Mary of his "implicit confidence in Madeline's sagacity . . . she is a very remarkable woman—I can say that to you—& her character is so strong that it must influence any children under her care." In contrast to the christenings of his sisters, Robert's was celebrated with pomp, at Babraham. The estate's laborers were given the day off. With characteristic diffidence the Adeanes had only let it be known that the service was not private. They were astonished and touched to find the church packed full. A large tea followed; plans were made for enhanced Christmas festivities in due course. With little Robert laughing and crowing in his cradle, everything for Madeline seemed more than perfect: "LOVE . . . seems to radiate around," she told her father.

TWENTY-THREE

The Souls in Power

Little over a week after the hollow peace of Vereeniging marked the end of a grueling guerrilla war, another political titan departed the public arena. In early June 1902, the elderly Lord Salisbury finally relinquished his post as Prime Minister. Arthur Balfour made his way to Windsor for a secretive meeting with the King. Two days later, his name was put forward for approval at the Unionist Party conference. It was a nominal gesture. No one was likely to oppose the man groomed for decades as Salisbury's successor.

As the news of Arthur's succession became public Mary was at Wilton in perfect weather, hugging to herself news that she had known since he was summoned to Windsor. "My dear P.M. & F.L.T., L.P.S., & L.H.C.," she wrote jubilantly to him, savouring the flock of titles that were now his: Prime Minister, First Lord of the Treasury, Lord Privy Seal and Leader of the House of Commons. Her old friend and rival Daisy White had already begun quizzing her about when exactly she had known of Salisbury's intention to resign; and when Daisy tried to show off her own inside knowledge by alluding to the still-secret resignations of various Cabinet ministers (part of the inevitable shuffle that accompanied the handover of power), "of course I took it as news," said Mary magnanimously.

Mary had given birth to Bibs less than a fortnight before, but she had no intention of recuperating quietly. She was the confidante of the most powerful man in the country, and she reveled in her role. Balfour's ascendancy marked Mary's heyday. They were "the great days of Mary Elcho at Stanway," in H. G. Wells's words. To say that Mary came to power when Arthur did is no exaggeration. She had the ear of the Prime Minister, controlling access by guest list and seating plans. Her invitations soared accordingly: she was asked to great houses of influence she had not visited for years, and made the guest of honor at London dinners, where the most influential and ambitious men in the country hung on her every word. She reported such triumphs to Balfour: the compliments on "gown, figure, face, prettiness" paid her by Lord Revelstoke, senior partner of Barings Bank—and an old admirer of Pamela's—until she hardly knew where to look; a confidence from Sir John ("Jackie") Fisher "that he had finished the Army thing" (Fisher was a member of the Esher Committee, which had been set up in 1903 to recommend reforms in the organization of the War Office in the wake of the Boer War) while waxing large on Balfour's fine treatment of Britain's naval force. Ten months later Jackie Fisher was head of the Royal Navy as First Sea Lord, implementing a radical restructuring and modernization of the navy and hurling Britain into a naval race with Germany.

"I appear to be having one of those odd and apparently causeless 'booms' of appreciation which some people have at intervals, they go in cycles regardless of any change of circs [*sic*]," Mary told Arthur in 1904, after a successful visit to imposing Chatsworth House in Derbyshire, the home of the social and political grandees the Duke and Duchess of Devonshire. The Dukes of Devonshire were one of the richest and most powerful of all the aristocratic families. Mary's host, the 8th Duke, known by his courtesy title the Marquess of Hartington, was the Whig leader of the Liberal Unionist Party. An invitation to Chatsworth was only bestowed upon those of the greatest social or political influence, and Mary's invitation to a house that she had not been to, on her own account, for many years was doubtless due to her new position of power. To Mary's delight she discovered, on Hugo's account, that the assembled company had been fulsome in their praise of Lady Elcho after her departure, talking "of how nice I was! Isn't that odd? And absurd—I *have* to tell you!" Disingenuous and delighted, Mary continued: "Of course I do think the discovery that I am a *well-informed* woman must greatly add to my assets—prestige! I really must try and live up to the part." The following month, she visited Dresden, where sixteen-year-old Cincie was being "finished." On the promise of a meeting with the Kaiser, she hastened on to Berlin, with only the oldest of gowns and without a maid. The meeting turned into a two-hour tête-à-tête. "You'd have laughed to see us," she remarked to Balfour. "Me on sofa, as if we were a play, and Fursts, Grafs and Admirals in the next room gazing and muttering! . . . [I] had quite a 'succès fou.'" At a time when Anglo-German rivalry was increasing, Mary, fearlessly, had "got" the Kaiser "onto our army and his army and of course as his soul is in that subject we got beyond making conversation and had a very interesting evening," discussing the recently published Esher Committee's reports. The Kaiser, unsurprisingly, was fiercely opposed to the proposals which recommended "divided responsibility" between an Army Council and the General Staff, and the abolition of the office of Commander-in-Chief.

Mary's social confidence gave her new confidence with Arthur. Their relationship had recovered from the blows of the births of Mary and Yvo Charteris. If anything, it put Arthur on his mettle, and gave Mary a sense of liberation. A year after Yvo's birth, Arthur told Mary of a recent trip to Germany, where he had found a bookseller offering "manuals of instruction in Latin on the best way to become a wife without also becoming a mother! I bought one of these last as a curiosity—I hope you are not going to allow all the blood to be sucked out of you by that Vampire Balfour," he added, making reference to Bram Stoker's recently published, best-selling *Dracula* (which Mary read to her children, defending herself to a disapproving Hugo on the basis that it was "quite harmless and most thrilling"). Mary scratched out the six lines that followed, but a letter she wrote to Arthur the following summer from Kissingen describing herself while taking her "cure" escaped censorship: "I do look *very pretty* in my bath, thousands of nestling bubbles that show off the modeling—breasts supported by water, of perfect shape with rosy tips! limbs of a ghostly whiteness—Really like a Venus or a Rhein maiden . . . Yesterday while reading George's Introduction [to Plutarch] I slipped into Venus and Adonis—my dear! *You* may consider yourself lucky—that's all I say!!! Write to me freely—I will destroy your letters," she told him. But for all that, Mary had been badly shaken by a visit paid to England by Mary Curzon in the summer of 1901 that was part convalescence from the harsh Indian climate and part reconnaissance, gauging for Curzon the political climate at home. Arthur did not trouble to conceal his obvious attraction towards the Viceroy's beautiful American wife. At a house party at Wilton, according to the Vicereine's report to her husband, Mary took Mary Curzon to her room for a "dentist" that was in fact a grilling as she tried to ascertain just how close she and Arthur were. She refused to accept Mary Curzon's protestations that she was "only in the galère with [Arthur's] other friends" and that Mary Elcho was "the only one that matters with AJB in the least. 'No' says she, 'I know when he is interested and he loves being with you.'" The return to London provided more gossip for Mary Curzon to relay. She and Arthur went to Cadogan Square to find Mary after she had failed to turn up to a lunch the three of them had arranged at Willis's Rooms, the social club previously known as Almack's in St. James's in London. Mary Curzon described what followed to her husband with some relish:

> We asked for her, and the footman went off to fetch her, while we waited in the library. Suddenly Mary appeared, wild-haired in a filthy dressing gown, and for two seconds we all stood quite still. Then Arthur said, "Well, why didn't you come?" "Come where?" said Mary. "To lunch" said A. "You never asked me," cried Mary and hurled herself on a sofa. Arthur said, "You must be mad." Then Mary said, "Don't you think I would have come if I had thought you wanted me? Would I miss an hour when I could be with you? I have suffered agonies to think you didn't want me, and you had promised to lunch alone with me."

Mary Curzon made her excuses and left, but not before Balfour, in front of a near-hysterical Mary, made Mary Curzon promise to dine with him alone at the Commons that night.

Was Mary Curzon exaggerating the anecdote to provide her husband with gossip? Perhaps—but the nugget of truth is there, and Balfour's "stern and cold" treatment of "his poor trembling wild Mary" is easy to believe. For all that she was flattered by his attention, Mary Curzon returned to India wary of Balfour. "When the sun shines and women smile, he is a picturesque, rare, enchanting creature . . . In times of stress he is, I think, harsh, and just a little selfish."

Mary when confident was a very different creature from the distraught figure in the filthy dressing gown. Her correspondence with Arthur opened with the same lack of ceremony as always: Mary's abruptly, with no heading, and signed off as "Melcho"; Arthur's addressed as always to "My dear Lady Elcho." But when confident, Mary continued coquettish, and at times explicit, with coy references to "punitive expeditions," and teases about long hours in bed in the morning, playing with a "beastly little 'Beast' of yr [Arthur's] own making." "2 hrs is what I like: one for boring things and one for putting you in yr place . . . on yr knees at my feet," Mary told Arthur in 1904, after managing to snatch two hours on a Sunday afternoon alone in his room at a house party in Oxfordshire. Three years later on Valentine's Day she sent him a sketch of "somewhat obscure objects . . . a birch rod . . . a brush and a tin bottle of squirting grease (smells of peppermint!)," taking childish glee in the nursery-punishment element of their relationship that appealed to her love of secrets and private jokes.

The "boring things" were "talking business"—the business of politics. Mary's children teased her that Balfour piled her letters unopened into his desk drawers, but in fact he seems to have sought, and greatly valued, the benefit of her wisdom and instinct. As Arthur's confidante, Mary operated in the manner of most political wives at the time: listener rather than adviser, a sounding board to be trusted implicitly where colleagues could not. Most political wives did not aspire to more and Mary was no different. Her own political foray onto the parish council was short-lived: depressed by a committee's inability to get anything done, and feeling as though she were "skinned alive," she abandoned her seat as soon as she could. Throughout Arthur's forty-one months as Prime Minister, the two discussed appointments, policy and crises. Mary's advice to him on appointments focused on personality as much as policy: the alchemy that could make a successfully balanced Cabinet work was not far off that required to make a house party "sing." "There must be some heaven-born Chancellor somewhere outside . . . Cromer or Dawkins, or *Hugo*!!" she told Arthur, as he began devising his new Cabinet in 1902, a mischievous reference to Hugo's unremitting gambling. She was more serious about her brother's prospects: "I suppose you know you won't have a happy or peaceful life—with me—until brother George is in the Cabinet!" Despite Balfour at first insisting that he could "see *no* chance of George having anything," George, while retaining his position as Irish Secretary, ultimately, and no doubt thanks in part to Mary's tenacity, was brought into the Cabinet.

Arthur peopled his Cabinet with Souls. Civil servants were aston-

Whittingehame House in Scotland, home of the Balfour family and where Arthur was born. Neoclassical Whittingehame was built from nabob money in the 1820s by Arthur's grandfather James Balfour, who had made a fortune in the West Indies and purchased the ten-thousand-acre estate in 1817. James's Scottish estates, which included rich coal seams in Fife, remained a vastly lucrative revenue source during Arthur's lifetime, but a series of unwise investments by Arthur and his brother Gerald (including an attempt to develop peat processing as a clean alternative to coal mining) depleted them. A mere fifteen miles from Gosford, Whittingehame provided a convenient escape for Mary from the oppressive presence of her father-in-law, although Arthur's sister and chatelaine Alice rarely welcomed the periodic intrusion of the Souls women into her domain. During the Second World War, the house became a school for Kindertransport refugees. Today it is divided into apartments.

ished to hear the Cabinet addressing one another by their first names, as the old friends they were. But their golden age was beset by problems. The new century had brought a new dawn, and, as the fog of jingoism cleared, a number of developments allowed the electorate to see the Unionists in a clearer light: as a party that did not seek to remedy the legal position resulting from the notorious Taff Vale legal judgment of 1901, which, by allowing employers to sue trade unions for damages arising from strike action, had a chilling effect on the ability of the laboring classes to protest; and as a party that, having compared Uitlanders to helots, was willing to import cheap indentured labor from China to work on the Rand, as the Witwatersrand plateau, location of South Africa's gold mines, was known. The "Chinese Slavery" scandal was a gift for the Liberal Opposition. St. John Brodrick's conduct as Minister for War during the Boer War began to be vilified and the Government's justifications for war looked shabby. In India, Curzon orchestrated a Coronation Durbar to mark Edward VII's ascension to the throne, which half of London society, including Hugo, Pamela and Eddy, attended. Yet for all its breathtaking grandeur, those who returned agreed that they had never heard of a more unpopular Viceroy. "Whether this is because his reforms are too good or his manners too bad seems doubtful," said Balfour. But he too was tiring of a Viceroy who treated anything less than absolute acquiescence to his proposals as a personal affront.

To her chagrin, Mary did not go to India. At the eleventh hour Cincie had fallen ill and Hugo went alone. Mary was so disappointed she refused even "so much as to look at a newspaper—I was much too angry at not being there." Instead, she took the children to Madeira, the clement Portuguese island in the North Atlantic Ocean, to recuperate and escape England's foul weather. Hugo was being characteristically uncommunicative and from there, she berated her husband for "the howling desert of loneliness & ignorance of all yr plans in which I have been living." Yet only in curiously oblique terms could she try to persuade him to refrain from behavior still more hurtful. A tiny "hinge" at the bottom of her letter reads: "I hope you have got a little offering for each child—it makes nurse cruel to Yvo if you have nothing for Mary she, nurse, cries all night about it. It's cruel & does such injustice to yrself." Only by invoking Yvo could Mary hope to make Hugo be kind to Mary Charteris. It is a small clue that, despite Mary's predictions, Hugo did not treat Blunt's daughter as he did his other children.

The Government of the Souls was already waning. That month, the Liberals moved a vote of censure (known now as a vote of no confidence) against the War Secretary St. John Brodrick over his conduct of the war recently concluded. Brodrick was saved only by George Wyndham's Land Purchase Bill making its way through the Commons, which provoked the Irish Nationalists to stand by the Government, knowing that if the Government fell so would the Bill. George seemed in fact the only minister to be credible: his Land Act, as it became once passed, instigated a workable land-purchase scheme that allowed tenants to buy the land they farmed from their landlords—unquestionably George's finest legacy, and one of the high legislative points of an otherwise unexceptional ministry.

To a large extent, the fault was Arthur's. For decades he had been held up as the future. Yet, in power, he already seemed out of date. His detached, intellectual approach did not suit a country anxious about imperial decadence; he was not able—or willing—to control the fire-and-brimstone elements of his Cabinet. By 1903 his Cabinet was riven over the question of "imperial preference" or "tariff reform": whether

Forty-year-old George Wyndham (seated) and thirty-eight-year-old Guy Wyndham (standing), 1903. The brothers had always been extremely close: upon George first being sent to boarding school aged eight, Guy became so unruly without his brother that his parents reluctantly sent him too, a year earlier than planned. Now the brothers were once more reunited following a separation: this time, due to war. After three years serving in South Africa in the Boer War, during which time he was promoted to the rank of lieutenant colonel, Guy received the honor of being mentioned in dispatches (in which a superior officer in an official report to high command drew attention to a particular soldier's bravery). He returned to England and his relieved family in 1902.

Britain should introduce protective tariffs on trade outside the Empire. Head of the tariff reformers was Joe Chamberlain, the Colonial Secretary, who believed it would forge imperial unity and provide revenue for social reform. Opposing Chamberlain with equal force were the Liberal Unionist Whig grandees, for whom protectionism was simply heretical. Balfour's own musings on the subject, *Economic Notes on Insular Free Trade*, published in pamphlet form in September 1903, sat firmly on the fence, advocating cautious protectionism. Possibly this was the only way he could hope to hold together two magnetically repelling forces. Balfour sent his notes to Mary in draft and discussed with her whether she thought the novel approach of publishing views not yet set out by him in Parliament was wise. Mary was in favor of publishing. Politics was changing: she thought the approach might sway young people's views and "you ought certainly to tell the important Press, they will surely review it." With Balfour's permission (and delighting in delivering such a confidential communication) Mary showed the notes privately to Hugo and Percy and indicated Balfour's thoughts of publication. To Balfour privately she mocked Hugo's old-fashioned response. While a firm protectionist, he believed policy should only be revealed by parliamentary speech: "[He] thinks sending these notes to the Press, a shocking idea! Odd, incorrect, altogether wrong. I thought I'd tell you that," added Mary.

In the late summer of 1903, Balfour and Chamberlain privately agreed that, if the Cabinet would not accept Imperial Preference, Chamberlain would resign and campaign for tariff reform outside the Cabinet to test the waters of public opinion, and his son (and proxy) Austen would become Chancellor. By skillful maneuvering in September, Balfour used the bluff of Chamberlain's resignation to rid himself of the most burdensome free traders of his Cabinet, including his Chancellor, Charles Ritchie. Momentarily, Balfour even seemed to have achieved his intended aim of keeping the Whig grandee, the Duke of Devonshire, in his Cabinet, but, bullied by his free-trade companions, the unhappy Duke resigned in October.

In a hurried meeting in London in the middle of the negotiations, squeezed in before Mary left for Ireland to visit George, Arthur confided in Mary the latest developments: his interview with Edward VII about Cabinet changes, St. John Brodrick's impending demotion to Indian Chief Secretary, Ritchie's departure. He gave Mary permission to tell Hugo "various items of the dramatic situation," which Mary duly did: "He was much thrilled and very grateful for being told . . ." she reported back. At Phoenix Park, Mary once again had the upper hand. Placing a marker for the future, George confided in her his hopes for the Chancellorship—"the heart's desire of his life." Mary "told him (for fun) without my saying anything to tell me his views. He hopes that St. John will stay at the War Office . . . I do wonder who will take his place? . . . It would be an amusing experiment to put in Arnold Forster but perhaps too much of an experiment." Hugh Arnold-Forster, erstwhile Parliamentary and Financial Secretary to the Admiralty, was indeed Arthur's choice as War Secretary, a significant promotion. He immediately rose to the task by setting up the Esher Committee, which considered War Office reforms, which the Boer War had so painfully demonstrated were needed.

Notwithstanding Arthur's maneuverings, by the summer of 1904 it was obvious "to anyone with Parliamentary experience that with the Conservative party torn with dissension and tottering to its fall, the coming Session would be its last," said George's private secretary Murray Hornibrook. The more immediate crisis was to be George's. His Land Act had been a triumph. His intellect had risen to the challenge of the job. His nerves, fed by his mania for work, had not. He began to drink and smoke ever more heavily, slept little and forgot to eat.

"I am undergoing a phase of nausea at politics, nostalgia for poetry," he told Pamela, declaring as he did to Wilfrid Blunt, that he was sick of office. His mental state in these months was described, with admirable honesty, by Guy Wyndham in George's *Life and Letters*:

> Between the engrossing demands of other political problems, the toil of constant effort towards keeping the shattered and mutinous party together, and the sickness at politics which continued during the summer months . . . he was losing his grasp over the machine . . . a machine so erratic in its working that it needed daily and almost hourly vigilance . . . Artificial stimulants and bursts of physical exercise only ran up the overdraft. He was, in the vivid phrase of a friend, "whirling rather than walking through his days"; and he could not stop.

George, always "over-engined for his hull," was more or less in the throes of a nervous breakdown, one so profound that even Sibell could not help but notice it.

As soon as the summer session of 1904 ended, George and Sibell went to the Continent for an "extended holiday" of six weeks. His secretaries were told not to contact him or to forward any papers which could await his return. In George's absence MacDonnell drafted, on Dublin Castle writing paper (signifying implicit government approval), a devolution scheme that was published by the Irish Reform Association (a body advocating limited self-government for Ireland but stopping short of full Home Rule) on 26 September 1904. It proposed an Irish Financial Council governing purely Irish expenditure and a new statutory body legislating on Irish business with which a Westminster Parliament "was unable or unsuited to deal." In the words of John Redmond, the leader of the Irish Parliamentary Party, it was "simply a declaration for Home Rule."

The result was political uproar. Ulster was enraged. The Unionist press, in the words of Murray Hornibrook, "went for it." On the opposite side of the political spectrum, the radical nationalist Michael Davitt considered it a "wooden-horse stratagem" that attempted by halfhearted reform to subvert and demoralize the nationalist cause. George wrote a letter to *The Times* the next day, claiming to be dumbfounded. He was ignorant of MacDonnell's scheme, and rejected it outright on behalf of the Government.

Whether George knew or did not know has never been clear. A decade later, Mary commented to Wilfrid Blunt that "it is *curious* how each

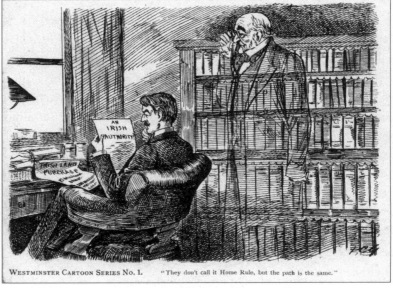

WESTMINSTER CARTOON SERIES No. 1.   "They don't call it Home Rule, but the path is the same."

The Conservative Unionist Party had been forged out of opposition to the Home Rule for Ireland advocated by the Liberal Prime Minister William Gladstone in the 1890s. Just how shocking was the suggestion that George Wyndham, a Unionist Irish Secretary, could now be advocating such a form of self-rule is evident from a contemporaneous cartoon. In it, George Wyndham sits reading a paper entitled "An Irish Authority?," doubtless a reference to MacDonnell's devolution scheme, while on the desk a sheet entitled "Irish Land Purchase" reminds the viewer of George's role in bringing about the Irish Land Act of 1903, which allowed Roman Catholic tenant farmers to purchase land. Over his shoulder, the ghost of Gladstone looks on approvingly. The caption reads "They don't call it Home Rule, but the path is the same." The implication is clear: George was a turncoat, betraying his party.

person wants to prove George to be the thing they love themselves or to twist him into their narrow horizon if they like *pink*! They say he *is* pink that he was a nationalist, that he was an R[oman].C[atholic]. this that & the other . . ." In 1911, George would inveigh against constitutional reform of the House of Lords and the removal of its absolute veto, claiming *inter alia* that it would pave the way for Home Rule. Yet this lay in his more extremist future. What brought him down when Parliament reconvened in February 1905, and an amendment to the King's Address was moved concerning his own conduct, was that he could not be pinned down at all on what he had meant, what he had known, what he supported and what he believed.

Five years before, George had made his name in response to an amendment to the monarch's Address on opening Parliament. Now, he "had to fight with his back to the wall under a hail of furious charges and envenomed insinuations, knowing that even on the benches alongside of him and behind him there was an atmosphere of sullen suspicion." He was accused of concealing "ugly facts," of using MacDonnell as a scapegoat or a Trojan horse. "Cannot the right hon. Gentleman give a plain answer to a plain question?" he was asked. George's family did not pretend that his conduct during those weeks in the Commons when he was under attack was anything other than a shambles. They had simply to wait for the horror to end. At the end of January, a leader in *The Times* declared that "the Chief Secretary, owing it is understood to enfeebled health, has seen little or nothing of the country for the administration of which he remains responsible." Of all the attacks, this, for the "Patriot" George, was one of the most bitter blows.

On 20 February 1905 he made his final speech as Irish Secretary in the Commons. He was shambolic, rambling and confused. On 6 March, George being too ill to appear in person, as was the norm, Balfour announced to the Commons "with the deepest regret" that he had accepted the minister's resignation. He refused to pronounce on the merits of George's decision, making his support for him as plain as he could, while adhering to instructions given by George the night before as from "not . . . a colleague but . . . one of your closest friends. I beg of you not to praise me to-morrow. It will do you harm. Perhaps that argument will not weigh with you. So let me add, it will do me harm."

George was at Clouds, knocked out on sedatives. Pamela came over from Stockton, bringing Bim and David to lighten the atmosphere in

The front page of *The Sphere*, 11 March 1905, reporting George's resignation as Irish Secretary. For many years, this pro-imperialist weekly had championed George as one of its heroes. In the context of his sudden fall, its reference under his portrait to George being the great-grandson of "the famous Lord Edward FitzGerald," a man who had notoriously fought for an Ireland independent of England, may well have been double-edged.

the house, and was appalled by the heavy, bowed figure she found masquerading in her brother's body. "I never saw such a strong vigorous life so brought to a standstill," she reported to Mary, likening it to seeing a horse fresh from hunting pulled to a halt, heaving, with sweating flanks, "only the horse was George." Pamela spent several days there. Madeline Wyndham was on "iron hooks" of anxiety, Percy silent. It was clear to Pamela that Percy was using every ounce of his self-control not to break out in recriminations against his son and the world for having disappointed him so. Sibell was "all she could be," Pamela told Mary, but they both knew that that was little more than the provider of a soft hand to clasp another's while she prayed.

Pamela treated George gently, taking him for long walks and talking over the old times. They played games of "do you remember" from their childhood, reminiscing over "old trivial happenings" at Wilbury and Isel. Every detail George remembered was greeted by Madeline Wyndham with silent relief that his crash had not permanently damaged his mind. Pamela and George spoke of Percy's unselfishness and "self-control"; of poetry. Prompted by George, Pamela recited to him lines by heart. "And there were only two long spells when he walked on as if he forgot things around him," Pamela told Mary. At dinner the family feigned normality, maintaining chatter as George sat silently. His scattered interjections— "Now go on, Pam, tell me some more stories"—were greeted with relief, "and once," said Pamela, "he had a real good laugh & said now that is excellent, in his tremendous emphatic manner, you know, and then, with a great sigh 'I've not been amused for so long, just go on.'"

"Never should the outside world know, willingly, from me that he had been knocked out of step, even for a day or two, by all this," declared Pamela, urging Mary to keep this letter private. Externally calm, Pamela was burning internally with "spleen and rancour," a white-hot rage at those who had brought down this beloved Icarus who had flown too close to the sun. And perhaps it was the Wyndham religion that prompted Mary's oddly pragmatic analysis of the matter in her letter to Arthur, sweeping under the carpet the destruction, public and private, of her brother. "George has profited by experience before . . . if he takes this right it may be a lesson to him . . . its [*sic*] very serious its *breaking* him so . . . but I think he will rebound all right," she said, anticipating that George's "nervous disposition" would act as a "safety valve."

Publicly, the Wyndhams refused to blame anyone for the incident, least of all Arthur. Katharine Tynan pressed Pamela and Mary on the issue several years later. "My brother is nothing if not magnanimous," said Pamela. Mary offered the same smooth façade: "She . . . had no condemnation for any of those who had hounded him out of his beneficent public life . . ."; her only comment was: "He was so full of all he was going to do for Ireland . . . that he could not help talking about it." But privately Mary thought that George had got into his secretary's "clutches somehow morally," and his lifestyle had not helped: "Alcohol and nicotine are more insidious that [*sic*] microbes! . . . You have never been influenced that way. Bless you! I wish you didn't Atlas all the world," she said to Arthur.

On 4 December 1905, torn between free-trading backbenchers and Chamberlain, who, despite increasing ill health, refused to abandon his vigorous campaign, Balfour resigned. He was replaced by Britain's first Radical Prime Minister—the Glaswegian Henry Campbell-Bannerman, known as "CB," who formed an interim Cabinet. In the election campaign of January 1906 the Liberals, united in their support of free trade, confidently on the moral high ground, were spoilt for choice on which issue to attack the Conservatives with first. They won by a landslide, gaining 200 seats to bring their number to 397, to the Unionists' 156. It was their last outright majority to date. In an unprecedented show of defiance by his constituents, Balfour even lost the Manchester East seat that he had held for twenty years, and had to be rushed back into the Commons via the more pliant electors of the City of London (made possible by the staggered election process that meant that constituencies voted at different times). "Dearest Chang here's a to-do," Percy wrote to his eldest daughter in his neat, backwards-sloping handwriting: "Arthur out with an enormous majority. I wonder what you think of it."

The ministry of Souls had failed, remarkably, almost cataclysmically, to live up to the hopes promised by these men when young. Still worse, the experience of government had fractured the Souls themselves, exemplified by the return, the day before Balfour resigned, of Lord and Lady Curzon. Britain's youngest, most glamorous, most brilliant Viceroy had been driven out of his post, and Balfour had let him go.

The occasion was a clash of egos between Curzon and Lord Kitchener, India's Commander-in-Chief. Tension had been building between the two men ever since Kitchener had taken up the post in 1902. In 1905 Balfour backed Kitchener over questions of military reorganization. Employing a by now habitual bluff, Curzon proffered his resignation, and was appalled when Balfour accepted it. Few thought that Balfour had behaved wrongly: the Viceroy's delusions of grandeur had reached near-megalomaniacal proportions. But Curzon never forgave Balfour for what he considered a stab in the back, and Balfour's failure to arrange a single representative of the Government or the monarch to meet the ex-Viceregal pair as they stepped off the train at Charing Cross on 3 December 1905 was pure cattiness. A gathering of Souls, including Balfour, was at Stanway. The party decided it was too far to travel to London for the occasion. "We were trying all Sunday to concoct a telegram of greeting which all, including A.J.B., could sign. Nothing less jejeune seemed to evolve itself than 'Glad you're back,'" Hugo Elcho said. "If we don't look out, it'll turn into 'Glad your back's worse,'" remembered Ettie Desborough, making reference to the corsets Curzon wore for his perpetually weak back. In the end, they sent nothing at all.

TWENTY-FOUR

Pamela at Wilsford

Eddy Tennant was one of the many new Liberal backbenchers to take their place in the Commons that spring. He had taken the constituency of Salisbury from the Unionists, benefiting from the landslide and from Pamela's charms: "There was many a Tory turned Liberal when they saw her—she was the most beautiful woman I ever saw," remembered one elderly constituent.

Although united on free trade, the Liberals remained split between Radicals and Imperialists. With Edward Grey, the new Foreign Secretary, and Asquith Chancellor of the Exchequer, Eddy and Pamela were in the inner circle of power. In fact, Eddy—the "moderate liberal"—was ambiguous about the direction of his party, and Pamela had long since ceased to feign any interest in politics. The Tennants' visits to Grey—a world-famous bird expert—at Fallodon were filled not with political talk but with walks along the seashore to watch for eider duck, curlew, whimbrel and dotterel and listen to "their plaintive attenuated cries"; evenings were spent listening to Edward Grey read aloud. Pamela's times at Fallodon revived her, as though she were filling her lungs with the fresh sea air. "I came back with a new stock of patience to hear wrangling voices with, and to cope with seeing the cook, & paying the bills and all the 'dreary intercourse of daily life' . . ." she told Charlie Tennant, a cousin of Eddy's, after one such visit in 1908. Eddy, Pamela and Grey had grown even closer since Dorothy's death, in February 1906, in a freak carriage accident. Pamela seems to have been the anonymous author of the obituary in *The Times*, paying tribute to "a friendship which has been one of the high privileges of my life." Thereafter Grey spent Christmases with the Tennants at Glen.

The birth of the Tennants' fourth child, Stephen, in April 1906 occasioned rumors that he was an "Aarons baby," the product of a Society doctor said to inseminate artificially women who could not conceive with their husbands, either by a stud of footmen or by the insertion of a teaspoon filled with sperm. None of this can be substantiated (although Jervois Aarons was indeed Pamela's doctor), but it speaks volumes about the state of their marriage that it was capable of generating such gossip. People were always willing to talk about the Tennants, particularly after the Bart's death in June 1906, whereupon Eddy inherited a "considerable proportion" of the Bart's £3,151,976 estate, and of the family empire, now no longer just chemicals but comprising another fortune in shares and mining.

Eddy sold the family house in Grosvenor Square and bought 34 Queen Anne's Gate, a picturesque cobbled street in the political heartland of Westminster, a stone's throw from St. James's Park and mere steps from the Foreign Office, where Edward Grey spent his days. The Tennants commissioned Blow to add on a wing to house the Bart's collection of principally English Old Masters previously housed at Glen. The gallery, which had a separate entrance, was opened to the public in May 1910, between 2 p.m. and 6 p.m. on Wednesdays and Saturdays. To Pamela's delight, it was a success from the first, with 150 people visiting in the first two hours alone. This was just one of many philanthropic gestures by the Tennants; Eddy's charitable "obligations" were considerable, all willingly undertaken.

In the summer of 1906, the Tennants moved into their new home, Wilsford Manor in Wiltshire. It was featured in a seven-page spread in *Country Life* on 29 September. A series of handsome black-and-white photographs accompanying the article showed an elegant stone house in the Jacobean style, with mullioned windows and graceful proportions. The gardens are mature, lush and well tended. The manor looks as though it had stood undisturbed in its idyllic location for centuries. In fact, explained *Country Life*, the house had only just been completed by the architect Detmar Blow, whose previous work in Wiltshire had

A pen-and-ink sketch of Edward Grey addressing the House of Commons during the first phase of his political career, sometime in the 1880s or 1890s. Despite being a dilettante undergraduate who managed only a third-class degree from Oxford (referred to both at the time and still as a "gentleman's first," meaning little work has been done), Grey became the youngest MP in the House of Commons when in 1885 he was elected as the Liberal candidate for Berwick-upon-Tweed, the Northern constituency that borders Scotland. He professed an ambivalence towards politics, but within less than a decade, Grey had a post in Government as Under-Secretary of State for Foreign Affairs. Within two decades, he was himself Foreign Secretary in Henry Campbell-Bannerman's Liberal government of 1905, a post he held for eleven years.

included the underpinning of the East Knoyle church tower some years before.

Wilsford's foundation stone had been laid by Madeline Wyndham in 1904. Two years later, the house was complete. The house, from birth, bore the patina of age It had been built using local labor, sand from a paddock two fields away, and all the stone of the small farmhouse that had originally stood on the spot. In the course of digging the foundations, the remnants of an Elizabethan stone-and-flint wall and fragments of old mullions had been discovered, suggesting that a grander house had preceded the farmhouse. Pamela had not been surprised. The beauty of the garden, with its yew hedges and great ilex trees, had always seemed more appropriate for a larger house. The fragments of stone and glass were incorporated into the new building. In the digging, the builders had also discovered boar tusks, a few "trifling coins" and numerous fossils, called locally "Shepherd's Crowns." Pamela would take the name for the title of one of her books.

To the side of the "Jacobean" main building was a long, low cottage-like nursery wing with thatched roof. It overlooked on one side a court-yard with a large old tree in its center, and on the other side the bowling green and lawns. At its far end was the "Stone Parlour," a room open on three sides to the elements, and furnished like a cottage kitchen with scrubbed pine table and dresser, where Pamela sat with her children to draw, play, paint and write, drinking in the sweeping views over the lawns down to the river Avon, which ran through Wilsford's grounds. As far as the eye could see, the land belonged to the Tennants.

The gardens were Wilsford's true glory, and the same process of strenuous preservation had taken place there in order to fit the ancient hedges and trees to the new house in the best way. Pamela described the process vividly to Wilfrid Blunt:

> transplanting enormous bushes & moving trees—Napoleonic measures in horticulture . . . You see my great desire has been to avoid, in our new building, the sight of bare walls. So to ensure this I have had the great big creepers moved, last autumn, & arranged onto poles, or racks (if they were voluminous) to support them. Then up went the walls, & then in March (when roses may wander) they were cautiously laid against the walls again—& there they now stand—vines, reaching to above the first floor—& roses topping the string course! My Delight! . . . well, I had one rose wheeled slowly up in a barrow by a stout gardener, three men holding her [the rose's] hair up in its wake, & staggering so you can imagine it has been worth doing.

Those Napoleonic efforts had paid off. The gardens photographed by *Country Life* are verdant. A plate illustrating "The House and Bowling Green" shows mature yew hedges and an ancient tree under which sit two small figures in wicker chairs: Pamela and a schoolgirl Clare, enjoying the peace of the garden so recently created—in Pamela's words, "a rambling farmhouse garden that has never been spoiled, and some yew hedges of a noble size."

While browsing through a little bookshop in London, Pamela had discovered a sundial, lying on its side in two pieces almost hidden away under dust and cobwebs, obscuring the words "come light visit me" inscribed on its dial. She restored it, and placed it in the garden: "So, there now it stands: 'where leaves spread out their budding fan to catch the balmy air' . . . I feel [it] is enjoying itself out in the open once more," Pamela told the curator Sidney Cockerell, erstwhile apprentice of Philip Webb, now the director of the Fitzwilliam Museum in Cambridge, and one of Pamela's many adoring acolytes.

It was a very large "Family Cottage" indeed, but Wilsford reflected Pamela and Eddy's aversion to ostentation. "I want to be heard if I shout for my boots," said Eddy. The Tennants employed surprisingly few staff—a collection of maids supplemented by help from the local village—although there were eighteen gardeners for the grounds. The house was furnished elegantly and comfortably, and was papered with Morris prints; its interior bore the marks of the Arts and Crafts movement, with finely turned wooden balustrades flanking wide staircases. Visiting Wilsford almost twenty years after it had been built, Cecil Beaton, a friend of Stephen Tennant's, and then just beginning to make his name as a photographer, recorded "a large long oak room, very comfortable and informal with enormous soft chairs, bowls of fat hyacinths, freesia & a lovely untidy litter of books." A profusion of bird cages was hung along the walls and the house, as always, was massed with the fresh flowers Pamela loved: she had named each bedroom after her favorites: Celandrine, Jessamine, Hyacinth. As at Clouds, guests often found, beside their beds, books specially ordered for them, but "life at Wilsford was not luxurious at all—it was comfortable, yes—but no luxury," said Susan Lowndes, daughter of Pamela's friend the novelist Marie Belloc Lowndes and her journalist husband, Frederick, and a frequent visitor to the Tennants.

Wilsford was not a political house *per se,* but most of its literary guests reflected a strongly imperialist view, including Arthur Conan Doyle, author of the *Sherlock Holmes* books, the poet Henry Newbolt (whose most famous work demanded that young men fighting in defense of the Empire "Play up! Play up! And play the game!") and the newspaper magnate Lord Northcliffe, as the *Daily Mail*'s Alfred Harmsworth had become. Another frequent visitor was a near neighbor, the spiritualist and physicist Oliver Lodge. Invasion scares were moving from fantasy literature to the front page. It was the age of the "dreadnoughts"—as England and Germany raced to build the behemoths introduced by Jackie Fisher that rendered all other battleships obsolete—and of a corresponding realignment of foreign policy by Edward Grey as Britain entered into ententes with France and Russia.

George—a frequent and honored guest at Wilsford—was fast becoming a figurehead of the naval lobby, coining the memorable phrase in respect of dreadnoughts at a by-election in Wigan, Greater Manchester, in 1908, where he was supporting the local Unionist candidate: "We

want eight and we won't wait!" His support for tariff reform, once tentative, was now ardent, even as Balfour refused to move beyond his cautious position. George had ostensibly recovered from his crisis of 1904,
but something had cut loose. He returned to the backbenches in 1906
"an incorrigible Tory!" glad to have "shed our Financiers and Brewers"
(signifying the new money he now despised) and eager to fight for "the
Church," "the Realm" and "the Empire of the English." He allied with
Marie's writer brother Hilaire Belloc over a mutual hatred of the "cor-
rupting influences" of "Levantine finance" and the plutocracy, and displayed an overt anti-Semitism hitherto no more pronounced than that
casually expressed by the rest of his class. Balfour laughed off George's
new stridency. Wilfrid Blunt found his cousin's alteration of character
repugnant. Pamela thought nothing of it. In her eyes George was a poet,
and a poet he remained.

Margot Asquith—a less welcome family member—made her first visit
to Wilsford in July 1906. She had to admit that the house was "perfectly
lovely," although she took pleasure in pointing out the impracticality
of the thatch on the nursery wing. It was "charming from the outside
[but] I cd hardly sleep for thinking of the heat of Clare's bedroom over
the kitchen," she noted in her diary. Relations between the sisters-in-law
remained strained. In 1903, Pamela had scored a palpable hit with an
allegorical short story, "in which Margot figures as a princess in a glass
house, herself as a beetle beloved by God, and my father [Asquith] as a
Muscovy duck . . ." Margot's stepson Raymond wrote in his diary, anticipating with interest a visit by the Tennants to the Asquiths at the Wharf,
their countryside residence in Sutton Courtenay, Berkshire. Yet the two
couples were tied closer than ever since the Bart's death, which left Eddy
in the peculiar position of holding the Chancellor of the Exchequer's
purse strings. Margot's marriage settlement had provided that she would
receive £3,000 per annum while her father was alive, £1,000 per annum
after his death. The loss of income hit the Asquiths hard, particularly
as Asquith's political duties became more pressing, and Margot's bridge
habit became more expensive. In 1919, Eddy estimated that he had given
Margot, by way of loans and extensions, around £25,000 in excess of her
allowance (well over a million dollars in today's money) since the Bart
had died.

Margot took the opportunity of her visit to draw a character sketch
of Pamela in her diary: "remarkably clever & very beautiful. Charm-

"Glen."

(Sir Edward Tennant.)

Eddy Tennant in his late forties or early fifties, caricatured in *Vanity Fair* shortly after he succeeded to his father's title of Baronet upon the Bart's death in 1906, becoming Sir Edward Tennant. This was before Eddy reluctantly accepted the title of Baron (or "Lord") Glenconner in 1911. As head of the Tennant family, Eddy commanded an impressive and international business empire as well as being the subject of requests by his siblings for money. Yet as the simple caption to this caricature demonstrates—the single word "Glen"—all who knew Eddy knew that his heart lay on the vast Scottish estate where he had grown up.

ing with other people's children & a wonderful mother herself but she lacks nature & humanness . . . she has not felt anything very deeply yet, she has always controlled her own destiny . . . She is not a citizen of the world . . . she lives in an adoring, uncritical milieu . . ." She thought that Pamela, "self-scanned and self-secure," would get "more heart when her own has been squeezed." Pamela often defended herself against accusations of remoteness, claiming that it was simply shyness. But her frostiness towards Margot stemmed from dislike, as Margot well knew.

Margot's sketch had much truth to it. Pamela surrounded herself with acolytes, whether family or minor literary figures. Her papers are crammed with their missives: breathless pages from Wommy declaring undying devotion; paeans from F. W. Bain, best-selling author of the fantasy *A Digit of the Moon* (which he claimed he had translated from ancient Sanskrit manuscripts but in fact had made up himself), addressing her as "Shri," the beautiful, sensuous princess heroine of one of his tales; a declaration from Sidney Cockerell that to him and Bain Pamela was "a Great Golden apple out of reach on the topmost bough." One of the more intriguing is a folded scrap of almost translucent paper covered in tiny penciled handwriting. It was written by an admirer in the gods at Covent Garden's Opera House watching Pamela in a box below. The author tracks her every move: her anxious studying of the program; fiddling with her glove and bracelet; her asides to the man beside her; the expressions fleeting across her face as the violinist played on. Pamela looked tired and lost in thought, thought her correspondent, who, presumably having tightly folded up this love letter, pressed it into her gloved palm as they met briefly in the buzzing, brightly lit foyer before going their separate ways. The signature on it is almost illegible, but appears to read "Sholto"—possibly Sholto Johnstone Douglas, a Queensberry cousin to whom Pamela was close.

To all these people, Pamela played the great lady, bestowing upon them the gift of her company. Most of them rhapsodized in turn about Wilsford's perfect simplicity. Pamela instructed her staff to give food and alms to vagrants so that in their underworld Wilsford would earn a reputation as a "safe house." She welcomed into the house Bim's troop of "village boys," sending off to Hamleys on Regent Street, London's most famous toy store, for quantities of cardboard armor and toy pistols for their games. She took her children on overnight excursions across the Downs in a colorful Gypsy caravan, burning sausages and pigeons that her children had shot over a campfire and singing them to sleep with folk ballads on her guitar. She entertained parties of youths, sending them off, with the caravan carrying their bedding, to sleep at Stonehenge overnight. She had a pet bullfinch, Chuffy, who sat on her dressing table whistling a tune she had taught him, and who tried to drink her diamond earrings, thinking them "water-drops."

The flip side is the many contemporary anecdotes that show Pamela in the worst possible light. Marie Belloc Lowndes recounted in her memoirs a dinner party at Queen Anne's Gate at which Eddy remarked to the assembled company in "quiet measured tones" that he could not conceive what jealousy might feel like. Pamela, perceiving the comment as a slur upon herself, fled into the garden, pacing up and down and sobbing in full view while her uncomfortable guests continued eating inside. Marie's daughter Susan recounted as a child at Wilsford catching sight through an open doorway of Pamela lying on the floor, literally bit-

Pamela, once again in white, offers a photographer a challenging gaze. She appears to be wearing the diamond earrings her pet bullfinch Chuffy once tried to drink.

ing the carpet in fury. In family legend, as recorded in memoirs written by her descendants, she has become little more than a narcissistic horror, spoiled, demanding, vain and destructive—a woman who, if she felt she was receiving insufficient attention, would rise from the table and implacably face the wall; who asked Eddy to remove the motto "Charles Tennant & Co., Chemical Manufacturers" emblazoned on the walls of Glasgow's Central Station, disliking this public reminder of the family's trade roots; and who so frightened her husband that he never charged her directly with her extravagance, but asked the company secretary to drop a gentle hint about her overspending.

Charlie Tennant, who became one of Pamela's protégés, was the recipient of the best of her nature. Her letters to him are honest, thoughtful and humorous. She fretted about his happiness while working for the family company (she feared he was "the square peg in a round hole, in Glasgow!"), made efforts to match him with "pretty girls," inviting him to attend the Peebles Ball with her goddaughter "Pammy" Adeane, and told him of the time that someone had asked her the date of Easter that year and she, lost in thought, had answered, "Oh, about the 18th or 19th of *Wilsford* I believe!" As with all her closest friends, it was a rare letter from Pamela that did not contain some discussion of her current reading, from the popular novelist Mrs. Humphry Ward ("[she] has a suburban way of describing life that doesn't hold one") to Gibbon's *Decline and Fall,* which Edward Grey had read aloud at Fallodon (she found getting her mind around Gibbon's complex sentences like trying to span the girth of an enormous tree: "You feel you can't quite get round it, or if you do, it is only *just* done").

TWENTY-FIVE

Mr. Balfour's Poodle

On a summer's morning at Stanway, in July 1907, Mary was bearded in her bedroom by a furious Hugo. Once again he charged her with excessive socializing, this time on behalf of their children, and expressed the hope "that the result of our dinners etc. will not be a double marriage, Violet [Manners]–Ego, Cynthia–Beb [Asquith]," adding "that Cynthia spends all her nights with Beb at balls, and that V. and B. both look very second rate and that he's going to tell Cynthia and Ego so—this is the really worrying thing," Mary reported to Arthur. The Duchess of Rutland (as Violet Granby had become) had a trio of daughters, known as "the Hothouse" for the highly strung fascination they exerted over men. The second of the three, Lady Violet "Letty" Manners, married Ego in 1911. Cincie and Beb, Asquith's taciturn second son by his first marriage, were already secretly engaged.

The children of the Souls, all well known to one another, were approaching maturity. They gave themselves the name of "the Coterie"— later renaming themselves "the Corrupt Coterie" as a mark of defiance. Mary's children were all, by their birth, part of the Coterie, although some had mixed feelings about it. Mary's three eldest were now young adults. The twenty-two-year-old Ego, recently graduated from Oxford, was "rather a darling," quietly humorous and diffident, and still politically naïve enough to have been devastated at Arthur Balfour's apparent

Mary and Hugo Elcho's eldest daughter, twenty-five-year-old Cincie, in 1912. A society beauty, Cincie had a keen interest in her own good looks (she agonized to her diary on the days when her face did not seem to be at its best) that was matched by her undoubted intelligence. In later life, she was a prolific and successful writer, renowned in particular for her blood-chilling ghost stories.

betrayal by his Manchester constituents in the elections of 1906. Mary wished he could spend more time talking to Arthur: "I should like him trained to be a good Unionist Conservative." Guy had suffered from his position as second son, and from the poor health he had endured since childhood. At Oxford he racked up large debts and barely scraped a third. Mary worried that whenever he was in a position of tension or stress he might "crack up" under the strain.

Cincie had an alien beauty, with wide-set eyes, and a razor-sharp intelligence left entirely unhoned by her education. Mary, with much agonizing, had dispatched the intellectual Miss Jourdain in 1896. She feared that Miss J's intense Catholicism was making Cincie overly religious, and was unnerved by the governess's own emotional attachment to Mary herself. She replaced her with Fräulein Moskowitz, a "dear, bird-witted little Viennese," known as "Squidge" for her resemblance to a squirrel. The expectation for Cincie was that she would "marry a country house," in the terminology of their set (meaning, marry an heir to a large estate, preferably titled), but while in Dresden, aged sixteen, she had met Beb Asquith, and in the two years since had appeared totally uninterested in any other man.

Cynthia's apparently inexplicable determination to be with the silent Beb placed Mary in a quandary. She found chaperoning a challenge—

"even if one is at the balls oneself . . . one cannot see what is going on," she said—and felt "low and rather helpless" in trying to determine ". . . how much to meddle? . . . Our system is confused and illogical. I dare say general results work out the same! whatever systems!!" she lamented to Arthur. Lord Wemyss—who, as head of the family, would determine what marriage settlement his granddaughter Cynthia would receive—was fiercely opposed to Beb because he was a Liberal. Mary and Hugo's objection was that Beb lacked the qualities needed to make a success of himself. Mary's duty as a mother was to see her daughter well provided for by marriage financially, as well as emotionally. Finding that balance was the alchemy.

Mary's visits to Gosford were normally spent trying to avoid lectures from her octogenarian father-in-law on the subject either of her children or of Arthur's leadership of the Unionist Party, both of which Lord Wemyss felt were being seriously mishandled. Mary found the former particularly enervating given Hugo's own conduct. "My children are *not* immaculate," Mary told Arthur with force, "but they have some conscientious feelings, they are warm-hearted, friendly, and essentially domestic. They love being at home, they do not remember always but they would be grieved at distressing one and would shut a door to please one and do tiresome things occasionally because they feel them to be right and they *want* to please one . . ." The comparison was pointed. Neither Hugo's gambling nor his infidelities had improved. A recent visit to the Devonshires at Chatsworth, when Mary had tried to befriend Hugo's latest mistress, twenty-five-year-old Peggy, Countess of Crewe (a daughter of Lord Rosebery's), had been a disaster. A horrified Hugo tried to freeze Mary out. "I ask you a perfectly harmless question—you jump as if you were shot, I come near yr room & you look at me as if I were a poisonous snake," wrote Mary afterwards in reproof. "I had really far rather that you spent the whole of every night with P. & behaved in a decent friendly way to me all day . . . but you are so aloof, so strange, so suspicious, so on wires—that you really make me inclined to . . . tell you that I think you an ass! . . . why should being pro her make you anti me?" Undaunted, Mary continued to offer quasi-maternal advice. "You exaggerate each other's peculiarities," she said, encouraging Hugo to "steady" the spoiled, witty, headstrong Peggy.

In the autumn of 1907 Mary took Ego and Cincie to Italy, hoping that with Beb "out of sight, out of mind" Cincie's infatuation would cease.

A photographic portrait of Percy Wyndham in his mid-fifties. As he grew ever more despairing about the direction of public life, Percy turned Clouds into his own personal fiefdom. He was particularly fond of putting up signs over the house and grounds, forbidding guests and family from minor infractions, such as leaving a door ajar.

The trip was exhilarating. "One . . . gets to know one's children more in 20 days in these circs than in many months at home," Mary told Arthur, although ". . . I feel rather as if my brain were lined with frescoes upon frescoes . . . and my mind is a jumble of Tuscan, Romanesque Gothic style!" On Mary's return she went to Birmingham, in the Midlands, to listen to Arthur address the annual conference of the National Union of Conservative Associations on party unity over tariff reform. She had not heard Arthur speak publicly for some time and thought it "*excellent*": touching his "top level qua 'platform speech,'" but she knew that "human nature is alas! silly and small," and that people would continue to think that Arthur, by not taking a firm position on the issue, was Chamberlain's puppet, trying to lay the ground for the party's adoption of the policy in due course.

Balfour's main political role in opposition, however, consisted of employing his Unionist majority in the Lords to filibuster the social reforms of CB's Liberal ministry. "New Liberalism," as it was called, was a scheme of social reform by which the state took unprecedented responsibility for the welfare of its people. In fact, due partly to internal divisions in the party, the reforms put forward between 1906 and 1908 were prosaic, focusing on implementing stricter liquor-licensing laws and reducing state funding of church schools: issues close to every Liberal's heart. Still Balfour's Lords filibustered every measure of any significance: killing them outright, or wrecking them with amendments so that the measures were "stripped and wounded and left half dead" as Lloyd George, now President of the Board of Trade, said bitterly of the mangled 1906 Education Bill. In 1906, Percy had gloomily asked, "We are now just where we were in 1885 on the brink of Democracy, when Gladstone saved us for 20 years by jumping into Home Rule. What will save us now?" The answer, it seemed, was Balfour and his House of Lords.

Thwarted and frustrated, in March 1908 Campbell-Bannerman put before the Commons proposals for constitutional reform: making the Lords' outright veto merely suspensory and reducing parliamentary terms from seven years to five. The Unionists howled that the Upper House was the watchdog of the people. Lloyd George gave one of his memorable ripostes: "A mastiff? It is the right hon. Gentleman's [Balfour's] poodle. It fetches and carries for him. It barks for him. It bites anybody that he sets it on to." The Commons voted in favor of the reform, but within a month Campbell-Bannerman had resigned, and he died still in residence at 10 Downing Street, from where he had been too frail to be moved.

Asquith was finally in power, although in order to kiss hands (the term for the monarch's appointment of ministers to office) he had to cross the English Channel incognito by night train and ferry since Edward VII had refused to cut short his holiday with his mistress Mrs. Keppel in Biarritz, the French pleasure resort on the Atlantic coast popular for its bracing air, golf courses and casino. Asquith's advancement, however, did not improve his son's prospects so far as Hugo and Lord Wemyss were concerned. Far from it. Lord Wemyss fulminated against Asquith's final Budget as Chancellor, which introduced the "socialistic" measure of pensions for the elderly. Like many, Lord Wemyss thought this sneaky since, by convention, the Lords could not veto fiscal measures such as the budget. Otherwise, Balfour's Lords continued poodle-like, in 1908 alone rejecting or mutilating bills for licensing, education and town planning, and two Scottish measures concerning smallholders and land values.

Mary was still encouraging Cincie to meet "fresh people." In the spring of 1908, Cincie brought a baffled young admirer to Stanway, who encountered an otherwise middle-aged house party reveling into the small hours of the morning. It began at around midnight on Sunday, when after a long dinner and much talk, the party was seized by "a frenzy of song, dance and improvisation." Arthur Paget—"the Stanway Minstrel" (and Pamela's youthful suitor)—seized his guitar; the carpet was rolled back; George Wyndham spouted Virgil while somersaulting across the floor; the "Professor"—Sir Walter Raleigh—crowned by a wreath of roses, did the cakewalk with Cincie. The party spilled out into the garden to serenade Arthur Balfour (who had gone to bed some three or four hours before) at his window. "Mary—I must tell you—asked me to come 'and see her quiet home life': I have never heard, and rarely made, more noise before . . . A. Paget is a 'Pied Piper of Hamelin' . . . and we were rats who danced in time to his music," George told Percy as he made his way back to London.

In the spring of 1909, Wilsford village was "rocked & shaken" by the revelation that its new Canadian curate, "so excellent it seemed in every way," was a bigamist with a "very bad past." With the curate in a state of "breakdown" and his wife in "misery," Pamela took in their "poor little boy . . . to get him out of the poor mother's way . . . He is lying looking at picture books on the rug now," she told Charlie Tennant. Meanwhile, Mary and Cynthia were setting sail on the *Empress of Britain* for the curate's native land, Mary equipped with a new grey-squirrel fur coat bought in London on sale for thirty pounds to insulate herself against the cold. Ego, trying out a stint in the Foreign Office and now serving as a diplomatic attaché in Washington, D.C., was to join them as guests of Canada's Governor General, Earl Grey (a distant cousin of Edward Grey's), and his wife. Ostensibly, Mary was making the most of an opportunity to visit old friends. Privately, she made no bones about the real reason for the trip: "for Cynthia: general indefinable hope that change may be beneficial physically, mentally, spiritually," she told Arthur; or, as she put it more candidly to Hugo, to keep their daughter out of "the arms of Beb!" Uncharacteristically, they traveled in some style, securing a double-berthed suite with a private bath and parlor, at a cost of fifty pounds. An extra fourteen pounds allowed first-class servant accommodation for Mary's maid. "If we are ill the whole time and never sit in our parlor I shall die of disappointment at the money wasted, unless I die of sickness,' said Mary.

Mary found Canada exhilarating. She admired its pioneer spirit, relished the wild open spaces that reminded her of Cumberland, and enjoyed the fact that post, routed via New York, took several weeks to arrive. She could breakfast in peace without Squidge or Nanny appearing with tales of domestic disasters. Now that she was in her late forties, the freshness of Mary's youth was long behind her, but she had not yet earned the respect and dignity of "*extreme* old age." Yet local self-made eminences fell over themselves to praise her at Government House dinners (everyone, she told Hugo mockingly, appeared to be a baronet and she had never heard of any of them). Invigorated, she began devising unrealistic plans for the future: she wanted to send her sons to the Macdonald Institute, a new and innovative agricultural college; to return in the summer and explore the Rockies; perhaps even to invest in land. "If I were a man I'd settle there [in British Columbia] & buy a fruit farm—in fact if I'd any capital, I'd buy a small valley right away—*I wish you would,*" she told Hugo, adding, in a dangerous tactic that appealed to his worst nature, "the difference between what you have & *pay* & what you *get* is positively El-Doradoish."

Mary's plans for a leisurely trip, passing through New York on their way back to London (where Mary had already arranged a dinner with William Astor, the property magnate and newspaper proprietor) were thwarted. Barely a fortnight away, she received a telegram. Percy had fallen badly in the early hours of the previous morning and suffered a "seizure." A doctor and nurses were treating him at Clouds, Pamela and George were making their way there now. There was talk of "brain leakage": it is most likely that Percy had suffered a stroke.

Just days before, Percy had written a long and chatty letter to his eldest daughter. The Wyndhams had paid an enjoyable visit to Petworth, but were now both plagued by colds; an unexpectedly large snowfall had offered temporary employment to London poor as street sweepers; George Wyndham had given a Commons speech on tariff reform that people were saying was the best thing he had done in recent years. The *Evening Standard* reported that Balfour was giving the issue of protectionism serious consideration, and Percy thought that even Lloyd George and Winston Churchill seemed to be recognizing its benefits.

However, Percy was not feeling at his best. "I am coming to a theory as to the way in which man & woman grow old," he told his daughter, illustrating with a sketch:

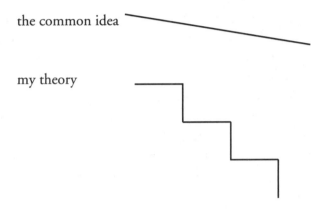

the common idea

my theory

Percy never really recovered from this first stroke, which was partly attributed to his splenetic anger over the direction of the country. Henceforth he was perpetually in the care of two nurses. His doctor banned him from any further public speaking on politics.

His resolve was immediately tested. On 29 April 1909, in a rambling four-hour speech Lloyd George, now Chancellor, introduced his first Budget: a "war budget" to "wage implacable warfare against poverty and squalidness." It introduced direct taxation on spirits, estates and higher incomes (a "supertax" of sixpence on the pound on incomes over £5,000 a year) and land taxes including a tax on the "unearned increment" of the value of land enhanced by the effort of the community. The landed classes saw it as a war on themselves. "This is not a Budget, but a revolution; a social and political revolution of the first magnitude" and "obviously intended as one," declared Lord Rosebery both from the crossbenches (the perpendicular benches in the Houses of Parliament where sat those who were neither supporters of the Government nor of the Opposition) and in *The Times*. He circulated among his Liberal League's executive body (a vehicle he founded to promulgate imperialist views) a fishing letter to see who might wish "to join a crusade against the Governments [*sic*] proposals if they knew that Lord Rosebery would lead the movement, and accept full official responsibility." Eddy Tennant and Edward Grey, both members, appear to have been tempted.

To join would be to break with the Government. They stopped short of that. But in a private letter to the league's secretary, Eddy's sympathy for Rosebery's position is clear enough. In an address delivered two days later at the National Liberal Club, Edward Grey defended the Budget inasmuch as he suggested that it was not quite the revolution Rosebery had claimed—but he did not directly endorse it.

For Unionist Mary, the Government had simply disgraced itself by allowing its policy to be dictated by "party enmity" while disregarding the country's wishes. Like Balfour, she thought the approach of dressing up a social measure in fiscal clothing was "unwise and dishonest" and constitutionally dangerous.

In the months that followed, Lloyd George did not trouble to conceal his contempt for the parasitical leisured classes. Yet his Budget seems primarily to have been expedient. The pension scheme had a £16 million shortfall; new social reforms required funding; local government was in financial crisis; naval expenditure was running out of control. If the Government could redistribute wealth at the same time as generating revenue, so be it.

Nonetheless, the Unionists could not stomach it. Yet all knew that if the Lords rejected the Budget, a constitutional crisis would ensue. The summer and autumn of 1909 were dominated by the issue. The undoubted star of the hustings was Lloyd George, addressing crowds of thousands. At Limehouse in East London in July he addressed his working-class audience on the landlord: "a gentleman . . . who does not earn his wealth. He has a host of agents and clerks that receive for him . . . He has a host of people around him to do the actual spending . . . His sole function, his chief pride, is the stately consumption of wealth produced by others." At Newcastle's Palace Theatre in October before another working-class audience he turned his guns on the peers of the realm. "'A fully-equipped duke costs as much to keep up as a couple of Dreadnoughts,' he said in the tone of one who is proposing a complimentary toast; 'and they are just as great a terror and last longer,' he added when the 4,000 had done laughing."

The genius of Lloyd George's rhetoric was the good humor with which he delivered his blows—but those blows were trenchant enough to prompt Edward VII to demand that Asquith control his excitable Chancellor; and for *The Times* to condemn the Chancellor for inciting class warfare—a demagogue, appealing only for "men who have the crude taste for ginger," more suited to the kind of soapbox oratory practiced at Speaker's Corner at Hyde Park or down the East End's Mile End Road (namely in Victoria Park, where public speakers on socialism included William Morris and the reformer Annie Besant). In fact, the tone of politics, gradually shifting since the Reform Acts of 1832 and 1867 and the legislation of 1884–85, had irrevocably changed. It was now impossible for a politician to make any kind of speech without "the constant expectation of interruption"—whether heckling or more aggressive interruption since the Women's Social and Political Union (known as the WSPU) had begun to employ violent tactics in its campaign for votes for women. At almost every venue at which Liberal ministers spoke over the summer and autumn, a jostling, heckling crowd of suffragists was massed outside. At Limehouse, a man wearing the WSPU's purple, white and green, was hauled down from a pillar by stewards and roughed up so badly by the crowd that he was hospitalized. In Newcastle, suffragists smashed all the Liberal Club's windows after a fracas with local youths. The next day, *The Times* looked back wistfully to days when political meetings required no more than a couple of policemen on the door: "The woman suffragists have changed all that. When a Cabinet Minister is announced to speak the local authorities close all the neighbouring streets to ordinary traffic, barricades are erected, and the county is scoured for extra police and quiet horses . . . no doubt, at a pretty cost to the ratepayers."

"I am very low about the future of this country and things generally. People are all on a wrong tack," Percy wrote to Mary at the year's end, in spidery writing noticeably shakier than the neat script that preceded his stroke. Mary was scarcely more cheerful. Her efforts to keep Cincie and Beb apart had failed. In October, Hugo got wind of the fact that the two had been seen together at a party organized by Letty Manners which Mary had chaperoned. Mary fought back:

Beb is very dogged & a hard worker . . . if money is to be confiscated from the "leisure" classes—it will be better for Cynthia to marry, a man with grit who is hardworking & able to *make* money than a member of the aristocracy of the Charteris type (yr sons)—you say everyone has to make money nowadays—Beb is about the only man she knows who seems able and willing to do so.

Mary timed her defense well. On 4 November 1909, after seventy days of parliamentary debate and 554 divisions (the Commons votes on an issue by "dividing": physically going into two different areas on either side of the House), the Budget passed its last stages in the House of Commons by 379 votes to 149. Three weeks later the Lords rejected it by 350 votes to 75. The Radical *Daily News* fired red rockets into the London sky in anticipation of the battle to come. The first skirmish was just days later, on 2 December. By the early afternoon the House of Commons was packed, with not a single vacant seat on the floor, the strangers' galleries full to overflowing and peers spilling over their reserved spaces into the side galleries. "One saw on every side rows upon rows of eager, attentive faces . . . mindful of the great issues at stake," reported *The Times*. Asquith entered the Chamber just after 3 p.m., and shortly afterwards was followed by Balfour, to cheering from his backbenchers because he had been ill and it had been feared he might not attend.

The debate itself was short, barely two and a half hours. To lusty support from the Government side, Asquith declared that the Commons would be betraying its heritage and traditions were it to brook such interference and usurpation for another day. Balfour "taunted the Government on having a perfect passion for these motions, which bound no one, hurt no one, probably encouraged no one, and certainly frightened no one." By 349 to 134 the measure was carried that the peers' action was "a breach of the constitution and an usurpation of the rights of the Commons." The House adjourned at twenty-five to six. Asquith went to the King, who, at his Prime Minister's request, dissolved Parliament, and a general election was announced for January 1910.

TWENTY-SIX

1910

In January and again in December 1910 the politicians went to the people, the elections bracketing a summer of secret talks between the party leaders as they tried to find a solution to the growing constitutional crisis. The January electoral campaign was twenty-six days in total—the longest in political history. Hugo threw himself into it, passionately advocating tariff reform on hustings from nearby Tewkesbury in the Cotswolds to Doncaster in South Yorkshire and haring from London's Chelsea to Stanway, then to Peebles over three days so as to cast his ballot in all his different constituencies. It seemed as though everyone had become politicized: Nanny Cliffe had manifested herself as "a great politician—hates Mr. Asquith & longs for Mr. Balfour to come in again." To Mary's distinct amusement, it appeared that her chauffeur, Turner, was a "socialist": "While Ego & I went up the hill [near Stanway] & were talking Tariff Reform inside the farms—we came out & found that Turner was having an impromptu meeting on the road! & doubtless more than neutralizing any results we may have achieved!"

Asquith had made it clear that, if reelected, his party intended to address the Lords' veto with constitutional reform, which everyone understood would seek to reduce the current powers of the upper House. As the election results came in, Mary was hopeful: "Things look healthier . . ." she told her father, "if only we can keep on at this rate—both sides may end up even—they will then be dependent upon the [Irish] nationalists who hate me budget and altogether their claws will be well cut & I think on the whole it's the best thing that can happen *just now* & Free Trade will be pretty well dead . . ." The night before, she had been seated by the King at a dinner for his brother the Duke of Connaught. The atmosphere was "amusing . . . [for] of course the King has to affect a kind of neutrality . . . yet all the time one knew that feeling was running high & everyone was acutely excited." Throughout dinner Edward VII received telegrams with the latest results from the constituencies. "All the Peers' eldest sons are being returned," he commented, which Mary took to "express . . . his relief . . . [I] think he begins to feel that the Gov. miscalculated the real feeling of the *Country* (whatever *party* feelings may have been) when they made such a fuss about the Lords—& I think the King must feel relieved for he was very agitated at one time."

In the final tally the two parties were almost exactly equal: Liberals 274, Unionists, 272. Eighty-odd Irish and forty Labour MPs held the balance of power. Eddy Tennant was one of over one hundred Liberal MPs to lose their seats. When Pamela expressed disappointment, Mary gave her short shrift. Salisbury was "a conservative town, if ever there was one," and besides, "Eddy . . . hates practically everything that this Gov. has done & he ought to be on his proper side or none at all." The Budget had been mandated, but only just. The country was uncertain. For Percy this simply proved how ill suited the masses were to make decisions about the future of their country: "Power has been taken from those who should hold power . ." he said, blaming patrician and upper-middle-class "vote hunting." Once again, he predicted the death of his class. "When the country has gone into the melting pot an aristocracy or governing Class call it what you will will arise, but it will arise from Trade and Commerce and our lineal successors are not likely to be among them. The grandsons of the Labour members more likely," he told Mary. George had a "splendid majority" and returned to Parliament, guns blazing, ready for an Armageddon-like battle to the death. Edward VII made almost straight for Biarritz. The Budget was passed without division by the Lords at the end of April.

In March, fearful of approaching Hugo, Beb Asquith had taken the unusual step of discussing his financial prospects with Mary. He had earned £800 in the past year, and his father had promised him £600 a year more—a sum he knew was "*most* moderate" but hoped might be "*just* possible." Mary was still concerned. Violet Rutland had just written her a "frantic private letter" revealing that her son John, now Marquess of Granby and heir to the Dukedom of Rutland, "admires C. much (great compliment for them to want a pauper!) and begging me to stem the Beb tide." A future Duke was a fine prize indeed, but Mary knew where her daughter's heart lay. She had long talks with George along "the 'Riviera,'" Clouds' river walk, "about Nyncie [*sic*] and Beb where they 'argued all about it and about' . . ." But she was instinctively sympathetic to the determined young lovers: "I do think that if poor old Squith [*sic*] can allow 600 it's awfully shabby if the Earl [of Wemyss] cannot give another 600. But his bitter politics will make him mad."

Weeks later, Asquith threw down the gauntlet with his Parliament Bill, which proposed to replace the Lords' absolute veto with a suspensory one—and removed the veto entirely on fiscal measures. As he introducted it to the Commons, he gave two alternatives. The Lords could pass it, castrating themselves, or they could veto it, in which case he would seek an immediate dissolution and recommend that the royal prerogative be used to create enough new peers to secure its passage.

In fact, unbeknown to all but Edward VII's private secretary Lord Knollys, the Archbishop of Canterbury (the senior bishop of the Church of England) and Balfour, there was another option. At a secret meeting between the three at the Archbishop's official residence, Lambeth Palace, which lay just over the Thames from Westminster, Balfour had indicated that he might be willing to form a government if necessary. Knollys told Edward VII of Balfour's offer in early May. The next day, history "rattled over the traces" with the King's sudden death. His son and successor, the forty-four-year-old George V, was politically naïve and totally ill equipped to deal with a crisis Asquith deemed "without example in our constitutional history." On hearing the news of the King's death Asquith, on board an Admiralty yacht nearing the Bay of Biscay, between France and Spain, was "bewildered . . . indeed stunned" by this terrible turn. He went up on deck to see Halley's Comet blazing in the night sky, a grave omen.

Edward VII's death flung the country into mourning—it was the summer of the famous "Black Ascot," when Society turned out to the races in funereal dress—and provoked the two parties to seek a resolution to the brewing crisis. Over the course of the summer eight senior Unionists and Liberals, including Balfour, Asquith and Lloyd George,

Cincie Charteris on her wedding day to Bob Asquith with her sisters and bridesmaids, fifteen-year-old Mary Charteris (seated to Cincie's left) and eight-year-old Bibs (on floor). The beleaguered look on Bibs's face suggests their mother's "quasi-greek" creations by way of bridmaids' dresses and gladioli bouquets may have been rather too much for her.

met more than twenty times in "constitutional conference." The fact of their meetings was public; everything else was secret, and the subject of frantic press speculation.

By the time of Cincie and Beb's wedding—held at Holy Trinity Church in Sloane Street, Chelsea, on 28 July 1910—tensions were such that guests arriving at the church were asked by ushers "Unionist or Liberal?" and seated accordingly. Mary, inspired by dancers she had seen at a show at the London Hippodrome (the popular West End variety theater), had designed the bridesmaids' dresses: "quasi-greek" drapery with belts of fine gold braid, and red gladioli in their arms—an "authorized classical style," she told Hugo, anticipating criticism. She emphasized that she had not gone for the full fashion, which involved a rope tied around the ankles: "It is too ugly the fat bridesmaids would look like tubs," she said, illustrating her words with a sketch—doleful tub next to her reed-like counterpart, the latter waving her gladioluses in triumph. The following summer, Balfour was amused to be asked by one concerned hostess whether he would object to being at a dinner where

Cincie and Beb were present. Mary's early fears about the match proved
sadly well founded. By the 1920s, with Beb debilitated by shell shock
and alcoholism, Cynthia was more or less singlehandedly supporting
their family as private secretary to the celebrated playwright J. M. Barrie
(author of *Peter Pan*) and what she could earn as a freelance writer.

Percy and Madeline Wyndham celebrated their golden wedding at
Clouds in October. Only Mananai was absent, from illness. They held
a large, celebratory tea as was customary and were presented with gifts
from their tenantry and East Knoyle's schoolchildren. In 1904, Percy
had commissioned the rising young Irish portraitist William Orpen to
paint both their portraits. Now a series of photographs taken in front of
Clouds' great doorway marked the occasion. In one, Percy and Madeline
stand, strangely formal, shaking hands, a curious dachshund by Madeline's feet. In another, seated, they gaze at each other, Percy clutching
a cane, Madeline swathed in shawls, her hand to her throat. Fifty years
after they had married, the Wyndhams' relationship was still strong.
Madeline's past infidelities never diminished Percy's devotion.

Although dapper as ever in these portraits, Percy's health was slipping.
He complained to Webb of "various distressing infirmities." He was
consumed by anxiety at the direction of the country, his class's apparently firm foundations turning to quicksand before his eyes. Had he
known of the "secret understanding" which George V "reluctantly" gave
Asquith in November, Percy would have been more splenetic still. In
November, Asquith told George V that the only solution to the deadlock
was Parliament's dissolution and a general election on the question of
constitutional reform. He extracted from his King the promise that if
the Liberals won that election, George V would use his prerogative (the
royal powers which may be exercised by the monarch alone, but usually
upon advice from his ministers) "to make Peers if asked for": ennoble
as many government supporters as would be necessary to pass the Bill.
Without that guarantee, Asquith told him, he and his entire Cabinet
would resign at once.

It was a shocking proposition, though not surprising in the circumstances. Faced with this ultimatum, fearful of the idea of debasing the
peerage in this way, George V sought the advice of his secretary Knollys.
Knollys, who had never told George V of Balfour's offer the previous
spring (presumably fearing that the novice King might accept it) now
assured him (with no evidence that this was the case) that Balfour would

One of a series of photographs taken at Clouds in October 1910 to commemorate the fiftieth wedding anniversary of Percy and Madeline Wyndham. Their marriage had survived Madeline Wyndham's long-ago infidelities. Together they had built a dynasty and a family seat to honor it.

decline to form a government. He told him that George V's only option was to give Asquith the guarantee and, crucially, that he would have given the same advice to Edward VII, who would have taken it. Coerced and deceived, George V reluctantly assented. "I disliked having to do this very much, but agreed that this was the only alternative to the Cabinet resigning, which at this moment would be disastrous," he explained to his diary on 16 November 1910.

The campaign itself was muted. Lloyd George did his best to keep the fires of class enmity burning, revisiting Limehouse to liken the aristocracy to cheese ("the older it is the higher it becomes"). At a convention held at the Royal Albert Hall, Balfour appeared to move slightly from the fence on tariff reform by announcing that he had no "objection" to a referendum on the matter—immediately alienating tariff reformers, who were furious that he would not adopt it outright. By and large apathy reigned. Candidates rehashed speeches made just a few months before. Poor weather kept people indoors. One-sixth of the men who had voted in January—over a million in all—declined to do so in December. The results, after a year of haggling, debating and gambling, were near identical. The Unionists had lost one seat, the Liberals three, and the Irish Nationalists and Labour Party each gained two. As Christmas approached, Percy wrote to Mary in anticipation of his daughter's visit to Clouds: "Arthur is very welcome here especially if accompanied by yourself. The door is closed to Socialists, Fabians or other and I cannot say Radicals are welcome unless near connections by marriage," he added meaningfully.

TWENTY-SEVEN

Revolution?

O
n Monday, 13 March 1911, Percy died in his bedroom at Clouds. He had been declining for days. His wife and four of his five children were with him; only Guy, summoned by telegram back from St. Petersburg, where he was military attaché, did not arrive in time. Percy's children agreed that their father was "absolutely himself to the very end . . . his mind clear as crystal." His friends were saddened, but not surprised. His frailty had been apparent at his last social appearance, Ego Charteris's wedding to Letty Manners the month before.

Percy, whose religious faith had wavered ever since he had read Darwin as a young man, appeared to have had some sort of deathbed enlightenment. "'God' *revealed* himself to Percy & gave him such a vision OF LOVE & HAPPINESS & glory that I can never forget it," Madeline Wyndham told Wilfrid Blunt. Her ardent polyglot faith gave her comfort. "The feeling that He *has left us,* never makes me *unhappy,* not half as unhappy as seeing Him suffering & *miserable Here*—that was *wretchedness*," she told Mary some six months later from Clouds as she passed her first birthday for fifty years without her husband on "a Heavenly day almost too Hot with a Peacock with head turned up to heaven piercing the air with his Cries."

Percy's body was cremated at Woking, in Surrey, just outside London, where the country's first crematorium had been in operation for around thirty years. His ashes were placed in an oak casket made from trees grown on the estate and buried after a funeral held at East Knoyle church on Saturday, 18 March, marked by a green sandstone cross. Percy's obituaries mourned the passing of the last of an age: an independent-minded aristocrat serving through paternalistic rule. Pamela immediately placed an order with the milliners Maison St. Louis in London's Halkin Street (a stone's throw from Belgrave Square) for a black straw quatre coin with chiffon veil, a coarse black straw and feather toque with veil, a widow's hat with crêpe veil, two chiffon hats, a black tagel picture hat with grey feather mount, a mercury in black straw-lined velvet with velvet trimming, and a grey straw with velvet lining and grey wing—£26 16s. 6d., in total.

Percy's estate was valued at £241,162 gross. He left Madeline Wyndham a lifetime interest in 44 Belgrave Square, his household effects and her jewelry, all to revert to George on her death. She received absolutely a lump sum of £1,000 and an annuity of £3,100 and his horses, carriages, personal effects and "consumable stores." Guy received £5,000 and a further annuity of £850 during his mother's lifetime. Percy's daughters received nothing—nor did Dorothy Carleton (on whom he had intended to settle £300)—for all, so he wrote in his will, were sufficiently provided for by settlement. The governess Bun received £100, so did Percy's land agent Edward Miles. Various other members of staff received small bequests. Everything else went to George. Increasingly, Madeline Wyndham divided her time between Clouds, Stanway, Babraham and Wilsford, a shawl-clad, mob-capped expansive figure, beloved of her grandchildren, known to them as "Gan-Gan" (the name has been passed down, and Madeline's female descendants are still known to their grandchildren by the same title).

George turned his substantial energy towards making his own mark upon Clouds. He arranged for electricity to be installed, and commissioned Detmar Blow to turn the old nursery into a large library for himself. The now redundant lamp room was made into a chapel for Sibell, paneled in old Italian dark wood with a redbrick floor and an arching whitewashed ceiling overhead. George assumed with relish, and somewhat ostentatious humility, the role of squire for which he had been preparing all his life: "All the work I have to do here only increases—if that were possible—my deep respect for his [Percy's] definite character and my admiration of his justice and generosity," he wrote to a friend. For the present, his full energies were focused on securing the future of his class.

For almost two decades the Souls had managed to separate politics from friendship. In 1900, Arthur had written to Mary recounting a heated "passage of arms" with Asquith in the Commons over Irish landlords, which took place directly after Arthur had dined with the Asquiths: "Asquith was the challenger, but I felt a mild awkwardness replying to a man on the strength of his own champagne!" Now the situation was forcing underhand behavior. In January 1911, Arthur dined with Lord Knollys and fell into the trap of giving him his views on the constitutional position and the creation of peers, not knowing either of the secret guarantee or that Knollys had promised Asquith to report back on the dinner. At the same time, Margot, who almost certainly had some idea of the guarantee, was leading Mary astray. Visiting her at Gosford, she came to her room for a talk after tea. While claiming to know no real details, she urged magnanimity from the Unionists with regard to the Parliament Bill about to be put before the Commons. As Mary wrote to Arthur:

> She was practically making a great appeal to "trust Henry" . . . I said but supposing we are disposed to trust Henry and accept the veto bill as the best way out, trusting to amendments and Henry's conscience or moderation, how can we tell that Henry would not be pushed much further than he wanted to go . . . She said Henry's not a bit afraid of his own party. She is horrified at the idea of having to create peers.

The Parliament Bill had its formal introduction to the Commons (known as the "first reading") on 22 February. During three readings over three months, nine hundred amendments were tabled—almost all from the Opposition—only the most minor of which succeeded. All knew that the real action was to come in the Lords, where a tribe of backwoods peers, who had never hitherto troubled the Upper House with their presence, were mustering under the leadership of their paradigm, Lord Willoughby de Broke. De Broke, a sporting peer from Warwickshire, has been described memorably by the historian George Dangerfield as being a man who "was not more than two hundred years behind his time." This reactionary force was given encouragement by more senior and serious politicians, including George Wyndham, Curzon and Lord Lansdowne, the Unionist Leader in the Lords.

It was shaping up to be a sweltering summer. George V's coronation, held on 22 June, was one of the few cool, cloudy days of the Season. Whenever he could, Balfour adopted flannels and straw hats; after work, Edward Grey and Winston Churchill splashed about in the marbled swimming baths at the private members' Automobile Club on Pall Mall. At a fancy-dress ball at Claridge's Hotel on London's Brook Street in Mayfair, given by Lord Winterton and the rising Unionist star F. E. Smith on 24 May, to general merriment Waldorf Astor, son of William Astor and a Unionist MP, appeared clad in a peer's robes of state and a tinsel coronet on which was balanced a placard: "499" read one side; STILL ONE MORE VACANCY read the other. Both Asquith and Balfour were present.

It was no laughing matter when the Lords massacred the Parliament Bill with amendments in July, and the news of the King's secret guarantee was finally leaked. It was a "shocking scandal," Arthur said to Mary. "I expect an anxious, but not a laborious week . . ." In fact, he was furious at Asquith's and Knollys's underhand behavior in securing and concealing the guarantee. For more rational Unionists, the guarantee's existence made continued obstruction of the Bill impossible: a House flooded with Liberal peers would destroy any remaining Unionist power in the Lords. Yet when on 21 July Balfour called his Shadow Cabinet to his house at Carlton Gardens to vote on what course the peers should take, there was no agreement: "indeed most violent differences," he told Mary. Standing against the "Hedgers," like Arthur, who recommended capitulation, were "Ditchers," like George, in a phrase of his own coining, determined "to die in the last ditch" defending the Lords.

For the first time in their long friendship, Arthur and George were on opposing sides, although that is to misrepresent their relative positions somewhat. George was zealous, and Arthur expressed almost no position at all. Privately Arthur thought resistance would only "advertise . . . the fact that we are the victims of a revolution." Publicly, he said only that he would stand and fall by Lord Lansdowne, Unionist Leader of the House of Lords. Lansdowne, the most reluctant of "Hedgers," advocated but did not demand from his peers the capitulation to the Bill that privately he too found "unpalatable." Passivity had settled like a blanket over the party leadership. The Ditchers were in full revolt.

The Commons was scheduled to address the Lords' wrecking amendments on 24 July. It was confounded by the "Cecil Scene," as Asquith, rising to speak, was drowned out by a full half hour of catcalls, jeers and howls of "Traitor," "Who Killed the King," "Let Redmond Speak" (an allusion to the fact that the Lords was considered the last bastion against Home Rule) and, more obliquely, "American Dollars." Eventually, without uttering a word, Asquith sat down. When Balfour rose, the Chamber fell embarrassingly silent. Nothing comparable to this had been seen since MPs brawled on the floor of the Commons over Home Rule in

PUNCH, OR THE LONDON CHARIVARI.—August 30, 1905.

SHELVED.

Chorus of the Resigned *(crowding up to make room for Lord Curzon).* "HULLO! HERE COMES ANOTHER OF THE OLD BRIGADE! WHY, ARTHUR 'LL SOON BE THE ONLY ONE LEFT."

A cartoon clipped and pasted by Madeline Wyndham in one of her "Clouds Books." This records George Wyndham's new role as a ringleader of the Diehards, who opposed Asquith's plans to limit the powers of the House of Lords and, in so doing, caused their own party leader, Arthur Balfour, considerable trouble George sits on a high shelf with other prominent Diehards, while his fellow Soul George Curzon climbs up to join them. The caption "Shelved" suggests their old-fashioned views. The title says "Hullo! Here comes another of the old brigade. Why, Arthur [Balfour]'ll soon be the only one left," indicating how many Unionists the Diehards were converting to their cause.

1893, but that had been born out of momentary passion. This was a plot organized by Balfour's Cecil relations: "As usual the leading lunatics are my own kith and kin," Arthur admitted to Mary wearily.

By tacit agreement, neither Mary nor Arthur mentioned George's part in events. The next day, Wilfrid Blunt stopped in at Belgrave Square to find George, F. E. Smith and George's stepson Bend'Or, now 2nd Duke of Westminster, ebullient at the Cecil Scene's success and planning their next line of attack. "Here you see the conspirators," cried George as his cousin poked his head round the door. "They are all in the highest possible spirits at the commotion they have caused and consider they have forced Balfour's hand," Wilfrid recorded in his diary; ". . . they are going to give a banquet to old Halsbury . . . as the saviour of the Constitution." The hastily arranged "Halsbury Banquet," celebrated the Diehards' figurehead, the eighty-seven-year-old Earl of Halsbury, Lord Chancellor under three prime ministers: Disraeli, Salisbury and Balfour. It took place at the lavish Hotel Cecil on the Strand two days later. Spirits among the six-hundred-strong crowd ran dangerously high. "They [the Government] have been playing, and they are playing a game of gigantic bluff . . ." declared Austen Chamberlain. It is hard not to see George's hand in the hastily devised plan at the evening's end for the banqueters to draw Halsbury in triumph from the Strand to his house in Ennismore Gardens, several miles away in Kensington. Halsbury's family stymied the plan, fearing the octogenarian might expire from the excitement. "The country is in revolt," George told Wilfrid. "They are ready for actual armed resistance, or rather, they would like that," Wilfrid told his diary, with certain disbelief.

The final reckoning began at half past four on the afternoon of 9 August, when the Lords convened to discuss the Commons' amendments made to the Parliament Bill. It was the final round of pass the parcel. If the Lords considered themselves "Content" with those amendments, the Bill would pass. If "Not Content," it was time for the guarantee—the precise terms of which were still unclear—to be put into action. After almost eight hours, the debate was adjourned just after midnight.

As it reconvened the next morning, 10 August, Balfour was making his way in baking heat to Paris, on the first leg of his journey to Bad Gastein in Austria. That the final act of a two-year saga was even now playing out at Westminster could not convince him to alter train fares booked some time back. He had washed his hands of the affair, which, he told Mary, was more "odious" to him "from the personal point of view" than any other episode in his public life. Asquith was also out of London, recuperating from laryngitis in Oxfordshire. But Asquith's party was not mutinous, and he had made contingency plans for an emergency Cabinet meeting the following day in the event that it was required.

When the session recommenced in the Lords that morning, the atmosphere on the Opposition benches was electric, the Government benches calm. The real fight, everyone knew, was not between the Government and the Opposition, but between Hedgers (many with buttonholes of white heather) and Ditchers (sporting red roses). On the Government side, Lord Morley, head of the Privy Council, which formally advised the King on the exercise of his Royal Prerogative, sat quietly, glancing frequently at a small piece of paper that he kept in the pocket of his frock coat. The debate recommenced. St. John Brodrick (now Viscount Midleton) began, taunting the Government that the proceedings were a sham. The call was taken up by Rosebery and Lansdowne for a clear statement by the Government about the nature of the guarantee.

At that point, Lord Morley stood up and read from the paper that he held in his hand: "If the Bill should be defeated tonight His Majesty could assent—I say this on my full responsibility as the spokesman of the Government—to the creation of Peers sufficient in number to guard against any possible combination of the different Parties in Opposition by which the Parliament Bill might again be exposed a second time to defeat."

Morley had barely finished speaking when a cheer rose up from the Government side. From the Opposition, Hedgers and Ditchers alike, there was dead silence. By request, Morley read the statement out one more time. It proved that the Government's stance was no bluff. If the Lords voted against the Bill, their number would be swamped until the Upper Chamber was so pliable as to vote through anything the Government might desire. In case anyone had not quite understood the implications of his words, Morley added helpfully, "Every vote given to-night against my Motion not to insist on what is called Lord Lansdowne's Amendment is a vote given in favor of a large and prompt creation of peers."

Outside, heat shimmered above warped railway lines; tarmac melted on the roads. It was the hottest day recorded in seventy years. In the

East End, the dockers were on strike. Inside the neo-Gothic splendor of the Upper Chamber, Rosebery attacked the Government for taking advantage of a "young and inexperienced" King; others denounced the Bill as sheer "revolution." But they knew they faced a choice of evils. As the Liberal Unionist Earl of Selborne put it, "Shall we perish in the dark, slain by our own hand, or in the light, killed by our own enemies . . . ?" At twenty to eleven at night, the division was called. As peers thronged the lobbies, a desperate Willoughby de Broke hid the top hat and coat of one duke to keep him in the Lords to vote. The duke bolted, preferring to commit the cardinal sin of appearing in public hatless and in shirtsleeves rather than make an impossible choice. In any event, one duke would not have made a victory. The final vote was as follows: Contents, 131; Not Contents, 114. The Government had won by seventeen votes, thanks to the support of thirty-seven Unionist peers and thirteen prelates, or, as George Wyndham termed them, "the Bishops and the Rats"—men, including George Curzon, who were henceforth hissed upon when entering the Carlton Club by the hysterical Diehards.

From the Ritz Hotel in Paris, Balfour wrote to Mary: "You must not ask me to tell anything about the last ten days. I am trying to forget it all." Mary replied immediately and sympathetically from St. Moritz: "I feel I do not understand [the situation] and I suppose never shall! This letter is only to remind you of what perhaps you know . . . that my heart goes out to you . . . I longed and longed to be able to come and comfort you—not by talking over the situation but by quite other means—a good smacking would brace you up I think!" Arthur's leadership would not survive the crisis. Succumbing to editor Leo Maxse's campaign in the *National Review,* a platform for the views of the Conservative Party, that "Balfour Must Go"—staccatoed to "B.M.G."—he resigned in November. The night before the announcement, he visited Mary, one of very few to have known his plans from the first, at Cadogan Square. Tired, sad, finding it difficult to speak, Mary stood on the steps of no. 62 to watch the motorcar "turn away with you buried inside, not looking!, and I had a serrement de Coeur as the car drove away for the last time—with you as Leader—after so long."

That August, both kept silent about George, who himself wrote to Sibell, incoherent from tiredness and emotion, mourning the death of his age:

Many things that I loved are shattered and some friendships gone . . . Now we are finished with the cosmopolitan press—and the American duchesses and the Saturday to Mondays at Taplow—and all the degrading shams. When the King wants loyal men, he will find us ready to die for him. He may want us. For the House of Lords today—tho' they did not know it—voted for Revolution.

TWENTY-EIGHT

1911–1914

As news of the vote reached India, F. W. Bain wrote to Pamela, "I suppose that you and your 'mountain-top' have been full of politics, rejoicing over the downfall of the Peers." In fact, at the time of the Liberal triumph Pamela was facedown on her bed in her darkened room, pillows sodden with tears, crumpled-up handkerchiefs strewn across the counterpane, succumbing to the grip of "the Glen mood," a mixture of "neuralgia," self-pity, depression and self-loathing that besieged her each year for several days on arrival at Glen, a place where even the weather seemed bent on victimizing her with "hard metallic sunshine" and "whipping wind."

"When I am in my Hinterland," Pamela explained to Charlie Tennant, "the chief feeling of it is a longing to be of use . . . not to spend so much money on the trivial things, and to do some tangible good. If you knew what a World there is in one, of a need to give . . . Money doesn't express it, I'm giving that away with both hands . . . & always will, so long as I have it, but that kind of giving doesn't express my need." Charlie was one of several confidants to whom she revealed at length her darkest feelings of worthlessness and despair. She drew for them comical pictures of herself, tear-stained, in her darkened room; recounted her imagined dialogues with God defending the insatiable need for affection and praise that He had bestowed on her; bemoaned her selfishness and vanity; complained how Eddy did not afford her "the smallest little sayings of praise"; and vowed to make the best of her life through the futures of her children: "If only I may make a good success of that, I shouldn't mind about my own rubbishy life. But sometimes the fear of failing, or the responsibility of it all floods over me, & I feel as if I were out on an open Sea—in the dinghi [*sic*]— . . . with a hair-pin for a paddle," she said, writing to another, unnamed, recipient.

Pamela had a magpie's knack for the picturesque image or phrase. Her "hair-pin" line seems to have been inspired by a Sanskrit translation sent to her by Bain from "the great Hindoo Poet" Kalidasa earlier that year: "I am desirous of crossing the impassable ocean, in my infatuation, in a tiny boat" ("You can remember the words when I am in India," Bain said). Pamela tweaked it in her letter to Charlie Tennant ("sometimes it seems to me as if I were on a great Sea, alone in a little boat; & all my love of poetry & books & great ideas, avail nothing. I only feel utterly useless, & of no value anywhere . . .") and to better effect here. The brilliant transposition is an indication of her flashes of real talent as a writer, but so easily did she lay her soul bare to numerous correspondents that her letters, ostensibly so anguished, become almost glib. It is hard not to agree with Elizabeth Asquith, sharp-tongued daughter of Margot, that Pamela gave her "essence . . . cheaply."

In March 1911, Eddy had been raised to the peerage as Baron Glenconner and appointed Lord High Commissioner to the General Assembly of the Church of Scotland. The Prime Minister's brother-in-law was now the King's personal representative to the Scottish Kirk's governing body: a true grandee. Edward Grey began to address him, affectionately, as "Your Grace." The Glenconners' official residence in Scotland was the ancient Palace of Holyroodhouse, lying at the foot of Edinburgh's Royal Mile. In fact, they spent ever more time at Glen, some thirty-odd miles south. In print, Pamela described Glen as a "paradise": with parties and lawn tennis, acting, charades and camping parties at Loch Eddy, the placid man-made loch on the estate named after Eddy, who loved to fish for trout there. She invited her Adeane nieces to parties of young people that she took to Peebles Ball, insisting on giving Mananai "money presents" (kept secret from Charlie) for their ballgowns. Privately, she never ceased to hate it.

Eddy's appointment reflected the considerable financial support provided by the Tennants to the Asquiths as well as the Liberal Party,

although he never sent Margot a check without an accompanying hom-
ily and protestations that he too needed to "be careful." Margot gave
this short shrift—"I wish I felt he & Pamela wd ever be in debt!" she
scrawled on one such letter of 1910. "Highly characteristic of my brother
on the subject of money," she wrote on another envelope from Eddy.
"They both owe Henry *everything*."

For over a decade, Margot had been devising ways to exploit her
brother's finances and his wife's social appeal to the party's end. From
the start, she tried to use the aristocratic Pamela to make the party "more
socially attractive." "I shall have a 'day,'" she told Eddy in 1900, "& with
Pamela's beauty . . . I'll show our party what we can do," planning also
to recruit Mananai to the cause. Margot thought senior Liberal wives
were socially lax: "Ly Harcourt & Ly C.B. [Campbell-Bannerman] do
nothing at all . . ." The construction of the gallery at Queen Anne's Gate
in 1910 facilitated the hosting Margot wanted Pamela to take on. She still
complained that the Tennants entertained far too little.

Pamela thought they entertained far too much. "The world of
Books . . . is more to me than any other," she told Sidney Cockerell,
drawing a little crown above the capitalized word to emphasize her
point. In 1912, her compendium, *The White Wallet*, was published, the
title a reference to her vellum commonplace folder where she kept writings that caught her eye. She included her poem "Fantasia—of a London
House Closed," in which she wanders through the shut-up great houses
of London, lamenting time spent in "tedious revelry," haunted by ghosts
of "murdered Summers" that

> *speak of Mays, strangled in Rotten Row,*
> *Of massacred Julys, whose glowing heads*
> *Hung on the lances of red-cloth Bazaars—("Society Bazaars" that kill*
>   *the soul . . .)*

Pamela refused to let the demands of her official engagements impinge
upon time spent devoted to the things she thought most worthwhile—
"her children, her village friends, poetry, the cultivation of her own considerable literary gift, and that life-long enthralling interest . . . her love
for, and study of, wild birds." It resulted in a certain ruthlessness where
everyone else was concerned. On occasion Mary became distressed by
how little the sisters saw of one another. She wrote to Pamela express-

ing this sentiment. "It is quite all right about you and me. I find I am able to love *operatively* (the italics are mine) from a distance," Pamela replied. Mary's children thought it "wonderfully typical" of their aunt, and urged their mother to "love operatively from a distance" whenever she proposed inviting disliked guests to Stanway.

When Pamela did entertain, she did it on her own terms. The rest of the family had long turned away from Bosie Douglas, on account not of scandal but of his character: "The kind . . . I most despise," Mary told Arthur privately—a weak aimless conspiracy theorist quick to exercise his vitriol against the world. Bosie had "converted" to heterosexuality and married Olive Custance in 1902. Pamela persuaded Eddy to give the Douglases a cottage on the Wilsford estate, and to offer Bosie, in 1907, the editorship of the *Academy*, a literary monthly recently bought by Eddy. Bosie used it as a vehicle to attack the Asquiths until his attacks became so extreme—he described Margot as "bound with lesbian fillets"—that Eddy, unable to fire him for fear of Pamela's fury, cut all ties with the publication, giving the entire enterprise to Bosie as a gift. In 1912, Bosie prompted another scandal when he came face-to-face with Robbie Ross, the executor of Wilde's literary estate, at a reception held by the Tennants at Queen Anne's Gate, and launched himself at him, shouting abuse. Ross hid behind a large table, and Bosie, sliding across the polished oak in pursuit, was hauled back by other guests, allowing Ross to dodge into the drawing room and bar the door. Roaring impotently with rage, Bosie remained glowering and huffing in the gallery's corner until his mother, Sibyl Queensberry, persuaded him out by requesting he escort her to her carriage. Meanwhile, Eddy Tennant moved quietly among his female guests, apologizing in his understated manner for the unseemly disturbance to which they had been subjected.

Pamela's regal indifference to convention provoked a certain cattiness—"an Olympian character, she floated to and fro between Wilsford and the Glen, appreciating their different beauties, and so well buttressed by wealth that she never had to catch a bus or think about the price of fish," said Susan Buchan, wife of the writer John—and provided ample anecdotage beloved of the press. She stopped her carriage in the middle of a state procession through Edinburgh, to buy up all the birds caged in a pet shop, ordering them to be delivered to Holyrood, then setting them free in King's Park, the royal park adjacent to the Palace. Mary recalled a visit by the sisters to London Zoo to visit a cockatoo of

Pamela's from which she had "parted . . . because its language was too shocking for words!" At the zoo she "outraged the authorities by taking her dog Roly into the gardens, she hitched the dog under her arm and disregarded the complaints and threats of the officials, who followed her protesting, and at last withdrew in despair!" When they found the disreputable bird, it recognized Pamela. "What would you think if I told you that I knew of a family of which the eldest son walks up to his waist in water when going out to dinner, & of which the mother, when she dines out, burns her pocket handkerchief in the dining room fire?" teased Edward Grey.

Each New Year's Eve—Pamela told Sibell—she trysted with the memory of her doomed love for Harry Cust, sobbing as she reread all his letters stored in her keepsake box. There are hints in Bain's letters that he and Pamela had some form of physical relationship—"when I die, Stonehenge will be found printed on my heart," he said—and Pamela always made clear to Bain that her invitations to Wilsford did not include his wife. But Grey was the constant, providing Pamela with the attention and reassurance that she needed, meeting her mind in the truest fashion. At Queen Anne's Gate, they shared firelight "knitting suppers," at which Grey read aloud to Pamela as she knitted the fearsomely complicated patterns at which she was so proficient, needles clacking furiously beneath her serene face. "Are you not more than Mary-Queen-of-Scots beautiful?" he asked her, and Pamela, mollified, receded from her hysteria. "Emma, You are very perverse in supposing that when I tell you of having refused bridge I do so with the object of conveying to you that I make sacrifices when I spend an evening with you. I tell you of these refusals to convince you how very much I prefer a K.S. [knitting supper] evening to other attractions," he wrote, addressing her as Emma Woodhouse from Jane Austen's *Emma,* and signing off as her fictional lover Mr. Knightley, after a stormy one-sided row in which Pamela had accused him of being motivated to see her by duty rather than desire.

On an early-summer Sunday in 1912, Grey wrote to Eddy from Wilsford; it was a beautiful day, with missel thrushes out in force, and the river flowing strongly and full. He recounted his anxious train journey from London, transporting in a slopping can of water six giant orfe fish ordered by Pamela for Dingley Cut, the pond at the bottom of the garden; the sight, at breakfast, of a stoat proceeding at a stately pace across the lawn, its mouth full of prey; and a long afternoon's walk with Pamela across the Downs featuring "the usual adventures; finding & negotiating precarious planks in unfamiliar water meadows." All the children were well, he continued, Clare reluctant to return to school in Salisbury the next day, six-year-old Stephen satisfied with his new gardening method: digging up the crocuses flowering in the other children's gardens and replanting them in his own plot. " 'Rousing up the bulbs' he called it." One would think that this letter came from the father of this family, such is Edward Grey's familiarity with the Tennants' quiet domesticity. Eddy, kept in Scotland by business and a mistress—a sweet-natured local woman about whom no one ever spoke—was an increasingly shadowy presence in that family's life, even to the extent that Bim was sent for public school from age thirteen to Winchester College, Grey's alma mater, rather than Eddy's Eton, with Grey making the necessary introductions to the suggested housemaster. It must be this which provoked Stephen's acidic claim in adulthood that he could scarcely remember what his dull father looked like.

The Glenconners' houses provided Grey with respite from his tussles at the Foreign Office. The Great Powers—France, Britain, the Russian Empire, Germany and Austria-Hungary—those states which had the military and economic strength to exert their influence on a global scale—were aligning themselves on opposing sides in a tangle of ententes and alliances. In 1911, France's designs on Fez in Morocco brought England within a whisper of war against Germany; in 1912, the frighteningly fast disintegration of the Balkans brought together the Great Powers in London at a conference of eight interminable months of petty disagreements and squabbles. Domestically, the bloody revolution that George had predicted, perhaps hoped for, had not come to pass, but the seeds of social unrest seemed everywhere. Bills proposing Home Rule for Ireland and the disestablishment of the Welsh Church were progressing through Parliament, their eventual legislative force apparently now only a matter of time. Suffragettes poured acid onto golf courses in green suburbia or chained themselves to the railings of Buckingham Palace; and, in front of dumbstruck crowds at the Epsom Derby, a young woman named Emily Davison, with a return train ticket in her pocket, stepped out in front of the King's horse, and died four days later from the injuries sustained. The sympathy of many was for the horse. At Wilsford, Nanny

Trussler read out to her charges at breakfast the *Daily Mail*'s dire warnings about the consequences of the coal strikes breaking out across the North Country; in East London, the dockers continued their protests.

Color, dissonance and the shock of the new assaulted English culture, from the discordant strains of Stravinsky to Chekhov's languid characters on West End stages. Society dressed in exotic costumes inspired by Sergei Diaghilev's astonishing Ballets Russes. Time seemed to be slipping ever faster past. Roger Fry's exhibition "Manet and the Post-Impressionists" opened to public outrage at the Grafton Gallery in the winter of 1910. Two years later, a second exhibition of Post-Impressionism (now containing contributions from English artists inspired by the first) barely raised an eyebrow. The *Titanic*'s sinking in April 1912 blindsided a society that thought itself technologically invincible. The disaster, remembered Cincie Asquith, "loomed . . . large in one's life for months." Invasion fears blossomed: Lord Roberts began campaigning for a Home Defense Army to protect England against the Germans. Summering at Baden-Baden in 1912 with Cincie, Mary noted with unease the effect of such speeches when reported in the German press. Only that morning, her German doctor had asked her in a truculent tone "if there was going to be a war in the spring . . . they are persistently, and absolutely convincing themselves that we want to fight them," she reported to Arthur.

In Baden-Baden, Cincie showed Mary a passage in the memoirs of Charles Greville, the celebrated diarist of the Regency and early Victorian years, concerning their ancestor the "Third Earl." Mary was thrilled to recognize in Egremont's patronage and open-handed hospitality qualities that "are me!" and was surprised that they stemmed "from my paternal English (stiff shy English) and not from my Franco-Irish (Celtic! Red rag to Balf) side!" Mary was fifty, with married children, and now with grandchildren (Cincie's son John was born in 1911 and Ego and Letty's son David in 1912). In 1913 Guy Charteris became engaged to Eddy's niece, Frances Tennant, another example, commented Mary, of the way in which "we Wyndhams . . . have dipped into the Tennant family as our marriage Lucky Bag."

Over the years, Mary and Stanway had melded into each other: the house was "a kind of material envelope—a shell—exactly fitted to your personality," declared Arthur; "a golden beehive of mellow stone and yellow grass with beautiful children and grandchildren swarming in and out," said Detmar Blow. "I am simply absorbed in happiness over my family!" Mary told Arthur on a September's afternoon in 1912, writing from the warmth of her "boudoir" as rain beat against the windowpanes. The fire was crackling in the hall, where Mary had arranged chairs for the "young females" to work and read; the boys were playing stump cricket in the barn; her mother was writing letters in her bedroom. As the house hummed with quiet activity, Stanway seemed to Mary "a wonderful center of Love and Vitality (Life) Radiance and Harmony, and I begin to see dimly that I have done something, or that to speak more humbly and truly . . . something has been done thro' me, for to have built up this home life is something and to have the radiating center from which people can draw something and pass it on, is like having founded a watering place!"

The house was short on creature comforts, even cleanliness: "Every horizontal object wears a coat of dust, like a chinchilla. It's a wonder the inmates look as clean as they do," commented Letty's sister Lady Diana Manners in 1909, and Mary was constantly battling to find enough space for all her guests. "When a man's tired he rests, when Mary Elcho['s] tired she moves furniture," Mary told Arthur. In 1913, Lord Wemyss (under some pressure from Connor, Gosford's land agent, whom Mary called "my Scotch champion") agreed to install electricity at Stanway and increase the Elchos' annual income to £1,000. When Connor telephoned to tell her the good news, Mary, at first so relieved she could only weep, then poured all her energies into cajoling, bludgeoning and wheedling her husband, father-in-law and agent into agreeing to build Stanway a new wing, frantic not to let this dreamlike opportunity slip out of her grasp. The resulting extension, built by Detmar Blow, was torn down by Mary's prescient grandson shortly after the Second World War, realizing it to be the only way the house might survive as a private residence.

Looking down over the assorted scrum of people at breakfast at these weekends, Mary was fond of saying that Stanway was like a lunatic asylum, although "sometimes . . . and this is probably true, I think it's I who am a mad woman keeping house for the sane . . ." she wrote. Certainly she anticipated this reaction from her "worldly" friends (Ettie Desborough and the like) when, in the spring of 1913, she hosted Hugo's latest mistress, Lady Angela Forbes, and her two young daughters at Stanway for several weeks, even going so far as to help Angela enroll the elder, Marigold, in the same Malvern girls' boarding school attended by her own daughters Mary Charteris and Bibs, which lay about thirty miles from Stanway. Angela was a chain-smoking, brash, hard-living divorcée. Mary could not resist the challenge—"this is a very hard nut ahead," she said, with an ill-concealed glimmer of excitement. Even so, she recognized the difficulties her instinct could lead her into. "It's very awkward living with a leg in each world. Some day I shall split and shriek like a mandrake!" she admitted to Arthur.

In the same letter, Mary reported the "great excitement" of the engagement of George and Sibell's son Percy "Perf" Wyndham to Diana Lister, daughter of Tommy and Charty Ribblesdale, just two weeks after they met. The wedding six weeks later was remarkable as a grand convention of "the Wyndham clan—all so beautiful and so well pleased with each other," commented an onlooker. The great hope was that Perf's marriage would restore life to Clouds. Percy's death had left Clouds "*awful*— haunted by vivid memories, presences you may almost say of Papa and Mama, myself! You! My children, Madeline, Pamela, Guy and *all*," Mary told Arthur. Madeline Wyndham, having handed over the reins to Sibell, "naturally won't" play the chatelaine "and Sibell apparently can't!" said Mary. "Let the young people in I say and give them their heads."

Six weeks after Perf's wedding George took a trip to Paris, accompanied by his mistress Gay Plymouth and her daughter, and planning to meet up with his old friend Hilaire Belloc while he was there. George's time in Paris was nigh perfect: he hunted through antiquarian bookshops for books for his library (which needed only the inscriptions on the walls to be complete), and enjoyed the late-spring sunshine on walks with Gay and Phyllis in the gardens of the Château de Fontainebleau, just outside the city.

At the Ledoyen, one of Paris's oldest and most famous restaurants, he dined, quite alone, on potage Saint-Germain—a fresh pea soup; a whole brill in mushroom sauce; a cold quail stuffed with truffles, garnished with aspic and parsley, with a salad; hot green asparagus, as thick and fat as the white ones, with a sauce mousseline; a cold salade russe, without ham but with a "perfect" mayonnaise; and the best strawberries that he could ever remember eating. The wine was a Richebourg of 1890 that was to other wines, George told Belloc, "in the relation of Homer and Shakespeare to other poets." He considered it a perfect evening: "No Jew was there. No American. No Englishman but myself. I had struck an oasis of civilization. There were few women, and that was fit. For how few women understand?"

With hindsight, George might have avoided the mousseline. Four days later, he was dead of a heart attack. The official version, in his *Life*, is of an entirely respectable demise, nagging heart pains, morphine injections by a nurse, a turn for the worse. The unofficial version is that George died not in the arms of a nurse in the Hôtel Lotti, where he was staying, but in those of a prostitute in a brothel. Perf Wyndham went to bring his father's body back to England. "He looks very peaceful and very beautiful," he told Sibell. "England has lost someone as valuable and precious to Her, as He was dear to us—it is an unfathomable callamity [*sic*]—but callamities must be borne and endured."

Wilfrid Blunt dedicated his poem "To a Happy Warrior" to George, sending copies to the Wyndhams. It immortalized George as poet, warrior, lover, chivalric knight of old, "the ultimate man . . . Whose keener sight / Grasped the full vision of Time's master-plan." Mary wrote to Wilfrid immediately, excusing the scrappy paper that was all she had to hand:

> I think yr poem to George most beautiful—quite magnificent & very fine—I am *so glad* you have done it . . . you speak of God & Paradise but it's *the* most gloriously Pagan thing that I've ever read but then I feel that *you* & George and I *are* pagans really . . . there is no mawkish sentiment about you, no cloying & seeing thro colored glass—but the broad horizon & the big sweep . . .

In the last decade of his life, George had separated from his party's leadership, moving ever rightwards. Yet his campaigns for tariff reform and naval reform and his position as a Ditcher had shown what influence the crusading knight could still wield. Wilfrid Blunt considered "George's politics . . . the least creditable part of him . . . it was George's other side that I loved and admired." But among his wider circle there was genuine disbelief that George, barely fifty, would not return from political exile to a second act. "I think all must feel that he has been cut off at a time of life when there was still before him the hope and promise of greater things in the future than ever in the past. These are the great tragedies of life," said Arthur in a eulogy delivered to a hushed House of Commons. Hilaire Belloc thought George's death the "end of honesty in public life."

Clouds and almost £20,000 of death duties still owing from Percy

A posthumous portrait of George Wyndham by Harold Speed. In the striking silver hair and bushy mustache, the resemblance to Sir Anthony Eden (later the Earl of Avon), Britain's Prime Minister from 1955 to 1957, is clear. Sir Anthony was rumored to be the love child of George and Sibyl, Lady Eden, one of George's many close female friends. Like his putative father, Eden was also a golden boy of politics brought down suddenly by a fiasco and allegations of collusion. In his case, the Suez Crisis in 1956 brought an end to his tenure as Prime Minister after twenty-one months, when he resigned, citing ill health.

Wyndham's death passed to Perf Wyndham, although George's foresight in insuring his own life for £30,000 meant that the estate was not financially crippled from the start. A stained-glass window in St. Mary's Church in East Knoyle was dedicated to George by his erstwhile parliamentary colleagues. In just two years, the charmed circle of the Wyndhams had suffered two shattering blows. Sending Mary *"fondest* Love" on her birthday that year, Mananai added: "These anniversaries make one *sad* yet one can be grateful & look back on happy times all of us together in the past."

More change came a year later when Lord Wemyss died, aged ninety-five, on 30 June 1914. He had tied up almost everything in trusts, even Gosford and Stanway's household effects. Almost the only thing that Hugo received outright was his father's London house, 23 St. James's Place. He promptly sold it. Mary's "General Account" was raised to £4,500 a year and Hugo's personal allowance to £2,000. But death duties which obliged the estate to pay out £28,000 a year for eight years and personal legacies left by Lord Wemyss made Hugo, paradoxically, feel more insecure financially than he had ever done before. He threatened to let Stanway at once and move to Gosford. "At present the Change of name seems only to have brought Trouble & the sense of fresh responsibilities & burdens and less freedom . . . !" Mary told Wilfrid, adding, "I simply *hate* my new name I feel that Romance & Poetry have fled with my old *pretty* name!" It took Lady Elcho of Stanway years to become accustomed to the cold, hard grandeur of the Countess of Wemyss of Gosford, and she often found herself absentmindedly signing off as "Melcho."

Stanway's reprieve came at a greater cost to Mary than she could possibly have imagined. Two days before Lord Wemyss's death came the news of the assassination of Austria-Hungary's Archduke Franz Ferdinand, heir-presumptive to that throne, in the faraway crumbling Balkans. On 23 July 1914, Austria-Hungary issued an impossible ultimatum to Serbia. The house of cards built on secrecy and paranoia began tumbling down. The ten days that followed were a blur of ultimatums; crisis talks between the diplomats of the Great Powers; mobilization orders issued, halted, partially revoked, reissued. Germany came out in support of Austria, Russia in support of Serbia, France in support of Russia. Sir Edward Grey appealed to Germany, through its Ambassador, Prince Lichnowsky, for peace; the Germans tried to persuade Sir Edward Goschen, Britain's Ambassador in Berlin, to stay neutral if an attack on France was routed through Belgium. For this was the basis of Germany's Schlieffen Plan, which was intended to wipe out French resistance in a matter of weeks. And Britain, since the 1839 Treaty of London between itself, Belgium and the Netherlands, had sworn to uphold Belgian neutrality at all costs. So, suddenly, war went from a remote possibility, which allowed Grey to spend his usual Sunday in Wiltshire on 26 July, to a probability in the week that followed, to a certainty, as Grey left the Foreign Office, brushing off in the doorway Prince Lichnowsky, who had come to make a final appeal, and went to address the Commons in a historic speech on 3 August. "Mr. Speaker," he said, as the cheers around him died down, "Last week I stated that we were working for peace not only for this country, but to preserve the peace of Europe. Today—but events move so rapidly that it is exceedingly difficult to state with technical accuracy the actual state of affairs—it is clear that the peace of Europe cannot be preserved."

Slowly and clearly, Grey laid out before the Commons the ententes and alliances to which Britain was party. He stressed that no secret engagement was to be sprung upon the country. He sketched for the MPs massed around him the nature of the 1839 Treaty by which Britain had promised to defend Belgium's neutrality, reminding them that Gladstone himself had upheld it some fifty years before:

> We worked for peace up to the last moment, and beyond the last moment. How hard, how persistently and how earnestly we strove for peace last week, the House will see from the papers that are before it. But that is over so far as the peace of Europe is concerned. We are now face to face with a situation and all the consequences which it may yet have to unfold.

The only step that Britain could take was to issue Germany with an ultimatum: unless Germany guaranteed Belgian neutrality by midnight the following night, Britain would declare war. So Britain did. That evening, so it was said, an exhausted Edward Grey stood at the window of his room in the Foreign Office. The dusk was gathering, and the gloaming pierced by the fireflies of warm yellow gas as the lamplighters moved steadily from one streetlight to the next. "The lamps are going out all over Europe," Grey said, turning to the man who stood beside him. "We shall not see them lit again in our lifetime."

TWENTY-NINE

MCMXIV

E arly in the evening of 4 August 1914, as news of the British ultimatum spread, crowds began to mass in Westminster, London's political heartland. Motorcars carrying men and women in evening dress waving the Union Jack wound their way slowly among the crowds thronging Whitehall, Parliament Street, Trafalgar Square and the Mall. People scaled the plinth of Nelson's Column and pedestals of Whitehall's statues; spectators eagerly leaned out of the windows of Government offices. Outside Buckingham Palace, where the Victoria Memorial was "black with people," the cheering and singing reached fever pitch at 7 p.m., and again at half-past nine, when the Royal Family appeared on the balcony. In Trafalgar Square, where two days before Keir Hardie had been shouted down attempting to address a socialist anti-war convention, the ebullient crowd was provoked to fresh heights of enthusiasm as the occasional field gun or ammunition wagon lumbered by. But, as the hour of the ultimatum approached, a "profound silence fell upon the crowd . . . Then as the first strokes rang out from the Clock Tower, a vast cheer burst out and echoed and re-echoed for nearly 20 minutes. The National Anthem was then sung with an emotion and solemnity which manifested the gravity and sense of responsibility with which the people regard the great issues before them," reported *The Times.*

At 10:45 the following morning, George V signed a formal proclamation of war against Germany. It is trite but accurate to say that most people truly thought the war would be "over by Christmas." Earl Kitchener, the hastily appointed War Secretary, discomfited the Cabinet when he predicted an engagement of several years. Mary had lunched with Kitchener the day war broke out. She and Ettie were at Alice Salisbury's house and Kitchener stopped by, having been urgently recalled from Dover—where he had been about to depart on a ship for Egypt—to see the Prime Minister at Downing Street. In other times, the Souls' talk would all have been of this dramatic development. But as mothers of adult sons their main preoccupation was with their children. That afternoon, Mary made her way back to Stanway. At Oxford Station she bumped into her sister-in-law Sibell on the platform. "Perf is getting ready," said Sibell, ashen-faced.

As a lieutenant in the regiment of the Coldstream Guards, Perf was a member of Britain's professional, full-time army, known as the Regular Army, of which six infantry divisions and five cavalry brigades were deployed to the Western Front as part of the British Expeditionary Force (the BEF) in the late summer of 1914. These professional soldiers termed themselves "the Old Contemptibles," after an apocryphal story that the Kaiser had vowed to wipe out Field Marshal Sir John French's "contemptible little army." By the end of the year the Old Contemptibles had been all but mown down at the battles of Mons, Le Cateau, the Aisne and Ypres. The BEF was now composed of the hitherto part-time voluntary troops of the Territorial Army (these regiments being known as the "Yeomanry") and Kitchener's volunteers, who flocked in their thousands to his imperious finger. Three hundred thousand men enlisted in the first month of the war, exceeding by 50 percent Kitchener's target. The total number of volunteers for the first week of September 1914 alone was 174,901.

Conscription was not introduced until 1916, when all men between the ages of eighteen and forty-one were called up. Instinctively, the British revolted against it. "It is repugnant to the mental constitution of a freedom-loving people and the British nation would never stand it," Eddy Tennant declared, addressing Liverpool's Liberal Reform Club on the subject of Home Defense in 1913. Hugo, blinded by patriotic fervor, was not of this mind. The day after war broke out, Mary breakfasted with him in Stanway's dining room. He was silent behind his newspaper, except for the occasional snort of disgust. After an hour or so, Angela

Forbes came into the room. Hugo looked up. "I'm afraid I've done something rather rash," he told his mistress. "I've dismissed all the servants."

Hugo had told his male household staff they must join the army, or be sacked. Mary was horrified: beyond Hugo's typical disregard for her and for the obvious logistical difficulties ("I shall have no chauffeur, no stableman, no odd man to carry the coals! I may have 100 parlor maids but someone must carry the coals!" she protested to Balfour, helplessly, seeking his advice), she felt that it smacked of the chain gang. Her footman's elderly father had "begged" his son not to go, but both Stanway's footmen, the odd-man, two gardeners, one carpenter and four keepers enlisted in that first wave.

All over the country, aristocrats were vigorously enjoining their tenants to fight, with generous terms: promising to keep jobs open; to house families rent-free; even to pay them part of their wages. "Are you a man or a mouse?" asked the Earl of Lonsdale, avid foxhunter and sportsman who had once hosted the Kaiser for grouse-shooting at his Cumbrian estate, Lowther Castle, in a recruiting poster of his own devising distributed throughout the Lake District. "If I had twenty sons, I should be ashamed if every one of them did not go to the front when his time came," said the Earl of Derby, a veteran of the Boer War and chairman of the West Lancashire Territorial Association.

This was doubtless true. The sons of the elite who were not already, like Ego, part of the armed forces—Ego had held a commission in the Gloucester Yeomanry, a Territorial Army cavalry regiment, since 1912, and left Stanway to join them on 6 August 1914—mostly joined up as soon as they could. Bim Tennant, who had quit Winchester in June, planning to spend several months in Germany before entering the Diplomatic Service, joined the Grenadier Guards at the age of seventeen—having, said Pamela, "the distinction of being the youngest Wykehamist to take up arms in defense of his country," and still a year younger than the official age for enlistment. Guy Charteris was gazetted into the Shropshire Light Infantry, subsequently moving to the Scots Guards. With difficulty Mary persuaded Yvo Charteris—who on 4 August had stood in a London street with shining eyes, reading the proclamation of war pasted to a lamppost—to see out his final term at Eton. In the early spring of 1915 he joined the King's Royal Regiment, and then the Grenadier Guards. Raymond Asquith's initial decision not to join up was seen as a dereliction of duty. By 1915 the pressure of the metaphorical white service in England and in France. The Winchcombe Hospital was a short drive from Stanway in the pony trap. Eliza Wedgwood, a nearby neighbor, was Commandant. Mary and her daughters (including Bibs, just twelve in 1914) all volunteered, as did Mananai's eldest, twenty-five-year-old Pamela Adeane, who stayed at Stanway for several months before being reluctantly dissuaded from going out to France ("I think everybody thinks France is too much for me, perhaps so"). She moved to the Queen's Hospital, a military hospital in Frognal, North London, specializing in "heads & jaws." It was hard work, requiring immense courage and a stomach of steel. Pamela thrived there: "I believe one is more useful in a military hospital . . . they do wonderful things here." She lost a lover in the war, spent it nursing and did not marry until 1919, when she was nearly thirty.

Winchcombe's atmosphere was informal and convivial. Cynthia chatted to Sister Awde as she stirred porridge on night duty; Bibs peeled potatoes in the kitchen, sulking at not being considered old enough to help in the wards. When funds ran low, Mrs. Patrick Campbell organized a charity matinée in London that raised £400, enough to keep the hospital going until the end of the war. In *Family Record,* Mary presented a rose-tinted view of the hospital as the family's second home, with Hugo taking convalescents for drives. In fact, Hugo was mostly with Angela in France, while Angela's daughters remained at Stanway: "He told me that he didn't care when I went to London[,] that he didn't mean to be there much!" Mary told Arthur in the spring of 1915. On the rare occasions he returned, he was "carping" and "critical" about efforts at Winchcombe and Stanway, conducting small feuds with Eliza Wedgwood. Mary reproached him for his behavior when he was "so full of admiration & sympathy about everything Angela does." She felt keenly that Stanway's war effort was less glamorous than Angela's.

Pamela Tennant recalled the war's opening months as possessing a curious sense of unreality, like "the early morning, before the world was numb with pain and broken, before things were stale and tired as they became." Both Bim and fifteen-year-old Kit, a cadet at Dartmouth Naval College in Devon, where the officers of the Royal Navy (then, as now) were trained, were still too young for combat—an officer could not officially go to the Front until the age of nineteen. There is a stillness to Pamela's descriptions of herself at the time, almost as if she were frozen. Reading her account in her memoirs of the mothers who "lay awake" at night and "listened" to "the quiet sound of feet, the measured beat of soldiers going by, company after company," thinking of what lay ahead, the sense is that she was speaking of her own experience.

In this limbo, one of the most curious incidents of Pamela's life took place. In October 1914, she wrote to Mary of "the adopted baby": "very good and nice—as far as he goes," in some ways even "better than [a baby] of my own . . . for one thing, it is such a relief . . . to be able to hear with perfect equanimity of a Baby having a rise of temperature!" Joking aside, Pamela said, "he is a great solace. I love babies—I like their ways & their ridiculous hands, & perfect feet," and he had "incidental value" for her "in deflecting some of dear [Nanny] Trussler's zeal from Stephen." This is Pamela's only letter to Mary mentioning this child, whose name was Oliver Hope.

Pamela had long had a habit of scooping up children. Bim's "village boys" were often more frequently at Wilsford than in their own homes. Pamela's granddaughter, the author Emma Tennant, has recounted her surprise on hearing from an elderly villager that her grandmother had "adopted four children in all: Mary and Tossie and Roger," in addition to Oliver. In Pamela's relatively few surviving letters to Eddy, she mentions at least two instances of taking in a child when their parents could not cope—the bigamous curate's son, and after the war a small South African girl whose mother, abandoned by her husband, was struggling to maintain her family and hold down her job at the War Office. Oliver was different. He was the only one of Pamela's patchwork assortment of strays who actually lived full-time at Wilsford, and the only one left an annuity in her will—fifty pounds per annum.

Wilsford Parish School—which Oliver attended briefly from summer 1918 to winter 1919—records in its register his birth date as 7 July 1912, meaning he was just over two when he was adopted. The official story, insofar as there is one, is that Oliver was the son of a "tinker woman" named Hope who died giving birth in Salisbury Infirmary. A search for boys born to a woman of that name between 1910 and 1915 yields no results in the England and Wales birth registers. While it is not impossible that the birth simply escaped registration (particularly in a Gypsy community), the hospital element makes a record more likely. It adds to the mystery surrounding this child, whose very name sounds like a fairy tale, and whose story peters out into a welter of rumor. He entered the Merchant Navy at a very young age (either running away, or being sent by Christopher, according to who is telling the story), and then disappeared so effectively that most of Pamela's descendants did not know of his existence. The surmise, by Emma Tennant, is that round-faced, dark-haired Oliver, similar in looks to both Bim and Pamela, was in fact Bim's illegitimate son, from a fling with an artist's model when he was little more than fifteen, already very good-looking and advanced for his years. While unproven, it is entirely plausible that Pamela would have scooped up her son's illegitimate child. A decade on, she tried to do exactly that with an illegitimate daughter born to her son David with the actress Hermione Baddeley. The timing—taking on this child exactly as Bim faced danger—may be coincidental, but it lends force to the supposition.

In September, when the war was barely a month old, Perf Wyndham was "shot *dead* through the head," leading his men on a charge out of a wood at the battle of the Aisne. "How *glorious* the death is," said Mana-nai, "*no* suffering, no *knowing* he must die." Bim echoed these sentiments in a poem that Pamela distributed to all the family:

Father and son have not been long asunder
And joy in heaven leaves mortals sad and wan
His death-salute was the artillery thunder
Praise be to God for such an Englishman!

Balfour heard the news from an acquaintance while lunching at the Travellers Club on Pall Mall. He waited to see confirmation in the casualty lists published daily in *The Times* before writing to Mary. "We live in the perpetual knowledge that our friends are in hourly peril . . . and we bear the news [of their deaths] as best as we can," he said. In those early days, when death was still a shock, not yet a near inevitability, it was strangely easy to believe in its heroic glamour. Cynthia Asquith later wondered how she had mourned these losses so intensely while still swallowing "the rather high-faluting platitude that it was all right for them—that they were not to be pitied, but were safe, unassailable, young, and glamorous for ever." Mary found it difficult from the start. After hours writing to her family in sorrow and loss over Perf's death, she wrote to Arthur last of all, with "a pen made of lead," unable to dissemble further:

It doesn't seem like sending youths to war, it seems more like a shambles . . . despite one's feelings of pride that they should "d.e in their glory" the lads that will never grow old . . . there are times when the feeling of "exaltation" ebbs and fades away and leaves one feeling utterly blank and flat and miserable and grim. It seems such a sickening waste . . .

In a devastating postscript, Perf Wyndham's will provided that if he died without issue his heir would be Dick Wyndham, the younger of Guy Wyndham's two sons. He thus doubly disinherited first Guy and secondly Dick's elder brother George—whom, the family presumed, he had overlooked simply because he got on better with Dick, and never thought this provision in the will would come into effect. "Dear Percy never realized that when a will is made it is facing the possibility of death at *any* time . . ." said Mananai. Clouds now belonged to Dick—barely eighteen years old. Guy and Minnie, who moved into Clouds with their teenage son (George was already serving in the army), were merely housekeepers until Dick came of age. It was a "crushing sadness . . . a mistake & absolutely contrary to the spirit of Papa's & George's Wills & in direct opposition to their wishes," lamented Mananai, who of all the sisters felt Guy's misfortune the most keenly. "I cannot bear to think that people might think this had been done intentionally & that there had been a split in our *united* family," she told Mary.

Mary busied herself, moving between London, where Yvo's Grenadier Guards were stationed in Chelsea Barracks, not far from Cadogan Square, and Ego and Guy Charteris's billets around the country. "I am living— here there & everywhere, like a soldier," Mary reported to Wilfrid Blunt in an undated letter written from Cadogan Square, recently returned from seeing Ego in Newbury in Berkshire, where Letty had taken "tiny little lodgings . . . like a dolls house" nearby. The night before, Mary and Mary Charteris had dined with them, Ego "so *beautiful* in his khaki," and George Vernon, a member of the Coterie and like another son to the family. Mary had brought down a picnic of "grouse! & *roses & champagne* . . . we had leopard skins stretched on a sofa, the piano acted as a sideboard . . . & we had a *feast* & talked camp shop—the arrival of transport, horses rifles—& the death of all the young friends who are giving their lives in France—it was a wonderful evening." A few months later, Mary and Bibs visited Ego in Hunstanton, on the Norfolk coast, staying at the Le Strange Arms. This time (in a turn of events that seems delightfully apposite given the du Maurieresque name of the inn), Bibs was suspected by locals of signaling to the enemy across the water when she left her window open, the light on in her bedroom and the blind flapping in the wind.

At Cadogan Square, Mary started a "War Salon" to amuse Yvo, filling the house with interesting guests—Hilaire Belloc, the *Observer*'s editor J. L. Garvin, Curzon and Balfour. At one of these gatherings in 1915, Cincie invented a new game: to discover everyone's secret complex. To general hilarity, she decided that Balfour, now advising Asquith's Government on defense, and attending meetings of the War Council, formed in November 1914, "was obsessed with the notion that he had caused the War and was feeling, secretly, very worried about it." At another, the Elchos, Charles Whibley and Lord Hugh Cecil debated Grey's Commons speech that had brought England into the war. Whibley attacked Grey "for shilly-shallying . . . he didn't even know himself which way his own speech was going to sum up"; Lord Hugh maintained that the war was "the inevitable, logical conclusion of the Entente Cordiale," the speech "an absolute masterpiece" of "Mark Antony oratory," which was the only way Grey could secure the support of the Radicals for the war. Cincie agreed with Lord Hugh on every point.

Mary found it difficult to engage in such discussions. From the war's very beginning, she had felt desolate. "Hopeless" reports of the war alarmed her—the "parallell [*sic*] lines & the germans [*sic*] living like trapdoor spiders—with the hills armed with Howitzers on cement floors!" She worried about Britain's shortage of artillery shells, which had been apparent almost from the war's outbreak, and fretted that she was not doing enough war work, which might serve as talismanic protection for her own sons. More than ever, she was drawn to her boxes of papers, but this correspondence was capable of making her break down, sounding "so still and small a note, so faint and futile in the midst of the bloody horrors and the Hellish Din." "Are all letters flattery?" she asked Arthur. "If not, they have built me a pretty monument, but are they worth keeping? Who cares? And does anything matter? Except explosive *Big* artillery! The one thing we have not got."

In the early spring of 1915, with Mary " 'out of sorts' mentally and physically," her doctor, Halliwell, prescribed a rest cure at Stanway. For three weeks, she was confined to her room in total isolation. Yvo was deeply amused to hear of this latest development: "How is your languid self," he wrote to his sister Mary,

> and how is Stanway, and how pray is that strange recluse or unspeakable monster, whom none may look on, closeted and communing with her spirit, dwelling on the heights until she emerge a full Mahatma? I suppose in the silence of the night the house echoes to the sound of beds, wardrobes and all manner of furniture being trundled round the room, and again to the rustlings of many sheet and blanket "manias." She will awake after a month and find Mockett [the butler] waiting with a sheaf of telegrams to the effect that her three sons are at the Front, her eldest daughter doing time for card-sharping, her second eloped with a young cavalry officer, her youngest truant from school and God knows where. But she will have forgotten them, so what matter? With renewed zest she will wheel the grand piano round in the drawing room and wander off over the hills with a pack of wild and aggravated chows, till Stanway falls in ruins about her. What a curious sight Halliwell must be, entering the forbidden room like the Steward of Glamis?

Shortly afterwards, on a cool April night, Mary, Mary Charteris, Bibs and Letty waved off "the Gallant Glittering Gloucesters" to Egypt in preparation for the Allied naval attack on Turkish forces in the Dardanelles. Allied control of the strategically vital strait would allow munitions to be shipped through to Russia. Britain's Government also hoped that victory in the Dardanelles might persuade the neutral states of Greece, Bulgaria and Romania to join the Allied side, and provoke the collapse of the tottering Ottoman Empire. The night before the Gloucesters left, the two Marys, Bibs and Letty had dined with Ego and his friend and fellow officer Tom Strickland. As part of their kit, the two had been issued with "little bottles of iodine" with instructions to apply instantly "to a fresh wound." "It would hurt a great deal to paint all round a very large wound," remarked Ego wryly. Letty followed them out a week later, taking nineteen-year-old Mary Charteris with her as a companion, ostensibly to do VAD work. Two months later, Mary returned from Egypt to announce that she was engaged to Tom Strickland. They married in Egypt, in December 1915.

A week after Ego's departure, Mary wrote to Arthur, distressed about the Gloucesters' shambolic artillery:

> These men have been mobilized since the very day war broke out, they contain the flower of England's nobility (what a flowery Daily Mail phrase) . . . and the flower of the darling yeoman men who left their crops—and their sheep at the most critical moment . . . they go with guns bought from (scrapped by?) the Germans after the Boer War. Now my dear! You are in with everything . . . all their councils and hob nob and gossip with Kitchener the God of War and with all the Bosses, just you order some nice little (or big) right little tight little guns to be dispatched at once, to reach them before their horses are fit.

Just weeks prior, Balfour had been recruited by the government to the Shell Committee, as the Cabinet Munitions of War Committee was known, working with Lloyd George to rectify the "deplorable" munitions output. Within weeks the "Shell Crisis" and disaster at Gallipoli would force Asquith into a Coalition government. Balfour was brought back into office proper, as First Lord of the Admiralty, replacing Winston Churchill, disgraced after the Dardanelles.

Arthur had always held the political fates of Mary's male family members in his hands. Now, in a sense, he held their lives. Yet the tenor of Mary's relationship with him during the war years was not markedly different to that of the decade preceding. At Downing Street, shut out by Asquith's infatuation with the young Venetia Stanley, a close friend of Asquith's daughter Violet, who had become the Prime Minister's confidante and obsession, Margot agitated to be told official secrets in order to boost her own sense of self. Mary discussed developments with Arthur and was honest in her views. She only ever pressed him for information when it directly concerned her sons, and even then her tone was measured and humorous. She understood if Arthur could not give her information. She knew that, if he were able, he would.

Many women—and men—were capable of compartmentalizing to mourn loved ones lost in a war negligently handled by generals that they nonetheless believed was just and necessary. Looking back, it is incredible, near impossible, that women of this generation and class watched their sons being sacrificed in a war governed by their husbands and lovers without ever once breaking faith. Pamela and Mary were two of these women. Yet, for different reasons, they did not. For Mary, Balfour was only ever trying to improve a situation rendered parlous by the neglect of others, drawn back into service by the need of the country. She mourned when he was brought back to the Admiralty: "so weary, reluctantly obliged to shoulder a heavy burden because all the nation trusts him."

After the war, Pamela helped Grey write his memoirs, *Twenty-Five Years,* his staunch, quiet defense of his conduct as Foreign Minister that took Britain into the war. That she seems never once to have considered Grey culpable is unsurprising; even had such thoughts occurred to her, she would have excised them before they took root. She defended her own, even down to rubbishing Margot's criticisms of Grey's and Eddy's wartime fishing habit. Margot proposed they should use the time in visiting the war wounded instead. Pamela replied, "I admit that the surface appearance of this fishing business, now, in Wartime, is ridiculous . . . I used to think the same as you—till I realized what a conventional view it was. It is not self-indulgence on his part, but relaxation—& [Eddy] needs relaxation . . . his way is in fishing, yours is in buying new clothes, mine is studying Psychological aspect of things." Unsurprisingly, Margot underlined the section alluding to her love of clothes in red pen.

In her own published works after the war Pamela maintained that the conflict had been glorious. "War . . . meant for Bim Romance," she wrote. "He had been playing at it, and dreaming of it, and writing about it . . . now it was his, and it brought him freedom, and self-expression, and joy . . . it was this that met him on the threshold of manhood, something as great as this. Not only illusive pleasure and the empty tyranny of little things . . ." If her private façade differed, it was only that Pamela did not engage with the war at all: not the munitions crisis, the change-overs in power, or the failings of the generals. She kept aloof, within her own world, frozen until her son came back.

Both Yvo—"a joy-dispenser," said Cincie—and Bim were part of a frenetic youth, squeezing out every moment of their lives. Pamela recalled that time as days of "color and purpose" for Bim, bombing around town in a two-seater crammed with people; arriving at Queen Anne's Gate in a flurry of hairdressers, tailors, buttonholes of white gardenias "in silver-foil and cotton wool," telephone ringing off the hook as he made plans for the next dance, the next dinner, the next play. They attended parties thrown by the American financier and adventurer George Gordon Moore, nicknamed the "Dances of Death," dancing all night to jazz and Hawaiian bands, fueled by "rivers of champagne" and surrounded by "mountains of red and white camellias," believing, as Iris Tree, another Coterie member, wrote, that there was "something of myth and legendary revival, the glory of Greece, the grandeur of Rome" in their antics. By night Diana Manners and Raymond Asquith's wife, Katharine, doped themselves on morphine and "chlorers" (chloroform). The Coterie's brittle vivacity and grim humor appalled Cincie. "I'm sure there is an insidiously corruptive poison in their minds . . . I don't care a damn about their morals and manners, but I do think . . . their anti-cant is really suicidal to happiness," she said. But Cincie was unusual in her sympathy for her parents' generation, who were "an object of ridicule" to the Coterie.

Time took on double speed. Within a space of ten months two of Mananai's daughters, Sibell and Madeline Adeane, clad in silk charmeuse and lacy veils, progressed up the aisle towards a khaki-clad groom in St. Peter's Church, near Babraham. Nineteen-year-old Clare Tennant married Adrian Bethell, an officer she had met barely weeks before in 1915. She was divorced, and remarried to another officer, Lionel Tennyson (grandson of the poet Alfred, Lord Tennyson), before the war was out. Margot complained to Pamela that the young were "uncultivated" and immodest. Pamela defended them:

> I think the "young females" of the present day *as a whole* have shown good quality. They have set to work & they go cheerfully without the gaieties of the world, which at 17 & 18 are, or might be looked on, as their right. Clare & her particular little world are exceptional, thank goodness, & she has a certain little exuberance of folly & [irreverence] of nature that must bubble to the top, like scum on ham.

In July 1915, worn out by his exertions, Bim came down to Wilsford on sick leave. He stayed for a fortnight, quietly recuperating. Pamela read aloud to her convalescent son. "Seeing him there again," she said, "among all the serene flowing of the currents of home life . . . it seemed to his Mother as if there must be some mistake, there could be no War . . . this must be the Summer Holidays, just beginning . . ." She took the opportunity to update the weight chart on which she recorded her family's growth: Bim, David, Kit, Gan-Gan (for Madeline Wyndham was staying with the family at the time), Eddy (a mere 9 stone 8 pounds, the same weight as Madeline Wyndham), Roly, the family dog, and at the bottom, "Oliver—2st 4lb."

A month later, Bim was specially selected to serve at the Front, despite being just eighteen. Edward Grey was honest with Eddy Tennant: "The selection of Bimbo . . . is a great honor & compliment but a great trial for you & Pamela. There is no way out of the trial & I pray that all may be well." The drumbeat was growing ever faster with George Vernon, Guy Wyndham's elder son George, Julian and Billy Grenfell, Frances Horner's son Edward and Charles Lister, son of the Ribblesdales, all among the recent dead. Bim left for France barely a week later, with a photograph of Pamela in his breast pocket. Less than a month after that, Mary suffered the same blow. She had stayed in London to be with Yvo, whose leave had been canceled. In the late afternoon, Yvo, "dog-tired," took himself to bed for a nap. Mary went to see Evelyn de Vesci for tea. When she got back to Cadogan Square at about seven, Yvo answered the door. Still in his "flame-colored, Turkish" dressing gown, his hair tousled with sleep, he held a scrap of paper in his hand. "I've got my warning," he said, "in a voice tense with suppressed excitement." All Mary could think was how young her son looked. She telephoned Evelyn. "Don't let him out of your sight," said Evelyn, "not even for a moment."

Plans were made for a fleeting visit to Gosford, where the rest of the family were making a last visit before the house was shut up for the duration of the war; that summer, Connor the agent had made it clear that this was the only way to meet death duties on Lord Wemyss's estate, and that it was "out of the question" to attempt "living in two houses." The night that Mary and Yvo were due to leave, London was cast into confusion by a Zeppelin raid. Mary was dining with Arthur when "the row" began. "I am responsible, and the guns are quite inadequate," said Arthur.

Zeppelins were still an awesome and eerie novelty, their strange beauty illuminated by the copper glow cast across the sky by flaming buildings and the boom of the defensive guns. King's Cross Station, from where Mary and Yvo were to catch the northbound train to Scotland, was pitch-black and plunged into confusion as Mary waited for Yvo, who had been at the theater with friends. They missed the sleeper, managing to get on a train that left at 4:55 a.m. Yvo slept on the train. Mary could not. "He looked so white and still," she later recalled, "and though I said to myself, he is still safe, he is still alive and under my wing, yet all the time as I watched him sleeping so peacefully there lurked beneath the shallow

A charcoal by John Singer Sargent, 1915, of Pamela and Eddy Glenconner's eldest son, eighteen-year-old Bim, in khaki, shortly before the young officer left the Grenadier Guards' barracks in London for the front line in France.

safety of the moment a haunting dreadful fear, and the vision of him, lying stretched out cold and dead."

They were at Gosford for just hours—arriving late afternoon and leaving at eleven that night. The party was avid for details of the "Zep" raid. Angela Forbes asked Yvo whether he had been scared. "Not a bit, after all why should one be presumptuous enough to imagine one would be killed?" Angela thought the reply typical of Yvo: "He was born with the rare gift of seeing things in perspective." That afternoon, Yvo went for a walk with Mary Charteris in the woods. The two were as close as twins, and Yvo could speak to Mary more frankly than anyone. "You know I probably shan't come back?" he said. "Oh *don't* say that!" she replied. They both knew the odds—as everyone there did, and the atmosphere of forced gaiety could not conceal it. "Poor Bibs looked too desperately miserable, never taking her eyes off his face," said Cincie. That night she slept with her little sister in their mother's bed. Recollecting Yvo's brief visit Angela Forbes later spoke of the "Spartan" courage of parents "who did nothing to thwart the enthusiasm of their boys." It epitomizes how insensitive Angela could be. For, short of pulling strings to get them out of combat and into a staff position—which would be considered a dishonorable and deplorable dereliction of one's patriotic duty—there was nothing these parents could do to stop their sons going.

Almost before Mary knew it, the day of Yvo's departure came. His train was scheduled to leave at 8:30 a.m., and they had a hurried, early breakfast at Cadogan Square, before making their way through the crisp autumn morning to Charing Cross Station. The station was a scrum, packed with English and Belgian soldiers, nurses in their starched white uniforms, luggage underfoot, and friends and family hanging over barriers to see their loved ones off. There Guy Charteris joined them, and friends of Yvo's, including the "hell-kitten" and Coterie member Nancy Cunard. Yvo's kit bag was stuffed so full that they had had to stand on it to squash it all in, and his mess tin was crammed with coffee, sugar and tea. In the melee, Mary spotted a doctor she knew. "I flew to him and said 'Yvo is here,'" she recalled. "Dr. Atkyns spoke most kindly and said I was to tell Yvo to go to him if he was ill or if he wanted anything." Mary was entrusting her tall fair son, still just eighteen, to the care of anyone she could find. Just before Yvo stepped up into the carriage, "he took out of his pocket the grenade [the ornamental badge worn by the Grenadiers] off his uniform, which was taken off when the less conspicuous ones were put on, and thrust it into my hand."

Mary stood among the waving throng, her arms hanging by her sides, the grenade clutched in her hand, and watched the train move slowly off amid clouds of steam. As the train picked up pace, the other officers in Yvo's carriage crowded to the windows to wave goodbye. For a moment Yvo was lost from sight. Then, wrote Mary, "Yvo leapt high into the air," allowing Mary "one more last glimpse of his beloved face."

THIRTY

The Front

Madeline Wyndham spent the war shuttling between Clouds, Stanway, Babraham and Wilsford to stay with her four surviving children; "the anxiety is almost more than I sometimes *can bear* . . . all *those* that I love best in the world Mary, Guy, Madeline & Pamela *all & each* one on the *rack* of anxiety & of *torture of heart & mind* . . ." she wrote to Wilfrid Blunt in October 1915, shortly after Yvo's departure. That spring, Mary had visited Clouds, arriving with Guy Wyndham to find their mother "waiting in the dusky hall; her darling eyes as big as an owl's with anxiety. Two telegrams lay waiting, she had watched them for hours without daring to open them, they were of no importance but I realized from the gulp in Guy's throat, after he had read them, what a strain it is nowadays to get a telegram."

Half a century later and in a different world, Tommy Lascelles, a Coterie member who considered the Charteris and Tennant families "the salt of my earth," wrote a cautionary note to his grandsons:

> If you read any of my war letters, you may feel that it wasn't as bad as it has been painted. Don't get that idea. In our letters, most of us deliberately omitted references to the many horrors and cruelties of war—to the dreadful sights one saw, to the hideous discomforts one had to endure, and the never-ending pain of the casualty lists. Such

things were, obviously, better not talked about to friends who understood them well enough; but they were there all right. So in letters home, one tried to recount only the lighter happenings, which, thank God, were there too.

To Yvo and Bim, war at first still did seem really like a great game. Yvo wrote to his family of having "one's legs swung onwards by a thousand singing men" on night marches, and forays under darkness across no-man's-land to look at the German trenches, returning with puttees torn from the barbed wire. He joked that, like a child waiting for Christmas, he could not wait for the cold weather to require him to use his new waterproof kit. He met up with Bim for "tea," and the cousins compared notes on their experiences thus far, enjoying the contents of the hampers from Fortnum & Mason ("the soldiers' twin saints," said Bim) that Pamela sent her son along with almost daily letters.

For the first month in France, Bim, known to his men as "the Boy Wonder," was well behind the lines of combat, digging trenches and learning how to set traps out of barbed wire. "It is rather fun making these entanglements and imagining the Germans coming along in the dark and falling over these things and starting to shout whereupon you immediately send up a flare . . . and turn a machine gun on to them as they struggle in the wire. It sounds cruel, but it is War," he wrote to his thirteen-year-old brother, David, in September.

Yvo likened war to a fairground. The German rockets were "as good as any Roman Candles I have seen on the 4th of June," he said. But it was a grotesque hall of mirrors that he evoked when he wrote to Cynthia from the ruins of Vermelles after a three-day stint in the trenches near Loos. A shell had landed on his billet that morning, almost burying him with falling earth and brickwork; and the town itself was little more than rubble. "I think one of the effects of this war will be that people will give up their feelings for ruins, qua ruins . . . there will be no more parties to Wardour Castle from Clouds," he predicted. He had a good mind to buy up the whole town and turn it into an amusement park like London's White City: "with flying-boats from the ruined shaft-heads—a maze made out of the trenches and rifle-ranges with dummy Huns peeping from the windows and ruined walls—shells filled with chocolate bursting at intervals throughout the grounds. I shall lay the suggestion before George [Gordon] Moore."

The devastation of the landscape had shocked Charlie Adeane when he visited France that summer in his capacity as Honorary Treasurer of the Royal Agricultural Society, investigating how agriculture in war-ravaged areas might be restored. The blasted landscape was even more desolate than he had anticipated. What shells had failed to bring to rubble, the Germans had burned. Charlie found villages deserted, only a few survivors living underground or huddled in the corners of a ruin. "The marvel is that cultivation should be carried on," he said, describing the sight of old men, women and children stoically loading carts and driving reapers through fields in which "the soldiers' red kepis [caps] hang on wooden crosses . . . where they fell, and show like red poppies above the corn." In a sun-bleached landscape, Charlie found himself outside a small church, almost the only building left standing, listening to the lusty singing of a congregation of French soldiers within. The service ended, the men streamed out, surrounding Charlie and his companions, while the shout rang out "Mort aux Boches!"

The trenches were still worse. Trench life was "an exact inversion of what is natural to man," said Yvo. Men lived underground, worked through the night, and slept, with interruptions for meals, at what intervals they could during the day. Their hours were punctuated by the sickening boom of shell fire ("an incomparably dreary sound, rather human—as though it loathed its mission") and the sinister death rattle of machine guns. Yvo, who turned nineteen while he was at the Front, was a platoon commander, the lowest officer's rank. He, like most, had already grasped the disparity between the shallow, stinking, swampy Allied trenches and those of the enemy. "The Germans have dug-outs 27 feet deep, with a long periscope going up the trench with a machine-gun run up and down on a winch and fired by means of a periscope at the bottom (at least so they tell me), so they don't stand to lose many men, even in a bombardment," he told Cincie. He had also grasped the essential futility of trench warfare. "I don't see that there is any military advantage in the line being a mile nearer Berlin, unless a gap is made through which troops can be poured to stop the enemy establishing himself in a second line," he said. "This war . . . seems weary of its own melodrama and does not know how to give up."

Still, ten days later, when Yvo was ordered to rally his men, holed up in a shallow trench, into a fresh—and clearly suicidal—attack, he did not demur. He led his men "over the top" and died in a fusillade of bullets: instantly, so his commanding officer said. He had been at the Front for not quite five weeks. Bim heard the rumor of his cousin's death the next day. "Osbert [Sitwell] and I are miserable about it, for no more lovable person ever stepped," he wrote to his mother, hoping against hope it might not be true.

But Bim himself was holed up in a frontline trench, under heavy bombardment from shell fire. He had had no more than four hours' sleep in seventy-two hours, and was sufficiently discomposed, as the ground around him shook and rumbled and debris showered over him, to allow his nerves to show, if only momentarily:

> I used to think I was fairly impervious to noise, but the crash upon crash, and their accompanying pillar of black smoke simply upset me, as they pitched repeatedly within 30 or 40 yards, and some even nearer. I don't think I showed I was any more frightened than anyone else. Perhaps I wasn't . . . I was very glad to get a letter from Daddy which seemed cheerful about the war. Please thank him for it . . .

Bim appears to have been entirely unconscious of the irony of this juxtaposition.

The news of Yvo's death reached his family the next day. Hugo's brother Evan Charteris, hearing the news first due to his position at the War Office, had arranged that the Elchos be informed by telephone rather than telegram. It took Cincie several moments to comprehend the full import of the blurred voice at the other end of the receiver telling her the call was "about Yvo Charteris . . . you must be prepared for the very worst."

Cincie's diary entry of that long, awful day records a family devastated: Bibs, huge-eyed, "petrified" and disbelieving; Mary Charteris, for whom Yvo was "practically her life," "frozen" at her dressing table, "mechanically greasing" her face with cold cream as she prepared to leave with Letty for Egypt the next day; "Poor Papa . . . most piteous—heartbroken and just like a child—tears pouring down his cheeks and so naïvely *astonished* . . . I think he really loved Yvo far the most of his children, and was so proud and hopeful about him"; and Mary, who had missed the telephone call while "closeted" in confabulation with Sockie, Bibs's governess, but guessed the news as soon as she saw Cynthia's face. "I think she really expected it . . . She was wonderful, quite calm after the first moment of horror. About five minutes afterwards she said something so sweet and natural, just what one feels when one is dazed: 'What a bore!'"

Ego wrote to Mary from Egypt, a frank letter that acknowledged in bald terms what this war had become:

> Darling Mum,
> I have absolutely nothing to say. When your own mother and brother are concerned it is futile to talk about sympathy, and the one consolation for me is that—if any comfort is to be extracted, or if the best thought is of any use, which of course it is—your soul is big enough, large enough for that purpose . . . The only sound thing is to hope the best for one's country and to expect absolutely nothing for oneself in the future. To write down everyone one loves as dead—and then if any of us are left we shall be surprised. To think of one's country's future and one's own happy past. The first is capable of vast improvement—as for the second, when all is said and done, we were a damned good family. Qua *family* as good as Clouds . . . I am so awfully sorry for Papa who loved him . . . He must write his sons off and concentrate upon his grand-children who thank God exist . . .
> Goodbye darling—I love you till all is blue.

For his family, Yvo's death was the point of no return. Whatever happened in the war, they could never go back to the lives they had lived before. For Cincie, it destroyed the familiar platitudes of glamour: "I am haunted by the feeling that [Yvo] is disappointed. It hurts me physically," she wrote in her diary. "Not little Yvo," Ettie Desborough wrote to Balfour. The following months felt to Mary as though "all the universe was rocking round one." She bore the return of Yvo's kit, his empty clothes "the most poignantly pathetic of all the heartbreaking angles & sharp turnings one has wearily to take," she told Wilfrid Blunt. "Mary has a lion-heart, it will make her able to triumph even over this, & prove herself indestructible," Ettie had written, but Yvo's death had eviscerated Mary, had "taken . . . all that I ever had of high worldly hopes & aspirations," as she put it to Blunt.

Mary refused to dissemble. "No one can maintain that it is not tragedy," she told Arthur from Stanway as the family faced its first Christmas without Yvo:

—pure and unadulterated, that it is draped in all the glamour of romance . . . does not mean the price is less to pay . . . and although the houses are not ruined or the harvests burnt here in England, still the long cruel tentacles of this deadly war has stretched its icy claw and reached each house and hearth . . . if you hold yr breath you hear the sound of widows weeping, sisters sobbing and the ceaseless falling falling of the mothers' tears, the whole air is stifled, surcharged with sadness, which eats into the soul . . . I will not believe that sadness is not sadness—or say it is God's will and all is for the best!

In the autumn of 1915, in her mid-forties, Pamela fell pregnant. She rejoiced in this late, unexpected pregnancy. It gave her "new courage & joy & hope—& bridged one over an Autumn & winter of [illegible] anxiety about Bim & Xtopher," she told Mary. In her poem "Hester," describing this time, she is Demeter-like, as fecund as the land around her during:

nine months' joy of happy life,
Of quiet dreams and blessed days,
Of peace that even calmed the Strife,
And steeped her in a golden haze . . .

Pamela was no longer frozen while the world moved around her. Now she was blooming while the world held its breath. Strings had been pulled and for the duration of Pamela's pregnancy, Bim was given a staff position under Brigadier John Ponsonby (commanding the 2nd Guards Brigade), away from action. The decision was justified by concerns about Pamela's health. Nonetheless, Bim took the position reluctantly. "My duties are to copy out recommendations for medals into books, and to check figures . . . Also I inspect the billets and rifles and gas-helmets of the Orderlies, telephone clerks and cyclists. Quite a large portion of my work is telling the General the date," he told his mother. He whiled away his time performing in shows for the troops: two-hour rowdy affairs each evening involving "Pierrot business," "Sketches" and songs. He procured a motorcycle and "tiff-tiff-ed" his way across the countryside; read the large packages of books Pamela sent him; and prepared his own poems for publication—*Worple Flit,* a slight, forty-page volume, published by Pamela's publisher Blackwell later that year. Pamela's son was safe; her child was about to be born. But the moment was to prove as fleeting as she might have feared. Hester was born on 24 May 1916, and died a few hours later.

"It has been dreadful—so overwhelming a sense of loss—at times I can hardly stand up against it," Pamela confessed to Mary. She had Hester photographed by H. C. Messer's studio in Castle Street, Salisbury—the waxen child, eyes shut, nestled among broderie anglaise—and sent the image to all her family and friends. Photographing the dead was not in itself uncommon: Percy Wyndham was photographed in his bed after death, surrounded by his favorite books and pictures. Pamela's widespread dissemination of the image at a time of mass grieving was.

Pamela had always established a monopoly on loss. During the Harry Cust episode, she never spoke, or apparently thought, once of Nina. When Drummy died, she acted as though she alone could have saved him, almost entirely ignoring the fact that he had been engaged to another woman. But her behavior on Hester's death, as her own family's sons died around her, tries the empathy of the biographer most. Pamela had suffered a terrible loss. She reacted as though she were the only person to have suffered loss in the world. She bombarded grieving families with pictures of her own dead child, and everyone who would listen, including Bim, in France, with pages about her grief. Perhaps the most difficult element is that Pamela paid lip service to self-awareness. "I try to dwell on how much all the World is suffering now—& how deep the sorrows of others," she said to Mary, but she employed these thoughts as consolation, not as perspective. It is doubtless this behavior that gave rise to another myth surrounding Oliver Hope's origins—disseminated, among others, by Susan Lowndes—that having buried Hester at Queen Anne's Gate, Pamela, retreating to Wilsford, from there made her way to the local hospital, Salisbury Infirmary, saying to the matron: "I've lost my baby, have you any orphans?" The Lowndes family had a strange fascination with laying claim to and denigrating Pamela's memory. This, as is evident from Pamela's earlier references to Oliver, is no more than a florid romance. But such was her behavior that the story of a high-handed aristocrat mad with grief could almost be true. She was not the

Pamela with her youngest son, Stephen, in 1916. The calm on Pamela's face and the faintest suggestion of a bump under her loose clothes suggests this may have been taken during her late, last pregnancy with little Hester.

monster of myth. She had simply been so long spoiled that she could not see anyone else as more than a circling planet and she the sun. But as she dwelt at length on her grief and pain in her letter to Mary she did rouse herself enough to recognize her sister's "anxiety—& dear Letty's" and add, "I long for you both to get good news."

Some six weeks previously, Mary had spent Easter at Stanway with a large group of family and friends. They had good weather, and games of tennis. But the "parliaments" in Mary's boudoir focused almost exclusively on the war; and a flippant discussion at lunch on the necessity of postwar polygamy now that all the young men of their acquaintance were being wiped out left thirteen-year-old Bibs, recorded Cincie, "seriously distressed." A further blow was struck at both sisters' hearts that afternoon on receipt of letters from Connor the agent enclosing the sum of ninety-seven pounds: their shares "of Ickey's [Yvo's] little fortune." In the gloaming, Cincie walked with a desolate Bibs up to the Pyramid. Stanway, as always, was magical in the dusk. But "Mamma is *miserable*—it's really like a broken heart. What *can* one do?" said Cincie.

That night Mary had a "dream-vision": "The atmosphere of the room seemed to quiver with excitement—I felt the stress and strain and *saw* as if thrown on a magic-lantern sheet, a confused mass of black smoke splashed with crimson flame . . . like a child's picture of a battle or an explosion." Among these "flames and smoke" she "saw Ego standing, straight and tall." His profiled face was set and stern, his eyebrows and mustache dark against his pale face. It seemed as though "he was exercising his forces with all his might and main." A brilliant golden banner swathed his chest in spiral folds, and "seemed to protect him." "I felt that something had happened," Mary said later, "but I knew not what, it was below the level of consciousness." She spent the rest of the weekend in a reverie.

Mary's dream was on the night of Saturday, 22 April 1916. Three days later *The Times* reported a small battle at Katia, in the Sinai, after a surprise attack by hostile forces at 5 a.m. on Easter Sunday. The day after that, Mary received a cable from Letty: the Gloucesters had been involved, Ego slightly wounded, and both he and Tom Strickland captured. "I can't bear it for Mamma," said a dismayed Cincie, knowing that Ego himself would be "miserable" at having been "captured at his very first engagement"—"so like his pathetic luck."

Stanway, 1916. The view is of the forecourt, looking towards the jewel-like gatehouse, built of mellow Cotswold stone in the calm decade before England's Civil War. The main house's oriel window is to the left. Almost three hundred years after the gatehouse was built, war was upon Stanway again. To the right, one of Mary's many chows keeps guard over the house's chatelaine in its darkest days.

But, despite best efforts, the details that trickled through over the next few days did not add up to any coherent story. *The Times* reported a "Stiff Fight" by British cavalry against enemy forces of up to three thousand— Germans, and Turks on camelback—in conditions of mist and fog. But the war correspondents' conjecture could not be confirmed because, as Mary said, "*all*" at Katia "were killed & taken," their fates obscured as much as the battleground that day. The trickle of news guttered out, to be replaced by "lots of confusing Egyptian rumours," prismed through the Chinese whispers of the well-meaning and those for whom Lord Elcho's fate was simply bavardage. At a dinner party in London Mary overheard Mrs. Keppel, once Edward VII's favored mistress, say that a syce (an Arab servant) had sworn that after the battle he had watched by Lord Elcho's body for hours.

Mary later said of her "dream-vision" that "it helped me to *wait* and kept me outwardly calm." But inwardly she was "terribly worried, over-tired and nervy." She pressed Balfour for "the private account of what happened to the Yeomanry (Glos. Worcs. and Warwicks.) on Easter Sunday . . . it's so maddening not knowing." Almost a month after the battle the Elchos were "inexpressibly relieved" to receive confirmation through the American Embassy that Tom Strickland was a prisoner in Jerusalem and being taken to Damascus. But the cable was silent about Ego. The next day, in early May, Mary went to Truro to stay in Miss Jourdain's convent "for a rest," taking with her a crucifix as an offering (the former governess had become a nun).

The uncertainty continued. A list procured by Hugo of prisoners at Constantinople did not bear Ego's name. More frustratingly still, Tom Strickland's letters to his wife, Mary, delivered by the Red Cross, made no mention of Ego. On 10 June the Red Cross telephoned with the message "Lord Elcho at Damascus. No details," which rendered the family "wild with joy." Two weeks later the message was countermanded: the Red Cross had sent the wrong name.

The final news came on 1 July. The French Red Cross confirmed Lord Elcho's death at Katia. He had been twice wounded, had had the wounds dressed and, despite his batman's entreaties, had gone back into battle. A shell had blown out his chest, killing him instantly. "Oh God—Oh God, my beautiful brother that I have loved so since I was a baby—so beautiful *through* and *through*! Can it be true that he'll never come back?" asked Cincie. Mary was at Clouds. Hugo wired through, asking

Guy Wyndham to break the news to his wife. For Mary it was confirmation of a still, small feeling in her deepest heart: "Ego told me—when he died . . . for I saw him in my dream," she told her mother. "I never really *felt* that he'd come home—from the War—but of course I didn't *know*." But so cataclysmic was the final confirmation of Ego's death that, ever afterwards, Mary could not remember whether it came on the first or the second of July.

Instances of people sensing a loved one's death from many miles away are not uncommon. It can be felt as a shift of energy, a ticker tape of images running through the mind, an inexplicable sense of discombobulation and loss. There is no rational explanation; many will think it simply imagination. But Mary thought that the vision—which seems to have coincided exactly with the time of battle—was the product of "a strenuous love." Ego had reached her at his time of greatest "mental stress and strain." She clung to that, determined "not to fail" Ego and to create for his sons the life that he now could not. "I'm *not* going to be wonderful! I'm sick of the word," she told Arthur. "But there is no other word for it," Cynthia said.

After Ego's death, Mary struggled—though she would never say it—with the fact that he had died in such a small battle, with no medals or mentions in dispatches to prove his valor. In a further wrench, the commander of the Egyptian Expeditionary Force, General Sir Archibald Murray's official report of the battle, published in *The Times* in September 1916, did not even mention Ego's name. The baldest account of Ego's death gave Mary the most comfort: a wire received from Hyatt, Ego's sergeant, now a prisoner of war, several months after Ego's death: "Lord Elcho twice wounded—then shell carried away chest. Acted magnificently." *"Acted magnificently"* Mary underlined, immediately sending to Ettie and Evelyn this last shred of news. Such words, from a "simple, unsuperlative sergeant," must mean something.

The day confirmation of Ego's death was received was—although this must have been reduced to the periphery of the family's thought—the first day of the battle of the Somme. It is strangely apposite: both such monumental tragedies, the difference only one of scale. Mary had heard the rumors of a new campaign back in January. "I suppose you know (I'm not asking you!) that there'll be heavy fighting in March or April," she wrote to Balfour at the time. Intended for spring, the campaign—a concerted Anglo-French offensive, devised, in the wake of Gallipoli and the British attack in the Eastern theater, to end the war on the Western Front once and for all—was delayed until July by the German offensive at Verdun. For a week beforehand the Allied forces had bombarded the German trenches with artillery. The sound was so loud that Asquith heard it in Downing Street. So confident were the generals that, as Raymond Asquith wryly wrote to his wife, Katharine, shortly before, "An order has just come to say that there is to be no cheering in the trenches when peace is declared. No one can say that our Generals don't look ahead."

At 7:30 a.m. on 1 July 1916 the first troops went over the top. They were assured by their generals that they could make their way across no-man's-land "with a walking stick," and that not even a rat could have survived the bombardment of the German trenches. At Angelina's, Angela fried eight hundred eggs in three hours. A short distance away, wave after wave of soldiers, weighed down by sixty-pound packs, walked steadily into a line of German fire, mown down, toppled like ninepins, entangled and shredded by barbed wire, pulped under the feet of the men who came up behind them only to fall themselves. A total of 19,249 British soldiers, including 993 officers, died that day; almost 40,000 more were wounded. The battle, which the generals had so confidently expected to be a rout, lasted in total 140 days. Nothing illustrates the generals' failure of intelligence and apparent disregard for human life more than the catastrophic Somme.

Bim turned nineteen on that first day of the Somme. His battalion was posted nearby, and in combat, on and off, that summer. But his letters home dwelt on "do you remembers," literary discussions and his anxiety about *Worple Flit*'s publication (Bim knew that his work was not "fashionable" and feared the critical response: "I daresay if I wore black shirts . . . and wrote verse that was quite incomprehensible, the reviewers would take it for genuine 'poesie'"). He wrote to Pamela, leaning on one elbow while lying on a blanket in a field surrounded by poplars, telling her about a nice new company commander who "laughs at my jokes," and alluding to a brief love affair with a young, "very pretty and very well-dressed" French woman called Ninette, promising to send his mother a photograph of her.

Bim's letters that summer were love letters, reassuring Pamela of her youth and beauty, mourning with her Hester's loss, marveling at her courage and strength. There are only brief hints at a darker truth, a pointedly casual reference to a corporal in his battalion who had received a "Blighty" wound only that morning ("He was hit in the ankle and forearm, and was simply jubilant. The other chaps envied him a good deal, and so did I"); a passing reference to the difficulty of sending mail ("We are moving around a lot"); a capitulation at the end of a long letter ("I would give the last ten years of my life for six months' rest now"); and, in August, a plea ("I do wish you would tell me what the High Brows think? The P.M. [Prime Minister] and sic-like . . .").

The war drove a rift between the generation that fought and those who sent them there, nowhere more so than among the elite. The mechanistic chain of command and incomprehensible orders gave the upper classes serving a glimpse for the first time of the impotence felt on a daily basis by most of Britain's populace. Suddenly there was a "They": generals and politicians who made decisions with no regard to what the men—even officers—thought. Those fighting were part of an anonymized mass, aristocrat and common man alike, buried where they fell. Many of those officers felt angered at the betrayal of their generation by their parents, and for the children of the Souls this was in many cases a literal statement—none more so than Raymond Asquith. The Coterie's acknowledged leader wrote to Diana Manners, savagely tearing apart the Souls who continued to chatter and talk:

> Their minds are almshouses . . . We do not hunt the carted hares of 30 years ago. We do not ask ourselves and one another and every poor devil we meet "How do you define Imagination?" or "What is the difference between talent and genius?," and score an easy triumph by anticipating the answer with some text-book formula, originally misconceived by George Wyndham in the early eighties at Glen, and almost certainly misquoted by Margot at the borrowed house of a Frankfort baronet, not because it was either true or witty or even understood, but because it was a sacred obligation to respect whatever struck the late Sir Charles Tennant as a cut above what he had heard in the night school at Paisley where they taught him double-entry . . .

Raymond's stepcousin Bim could not say this—he could not yet comprehend this. But he was no longer the child who had gone to war and who wrote to his mother, "I think I shot a German the other day; if I did, God rest his soul." In the dog-eared *Oxford Book of English Verse* that he carried always with him, the poems underlined all dwell on farewell and longing. In June, while at Poperinghe, he wrote "The Mad Soldier." Written in the vernacular, it is the voice of a dead soldier, decaying beneath a heap of bodies in the trenches where "rats eat Body-meat!"

> *... It's a sin*
> *To say that Hell is hot 'cause it's not:*
> *Mind you, I know very well we're in hell.*
> *In a twisted hump we lie heaping high,*
> *Yes! an' higher every day ...*

Bim's innocence had been corrupted—although it has been rightly noted that he could still only express this horror in a voice very different to his own. He sent it to Pamela, with anxious inquiries about whether she liked it. He had to ask her view several times before she gave it. Eventually, she appears to have replied with praise, but the delay is indicative. To read "The Mad Soldier" would be a shock for any mother. For Pamela it must have been a striking blow to her worldview.

Bim's battalion was sent up to the front line of the Somme on 9 September. His first three days in the trenches were spent under intense shelling: "We have had all the kicks and none of the ha'pence in this show, as other batt[alion]s had the fun of repulsing attacks and killing hundreds, while we had to just sit and be shelled ... the C.O. [Commanding Officer] is very envious of what he calls the 'other chaps' hellish good shoot,'" he wrote home. After three days behind the front line, his battalion returned to the trenches again as support. This time Bim was shaken—or wired—enough to reveal details he normally kept hidden. He had been directed to follow the Guards to their new location and then bring his battalion, which was in support, alongside. It required three trips back and forth along no-man's-land. During the first, he was "shot at by Boches on the high ground with rifles ... with bullets that scuffed up dust all around with a wicked little 'zump.'" The second was "an unpleasant journey" of "about half a mile over nothing but shell-holes full of dead and dying, with any amount of shells flying about" and with only an orderly beside him. Intercepted during the third, he spent "that afternoon, evening, and night in a large rocky shell-hole" with his commanding officer, the adjutant and the battalion's doctor under severe shelling: "about four men were done in in the very next shell-hole a couple of yards away. That night was one of the coldest and most uncomfortable it has ever been my fortune to spend with the stars to see."

There was another day still of leading, dodging, weaving to go. "My worst job was that of taking messages down the line of trenches to different captains. The trenches were full of men, so I had to go over the open. Several people who were in the trench say they expected every shell to blow me to bits." His battalion were relieved at midnight, and got back behind the lines at 2:30 a.m., "dog-tired," to "soup, meat, champagne, and cake . . . That is the time one really does want champagne, when one comes in at 3 a.m. after no sleep for fifty hours. It gives one the strength to undress." Already, from along the lines had come rumors of the dead: "Guy Baring, Raymond Asquith, Sloper Mackenzie, and many others . . . Death and decomposition strew the ground . . . I must tell you of other things."

And so Bim retreated into memory. He told his mother of a pleasant walk of a few hundred yards taken a few days earlier with a Corporal Jukes, who, it transpired, was the son of a former keeper at Clouds. Corporal Jukes remembered Pamela's wedding; remembered when Icke the butler was a mere footman—his sister had been housemaid at Glen under the Bart: "And so he is altogether a great family friend . . . We had a very good talk about people like Mr. Mallet, Mrs. Vine and suchlike hench-folk. Do write and tell me if you remember him?" So Bim ends an account of forty-eight hours of hell with an inquiry more suited to a polite dinner party.

Raymond Asquith's death—shot in the chest as he led his men out in an advance from Ginchy, lighting a cigarette to reassure them, and dying before he reached the dressing station—made headlines in England. "It seems to take away one's last remains of courage," said Cincie. Everyone had thought that Raymond would be the man to lead his country into a new era. "What a glorious company they are by now, recruited every week from our best and most radiant," Asquith said to Ettie, "those who, we fondly imagined, were going to make & guide the future here." If Asquith regretted not once writing to his eldest son while he was at the Front, he did not show it. It appears he did not, for he never once wrote to Beb either.

Four days later, Bim's battalion were ordered back into the trenches.

They were to go "over the top" the next day in an attack over 1,200 yards. Bim wrote to Pamela. He knew, in all likelihood, it would be his last letter. "Our Brigade has suffered less than either of the other two Brigades in Friday's biff (15th), so we shall be in the forefront of the battle," he explained. He had taken Communion that morning, slept "like a top" the night before, and was "full of hope and trust." He invoked the spirit of his "fighting ancestors," buoyed up by the thought of "all the old men . . . in the London clubs . . . thinking and hoping about what we are doing here!" "I have never been prouder of anything, except your love for me, than I am of being a Grenadier," he added. Bim told Pamela that on going into action he would carry as always "four photies [*sic*]" of her, and that "that line of Harry's" from "Non Nobis" rang through his head: "High heart, high speech, high deeds 'mid honouring eyes." "Today is a great day for me," he ended. "Your love for me and my love for you, have made my whole life one of the happiest there has ever been . . ."

Bim played the role expected of him by Pamela to the last, even invoking lines written about her own great romance with Harry Cust. Doubtless puppy-doggish, sweet-natured Bim genuinely believed the sentiments he invoked: the aristocrat worthy of his ancestors and the Guards who went before him. But this was also the officer who had dodged bullets and cowered inwardly in shell holes through long, freezing nights while trying outwardly to appear unmoved; who wrote "The Mad Soldier," and who in "A Bas la Gloire!" mocked the stout generals in their gleaming cars behind the lines. This is the generous spirit of the boy who on first getting a motorcycle drove along Wiltshire lanes with a cardboard placard attached to the back on which was written, in letters three inches high, "Apologies for the dust," one who feels, as Bim wrote in his letter, "rather like saying 'If it be possible let this cup pass from me' " but then invokes God's will and the "triumphant finish . . . [that] steels my heart and sends me into this battle with a heart of triple bronze."

On 22 September, Bim was among his company, sniping in a "sap"—a short trench dug from the front line into no-man's-land—when he was killed by a German sniper: "absolutely instantaneously," said his commanding officer. He was buried in the Guillemont Road Cemetery, a few graves along from Raymond Asquith, two of four hundred thousand

British casualties lost in the 140 days of the battle of the Somme. A total of 1.3 million men died on both sides in all. At the end of it, the British had advanced six miles.

The death of "Lord Glenconner's heir," "the 55th heir to a peerage who has lost his life in the war," headed *The Times*'s list of casualties the next day. The paper, noting that his death came just a week after that of his cousin Lieutenant Mark Tennant, reprinted lines from Bim's final letter: "Your love for me and my love for you have made my whole life one of the happiest there has ever been. This is a great day for me." Two days later, at Pamela's behest, *The Times* published Bim's "Home Thoughts in Laventie," a gentle, wistful poem in which a soldier buries his head in flowers found growing in the ruins of a blasted, shattered town. Inhaling their scent, he steps back onto the Downs: "Home, what a perfect place!"

THIRTY-ONE

The Remainder

I t has been forcibly demonstrated by statistics that the legend of "the flower of England's aristocracy" falling in the war was no mere myth. One in five of the British and Irish peers and their sons who fought in the war died, compared with one in eight for all members of the fighting services. There is no mystery to this: junior officers, leading their troops into battle, were the first in the line of fire; concepts of honor meant patrician males were among the first to join up or were already in the forces when war broke out, when casualties were proportionately at their worst. The Upper Ten Thousand's exclusivity meant that such losses were almost as acutely felt as in the decimated communities of the "Pals' Battalions"—for when these specially constituted units that allowed the men of a locality to serve alongside one another were wiped out in battle, so too was the male population of entire towns. Out of the Coterie of some thirty or forty men and women in total, fourteen died. "Oh why was I born for this time? Before one is thirty to know more dead than living people? Really, one hardly knows who is alive and who is dead," Cynthia wrote in her diary, expressing the sentiment that every woman of her acquaintance felt.

The historian David Cannadine has said that "it is not necessary to join the clichéd cult of the Wyndhams, the Grenfells, and the Charterises, to recognize that they were uncommonly gifted and promising young men, whose greatness had been predicted before they died and was not just invented afterwards." Enough Souls had demonstrated that predicted greatness could come to disappointing ends. Yet to an extent the mythologization of the "Golden Generation" by their mothers has done them a disservice. This generation had wit and talent. Many had integrity. "He had George's cleverness plus—great scholarly learning & absolute freshness[.] I looked to him to save the world!" said Mary of Yvo. Their true gold is rendered almost indiscernible under the thick layer of gilt. In 1916, Ettie Desborough's *Pages from a Family Journal, 1888–1915* was privately published (250 copies by Spottiswoode of Eton High Street at a total cost of £375). It was a scrapbook of reminiscence and letters, saccharine and utterly sanitized. "I find Ettie's book thrilling, it tells of our children's (the children of the Souls!) Golden Age," Mary told Balfour. Yet Raymond Asquith, receiving a copy at the Front, was weary of the Souls' cant, and criticized the way Ettie doctored the book to remove all trace of her sons' undoubted insolence, arrogance and aggression. "Ettie is a snob in [a] harmless sense . . . She meant to give her sons the best mise-en-scène from a worldly point of view which could be had . . ." Eleven days later, Raymond was killed on the Somme and became mythologized himself as "this star of England." The words, from Shakespeare's *Henry V,* are inscribed on his tombstone.

Edward Wyndham Tennant, Pamela's memoir of Bim, was published in 1919. She first began sending chapters to her publisher, John Lane, in 1917. Writing her son's life was "like bearing him over again, a moral parturition," she said. She did not have to edit too much to provide the mise-en-scène she wished for Bim. "The Mad Soldier" and "A Bas la Gloire!" were included—quite possibly Pamela was trying to show that Bim, in 1916, was already moving towards work worthy of the greatest war poetry, and would have achieved work similar to Wilfred Owen's "Dulce et Decorum Est" and that of Siegfried Sassoon had he lived. She maintained that "War" was, for Bim, "Romance," and that he had died in the best, most fitting way, too exalted for the life of an ordinary mortal.

Mary first began collating material for her own memoir in January 1917. Sitting on the floor, "amongst heaps of 'dead leaves' fluttering papers of the past . . . has almost killed me with misery," she told Balfour. "I know I ought to feel grateful for the many happy years, but . . . I see . . . life's hopes and aspirations—and incidentally one's own heart!—

lie bleeding in the dust." Rereading all these letters, Ego's times from school to university, "the sweet short track of little Yvo," Mary could see only "the long years of preparation leading up to the holocaust."

Lacking Pamela's facility for writing for publication and Ettie's facility with emotion, Mary labored over *Family Record* for fifteen years, looking up to the Pyramid for inspiration from her boudoir at Stanway, struggling to avoid the "dragon's teeth" of cliché and hyperbole. She was terrified she might not do justice to her sons—worse still, might expose them inadvertently to criticism. It was written, so she told Ettie, "in heart's blood . . . !" and was published privately in 1932. Of the three memoirs, Mary's is the most painful, truthful reading. Her sons "emerge luminous," as she had hoped.

Since the war's start Mary had questioned the assumption of a glorious death. Yet, except to Arthur, it took courage to give voice to the heresy. When she first began working on the memoir she had asked Ettie to write a tribute to Yvo for inclusion. This was fairly common. Ettie did so willingly and ended by proclaiming Yvo's death "the only end worthy of his beginning." Revisiting these words in 1931 Mary balked. "Lovely as every word of it is," she wrote, tiptoeing carefully towards her point, ". . . during the passage of years does not one slightly change not one[']s point of view—but perhaps the manner of expressing it? . . . I only feel that . . . (altho' we know that it was wholly glorious right and noble what they *did*) we do not quite think that any other way (their darling lives, lived out here) would have been *unworthy of their beginning*? Perhaps you'll think me mad . . . but they *might,* as thank God, many did—they might have fought & lived? . . ."

In December 1916, Asquith's Coalition collapsed. Balfour replaced Edward Grey as Foreign Secretary in Lloyd George's ministry—although without a seat in the new Prime Minister's streamlined War Cabinet. Grey, since July Viscount Grey of Fallodon, retreated gratefully to his Northumberland estate. "I read nothing remotely connected with the war except the newspapers," he told Eddy Tennant, expressing his relief at being able to share "general anxiety" without feeling personal responsibility for the events that took place.

Grey had worried daily about Bim's welfare when at the Front, and was devastated by his death. On first hearing the "terrible news," he sent Eddy two letters in as many hours: "I will come to you at a word whenever you want me . . ." In April 1917, a fire at Fallodon all but destroyed the house, and all Grey's papers. It was "a melancholy business"—although he was the first to admit that it was nothing to compare with that suffered by the Glenconners. There was no question of rebuilding until after the war. In the interim, Grey stayed with the Glenconners at Queen Anne's Gate, and at Itchen Abbas.

It is still debated how far Grey, a Foreign Secretary who spoke no French and never once visited Germany, could have avoided Britain's entry into the war. Diana Bethell, Clare Tennant's daughter who more or less lived at Wilsford in the postwar years, remembered as a small girl tugging at Grey's sleeve asking, "Will there be another war? Will there be another war?" "The subject always made him shake, and brought the same answer: 'There will never ever be another war' he would repeat." What is clear is that neither Pamela nor Eddy ever held Grey responsible for the war that caused their son's death. Perhaps that was also because, to Pamela, Bim was not lost. As she explained in *The Earthen Vessel*, published by John Lane in 1921: "When the time came to need the comfort offered by Spiritualism, I turned to it . . . in just as common-sense and practical a manner as I would have gone about to book a passage or to send a cable to New Zealand, had it so chanced that my son had gone to that quarter of the globe."

The spiritualist craze that arose in the war years and continued throughout the 1920s was a bereaved society's response to incomprehensible loss. In post-Reformation England, people began to believe in witchcraft when Puritan austerity stripped them of Catholicism's amuletic defenses against evil. Now, a society shorn of its husbands, brothers and sons reached out for mediums, book tests and séances as solace in its pain. In 1915, Cincie had predicted that the great numbers of casualties would force a change in the way society treated its dead. "Now they are so many one *must* talk of them naturally and humanly, not banish them by only alluding to them as if it were almost indelicate." Instead, society began talking to them.

The Earthen Vessel, its subtitle *A Volume Dealing with Spirit-Communication Received in the Form of Book-Tests*, records the results of Pamela's book tests carried out between 1917 and 1920 with Mrs. Leonard, a medium on a salaried position with the Society for Psychical Research who communicated through her spirit guide, Feda. From January 1918, the sittings were paid for by the SPR, who sent a professional notetaker to attend the sittings "in the interests of investigation!"

said Pamela, thrilled to have the accuracy of "dear Bim's book tests & messages" recognized in this way, happier than at any point since Bim had died. As a child, "Step fearless into the dark" had been one of Bim's favorite expressions. Now Pamela found the phrase running round her head. "It seems to match the endeavor somehow," she said.

A book test involved a medium, acting on spirit information, directing the sitter to a line of a page of a book in a room in a house. The sittings were conducted mostly at Clouds, Wilsford and Queen Anne's Gate, attended by Pamela and Eddy, their sons, bereaved cousins and close friends. Pamela recounts an intensely loaded atmosphere: the receipt of the message from Feda, the hunt for meaning, the triumph when a book corresponding to the description was found, the relief and joy when the extract produced a message. Later Stephen recalled Pamela's face when she received a book test that worked: "so wonderful, so uplifted & happy."

Pamela claimed always to have held spiritualist beliefs. But there is little evidence of her ever employing them until she was confronted with death. Her early letters dwelt long on Christ, those in her middle years on her children. Only when Hester died did Pamela seize upon Lady Betty Balfour's suggestion that Hester's touching "Earth through me" might have been "necessary to her development in another life," as giving her hope. After Bim's death, spiritualism became an obsession for her: scarcely a letter goes by without Pamela recommending the latest spiritualist tract or recounting a message received.

As the number of mediums and sittings proliferated (by 1918, Mrs. Leonard had a three-month waiting list for sittings), the War Office became concerned, fearing that officers, caught off guard, were leaking confidential material in sittings. The *Daily Mail*'s Harold Ashton began a campaign to expose fraudulent mystics. Pamela appeared as a witness for the defense in one of the first trials, that of the American Mrs. Brockway, "charged with professing to sell fortunes," in December 1916. It was a sensation, ending in a furor when the defense counsel, Ernest Wild KC (King's Counsel), came to verbal blows with the skeptical magistrate and stormed out of court. At Pamela's behest Eddy exerted his influence to have Mrs. Brockway's deportation order sending her back to the United States commuted to one to Paris, a safer journey than across the submarine-infested Atlantic.

Margot was scathing: "Pamela, poor dear, has reached her religion through spiritualism . . . a random slap on the ear in a dark room has convinced her of the existence of God." Yet reports of these trials, in which magistrates tried to get to grips with whether "spirits" might be "lying" to the mediums who were their conduits, showed the ambiguity of society's attitude towards spiritualism. It suspected it was nonsense— but it could not quite be sure. Pamela, seeing herself as a guide for others, wanting to allow them to enjoy the "supreme joy" she found in this communication, encouraged those still unsure. In November 1916 she took Mary to a séance with a man in Tavistock Square in London's Bloomsbury. Mary told Cincie she was "agnostical," thinking "perhaps one ought just to give a chance to the theory that the middle-man may still be necessary for communication—more on account of Yvo than Ego." In fact, Mary wanted to believe far more than she let on to her cynical daughter. In December, she took Cincie to a further session at Tavistock Square. It was disastrous. The medium accused a mistrustful, uneasy Cincie of acting as a mental "screen" and "got hopelessly on the wrong track about me, thinking my husband had been killed," said Cincie. Mary could not stretch her credulity further. Pamela indefatigably continued to send her reports of sittings with Mrs. Leonard whenever Ego and Yvo made an appearance.

In 1914, Pamela had responded to war's outbreak by scooping up another child. An exchange from 1918 suggests that she responded to Bim's death in a similar way. In 1918, the academic Marie Stopes (who had begun looking into issues of sexual compatibility and the married relationship when her own unsatisfactory marriage to a fellow scientist— it was never consummated—fell apart) published the sex manual *Married Love,* and shortly afterwards *Wise Parenthood,* a birth-control manual popularizing the contraceptive diaphragm. One of *Married Love*'s controversial propositions concerned artificial insemination. Stopes believed that for many reasons—"the husband's actual sterility or the lack of mutual adjustment in their organs, or from an ill-understood lack of chemical affinity"—an otherwise loving couple might not be able to have a child. Since husbands might object to their wives "yielding" their bodies to another man, Stopes's solution was artificial insemination: "There are sufficient records in the medical profession of success . . . for it to offer much hope." She added, helpfully, that "where the injection is undertaken by a woman doctor, the husband need have no feeling that his wife has been violated" at all. Her theories were contested in the preface by her editor, William J. Robinson, informing readers that successful artificial insemination was so rare that the method "is never likely to acquire a great vogue."

Among Stopes's papers in the British Library is a tantalizingly brief exchange of just two letters between her and Pamela in July 1918, shortly after publication. In the first, Stopes refers to an intimate conversation between the women the day before:

> The more I think of it, the more undecided I am. You ask a thing I could only do for a most *intimate* friend, as *so* much is involved—I really do think you should find the right person *yourself* because you know *heredity* is a very very important factor—& how could I take such a responsibility? Supposing you were ever to regret any developing trait how would you prevent a feeling that you trusted me & I was somehow responsible?

Pamela replied that day:

> I quite see that you might view the matter we discussed *as you do*. It is worthy of you—and as I might expect . . . Thank you with all my heart . . . I don't yet fully know how much tension I am undergoing in keeping this longing in control, because I have a strong will! I must just wait & see. Meanwhile because of my talk with you I have felt much helped, & happier . . . I have never spoken to anyone as I did to you. I believe I was not misguided in my confidence?

With Pamela, almost nothing is too strange. These letters fit exactly a surmise that she had, however tentatively, suggested that Stopes should artificially inseminate her with sperm from a donor of Stopes's choosing, and Stopes shrank from being responsible for determining the paternity of any child Lady Glenconner might bear. So far as it is possible to tell, the idea was dropped, but there remained an understanding between the two women, and a deep gratefulness towards Stopes on Pamela's part.

The young continued to die—and the old. Harry Cust succumbed, suddenly, to pneumonia in 1917, and a death that once would have been seismic for the Souls passed almost unnoticed in the context of seas of crosses in France. Pamela placed memorials to Bim in Salisbury Cathedral, in the church at Wilsford and in the kirk at Traquair near Glen.

Madeline Wyndham raised a plaque in East Knoyle church: "In Memory of my Five Grandsons who were killed in the Great War." Her faith had become ever more determined in the war's bleak years. She now lived, said Pamela, "in close communion with all those who had gone before."

Mary suffered the evisceration of public appearances, laying foundation stones for a Garden City for disabled soldiers at Longniddry in Scotland, near Gosford, and memorial stones to her sons at Stanway and Gosford itself. Solace for her was Stanway—a place saturated with her sons' spirits—playing over "might-have-beens," trying to work out what would have happened with better scouting at Katia, or if Yvo had never switched from the Rifles to the Guards. She and Ego's widow, Letty, cherished David and Martin, Ego's two small sons. "I get through *bit by bit* (and nobody *need* ask one how, because one cannot tell them)," she told her mother. But after 1916 everything was an afterthought.

At 11 a.m. on 11 November 1918 came the Armistice, and the guns finally fell silent. Once again raucous crowds filled the streets. Yet for those who had fought, the forced celebration was far removed from the innocence of four years before. "This was the moment to which I had looked forward for four years, and now that it had arrived I was overcome by melancholy. Amid the dancing, the cheering, the waving of flags, I could think only of my friends who were dead," said Duff Cooper, one of the few Coterie members to survive, who married Diana Manners the following year; "I had expected riotous excitement, but the reaction of everyone, officers and men, seemed the same—flat depression," said Oliver Lyttelton, son of Alfred and D.D. "Even when you win a war you cannot forget that you have lost your generation," said Tommy Lascelles, who, like Duff Cooper, had seen most of his friends die.

So these officers stood frozen among the celebrating crowds, and the mothers of the dead thought only of the sons they had lost. "All day the thought of you has burnt in my innermost heart. Victory, & you & I look in vain for our Victors," Ettie wrote to Mary. "No one can feel light of heart . . . we miss our shining victors in the hour of victory," echoed Mary in her diary. The survivors had now to endure the peace, which Cincie thought "will require more courage than anything that has gone before. It isn't until one leaves off spinning round that one realizes how giddy one is. One will have to look at long vistas again, instead of short ones, and one will at last fully recognize that the dead are not only dead for the duration of the war."

THIRTY-TWO

The Grey Dawn

Among Pamela's papers is a printed pamphlet from July 1920 issued by one F. S. Graham, a North Yorkshire game dealer. Mr. Graham was pleased to announce that he would be importing Hungarian partridge from Czechoslovakia, and French partridge eggs. The widespread shortage of wild duck eggs—the result of farmers having to kill off wild ducks during the war—was also being put right. There was one further message: "The late war has brought about such a wonderful change in the titles and names of proprietors and tenants of shootings, and in gamekeepers names that it is necessary for me to revise my list of customers names and addresses . . . therefore my annual booklet will, this year, reach many addresses for the last time, unless I hear of a desire to have it continued." In 1918, Mary was fifty-six, Mananai and Pamela in their late forties. The war had brought an end to their way of life as conclusively, and briskly, as shutting the covers of an old hardback book.

Dick Wyndham, Clouds' heir, survived the war, although his elder brother George did not. In 1919, his mother, Minnie, died in the Spanish Influenza epidemic. Guy was bereft. "Bitter waters have rolled over Clouds," said Mary. "It began with the death of a little child—my Colin—then Papa George Percy—and four other grandsons of mamma—and now Minnie—most unexpected (and I venture to say uncalled for!) & soon we shall have to lay here the tired heart & body of darling Mamma," Mary told Arthur.

Madeline Wyndham was now over eighty, and ever more living in another world. Weeks before, Mary had spent "2 nights holding my mother's hands, talking of people long since dead and roaming with her through strange realms of phantasy and delirium in what *seemed* a *death chamber*, or birth into *another* world." It was decided that she should live permanently at Babraham, since the Adeanes, with ever-increasing duties within the county, were the most frequently at home. In 1915, Charlie had been appointed Lord Lieutenant of Cambridgeshire (an honorific post whereby the holder is the monarch's personal representative in each county), and in 1917 President of the Royal Agricultural Society, a body promoting the scientific development of agriculture, thus turning his energies towards "matters concerned with food production." Mananai proved herself indefatigable in her work throughout the war, always conscious that what had caused her such pain for so long—her inability to bear a son who lived—had saved her from seeing a grown son die. Nonetheless, the Adeanes still visited London, and could no longer afford to keep two houses running full-time. The sisters agreed that when their mother was in sole residence she would pay for the kitchen staff, and her guests would pay their own way. Charlie, who had darkly visualized his house being turned into a permanent rest home for his mother-in-law's multitude of elderly relations and friends, was relieved. Mananai was scrupulously fair: "When I come down to see Mamma I will pay my Board as she will be running the kitchen," she explained to Mary.

A decade before, such a proposal would have been unthinkable. But now death and taxes, which had risen throughout the war and were increasing once again, seemed to herald the breakup of estates everywhere one looked. The wrecking ball was a familiar sight in the streets of Mayfair and Piccadilly, demolishing the private palaces in which the Wyndhams had danced to make way for natty blocks of flats with ensuite bathrooms and all mod cons. "England is changing hands . . . Will a profiteer buy it? Will it be turned into a school or an institution? Has the mansion house electric light and modern drainage?" asked *The Times* in 1920. Even Eddy was feeling the pinch. "I could afford to give you a large allowance when taxation was upon a more moderate scale than it is now . . . [but] income tax and super tax are for me about 11/ in the pound so you will see . . . how I am financially situated," he said to Margot in 1919, explaining why he could no longer accede to her persistent requests for more money. "Unfortunately everyone thinks that I am very rich and forget the obligations under which I stand . . ." The Glenconners' charitable obligations and benefactions were considerable. Most recently, in 1918 Eddy had gifted to the nation Dryburgh Abbey, the monastic ruins by the Tweed River in Scotland where Sir Walter Scott is buried. The only condition was that an existing annual service of thanksgiving be maintained. Scott was one of Pamela's favorite writers, and the decision was undoubtedly precipitated by her.

Mary spent the postwar years fighting for her past. From the moment the war had ended, Hugo was itching to reopen Gosford. In the autumn of 1919, Stanway was let for the first time. Mary spent a fortnight there prior to the letting, "working like a galley slave a charwoman and a cabinet minister all in one" to prepare the house; "now poor Stanway is swept and garnished and the people come in October," she told Arthur. During the war, and in reflection of her greater responsibilities as Countess of Wemyss, Mary had begun to employ a personal assistant, Miss Wilkinson, known (like her maternity nurse) as "Wilkie," who stayed with her for the next twenty years. Wilkie became invaluable to Mary as she struggled with the Sisyphean task of trying to maintain 62 Cadogan Square, Stanway and Gosford. "Three houses in these days, will take every drop out of my body, every grain of energy out of my soul I never go out of my office, night or day," Mary complained to Arthur in 1920, contemplating an American let of Gosford for five weeks in August that would allow the Wemysses to live there for September and October, but required Mary to supply the servants: "an awful task—but not I think quite imposs [*sic*] if one puts one's back to it."

Now that she was Countess of Wemyss, and no longer had to kowtow to a difficult father-in-law, Mary refused to stay at Gosford. She rented instead Craigielaw, a small house a short way down the coast. She justified her "bungalow" on financial grounds. It allowed one wing of Gosford to be let, and "even the most ill-natured cannot pretend that Hugo & I have quarrelled if we lunch or tea together every day!" Craigielaw made East Lothian just bearable, limiting her exposure to "Hugo (the biggest child of them all)," the "Angel in the house!" as she called Angela, "the dull neighbor and the clergy, the disgruntled farmer or the Beggar at the Gate." Mary left Frances Charteris, Guy's wife, to keep the peace. "She is the only woman I could count on to do everything in the

Charlie Adeane's benevolence is apparent in this 1929 portrait, taken when he was in his mid-sixties. His grandchildren recollected a considerably crotchetier side which, when roused, Mananai was inevitably required to mollify.

home exactly as I would have it done only a great deal better!" Mary told Arthur.

In 1921, Stanway was redeemed. J. M. Barrie, the dramatist beloved of the nation as the author of *Peter Pan,* to whom Cincie had been indispensable as a private secretary since 1918, would take it each August, with Cincie acting as his hostess, allowing Mary to live there for the rest of the year. The system continued for over a decade, and brought further artists and writers to Stanway. Mary returned to Stanway that autumn, at the time that the Anglo-Irish Treaty ending the bitter War of Independence and providing for the division of Ireland into an Irish Free State and Northern Ireland was signed. She wrote to Arthur while unpacking her "household Gods" of photographs and trinkets: "Now our home will be here," she said staunchly. She recounted her previous night's drive in her "pony shay" with Wilkie and Eliza Wedgwood from a musical party back to Stanway: "the stars shining brightly out of the velvety deep blue black & so far away sky & the Didbrook church bells ringing for Peace between England & Ireland . . . All the many different times the bells have pealed or tolled—I feel that I shall hear them when they peal I hope (not toll!) for me . . . I felt very near to all I loved both those who have gone—so many & the precious few that are left . . ." It is a love letter to Stanway and to her past.

By the 1920s Arthur, author of the 1917 Balfour Declaration promising a national home to Jews in Palestine, and negotiator of the 1919 Treaty of Versailles, which formally concluded the First World War, had been propelled to international statesman: "You are the World's Chef making an apple pie of the universe," Mary wrote proudly as he attended the World Disarmament Conference in Washington, DC, in 1921. She made light of the contrast with herself, "all hoary and moss grown in Gloucestershire struggling with my Village Women's Institutes and War Memorials and looking after my . . . grandchildren." She remained mischievous and irreverent. At the birth of Mary Charteris (now Strickland)'s first child in 1919, Mary, summoned from her bed at Cadogan Square at 3 a.m., was, to her delight, permitted by the doctor to administer the chloroform to her daughter. "I had the time of my life," she said. At Stanway she composed melodramas for her grandchildren's Christmas theatricals in which she appeared as a pirate in turban, "Moorish coat & riding boots." She redoubtably sat down on the stairs at the formal reopening of Westminster Hall (the oldest part of the Palace of Westminster, which houses Parliament) in 1923 when she was tired—the only one with common sense enough to do it, she told Arthur stoutly. Mary Strickland recalled her kneeling on London's Paddington Station platform to finish writing a letter begun on the train while all about her streamed the disembarking hordes. Mary hustled to provide the funds she needed to keep up Stanway, importuning her friends to provide her with their old finery for a rummage sale to raise the fifty pounds required for electric lighting in Stanway's barn. "Ettie sent me 20 old Hats—& 16 prs of shoes!" she triumphantly informed Arthur of the event where the servants manned the stalls and Hugo's valet was auctioneer. In 1923, cautioned by Cincie's experience, Mary echoed history and shepherded a reluctant Bibs into a match with Ivor Windsor-Clive, a shy, awkward man thirteen years Bibs's senior. Ivor was heir to the earldom of Plymouth, the eldest surviving son of George's mistress Gay. "It warms my heart to think how George would have rejoiced—and my mother . . ." said Mary.

Madeline Wyndham had died at Babraham on 8 March 1920 at the age of eighty-four. Mary and Mananai were with her in her final weeks as she slipped in and out of consciousness and her mind wandered through

Seventy-seven-year-old Arthur and sixty-three-year-old Mary in 1925 with one of Mary's chows. The snapshot was taken by Lady Ottoline Morrell, the renowned hostess of the Bloomsbury Group and lover of the philosopher Bertrand Russell.

her past. "She has gone even further away into the borderland & only returns for short intervals, she still knows Madeline & me but no one else for long," Mary wrote to Dorothy Carleton. Dorothy had sent Madeline Wyndham a letter: "She held it in her hands all day together with some things I cut out for her . . . She has no anxiety now & says 'I am quite well' & she has no pain just . . . grows steadily weaker." Dorothy had also sent a message from Wilfrid Blunt. Whatever it was, it pulled Madeline Wyndham momentarily back half a century to a handsome cousin's flattery, for on receiving it "she said 'he means it!' her smile has been too wonderful," Mary reported to Dorothy.

Madeline Wyndham's body was cremated at Golders Green Crematorium in North London, her ashes buried in the family plot at East Knoyle on 12 March. She was the last Wyndham to be buried there. Pamela was not among the large crowd of mourners. For several months the Glenconners had been touring America, visiting Grey, who had come out of near retirement to serve as Ambassador to the United States.

Pamela decided not to cut short their trip. "I was absolutely convinced she was going to die before I returned so it was no extra grief to me," she explained to Mary from the Biltmore Hotel in New York, adding that she had taken the precautionary step of leaving an obituary she had written with Frederick Lowndes, who edited *The Times* obituary section, so that he could publish it if her mother died while she was away. Pamela's spiritualism had rendered her strangely impervious to grief. She had sought out mediums in every place the Glenconners visited, from Chicago to California (Eddy had privately chartered a Pullman to make the journey). Her first act upon hearing the news of her mother's death—in Boston—had been to go, anonymously, to a medium named Mrs. Chenoweth. It was a "very beautiful" sitting, she told Mary, "and the very first person who came was darling Mamma, it gave me such a great comfort . . . I can truly say I am thankful she is released—into the fuller Life, which I *know* is now hers! . . . I dwell in the thought of her joy."

America had given the spectacularly wealthy Glenconners a rapturous reception. "I never knew I was so delightful! or could be so clever!—how overlooked I have been until now! What have the people in London been thinking about?—didn't they know that when I was with them? . . . my room is a bower of roses, the table groans under cards . . ." Pamela wrote in her diary as they arrived in New York. They were fulfilling a semi-ambassadorial role, helping promote relations between the nations (the subject of an address made by Eddy to New York's Sulgrave Institution). Their every step was followed by pressmen, fascinated by the "Scottish Magnate" and his eccentrically beautiful wife, who organized her thirteen-year-old son to give dance recitals at their hotels.

In England the work of the press barons—both Lord Beaverbrook of the populist *Daily Express* and the *Evening Standard* and Lord Northcliffe of the equally successful *Daily Mail* were friends of Pamela's—was coming to fruition. The public was avid for tales of upper-class eccentricity. Pamela and her family provided it to perfection. Less than six months after their return to England Eddy died, aged sixty-one, in a private nursing home after suffering complications from what was intended to be a routine operation. He left Wilsford and Queen Anne's Gate in trust to Pamela. Christopher, now the 2nd Baron Glenconner, inherited Glen. The remainder, valued at £814,479 gross (a sum of over $36 million in today's money), was divided predominantly between David and

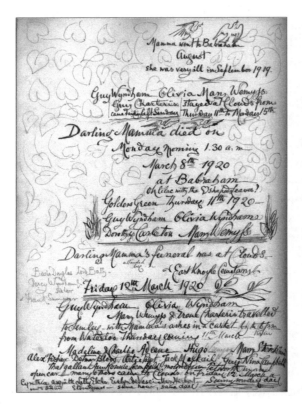

Throughout her life, Madeline Wyndham filled stacks of vellum-covered albums. In some she pasted letters. Others were used as visitors' books, recording guests at house parties at Clouds, press cuttings and mementoes from their stay. In her mother's last "Clouds Book," and in her most carefully flowing script, Mary set out the final illness, death and funeral of her "Darling Mamma."

Stephen, with a large lump sum to Clare, a bequest to Edward Grey and an annuity to Nanny Trussler.

Pamela, a widow not yet fifty, proved her mettle. She let out Queen Anne's Gate to a shipbuilding magnate and his wife on a rolling seven-year lease, so that Christopher could move back in when he married, and took a smaller nearby property. Four Buckingham Street was a "dear little house" two doors down from Guy and Frances Charteris on a street of seventeenth-century houses just off the Strand leading down to the Thames, "like Quality Street in its prettiness." Pamela decorated the house with cream-colored walls, "dark Columbine blue" curtains and carpet, and chintz sofas and chairs; the "dark red roses & pink roses look so lovely against the . . . blue curtains," she told Dorothy Carleton. The magnate and his wife had been happy to caretake the larger pictures in the gallery, so Pamela had brought "*only* a picked few of the smaller canvassed pictures" with her to the new house. She listed them for Dorothy and Wilfrid: two Turners, two Bonningtons, a Constable, three Nasmyths ("great favorites"), two Lancrets, two Hogarths, one Floris, the Orpen of Madeline Wyndham, the Lawrence crayon of Charles Dickens, *The Leslie Boy* by Raeburn, Mignard's portrait of Colbert, the Reynolds of "the dew bird," *Miss Stephens* by Zoffany, *Uncle Toby and the Widow Wadman* by Leslie, a woman's head by Angelica Kauffmann, the Millais of Lady Millais as Marguerite, the Natier of the Duc de Guise, Morland's *Industry* and *Idleness* "and a Fragonard."

From the moment of Eddy's death, Margot had scrutinized the Tennants, hawk-like, for sufficient distress. Mary described to Ettie Margot's behavior during a fraught visit to the Tennants at Glen, where they had repaired immediately after Eddy's death; "no tears, no heart, the dry-eyed are relegated to an everlasting limbo of callousness & cruelty," she added wryly. As for Pamela, who refused to break down in front of Margot: "I think one may as well . . . be thought 'to have done one's husband to death.'" Shortly afterwards, Pamela began to hear reports from friends of a "story of falsehood" and neglect reeled out by Margot at dinner parties—that Pamela and her children had shamefully abandoned Eddy to die alone in his nursing home.

Pamela confronted her sister-in-law: "Margot, I do not open my letter with the conventional term of endearment, as I cordially dislike you. Will you write me your apology for perverting the truth of my conduct towards Eddy on his death bed? I do not require a long letter; having neither time nor inclination for anything beyond the apology for which I ask. Yours, in utter sincerity . . ." Pamela subsequently explained that she had been with Eddy on the day of his death for almost fourteen hours straight, from "4 a.m. till about 6:30 (or 6 . . . I cannot recall accurately)." She was only absent at the moment of death because she had "fainted through anguish and lack of food" and been taken back to Queen Anne's Gate by Eddy's brother Jack to eat and change. Margot backtracked enough to give a semblance of apology, and Pamela graciously accepted it as though it were fulsome: "We will not quarrel for Eddy's sake," she told her sister-in-law.

To Pamela's mind this was still very much a present obligation, as she remained in close contact with her dead husband. "I have received two most excellent Messages in Book Tests from Bim & Eddy together . . . they are singularly *Good* and made me happy," she wrote to Mary three months after Eddy's death. She spoke of her dead as though she had just put down the telephone to them. Her granddaughter Diana Bethell remembered her sitting on her bed each morning, recounting the previous night's conversations with Bim. More bitterly, Stephen recalled arriving back at Wilsford, having been taken by his friend (and lover) Siegfried Sassoon to meet the elderly Thomas Hardy. He burst into the house, eager to tell his mother about the encounter with the legendary author of *The Mayor of Casterbridge, Tess of the d'Urbervilles* and *Far from the Madding Crowd*. Pamela, according to Stephen, barely looked up from her spiritualist tract.

In February 1922, *The Times* reported that it was "authorised" to announce that Pamela and Grey would marry in the early summer of that year. At half-past eight on the morning of Sunday, 4 June, Pamela and Grey were married at St. Michael's Church in Wilsford. Christopher Tennant gave Pamela away; Edward's sister Mrs. Curtis was the only other witness. The ceremony was kept so secret that the villagers of Wilsford did not even know of it until it was over. Grey had in fact proposed on Whitsunday a full year before, cycling over to Wilsford after an "odious paragraph" of speculation in the press. Then, Pamela had refused. At the time she told Lucy Graham Smith that it was because her sons still needed her, and expressly asked Lucy to tell "your immediate circle"—meaning Margot—that Grey "would not have suggested a thing so early had he not thought that the paragraph in the Press had worried me." A year later, Pamela had decided to bow to her sisters-in-law no longer. "The great step was taken, at last, by me," she told Wilfrid.

> I had no really valid reason for refusing any longer, and now that it is taken, I am quite certain it was right. Edward is so very fond of me, and I can be of use to him: and he is a wonderful LOVER and makes me very happy in a hundred ways . . . I feel—like Philip Sydney's mother—who made her second marriage so late in life that, like her, I could inscribe inside my wedding ring "NO Spring till now" . . .

The press leapt on the news. *The Times* on 6 June reported "A 'Marriage of the Minds,'" talking of the newlyweds' many shared interests (the correspondent is anonymous, but the tone smacks of Marie Belloc Lowndes). A double-page spread in the American press, on "The Romantic 'Miracle' of England's Loneliest Man," claimed that Grey's sight had been cured by his nuptials: "Now all of England is saying that the healing touch of the woman he loved brought life to the stricken nerves that had been pronounced dead by surgery."

Grey's sight had continued to deteriorate to the point that he was practically blind, and neither operation (which he tried) nor love (which he had) was going to fix it. But the marriage was very happy. The Greys moved, in London, to Mulberry House, an elegant Lutyens house on gaslit Smith Square in Westminster, but on the whole they divided their time between Wilsford and Fallodon. Pamela was spotted shopping in Newcastle with a green parrot on her shoulder (the same parrot was walking on her bed at Mulberry House the last time that Mary saw her sister). "He was sometimes a long-suffering husband," recalled David Tennant's wife, Hermione—but the example she gave was simply of Pamela, "not renowned for her punctuality," keeping a resigned Grey waiting by the car, a far cry from the tales of Pamela terrorizing Eddy. A "very perfect friendship" had become a still better marriage. "I feel I can write to you . . . telling you that I am happy, I was going to say—*at last,*" Pamela told Wilfrid, remembering distant Stockton days when her cousin had asked her if she was happy, and she had been unable to reply.

Pamela and Grey undoubtedly had a sexual relationship. Marie Belloc Lowndes, who never let a confidence go unbetrayed, said in her memoirs that Pamela had a miscarriage shortly after her marriage, which she attributed to an overlong drive to a political meeting. This was in the early spring of 1923. At fifty-two, older than what is now the average age for menopause, Pamela's chances of miscarriage were extremely high. Her doctor prescribed three weeks of bed rest, and no exertion for a further three months: "a holiday for 3 months! A lovely prescription! . . . I believe Dr. Aarons is going to combine a douching or ichth[y]ol treatment during the 3 weeks to increase the slender hope for the future," Pamela explained to Marie Stopes from Wilsford in March.

Pamela had not forgotten her debt of gratitude to Stopes. She agreed with pleasure (when most other grandees who were approached regretfully declined) to become a patron of Stopes's first birth-control clinic, the Mothers' Clinic, in poverty-stricken Holloway, North London, on its opening in 1921. She even hoped to connect that "fine work" with her Home for Working Mothers in her neighborhood of Westminster, where "I have the Infant Welfare scheme . . . The mothers who attend there, & they are continually increasing, would benefit by your work being made known to them." Throughout the 1920s, Pamela arranged for contraceptive devices to be provided to Wilsford's villagers. In some instances, this was to help women who already had large families. "I want to help [her] to feel secure . . . can I get one of the little rubber fitments you invented? If so where—" she said of one early case. Yet Pamela, like Stopes (and many more, including John Maynard Keynes, Havelock Ellis and Balfour), was an advocate of eugenic theory, then part of a progressive ideology. Eugenics applied in this context meant the use of birth control to prevent breeding among, in Stopes's words, the "inferior, the depraved, and the feeble-minded." In an undated letter to the Stopes Society, Pamela asked for "some appliances" that she could "take down . . . & explain . . . the use of" to a woman in Wilsford village: "She is not of very high intelligence, & it is really of importance that she should not bear a child. She has just married . . . I should be glad to be of use to her."

Despite her belief in Stopes's work, Pamela always gracefully resisted appearing on platforms at Stopes's meetings. Possibly this was her old fear of public speaking. She was probably also reluctant to become the controversial movement's figurehead that Stopes clearly wished her to be. On her remarriage, she gave up public support entirely. "I have been a breaking reed, I fear: not in conviction, but in supporting you in public," she told Stopes, explaining that "Lord Grey is averse to my taking

The American press reports on Pamela and Edward Grey's love story, or as this double-page spread put it, Edward Grey's "Love for the Widow of His Best Friend," explaining that Pamela had "Guided Him About the Streets When Failing Vision Made Him Helpless" and that her "Betrothal to Viscount Grey Fills Out the Life Friendship of Two of England's Greatest Families and Brightens Sir Edward's Later Years with Romance."

up public work, though he knows & admires your work . . ." It is most likely that Grey could not countenance Pamela having public involvement in work of this type.

Pamela was not to have another child. In 1925, she wrote to Mananai recounting another prolonged period of bed rest, with troublesome heart symptoms and raised blood pressure. She explained that the underlying cause was "the change"—menopause. "She has had to give up doing everything & live the life of an invalid," Mananai told Mary. The Greys and Stephen spent the winter in Madeira and the spring in Vernet-les-Bains, in the Pyrénées in southern France.

Grey's *Twenty-Five Years* had just been published, to remarkable commercial success (six impressions in six months) and critical acclaim. It was widely considered to vindicate Britain's entry into the war. Grey's dedication to Pamela explained that she had read over what he had written each day, offering suggestions and improvements. It seems that this amounted, in some cases, to rewriting. *Twenty-Five Years* contains an anecdote of Grey, as a child, seeing the Northern Lights and thinking them Paris burning in the 1870 Siege. It replicates almost exactly a supposed childhood memory of the Wyndhams, published in George's *Life and Letters* a decade before. In one biography of Grey Pamela has been presented as a society dalliance who had no impact on his life and work. This is emphatically not so.

An added frisson of interest for the popular press was that this elder statesman breakfasted with stepchildren who were leading lights of the Bright Young Things, the gilded youth whose antics fascinated and scandalized the British public in the 1920s. Immense wealth, good looks ("Of course, we have the fatal gift of beauty, darling," Stephen commented) and utter disdain for convention made Clare, David and Stephen irresistible to the press. David founded the notorious Gargoyle Club, a louche Soho nightspot that drew into its mirrored rooms everyone from the Prince of Wales to the silent movie star Tallulah Bankhead and the free-loving intellectuals of the Bloomsbury Group. He married, in 1927, the pint-size revue star Hermione Baddeley, famous for her rendition of Noël Coward's "Poor Little Rich Girl," written especially for her. Clare was an icy Society beauty, regularly featured in the press. Stephen was the androgynous beauty immortalized by Cecil Beaton, whose "Silver Room" in Mulberry House, wallpapered in silver foil, with a polar-bear-skin rug on the floor, was the subject of a *Vogue* spread (Pamela said it looked like an iceberg). Several of Beaton's most famous photographs of the Bright Young Things were taken at Wilsford, including that, in Pamela's drawing room, of Beaton, Stephen, Baby and Zita Jungman, Osbert and Sacheverell Sitwell, Rex Whistler, Elinor Wylie and Rosamond Lehmann lying on a rug underneath a tiger skin. In another, on the bridge over the Avon, men and women alike are dressed as Regency dandies in breeches with powdered faces, the river still as glass below them.

In *Broken Blood,* a family biography, Pamela's descendant Simon Blow alleged the corruption of an industrious, Presbyterian line by Pamela's blue blood. Certainly her extraordinary self-possession infected her children, but the way that David and Stephen Tennant, in particular, fascinated, titillated and outraged the press is redolent of the impact Eddy's

Pamela in her mid-fifties, with parrots, a few years after her late second marriage. She and Edward Grey had bought a number of parakeets on their trip to Madeira, including Pamela's personal favorite, an African grey named "Poll Squallor" or "Poll Squoll" for short. Her son Stephen brought back with him a green Amazon called "Jonathan Jewel." On first meeting Pamela at Wilsford at around this time, Stephen's friend the photographer Cecil Beaton thought his hostess's face, with her small, bright eyes, a little like a parrot's itself.

sisters had had upon launching themselves in Society forty years before. Perhaps Wyndham blood melded with generation-skipping Tennant insouciance.

Moving in and out of their circle was Dick Wyndham, who had lived at Clouds for only a couple of years, during a disastrous early marriage. After his divorce in 1924, Dick, a playboy with artistic pretensions, moved to the French Riviera and let Clouds, first to Sibell's son Bend'Or, then to a wealthy Dutch couple, Adriaan and Nancy Mosselman. Despite a substantial income, Dick had developed a habit of selling off a painting a year to keep his funds buoyant. In 1927 it was *The Wyndham Sisters.*

Dick justified the sale as providing an annuity for Guy Wyndham, who had remarried in 1923 and had two small sons with his wife, Violet (née Leverson). Sargent was rapidly falling out of fashion, but Dick thought he could get £20,000 for the painting—"an entirely artificial value over and above what Grandpapa payed [*sic*] for it"—which, invested, would provide an income of £1,200 a year. He explained to Mary:

> I look upon this painting as really belonging to you and Aunt Madeline & Pamela, so would do nothing without your consent. Personally I feel very strongly that it ought to be sold . . . The alternative is keeping a picture in a house, where neither I nor any heirs will ever be able to live. I feel sure that Grandpapa would have been the first to chuckle at his good buy—the painting is "sentiment" and I feel that Father's income is a more practical sentiment, particularly as none of the family get any advantage from the picture.

The Wyndham Sisters was sold to New York's Metropolitan Museum of Art in 1927 for £20,000. There is no evidence that any of the money did go towards supporting Guy. Pamela later heard from the Mosselmans that Dick had not even bothered to tell his tenants that he was intending to remove the painting. "The first they knew of the matter was the men trampling in to unhook it! What a lack of *touch*," she commented to Mary.

Pamela in later life was as ripe for anecdote as ever. She appears in Hermione Baddeley's memoirs as an imperious grande dame, whisking David off on Alpine tours with more suitable young women, and recruiting the press baron Lord Beaverbrook to have a quiet word with Hermione over lunch. "Marriage is not for a clever young actress like you . . ." he advised. "You keep your mind right there on your career. Don't get married. D'you hear me?" In Hermione's account, on discovering that David and Hermione had had an illegitimate daughter, Pauline, Pamela swoops in: " 'By the way,' said David, 'you know how fond she is of babies. She asks if you'd like Pauline and her nanny to live at Wilsford?' I couldn't believe my ears. Not only was she trying to marry David off to some suitable girl, but she wanted my baby too . . ." The story has a happy ending. After pitching up at David and Hermione's low-key wedding at London's Chelsea Registry Office in April 1928, draped in fox, with a feathered toque and Christopher and Stephen in morning suits, Pamela softened. She approached Hermione at the reception held at the Gargoyle "and pressed the most beautiful pearl, emerald and diamond ring into my hand. 'This is something very precious from me to you' she said. 'The first man I ever loved gave it to me.' "

Hermione and David threw a party to celebrate their marriage, requiring their guests to dress in nightwear. The press went to town. "Hasn't all this racket about poor Hermione's 'Bottle & Pyjama Party' been silly?" Pamela said to Mary, "the occasion really being nothing different to an ordinary Fancy Dress Party—& 'bringing a bottle' being one of the rather good 'short-cuts' I think of modern days, that facillitates [sic] impromptu entertaining! But the Press must have copy—so they invent long interviews." A month later, the long interviews were about Stephen, one of the protagonists in the "Great Mayfair War," in which he brought uninvited guests to a ball given by the Countess of Ellesmere, who then threw the "gate-crashers" out. Violet Ellesmere was only in her late forties, but she was indisputably part of a prewar generation, seeking to restore the old ways. The Old Guard, of which she was part, were fighting a rearguard action. Society had changed irrevocably since 1914. But Pamela's concern was for Stephen. Shortly afterwards, Edith Olivier found her at Wilsford "in a panic, quite broken . . . She and Lord Grey have been warned that it's the beginning of a 'Round-Up' of Stephen and his foppish friends," and Pamela was afraid that Stephen "would be suspected of real immorality if he continues to be written of in the papers in this company."

Pamela's concerns for Stephen were amplified by those about Clare, who was in the throes of a second divorce and lining up James Beck, her co-respondent, to be her third husband: "They quarrel as if they had been already married for ten years (!) cynical this—but you know what

I mean . . . poor little Clare she looks so worn and cross and miserable that I am anguished for her." Pamela told Mary. For some time Pamela's doctor had told her that she had a "hard patch in my Aorta . . . [which] gets affected by any emotional strain." In May 1928 she suffered a bout of illness after a "grueling week" in London in which she presented two young cousins at court (the Queensberrys' girls), gave a paper on spiritualism at the Forum Club and chaired a Sunlight League meeting (the organization campaigned for the health benefits of sunlight, and was closely linked to both the eugenics movement and a utopian view of progress) in a stiflingly hot room at Sunderland House: "I really did too much and my heart cried out against me." The following month, further anxiety about Clare "threw" her "back again [with] rather heightened B.P. and a sense of troubled circulation in my breast." She assured Mary that she was at Wilsford, "happily, *wisely resting*—& holding as well as I can a quiet Center of my own—in the midst of these troubles." She had adopted a raw diet, and was enjoying the latest biography of Emily Brontë, written with a fashionably new psychoanalytical slant.

Some five months later, on a Sunday afternoon in November, Pamela was alone in her garden at Wilsford when she suffered a stroke. She died a few hours later without regaining consciousness. She was fifty-seven. David and Christopher reached Wilsford in time. Stephen, who was summoned back from France, where he had been holidaying with Siegfried Sassoon, and Clare, now married to Beck (she had sobbed, "It's the end of my childhood" when told the news), were both too late. So was Edward Grey. He had been at Fallodon when he was telephoned on Sunday evening. Just before 10 p.m. that night the Edinburgh–London express train was stopped at the little private railway station on the estate and Edward Grey boarded. He reached King's Cross at 5:15 a.m., grey-faced, to be met by Christopher with the news that Pamela was dead.

Mananai would never forget the ghastly shock of the telephone call the next morning. In the days after their sister's death the three remaining Wyndham children, the survivors of Percy's "remarkable quintette," cleaved together for "heavenly days of *healing* and *comfort*" at Babraham. The Bishop of Salisbury conducted a bleak funeral at Wilsford, and a grim memorial service was held in London at St. Margaret's Church, the smaller church in Westminster Abbey's grounds known as the parish church of the House of Commons. Those attending had to fight their way through pouring rain and packs of pressmen eager to catch sight of the Bright Young Things in mourning, and the widowed elder statesman.

Pamela did not cease to demand attention even in death. At Glen that Christmas, Stephen said that his mother had "rained messages on me!" Shortly after she died, headlines were splashed across the popular press. Hermione had told friends of a ghostly experience the night Pamela died, and they had leaked it to the papers. The press tenor is exemplified by Utah's *Ogden Standard-Examiner,* which asked, referencing David's rakish lifestyle, "Did the Ghost of Viscountess Grey Return to Rebuke Her 'Naughty Boy'?" with a mock-up of Hermione with hair standing on end. Yet the incident, recounted in Hermione's memoirs, is curiously touching. She described being woken in the night by the sound of her bedroom door opening, and someone walking over to David's side of the bed:

> "Is that you, Stephen?" I whispered. No one answered. There was complete quietness in the room. I sat up terrified . . . "David," I said hoarsely, "someone's been in here." My heart was thumping. "There's someone in the room . . . whoever it was bent over you." David lay back. "Don't worry darling," he said sleepily. "It must have been Mummy coming to wish us goodnight."

The *Ogden Standard-Examiner,* Utah, reports on "the Best Explanation London Society Can Give for the Mysterious Footsteps Heard in the Staid Dowager's Bedroom in Old Wilsford Manor": namely that Pamela's ghost must be haunting her son David Tennant and his wife, Hermione. Pamela and Eddy's trip across the United States in 1920 did not take in Utah, much less Ogden, but Pamela would have been delighted to know that her fame had traveled this far. She would have been less happy at being described as either "staid" or a "dowager."

THIRTY-THREE

The End

The force of Pamela's personality made it difficult for her sisters to believe that she was really gone. "It seems . . . so bewildering & less easy to realize somehow to me now than when the blow first fell," Mananai wrote to Mary, three weeks after Pamela's death. For years, her instinct was to write to "Darling Pamela" with every piece of family news: "[She] still seems here to share as I know she would our family happenings."

The lives of the Adeane children—albeit without the column inches—also reflected how dramatically the war had changed their class's ways. Mananai rejoiced when Sibell Adeane and her second husband, Charles Lyttelton (brother of Pamela Adeane's husband, George), moved out of Hawarden Castle, once home of Prime Minister Gladstone, "that huge cold gaunt house with miles of basement!," into the recently deceased Helen Gladstone's "lovely sunny central heated—lit—modern house The Rectory." She mourned when Sibell, four and a half months pregnant, was obliged to undergo an induced miscarriage in "a little absolutely new & up to date Maternity Home" after the doctor said that she would never carry the child to full term. In 1929, Robert Adeane married Joyce Burnett. That November, Mananai was overwhelmed, even tearful, when she found out that they were to have a baby: "Isn't it *wonder-*

ful? it seems so somehow to me I don't know why—*Robert's* child," she wrote to Mary.

As that Christmas approached, Mananai was wrestling with the implications of the impending Local Government Act for her county council business. It was to come into force on April Fools' Day 1930, and had given her "much extra . . . work . . . but *most* interesting." She was also carrying on her Red Cross work, trying to launch an "orthopoedic [*sic*] scheme" to add to that of massage already existing. Mananai's letters were, as always, enthusiastically loving and short on reflection. She had escaped, by disposition, the fragility and nerviness of her sisters: she had also been helped by a happy marriage, and finding work that she loved.

From the late 1920s, Mary frequently asserted that she had not long to live. Crippling arthritis in both hips required her to walk with the aid of sticks, and left her in near-constant pain. She had been crushed by the sudden, early death, in 1925, of Frances Charteris, Guy's wife. "With Frances there . . . I felt 'safe' about them ALL and could have died tomorrow without a tremor," she told Arthur. Now, "I feel I must— more broken-winged than ever—trudge on like a snarling wrinkled char- woman, old and harsh with years! A crippled witch groping about with the Fairy Princess gone who ruled us with her gentle gracious sway." Others disagreed. An anonymous correspondent, paying tribute to Mary in *The Times* after her death, wrote:

> Many who remember with admiration and love the brilliant, vivid woman portrayed in Sargent's "Three Graces" may think that the last phase was the loveliest of all: the frail, shrunken, halting figure, dependent on the two sticks which were always losing themselves, and the monkey-headed hot-water bottle Pongo: the laces and muslin, fastened with little glimmering brooches, framing the finely modelled, deep-lined, ivory face in which the eyes of a young girl shone with inexhaustible fun.

Throughout the decade, the publication of memoirs sporadically flung the Souls back into the public eye. The first occasion was early on in the decade, when Margot released the first volume of her autobiography. Gossipy, indiscreet and ludicrously self-important, it provoked a "controversial maelstrom," in Balfour's words. "All the things that people quote to me from it as containing observations of mine seem to be quite untrue but not intentionally malevolent," he said to Mary, declining to even read it. There was another flurry in January 1929, when *The Times* serialized extracts from Richard Haldane's forthcoming memoirs, which criticized the Souls for taking themselves on occasion "much too seriously . . . on the whole it is doubtful whether their influence was on balance good." A number, including Ettie Desborough, wrote anonymously to the editor to protest. "When Lord Haldane says that . . . he is taking himself too seriously. [The Souls] were not concerned with chaperoning the conscience of anybody. They shared different ideas, different ambitions and different politics," said "Q" in a forthright riposte. All these letters emphasized the cross-party nature of the group, their lifelong devotion and loyalty to one another. The Souls continued to deny that they were a "set," maintaining, in a distinction perhaps only they could see, that they were simply a group of good friends. It left them in the somewhat awkward position of defending the character of a clique they claimed had never existed.

The previous spring had been the longest period Mary and Balfour ever spent under one roof, when Balfour came to Stanway for five weeks to recover from a mild stroke. Ettie was also there: a trinity of Souls, as of old. That year, Mary wrote to Arthur imagining what people might say about them: "How pathetic to see Arthur and Mary Wemyss. How sad is the end of life—the necessary onslaught of illness and old age. How sad to outlive Romance. I believe they were lovers once, tho' nobody knows the truth about these things!"

Arthur died at Fisher's Hill, Woking, home of his brother Gerald, in 1930. Mary was at Hyères. Two days before that, she had woken feeling out of sorts, edgy, nervous and tearful. From Hyères she sent a bunch of rosemary and thyme, the only flowers, besides family flowers, thrown into his grave. "I cannot yet realize how great the blank will be," she wrote, upon the loss of her "unfailing friend." Her lifelong confidant had gone. With the publication of *Family Record* in 1932, she began work on her Souls memoir in earnest. Ettie and Evelyn de Vesci, friends spanning fifty years, continued to marvel at Mary's energy. She was as "Napoleon-like" as ever, said Ettie, as Mary planned a day that involved leaving Stanway after breakfast, lunching in London and dining with Ettie at Taplow Court, stopping off in Surrey for tea. Yet Mary was also prone to fits of depression and gloom, and mental demons could drive her into fits of anxiety. She reached such a crisis in 1936.

In 1932 Dick had put Clouds—estate and contents—up for sale. Only the most precious objects—the Orpens of Madeline and Percy, the Watts of Madeline, George Wyndham's bust by Rodin—were kept in the family. Everything else—from eighteenth-century Italian cabinets to a pair of ice skates—was auctioned off over the following months. "The prices weren't too good—but not *too* bad," Dick Wyndham told his father. It took four years for Knight, Frank & Rutley, the estate agents, to find a buyer for the "dignified mansion" and its three thousand acres. In 1936 it was sold for a little over £39,000 to a property developer, who parceled it up. The eventual buyer of Clouds—now marooned on just twenty-six acres—demolished a third of the house before the Second World War, just to make it manageable.

Mary, adrift without Balfour, the *Family Record* that had accompanied her for fifteen years complete, Clouds sold, and agitated by Margot's prolific publications, began to try to pin down her past. Her progress on her memoir of the Souls had been faltering. Now she reattempted it, as an article which she intended for publication under the title "Friendship's Garland." Becoming frantic at her inability to capture it properly, she sought the help of Evelyn and her brother-in-law Evan Charteris. The manuscript horrified them. The article was meant to be "character sketches" of "ball throwers" that Mary had admired, but in reality it was full of titles, names and "unsubstantiated assertions," said Evan. "I think it is an *impossible* document for the *public* to play about with," said Evelyn. She thought it could attract only "unkind derision & criticism . . . a *saddening* document." Yet their attempts to dissuade Mary—now "verging on a nervous breakdown" in their view—failed. Evan agreed to go to Gosford to help her edit the work. Mary had told him that she would "go mad" if he did not, "& she looks a wraith—& agonized & distracted," he explained to Evelyn.

On arriving at East Lothian, Evan was dismayed by what he saw. Gosford had reached its nadir with Angela and Hugo's decision to turn it into a hotel of sorts, taking in paying guests. Evan's description is redolent of Fawlty Towers: "the little dining room (marble hall end)— now a gaudy cocktail bar—with a rather pretty barmaid—cheap little tables—& cheaper chairs—disposed in the true bar manner," Hugo "sulky as a bear" striding the corridors, barking at a man in plus fours turning into the saloon to ask him what he was doing there. Angela was "always in the house—usually in the Bar—following guests about, spying what she can & giving them fits with a monster Alsatian which barks & bays along the corridors"; while Connor, "in great distress about the situation financial & social . . . weeps for the good name of the Brigadier & Mumsey [the 10th Earl and Countess of Wemyss]." There was only one guest when Evan arrived, "& it has now got so bad a name locally & I believe universally that it is commonly regarded as doomed." No one escaped Evan's furious eye: "Guy [Charteris] with no more manners than a fish hook . . . wraps—papers—cards—bridge scores strewn about—dogs fighting and being screamed at—never a moments [*sic*] serenity or peace—everyone snapping & scrapping. I have paid my last visit there."

Evan's attempts to help with editing had been futile. "M is incorrigible . . . she concedes an exclusion of a name or the alteration of a sentence or paragraph & the next day it is returned—she is a naughty child up to every sort of subterfuge & dodge secretly determined to get her own way." He was more concerned about Mary's mental state:

[She] has been undone by coming here . . . the Souls & Moby Dick [Wyndham] have played havoc—& her state of mental agitation is worse than I can recall it to have ever been . . . I wonder if she ought not to try psycho-analysis . . . ? I know nothing about it beyond its claim to reduce complexes—& here at any rate are the complexes all-right [*sic*]—complexes which are biting into her reason—dominating her outlook & blotting out all other considerations.

The article was never finished. The following February, Mary's children and grandchildren held a "Family Banquet" for her at her club, the Albemarle, on London's Dover Street as her seventy-fifth birthday approached. The Adeanes did not attend: Mananai was recovering from the flu and Charlie had duties as Lord Lieutenant which he could not miss. "We don't want to complicate things (which leaving things open does) so I feel we ought to say no," said Mananai. Two months later, Mary had a small house party at Stanway: five or six of her oldest friends, and a new young writer and his artist sister whom "she had newly taken to her heart." To her guests she seemed as vibrant as ever—although she confided to one of them that she did not think she had long to live. This time she was right. She died a week later on 29 April 1937, at the age of seventy-four. She had been taken ill at Stanway in the afternoon, and died that night with "a swiftness merciful to her," wrote the anonymous

From left to right: Cincie's son Simon Asquith, the author J. M. Barrie, Cincie's son Michael Asquith, Queen Mary (wife of King George V of England), Mary, Mary Charteris and the journalist and author Charles Whibley during a royal visit to Stanway during Barrie's tenure. Barrie's renting of Stanway each summer for a handsome sum allowed Mary to stay in the house she adored long after Hugo had moved north to Gosford. Mary here looks more tenacious, mischievous and eccentrically dressed in old age than ever.

correspondent in *The Times*: "A rare spirit has passed away." Hugo lived another two months, rivalrous to the end, and died in his sleep at Gosford, in his eightieth year.

Mananai and Guy, the two quietest of Percy's "remarkable quintette," lived long enough for the sadness of seeing the world once more descend into war. Guy Wyndham died in the darkest days of the Blitz, on 17 April 1941, peacefully in his sleep in Wiltshire. Two months later, on 31 July, Madeline Adeane at the age of seventy-two suffered a fatal heart attack at Babraham. She had been engaged "literally" to the very day of her death in her county council and charity work. "The gap she leaves there . . . cannot be filled," wrote a correspondent in anonymous tribute. Under the headline, "One of 'The Three Graces,'" *The Times* noted the passing of a dynasty: "She was the last survivor of the gifted family of the Hon. Percy and Mrs. Wyndham, whose home at Clouds in Wiltshire, was, during the 30 years before the last War, a delightful social and intellectual centre."

And so it ends. But not, perhaps, if one takes Pamela's word for it. In 1928 she had made a "pilgrimage" back to Clouds, taking David, bearing wreaths for the graves of her parents and George. They had found the graveyard "profoundly beautiful & peaceful." Except that the rosemary on Madeline Wyndham's grave was overgrown, everything was as it should be. David had read aloud from Shelley's *Adonais* for George; Pamela had recited lines for her parents: a "little Persian rhyme" that Madeline Wyndham had loved, and for her father a biblical passage: Proverbs 4:18—"But the path of the just is as the shining light, that shineth more and more unto the perfect day."

Pamela and David had gone into the house, to be greeted kindly by Mrs. Mosselman, and wandered around the place. The house was warm and lived in, Pamela told Mary, and scattered with children's toys. In the library, Pamela had stood by the Rodin bust of George and "received a fine, and convincing RAP (—one of my *raps* that are so astonishingly apposite!) . . . I laughed, & said '*All Right!*—Message received!'" The atmosphere of the house was still overpowering, "like a tangible, all encompassing actuality! Just like great mid-summer Lilies or Honeysuckle, come towards you . . . on the air in Summer evenings."

Walking through the house, Pamela felt like Kai in Hans Christian Andersen's "The Snow Queen," a fairy tale she had read with her sisters long ago, in which dreams and vapors passed the boy that only he could see. She relived the sight of Madeline Wyndham, making her way across the hall, arms piled high with shawls for music listeners, of Percy in his flapping slipper heels slip-slopping his way across. She heard the sound of herself on her guitar. She saw themselves as children impatiently tapping the weather glass, longing for snow and ice to go tobogganing; saw the great teas where thirty or more sat and waited for toast, always cold and curling after the servants' trek down miles of corridor. She saw Mary and Madeline Wyndham, desperately trying to battle up the narrow stone staircase through gathering smoke, thinking the children still above, that January night that Clouds was ablaze; she saw too in the empty, rebuilt hall herself and Harry Cust standing on the hearthstone in that final interview at the end of the summer—the end of their affair. Clouds' atmosphere, like the scent of the wildflowers that once filled it, was still strong.

"Just as there are long strands of Time, here, on the Earth Plane which we live through & then fold up & lay away, so I believe, in the next phase of Consciousness, there are long sweeps of Earth Life, to be lived over again, to be more fully realized perhaps," Pamela told Mary. The only difference she thought likely was that "sad facts" might be hidden from "dead eyes." "And so," Pamela concluded, "it might be that Mamma may quite well be happily unconscious of any disturbing or chilling factors in the present history of Clouds, and be—possibly—safely and joyously tucked away again into a nest of lovely sisters, and visiting Mrs. Curragh with Lord Odo Fitzgerald [*sic*] . . . or shining in an equipage of old Lord Carlisle's, with outriders, driving through the gates of Dublin Castle . . ." on her way to meet, perhaps, for the first time, the young, uncertain Percy Wyndham, and let the whole story unfurl once more.

ACKNOWLEDGMENTS

Writing thanks for a project that has taken some eight years from inception to publication is a daunting prospect. My first debts are to Anthony Cheetham, who came up with the idea for this book, and my incomparable agent, Georgina Capel, who with extraordinary tenacity has brought that idea to fruition. Without them, this book would never have come into being. Then thanks are to my clear-sighted editor Arabella Pike at William Collins, whose incisive comments have immeasurably improved the work; to all her team for their hard work and endless patience, in particular Stephen Guise, Joseph Zigmond, and Katherine Patrick; and to Peter James, for his sympathetic copyediting.

The research for this book has taken me to libraries, archives, record offices and private homes all over the country. The following institutions and archives generously gave me access to, and permission to quote from, their collections, and their staff were unfailingly helpful: the Bodleian Library; British Library; Fitzwilliam Museum, Cambridge; Hertford Archives; National Records of Scotland; National Library of Scotland; and Somerset Record Office. Thanks also to the staff of the Cheshire Record Office and the West Sussex County Council Record Office for allowing me to read private collections on site. For access to private collections, I am grateful to the Earl of Egremont; Hugo Vickers; the Whittingehame Estate; Francis Wyndham; and others. Lord Wemyss has been generous beyond measure in allowing me access to the Stanway archives, as have James and Olinda Adeane. I cannot thank them enough. The Bonham Carter Trustee and Christopher Osborn were kind enough to grant me permission to quote copyright work of Margot Asquith. Others to whom I am grateful are the Earl and Countess of Oxford and Asquith for showing me material relating to Raymond Asquith and Frances, Lady Horner; Lady Glenconner; Philip Hoare, for answering last-minute, anxious requests; Melissa Wyndham and Susanne

Lobel, for their enthusiasm for the project; and Sarah and Duncan Farrar, who fed and housed me on my many trips to Edinburgh.

Certain people have helped this book immeasurably along its way. Philippa Brewster, Dan Jones and Hugo Vickers have all been the most sympathetic and helpful of ears in various times of crisis. Juggling writing with my other career as a barrister has only been possible thanks to the support of those at Essex Court Chambers, in particular, my clerks David Grief and Jack Wood; and my erstwhile pupil supervisor Nathan Pillow. To all my friends: especially Will Gresford, who encouraged me to take on the project and whose connections set me on the way; Laura Hamm, my wingman in every coffee shop in New York; Lauren Aguilar, who lived with the book for two months across Sri Lanka; Ollie Marre, Joanna Buckley and Henry Day, my lifelines through law school; Lucy Davis; Maggie Asquith; Phoebe Barran; and Charlotte Evans, whose support has been unfailing since we were eighteen years old. My godparents, David and Angela Neuberger and Alex Gordon Shute; Jonny and Gabrielle Levy, for their immediate, over-whelming support in the darkest of times. To all those who have lived with me and my boxes of books (in chronological order): Sarah O'Reilly, Sophie Elmhirst, Raya al Bader, Patrick Hennessey, Viva van Loock, Becca Ratcliffe, and Nicky Sayers—thanks for listening to me bang on and I'm sorry about the mess. To Mark Lobel, who has now so gracefully taken on their mantle—thank you.

To list my myriad, ever-expanding family requires a deep breath, so here goes: my father, Simon Renton, stepmother, Rachel Smith, and sister, Izzy Renton; my grandmother, Lavinia Hankinson; my stepfather, Derek J. Content; Judy Englender; my sister Philippa Content, and her clan, Chris, Arlo and Nina Winterbourne; my South African family, Jonathan, Gail, Kate, Nicky and Matty Schrire; Toby Colegate-Stone, the most patient and tolerant of brothers-in-law; and Imi and Mabel, the next generation of (head)strong women. Thank you all, beyond measure.

Finally, I come to the hardest, and the easiest thanks of all. To my brilliant, bold and beloved mother, Amanda Content, who died in October 2009, as I was halfway through this book, and my sister Julia Colegate-Stone, who has helped me every step of the way before and since. I could not have begun to understand the ties that bound the Wyndham women together without my own experience to draw on. To my mother and my sister, this is for, and because of, you.

CLAUDIA RENTON
LINCOLN'S INN FIELDS
DECEMBER 2013

Four years on from this book's publication in the U.K., I now prepare with enthusiasm for its publication in the United States. My thanks in addition to those set out above are to Georgina Capel and to Vicky Wilson, my brilliant editor at Alfred A. Knopf, for making this happen. It has been a pleasure to work with Vicky: her suggestions have encouraged me to look at the book with fresh eyes and her sage advice has been invaluable. Many thanks to her and to all the team for their hard work, in particular Chayenne Skeete, who was indefatigably enthusiastic throughout the process of collecting the images for this book, and Marc Jaffee. I am extremely grateful to all those who kindly gave permission to reproduce images in this book, in particular to Camilla Shivarg, Jonathan Ross and Hugo Vickers for their generous help.

A lot can happen in four years. I am, as always, beyond grateful to my family and my friends who are family. Most of all to my husband, Mark Lobel, who has cheered me on throughout, tirelessly encouraging in this and every endeavor—you are the best. And our son, Jack, timed his arrival beautifully to allow the finalization of this edition. Markus, Jackeleh, here's to the next chapter, my loves.

CLAUDIA RENTON
OLD BROMPTON ROAD, LONDON
DECEMBER 2017

NOTES

A note on the references:

The correspondence between Mary Elcho and Arthur Balfour lies principally in the Stanway archives at Stanway House in Gloucestershire and the Whittinge-hame archives. Professor Jane Ridley and Clayre Percy have edited a wonderful collection of this correspondence in *Letters of Arthur Balfour and Lady Elcho, 1887–1917* (Hamish Hamilton, 1992). For the reader's ease, where the letter I have referred to also appears in this published collection, I have referenced it according to the page at which it may be found in the *Letters*.

A note on the monetary values:

Where I provide calculations of money values in today's term, I have con-verted the original sum in British pounds to the closest available current-day value (2014) in US dollars, using www.measuringworth.com. This gives two val-ues, that calculated on Consumer Price Index (CPI)/Retail Price Index (RPI), which is more relevant to consumer goods, and that calculated on Gross Domes-tic Product (GDP) deflator, which is more appropriate to capital investments or government expenditure.

Place of publication is London, unless otherwise stated.

PROLOGUE

4 company of her children: Pamela Glenconner, "Fantasia—of a London House Closed," in Pamela Glenconner, *The White Wallet* (T. Fisher Unwin, 1912), pp. 211–12.

4 "talking about his pictures": Frances, Lady Horner, to Edward Burne-Jones, quoted in Caroline Dakers, *Clouds: The Biography of a Country House* (New Haven: Yale University Press, 1993), p. 163.

4 generals and politicians, gathered: The phrase is that of William Lethaby,

the architectural historian, and friend and biographer of Philip Webb, cited in Dakers, *Clouds*, p. 83.

5 "perhaps this is better": Percy Wyndham to Pamela Tennant, 7 February 1900, Glenconner Papers, NRS GD510/1/26.

5 "the public sees it": Pamela Tennant to Percy Wyndham, quoted in Dakers, *Clouds*, pp. 164–65.

5 "he got quite excited": Pamela Tennant to Percy Wyndham, quoted in ibid., p. 164.

5 "disturbing to the *scheme*": Ibid.

6 announced her sartorial intentions: Mary Elcho to Madeline Wyndham, 18 January 1899, Stanway Papers.

6 "it shouldn't be managed": Pamela Tennant to Percy Wyndham, quoted in Dakers, *Clouds*, pp. 164–65.

6 "Charlie can be there": Madeline Wyndham to Pamela Tennant, 16 February 1900, Glenconner Papers, NRS GD510/1/26.

6 of an artist's studio: William Howe Downes, *John S. Sargent: His Life and Work* (Thornton Butterworth, 1926), p. 17.

6 in the same light: James Lomax and Richard Ormond, *John Singer Sargent and the Edwardian Age: An Exhibition Organized Jointly by the Leeds Art Galleries, the National Portrait Gallery, London, and the Detroit Institute of Arts* (Leeds: Leeds Art Galleries, 1979), p. 53.

6 "she sits to him": Pamela Tennant to Percy Wyndham, quoted in Dakers, *Clouds*, pp. 164–65.

7 "and a sick nurse": Arthur Balfour to Mary Elcho, 22 September 1900, quoted in Jane Ridley and Clayre Percy (eds.), *The Letters of Arthur Balfour and Lady Elcho, 1885–1917* (Hamish Hamilton, 1992), p. 176.

7 "has unquestionably slipped in": Quoted in Downes, *John S. Sargent*, pp. 188–89.

7 "fascinated by its life": Quoted in ibid., p. 50.

7 "I do not judge": Quoted in ibid., pp. 109–10.

7 "face in your hands": Quoted in Lomax and Ormond, *John Singer Sargent and the Edwardian Age*, p. 55.

CHAPTER 1: "WORSE THAN 100 BOYS"

9 "written on his Countenance": Constance Leconfield to Madeline Wyndham, 15 March 1909, Petworth Papers.

9 as "the Sunny Baby": Emily Eden, *Miss Eden's Letters*, ed. Violet Dickinson (Macmillan, 1919), pp. 250–51, n. 423.

9 "one feel her immortal": Quoted in Fiona MacCarthy, *The Last Pre-Raphaelite: Edward Burne-Jones and the Victorian Imagination* (Faber & Faber, 2011), p. 324.

9 reserve—"you sweet mystery": Percy Wyndham to Madeline Wyndham, 31 July 1860, Petworth Papers.

10 "have gone so well": Percy Wyndham to Fanny Montgomery, 3 August 1862, cited in Dakers, *Clouds*, p. 20.

10 "executive in the world": Quoted in D. G. Boyce, *The Irish Question and British Politics, 1868–1996* (2nd ed., Macmillan, 1996), p. 1.

10 aristocracy were technically absentee: Lawrence James, *Aristocrats: Power, Grace and Decadence—Britain's Great Ruling Classes from 1066 to the Present* (Little, Brown, 2009), p. 314.

11 "Fenians of the family": Katharine Tynan Hinkson, *The Years of the Shadow* (Constable, 1919), p. 256.

11 "race girdling the earth": John Darwin, *The Empire Project: The Rise and Fall of the British World System, 1830–1970* (Cambridge, Cambridge University Press, 2009), p. 26, n. 1.

12 "meet her in it": Mackail and Wyndham (eds.), *Life and Letters*, 1:153.

12 "of the soft cheeks": Percy Wyndham to Madeline Wyndham, 1 August 1860, Petworth Papers.

12 "paper in the world": Percy Wyndham to Madeline Wyndham, 5 August 1860, Petworth Papers.

12 all trace of it: Conversation with Mrs. James Adeane, ca. 2008.

12 on her mother's death: Lady Campbell to Lord Leconfield, 12 July 1860, quoted in Mackail and Wyndham, *Life and Letters*, 1:17.

13 and Madeline's marriage settlement: See the correspondence between Henry Brydon, the lawyer responsible for the transaction, Percy Wyndham and Lord Leconfield in September and October 1860, Petworth Papers. The money, £35,727 16s. 5d., was transferred from Lord Leconfield's account at the Bank of England on 19 September 1860. The equivalent in US dollars is $4,050,000 (CPI/RPI) and $4,190,000 (GDP). Lord Leconfield was charged £1 1s. 6d. for the transaction. On 10 October, it was transferred to the trustees of the marriage settlement—Percy's elder brother Henry and Adolphus Liddell, a lifelong friend of Percy and Madeline's, and in time a close friend of their children. The settlement was signed by Percy and Madeline either the day before or the morning of their marriage.

13 herself to the marriage: "Heads of Settlement by the Honourable Percy Scawen Wyndham on his marriage with Miss Campbell of Woodview, Stillorgan near Dublin, daughter of the late Sir Guy Campbell, Bart., of £35,000 consols," Petworth Papers. When Percy's brother Henry married Constance Primrose, granddaughter of the Earl of Rosebery, some seven years later, Lord Leconfield provided the same amount for her. However, Constance matched this with the dowry she brought to the marriage herself.

13 "in all your sorrows": Madeline Wyndham to Pamela Tennant, 14 January 1898, Glenconner Papers, NRS GD510/1/32, f. 24r.

13 highest form of praise: Mary, Countess of Wemyss, *A Family Record* (Plaistow: Curwen Press, 1932), pp. 19–20.

14 Wyndhams was almost bourgeois: Nancy Waters Ellenberger, "Constructing George Wyndham: Narratives of Aristocracy in Fin-de-Siècle England," *Journal of British Studies* 39:4 (October 2000): 487–517, 496.

14 "the country at large": Bernard Cracroft, "The Analysis of the House of Commons, or Indirect Representation," in *Essays on Reform,* quoted in Lawrence Stone and Jeanne C. Fawtier Stone, *An Open Elite? England, 1500–1880* (Oxford: Clarendon Press, 1984), p. 422.

15 "of art and literature": Quoted in Leonore Davidoff, *The Best Circles: Society, Etiquette and the Season* (Croom Helm, 1974), p. 64.

15 one after each meal: Ridley and Percy (eds.), *Letters of Arthur Balfour and Lady Elcho,* p. 11.

16 "my heart to bursting": G. F. Watts to Madeline Wyndham, quoted in Mary S. Watts, *George Frederic Watts: The Annals of an Artist's Life,* 2 vols. (Macmillan, 1912), 1:239–41.

17 mother's long flowing skirts: Mackail and Wyndham, *Life and Letters,* 1:20–21.

17 skirts armfuls of flowers: Dakers, *Clouds,* p. 35.

17 perched on the mountainside: Mary Elcho to Wilfrid Scawen Blunt, 16 August 1921, Blunt Papers, FM 225-1976.

17 "*Skiddaw*—against the sky": Ibid.

18 "the girl last year!": Lady Campbell to Percy Wyndham, quoted in Dakers, *Clouds,* p. 20.

18 when they were toddlers: Mary Elcho to Madeline Wyndham, 7 December 1899, Stanway Papers.

18 "not see the fox": Mary Elcho to Madeline Wyndham, 17 February 1871, Petworth Papers.

18 by her brothers' tutor: Mary Elcho to Madeline Wyndham, 8 October 1874, Petworth Papers.

19 "his two hind legs": Mary Elcho to Madeline Wyndham, n.d. [1874], Petworth Papers.

19 to tire them out: Mackail and Wyndham, *Life and Letters,* 1:21.

19 with "those wild Wyndham children": Ibid., 1:19.

19 "worse than 100 boys": Mary Elcho to Arthur Balfour, 16 August 1895 (*Letters,* pp. 138–39).

19 up to a quarter: Christine Kinealy, *This Great Calamity: The Irish Famine, 1845–52* (Dublin: Gill & Macmillan, 1994), p. 357.

19 "supreme value for her": Edith Olivier, *Four Victorian Ladies of Wiltshire* (Faber & Faber, 1940), p. 92.

19 "but comforts we despise": Ibid., p. 93.

19 "the 'King of Glory'": George Wyndham to Edward Clifford, September 1895, quoted in Mackail and Wyndham, *Life and Letters,* 1:287.

20 puffed across the sky: Percy Wyndham to Madeline Wyndham, 12 August 1860, Petworth Papers.

20 "phenomena of his family": Ellenberger, "Constructing George Wyndham," p. 497.

20 "have never imagined life": Mary Elcho to Margot Asquith, 3 May 1911, Bodleian, Asquith Papers, MS. Eng. d. 3283.

20 to pronounce her name: As she grew older, the Wyndhams' second daughter more frequently used "Madeline." In order, however, to distinguish between mother and daughter, I refer throughout to Madeline (daughter) as Mananai, except where I use her married name, Madeline Adeane. Doubtless Mananai would have understood, as even she was capable of being caught out on occasion by the family's faithful adherence to a mere handful of names: "There were two Madelines in the house, two Pamelas, two Percys. . . . three Guys . . . so it was rather confusing," Mananai commented of a visit by the Campbell cousins to Wilbury in 1883 (Madeline Adeane to Mary Elcho, 16 September 1883, Stanway Papers).

20 roads and gas companies: Dakers, *Clouds,* p. 36.

20 for almost a decade: Ibid.

20 Lord Mayo, was Viceroy: Mackail and Wyndham, *Life and Letters,* 1:16.

21 she died, was bereft: Mary Elcho to Madeline Wyndham, n.d. [November 1869], Petworth Papers; Madeline Wyndham to Mary Elcho, 25 October [1869], Stanway Papers.

21 for them to end: See G. F. Watts to Madeline Wyndham, in Watts, *George Frederic Watts,* 1:239–41, 325–26.

21 "thirty thousand a year": Quoted in Dakers, *Clouds,* p. 57.

22 "lay siege to it": David Marquand, *Britain Since 1918. The Strange Career of British Democracy* (Orion, 2008), p. 53.

22 bombing of Clerkenwell Prison: Jerry White, *London in the Nineteenth Century* (Vintage, 2008), pp. 371–72.

22 "defer[ring] to their decision": Quoted in Marquand, *Britain Since 1918,* p. 33.

22 sitting down to lunch: Cynthia Asquith, *Haply I May Remember* (James Barrie, 1950), p. 138.

22 in pony and trap: See Pamela Tennant's recollection in her letter to Mary Elcho, 13 March 1928, Stanway Papers.

23 their connections and titles: Madeline Wyndham to Mary Elcho, ca. September 1884, Stanway Papers.

23 "She is a humbug": Philip Burne-Jones to Lady Frances Balfour, 15 October 1889, Whittingehame Papers, NRS GD433/2/301, f. 72.

23 child with some "defect": See Madeline Wyndham's response to Mary Elcho's miscarriage in 1884 and Madeline Adeane's stillborn child in 1899.

23 estate just outside Cairo: Elizabeth Longford, *Pilgrimage of Passion: The Life of Wilfrid Scawen Blunt* (Weidenfeld & Nicolson, 1979), p. 172.

23 Blunt, even in England: Frederic Harrison, *Autobiographic Memoirs*, 2 vols. (Macmillan, 1911), 2:166, 173.

23 through the beautiful grounds: Katharine Tynan Hinkson, *Twenty-Five Years: Reminiscences* (John Murray, 1913), pp. 302–3.

23 "are the fashion now": Wilfrid Scawen Blunt, diaries, quoted in Longford, *A Pilgrimage of Passion,* p. 102.

24 "strength . . . proving its wealth": Wilfrid Scawen Blunt, "Alms to Oblivion," Part V, Chapter III, Blunt Papers, FM 311-1975.

25 "I have no courage": Blunt Papers, K6115.

25 and reasonable trout fishing: Dakers, *Clouds,* p. 45; Mackail and Wyndham, *Life and Letters,* 1:24.

25 "her goodness too selfish": Wilfrid Scawen Blunt, diaries, quoted in Longford, *Pilgrimage of Passion,* p. 102.

25 "not grieve for me": Wilfrid Scawen Blunt, "Alms to Oblivion," Part V, Chapter III, Blunt Papers, FM 311-1975.

25 the regret "that kills": Madeline Wyndham to Pamela Tennant, 1 June 1896, Glenconner Papers, NRS GD510/1/30.

CHAPTER 2: WILBURY

26 "in a cousinly way": Longford, *Pilgrimage of Passion,* pp. 157, 310.

26 of Percy's "remarkable quintette": Percy Wyndham to Mary Elcho, 22 November 1900, Stanway Papers.

26 of "the Wyndham-religion": George Wyndham to Pamela Tennant, 23 December 1896, Glenconner Papers, NRS GD510/1/32.

26 "religion with the Wyndhams": Cynthia Asquith, *Remember and Be Glad* (James Barrie, 1952), p. 192.

26 the table his views: Wemyss, *Family Record,* p. 20.

26 the pride of Plantagenets: Richard Davenport-Hines, *Ettie: The Intimate Life and Dauntless Spirit of Lady Desborough* (Weidenfeld & Nicolson, 2008), p. 83.

27 her pet rat Snowy: Mary Elcho to Guy Wyndham, 11 May 1877, Stanway Papers. For Mary's recollection of herself at this time, see Mary Elcho to Arthur Balfour, 16 August 1895 (*Letters,* pp. 138–39).

27 part dog, part wombat: MacCarthy, *The Last Pre-Raphaelite,* p. 308.

27 "was there so much": Mackail and Wyndham, *Life and Letters,* 1:21.

27 "both in righteous wrath": Mary Elcho to Arthur Balfour, 16 August 1895 (*Letters*, pp. 138–39).

28 "morning, came green bile": Mary Elcho to Madeline Wyndham, 14 October 1880, Stanway Papers.

28 "consequences *when* they came": Mary Elcho to Madeline Wyndham, 3 June 1885, Stanway Papers.

28 "unconcern baffling the curious": Wilfrid Scawen Blunt, diary entry, 9 January 1895, quoted in Longford, *Pilgrimage of Passion*, p. 310.

28 closest friends truly knew: Asquith, *Haply I May Remember*, p. 155.

28 "air of Bohemian quasi-culture": Alfred Lyttelton to Mary Gladstone, 31 December 1886, quoted in Nancy Waters Ellenberger, "The Souls: High Society and Politics in Late Victorian England," PhD thesis, University of Oregon, 1982, pp. 62–63.

29 "days was through marriage": Mabell, Countess of Airlie, *Thatched with Gold: The Memoirs of Mabell, Countess of Airlie*, ed. and arranged by Jennifer Ellis (Hutchinson, 1962), p. 40.

29 history and public speaking: George Wyndham to Madeline Wyndham, 15 October 1874, Petworth Papers.

29 vocabulary in the latter: Mary Elcho to Madeline Wyndham, 4 September 1883, Stanway Papers.

30 "some sort of foliage": Mary Elcho to Madeline Wyndham, 19 November 1876, Petworth Papers.

30 "all spent at Wilbury": Mary Elcho to Madeline Wyndham, 7 December 1889, Stanway Papers.

30 friends and neighbors nearby: Mackail and Wyndham, *Life and Letters*, 1:26.

30 "hopes in the air": Philip Burne-Jones to Mary Elcho, quoted in Dakers, *Clouds*, p. 176.

30 and married to Prospero: Mackail and Wyndham, *Life and Letters*, 1:27–28.

30 Bloomsbury's Red Lion Square: Mary Elcho to Madeline Wyndham, 6 October 1880, Stanway Papers.

30 "of nonsense" in "Spression": Dakers, *Clouds*, p. 42.

30 possibly never even visiting: Ibid., p. 44.

30 for just over £100,000: Ibid., p. 48. The modern-day equivalent is $11,200,000 (CPI/RPI) and $11,000,000 (GDP deflator).

31 "for generations to come": Mackail and Wyndham, *Life and Letters*, 1:31.

31 "barley, 6 of oats": Mary Elcho, diary entry, 16 September 1873, quoted in Dakers, *Clouds*, p. 114.

31 "those of his party": Mackail and Wyndham, *Life and Letters*, 1:32.

31 Percy to higher office: Ellenberger, "Constructing George Wyndham," pp. 487, 496.

31 his party's temperate nonconformists: Quoted in Geoffrey Wheatcroft, *The Strange Death of Tory England* (Penguin Books, 2005), p. 31.

32 was in the ascendant: Lawrence James, *The Rise and Fall of the British Empire* (Abacus, 1995), pp. 196–99.

32 his decade of labor: Dakers, *Clouds,* p. 64.

32 used in the stables: Ibid., pp. 67–68.

32 epitaph for the gravestone: Mary Elcho to Guy Wyndham, 11 May 1877, Stanway Papers.

32 Germany, to be "finished": Mary Elcho, diary entry, 30 June 1878, Stanway Papers.

32 and the Jewish Quarter: Mary Elcho to Madeline Wyndham, 15 July 1898, Stanway Papers.

32 "you are coming home": Madeline Adeane to Madeline Wyndham, 26 July 1878, Petworth Papers.

33 "won't let you GO": Pamela Tennant to Madeline Wyndham, 11 December 1878, Petworth Papers.

33 "one she tore yesterday": Pamela Tennant to Percy Wyndham, 13 November 1878, Petworth Papers.

33 public for a shilling: *The Times,* 10 May 1887.

33 very expensive private house: *The Times,* 1 May 1877.

33 Lady Lindsay's "magnificent banquet": *The Times,* 10 May 1887.

33 opening made Burne-Jones famous: MacCarthy, *The Last Pre-Raphaelite,* p. 281.

33 a green carnation buttonhole: For a fuller account of the Aesthetic movement and its impact upon society, see Charlotte Gere, *Artistic Circles: Design & Decoration in the Aesthetic Movement* (V&A Publishing, 2010), and *The Cult of Beauty: The Aesthetic Movement, 1860–1900,* ed. Stephen Calloway and Lynn Federle Orr (V&A Publishing, 2011).

34 "in the *witness* box": Mary Elcho, diary entry, quoted in Dakers, *Clouds,* p. 57.

35 "prone at his feet": Mary Gladstone, quoted in R. J. Q. Adams, *Balfour: The Last Grandee* (John Murray, 2008), p. 29.

35 "of their youngest child": Harold Begbie (as "A Gentleman with a Duster"), *Mirrors of Downing Street: Some Political Reflections* (Mills & Boon, 1920), pp. 76–79.

35 "wonder . . . Thinks him good": Laura Tennant to Lady Frances Balfour, 9 October [1885], Whittingehame Papers, NRS GD433/2/477.

35 crowds at Leighton House: See Arthur James Balfour, *Chapters of Autobiography,* ed. Blanche Dugdale (Cassell, 1930), p. 234. *Chapters of Autobiography* has seventeen chapters. The first sixteen concern Balfour's political youth. The final words of this section recollect meeting Mary, Madeline

and George Wyndham at Sir Frederic Leighton's studio. The seventeenth chapter, tacked on somewhat incongruously, covers Balfour's first trip to the United States in 1917 and his subsequent diplomatic work there.

CHAPTER 3: "THE LITTLE HUNTER"

36 Room in Buckingham Palace: Mary Elcho, diary entry, 12 May 1880, Stanway Papers.

36 Mary's "passport to Society": Davidoff, *The Best Circles*, p. 25.

36 up in the hall: Dakers, *Clouds*, p. 59.

36 "fortunate to be fortunate": Quoted in Max Egremont, *The Cousins: The Friendship, Opinions and Activities of Wilfrid Scawen Blunt and George Wyndham* (Collins, 1977), p. 33.

36 its sovereign power decreased: See, in particular, David Cannadine, "The Context, Performance and Meaning of Ritual: The British Monarchy and the 'Invention of Tradition' circa 1820–1977," in Eric Hobsbawm and Terence Ranger (eds.), *The Invention of Tradition* (Cambridge: Cambridge University Press, 1992).

37 blazoned across the press: Piers Brendon, *The Decline and Fall of the British Empire, 1781–1997* (Jonathan Cape, 2007), pp. 165–66.

37 Minister a second time: Christopher Hibbert, *Queen Victoria: A Personal History* (HarperCollins, 2000), pp. 320, 362, 367.

38 result of mass enfranchisement: White, *London in the Nineteenth Century*, pp. 373–74.

38 rather than expressly arranged: Davidoff, *The Best Circles*, p. 49.

38 50 percent in 1891: David Cannadine, *The Decline and Fall of the British Aristocracy* (rev. ed., Penguin Books, 2005), p. 347.

38 "of the last century": Quoted in Ellenberger, "The Souls: High Society and Politics," p. 72.

38 "scum and nouveaux riches": Cannadine, *Decline and Fall*, p. 346.

38 great-great-granddaughters of a crofter: Davidoff, *The Best Circles*, p. 25.

38 "hats and low curtsies": Margot Asquith, *More Memories* (Cassell, 1933), pp. 219–22.

39 "patiently sitting as chaperone": Mary Elcho, "The Souls," unpublished memoir, quoted in Ellenberger, "The Souls: High Society and Politics," p. 45.

39 "in draft, rested, black": Mary Elcho, diary entry, 8 October 1884, Stanway Papers.

39 "and her plain sisters": Mary Elcho, sketches, n.d., Stanway Papers.

40 "& to be admired": Phrenological Reports, n.d. [ca. 1880 and 1883], Stanway Papers.

41 "Maid became a reality": Airlie, *Thatched with Gold,* p. 40.

41 "wanted me to wife!": Mary Elcho to Arthur Balfour, 14 February 1905 (*Letters,* p. 218).

41 "of 'grown-up conversation'": Mary Elcho to Madeline Wyndham, 3 October 1883, Stanway Papers.

41 her a little backward: Ridley and Percy (eds.), *Letters of Arthur Balfour and Lady Elcho,* p. 13.

41 "of my little efforts": Mary Elcho to Arthur Balfour, 14 February 1905 (*Letters,* p. 218).

41 "were afraid, afraid, afraid!": Ibid.

41 gay, even a hermaphrodite: The claim was famously made by Lord Beaverbrook: see Ruddock F. Mackay, *Balfour: Intellectual Statesman* (Oxford, Oxford University Press, 1985), p. 8; Davenport-Hines, *Ettie,* p. 54.

42 close friend May Lyttelton: Balfour was close friends with May (a niece of Gladstone's and a cousin of Mary Gladstone's), who died in 1875, and he mourned her all his life. He was a keen spiritualist (later in life, he became President of the Society for Psychical Research, a body founded in 1882 to use scientific analysis to "prove" the existence of a spirit world), and he tried several times to contact May through a medium. There is no evidence that Balfour and May were secretly engaged—or, whatever Blanche said, that Balfour asked for a ring to be put in her coffin (see Adams, *The Last Grandee,* pp. 29–31). Contemporaries, however, certainly believed the story to be true: see Maud Wyndham to Ettie Desborough, n.d. [1944], Desborough Papers, HALS DE/Rv/C2806, f. 2, recalling at length the affair: "He [Balfour] put what I believe had been his mother's engag[ement] ring into May's coffin, saying 'she wd [*sic*] have been my wife . . .'"

42 beyond Balfour's lodge gates: Begbie, *Mirrors of Downing Street,* pp. 76–79.

42 "even at their desire": Arthur Balfour to Mary Elcho, January 1894 (*Letters,* pp. 98–99).

42 "a very funny voice": Mary Elcho to Madeline Wyndham, 7 December 1880, Stanway Papers.

42 "the Brigadier," thought him feckless: Lord Elcho invented an Elcho boot, bayonet and military shovel and was a founder of the Volunteer Rifle Force, a forerunner of the Territorial Army, established in the late 1850s in response to invasion scares in the wake of the Crimean War (Wemyss, *Family Record,* p. 11).

42 wrong sons had died: Ibid., p. 10.

42 "she done for years": Hugo Elcho to Mary Elcho, 12 October 1887, Stanway Papers.

43 a friend might attend: Mary Elcho to Madeline Wyndham, 23 February 1881, Stanway Papers.

43 "sage, large-minded and kind": Mary Elcho to Hugo Elcho, 3 August 1881, Stanway Papers.

44 "at parties and balls": Quoted in James, *Aristocrats,* p. 307.

44 swore Hugo to secrecy: Evan Charteris to Hugo Elcho, 1 October [1881], Stanway Papers.

44 "refused is very funni": Hugo Elcho to Mary Elcho, 31 August 1887, Stanway Papers.

44 "with a clean nose!": Mary Elcho to Hugo Elcho, n.d. [summer 1887], Stanway Papers.

44 "many books for me": Quoted in Simon Blow, *Broken Blood: The Rise and Fall of the Tennant Family* (Faber & Faber, 1987), p. 42; Abdy and Gere, *The Souls* (Sidgwick & Jackson, 1984), p. 11.

44 her into marrying Hugo: Ellenberger, "Constructing George Wyndham," pp. 496–97, n. 34; see also Mary's first cousin Maud Wyndham to Ettie Desborough, 3 March 1944, Desborough Papers, HALS DE/rv c2806, f. 3: "Her mother had pushed her [Mary] into marrying L[or]d Elcho—so one used to be told at least."

44 "in love with you": Mary Elcho to Hugo Elcho, n.d. [summer 1887], Stanway Papers.

44 "followed her own trail": Ibid.

44 of the Conservative Opposition: Hugo Elcho to Madeline Wyndham, 1 November 1881, Stanway Papers.

45 "could shove somebody somewhere": Mary Elcho to Madeline Wyndham, 1 April 1882, Stanway Papers.

45 "keep one's hand in!": Mary Elcho to Hugo Elcho, n.d. [summer 1887], Stanway Papers.

45 disseminate the appalling news: Adams, *The Last Grandee,* p. 55.

45 "cads of the lobby": Quoted in Longford, *Pilgrimage of Passion,* p. 180.

46 illegal and oppressive behavior: Ibid., p. 190.

46 of Egypt's Consul General: *The Times,* 27 November 1882.

46 and Mary said yes: Mary Elcho to Hugo Elcho, 28 June 1883, Stanway Papers.

46 "made her love you": Percy Wyndham to Hugo Elcho, 2 July 1883, Stanway Papers.

47 "rather nervous about it": Unknown correspondent to Percy Wyndham, 11 July 1883, Stanway Papers.

47 "you all nearer together": Hugo Elcho to Mary Elcho, n.d. [July 1883], Stanway Papers.

47 from Hugo's desultory rivals: Mary Elcho to Arthur Balfour, 6 December 1913 (*Letters,* p. 307).

47 bemusement at the match: See, for example, the letters of Godfrey Webb to

Percy Wyndham, and Constance Mure to Percy Wyndham, both n.d. [July 1883], Stanway Papers.

47 not quite good enough: Mary Elcho to Arthur Balfour, 6 December 1913 (*Letters,* p. 307).

47 "six weeks of racket": Mary Elcho to Madeline Wyndham, 11 August 1883, Stanway Papers.

47 "house about bothering clothes": Mary Elcho to Hugo Elcho, n.d. [July 1883], Stanway Papers.

47 "halcyon days of muslins": Hugo Elcho to Mary Elcho, n.d. [July 1883], Stanway Papers.

47 great change before her: Mary Elcho to Hugo Elcho, 2 July 1883, Stanway Papers.

47 "nearer what you are": Hugo Elcho to Mary Elcho, 1 July 1883, Stanway Papers.

48 even embarked on it: Mary Elcho to Hugo Elcho, 18 July 1883, Stanway Papers.

48 "bottom of my heart": Ibid.

48 "take it to heart": Mary Elcho to Hugo Elcho, n.d. [ca. 17 July 1883], Stanway Papers.

48 "palpitated" over their marriages: George Wyndham to Mary Elcho, 15 February 1913, quoted in Mackail and Wyndham, *Life and Letters,* 2:737–38.

49 "even two hours old!": Mary Elcho to Hugo Elcho, 31 July 1883 [*sic*], Stanway Papers.

49 her side shouting "hurrah!": Hugo Elcho to Mary Elcho, 9 August 1883, Stanway Papers.

49 and became his wife: *The Times,* 10 August 1883.

49 "played louder & louder!": Madeline Wyndham to Mary Elcho, 10 August 1883, Stanway Papers.

50 "all the lovely flowers!": Ibid.

CHAPTER 4: HONEYMOON

51 "to being without you": Madeline Wyndham to Mary Elcho, n.d. [ca. August 1885], Stanway Papers.

51 that Hugo fell over: Mary Elcho to Guy Wyndham, n.d. [1883], Stanway Papers.

51 in the British Library: Andrew Marr, *The Making of Modern Britain* (Macmillan, 2009), pp. 74–75.

52 vigorously with black pen: Mary Elcho to Madeline Wyndham, 11 August 1883, Stanway Papers.

52 as Mary put it: Mary Elcho to Hugo Elcho, n.d. [ca. 1903], Stanway Papers.

52 considered his attitude unremarkable: Lambert, *Unquiet Souls,* p. 143.

52 the spring of 1884: Mary Elcho to Hugo Elcho, n.d., Stanway Papers; Mary Elcho to Madeline Wyndham, 7 September 1884, Stanway Papers.

52 "have any[thing] at all": Hugo Elcho to Percy Wyndham, 14 August 1883, Stanway Papers.

52 as was the convention: Pat Jalland, *Women, Marriage and Politics, 1860–1914* (Oxford: Oxford University Press, 1988), pp. 59–64.

53 "of it to lose!": Asquith, *Haply I May Remember,* p. 21.

53 the Elchos' common expenses: Percy Wyndham to Mary Elcho, 13 and 18 May 1888, Stanway Papers.

53 Hugo's master was "Mammon": Mary Elcho to Arthur Balfour, 6 December 1913 (*Letters,* p. 308).

53 in a "complaining chorus": Wemyss, *Family Record,* p. 16.

53 on two vast wings: Daker, *Clouds,* pp. 136–37.

54 over a bare landscape: Mary Elcho to Madeline Wyndham, 27 September 1888, Stanway Papers.

54 "dead & empty Cage": Mary Elcho to Wilfrid Scawen Blunt, 11 August 1915, Blunt Papers, FM 758-1975.

54 "has no living atmosphere": Cynthia Asquith, diary entry, 1 August 1918, quoted in Cynthia Asquith, *Diaries, 1915–1918,* ed. E. M. Horsley (New York: Alfred A. Knopf, 1969), p. 464.

54 "the King" sung flat: Dakers, *Clouds,* pp. 136–37.

55 "Mogs feels very sad": Mary Elcho to Hugo Elcho, 16 October 1883, Stanway Papers.

55 she could *"remove Mountains!"*: Mary Elcho to Madeline Wyndham, 17 October 1883, Stanway Papers.

55 work to be completed: Mary Elcho to Madeline Wyndham, 19 April 1884, Stanway Papers. Until mid-March 1884, Mary's letters from London are on writing paper headed 44 Belgrave Square (the Wyndhams' house). After that, they are headed 12 North Audley Street (see, for example, Mary Elcho to Madeline Wyndham, 10 and 27 March 1884, Stanway Papers).

56 in "nice long talk": Laura Lyttelton to Arthur Balfour, n.d. [ca. 1885], Whittingehame Papers, NRS GD433/2/477/4.

56 as their "court jester": Abdy and Gere, *The Souls,* p. 150.

56 "pouring out the tea": Hugo Elcho to Mary Elcho, 31 August 1887, Stanway Papers.

57 "are a domestic couple": Mary Elcho to Hugo Elcho, 28 January 1886, Stanway Papers.

57 "afresh! It's very funny": Mary Elcho to Madeline Wyndham, 10 March 1884, Stanway Papers.

57 still pregnant in September: Madeline Adeane to Madeline Wyndham, ca. 1902, Adeane Papers.

58 "and laps one about": Mary Elcho to Madeline Wyndham, 1 August 1884, Stanway Papers.

58 made by the housekeeper: Wemyss, *Family Record,* p. 35.

59 "livers," insomnia and indigestion: Mary Elcho to Madeline Wyndham, 5 September 1884, Stanway Papers; Wemyss, *Family Record,* p. 7.

59 urge, could paint it: Madeline Wyndham to Mary Elcho, September 1884, Stanway Papers.

59 "gown & your sofa": Ibid.

59 "words & reasonless rhymes": Quoted in Kenneth Young, *Arthur James Balfour: The Happy Life of the Politician, Prime Minister, Statesman and Philosopher, 1848–1930* (G. Bell, 1963), pp. 81–82.

59 "the verge of tears!": Mary Elcho to Percy Wyndham, 30 November 1884, Stanway Papers.

59 the games they played: Mary Elcho, diary entry, 23 November 1884, Stanway Papers.

60 "the night or morning": Ellenberger, "The Souls: High Society and Politics," p. 53.

60 party of the Souls: Ibid., p. 50.

CHAPTER 5: THE GANG

61 Wilbury on 28 December: The dates suggest that Ego was a "new thread," and Mary fell pregnant almost immediately after she miscarried in the spring of 1884.

61 "baby in the house": Pamela Tennant to Mary Elcho, n.d. [ca. January 1905], Stanway Papers.

61 effect a British withdrawal: For a full account, see Jan Morris, *Heaven's Command: An Imperial Progress* (Harmondsworth: Penguin Books, 1979), pp. 491–513.

62 Mahdi on Gordon's behalf: *The Times,* 24 December 1884.

62 Leader in the Lords: *The Times,* 31 December 1884.

62 was quietly let drop: Longford, *Pilgrimage of Passion,* p. 212.

62 "baked apples for luncheon": Mary Elcho, diary entries, December 1884, Stanway Papers.

62 "sitting on the Commode!": Mary Elcho to Madeline Wyndham, 30 July 1889, Stanway Papers.

62 "a most important *personage*": Madeline Wyndham to Mary Elcho, February 1885, Stanway Papers.

62 "spirits go down! Down!": Mary Elcho to Arthur Balfour, 15 March 1899 (*Letters,* pp. 60–61).

62 "but that's not strange!": Mary Elcho to Madeline Wyndham, 13 February 1885, Stanway Papers.

63 "called a milk *leg*": Madeline Wyndham to Mary Elcho, February 1885, Stanway Papers.

63 "death in our hearts": Madeline Wyndham to Mary Elcho, February 1885, Stanway Papers.

63 "life is thrown away": Percy Wyndham to George Wyndham, 19 February 1885, quoted in Mackail and Wyndham, *Life and Letters*, 1:29.

63 "grief" at the news: Madeline Wyndham to Mary Elcho, February 1885, Stanway Papers.

63 "she bares [*sic*] it wonderfully": Madeline Adeane to Mary Elcho, 18 February 1885, Stanway Papers.

63 "rejoice in his joy": Madeline Wyndham to Mary Elcho, February 1885, Stanway Papers.

64 "crying these last weeks": Madeline Wyndham to Mary Elcho, March 1885, Stanway Papers.

64 "six o'clock in the morning": Pamela Tennant to Mary Elcho, 6 March 1885, Stanway Papers.

64 augury of George's fate: Madeline Wyndham to Mary Elcho, March 1885, Stanway Papers.

64 "she came into contact": Quoted in Margot Asquith, *An Autobiography*, 2 vols. (Thornton Butterworth, 1920–22), 1:60.

64 "into a quiet pool": Mary Elcho, "The Souls," unpublished memoir, quoted in Ellenberger, "The Souls: High Society and Politics," pp. 49–50.

64 "their own good hearts": Quoted in Blow, *Broken Blood*, p. 88.

64 when she married Alfred: Ellenberger, "The Souls: High Society and Politics," p. 53.

64 "ladies and vulgar parents": Quoted in ibid., p. 51.

65 "for a sporting 'mees' ": Mary Elcho to Percy Wyndham, 12 April 1885, Stanway Papers.

65 they "walked home afterwards": Mary Elcho to Percy Wyndham 12 April 1884, Stanway Papers.

65 not Hugo but Arthur: Mary Elcho to Arthur Balfour, 26 May 1905 (*Letters*, p. 223).

65 that Mary openly blushed: Ibid.

65 as a "little flirt . . . !": Mary Elcho to Hugo Elcho, 14 August 1887, Stanway Papers.

66 "take one to task": Mary Elcho to Hugo Elcho, December 1886, quoted in Ellenberger, "The Souls: High Society and Politics," p 201.

66 "sees things in embryo": Laura Lyttelton to Lady Frances Balfour, 9 October [1885], Whittingehame Papers, NRS GD433/2/477, f. 10:13L

66 alone, could cause havoc: Ibid.; see also Laura Lyttelton to Arthur Balfour, n.d. [ca. 1885], Whittingehame Papers, NRS GD433/2/477, f. 8r, in which Laura declined, on behalf of herself and Mary, Arthur's suggestion that they

dine at the New Club with Hugo Elcho and Arthur Lyttelton out of town: "Dear Mr. Arthur I wd not go to the new Club anyhow with the awful protection of 10 Alfreds & 15 Hugos because it is full of gratuituous gossip & I think it wd be idiotic . . ."

66 "from one['s] moral mirror": Mary Elcho to Madeline Wyndham, 3 June 1885, Stanway Papers.

66 a stop to things: Laura Lyttelton to Lady Frances Balfour, 9 October [1885], Whittingehame Papers, NRS GD433/2/477, f. 10:13r.

67 "again as she did": Madeline Wyndham to Mary Elcho, May 1885, Stanway Papers.

67 "do the right thing": Mary Elcho to Madeline Wyndham, 3 June 1885, Stanway Papers.

68 or something more innocent: Ellenberger, "The Souls: High Society and Politics," p. 244.

68 "separated in *your lives*": Madeline Wyndham to Mary Elcho, August 1885, Stanway Papers.

68 "I worship you": Madeline Wyndham to Mary Elcho, 10 August 1885, Stanway Papers.

68 "& disappointed in me": Mary Elcho to Madeline Wyndham, n.d. [August 1885], Stanway Papers.

68 pregnancy as an excuse: Laura Lyttelton to Lady Frances Balfour, n.d. [autumn 1885], Whittingehame Papers, NRS GD/433/2/477/4, f. 17r.

CHAPTER 6: CLOUDS

69 their "scrumtious" [*sic*] new domain: Quoted in Dakers, *Clouds,* p. 81.

69 could manage was "delightful": Ibid.

69 "inside and windows outside": Georgiana Burne-Jones to Mary Elcho, November 1885, quoted in Dakers, *Clouds,* p. 81.

70 and a model laundry: Dakers, *Clouds,* p. 225.

70 in the plate closet: Ibid., p. 106.

71 ton and half ton: Ibid., p. 104.

71 bamboos, magnolias and rhododendrons: Ibid., pp. 87–89.

71 "a common warm bath": Percy Wyndham to Mary Elcho, September 1886, quoted in Dakers, *Clouds,* p. 82.

71 "heads on one side": Quoted in Dakers, *Clouds,* p. 81.

71 wood, beeswax and magnolias: Asquith, *Haply I May Remember,* pp. 40–41.

72 by Percy at auction: The auction was of the collection of William Graham, Frances Horner's father and an eminent art collector. In fact, the painting was by Pseudo-Pier Francesco Fiorentino. This was only discovered later. Dakers, *Clouds,* p. 142.

72 for trundling them about: Ibid., p. 94.

72 "moving among her guests": Pamela Adeane, daughter of Madeline and Charles Adeane, quoted in ibid., p. 91.

73 "surrounded by the Arch-Angels": Dakers, *Clouds,* p. 130.

73 pair of African jackasses: Wemyss, *Family Record,* pp. 20–21.

73 freely about the rooms: Asquith, *Haply I May Remember,* pp. 40–41.

73 legend "Miss Wyndham's bedroom": Madeline Wyndham to Pamela Tennant, 19 August 1897, Glenconner Papers, NRS GD510/1/26, f. 33r.

73 Sudanese prisoner of war: Mackail and Wyndham, *Life and Letters,* 1:31.

73 family safe and well: Dakers, *Clouds,* p. 81.

73 followed the next day: Ibid., p. 81.

73 "I have ever met": Violet Bradby, *A Family Chronicle,* quoted in ibid., p. 116.

74 the sick "nearly everyday": Madeline Adeane to Mary Elcho, 18 December 1885, Stanway Papers.

74 lawns—a very heaven: Dakers, *Clouds,* p. 119.

74 a new, warm jumper: Ibid.

75 maids displayed their talents: Ibid., p. 107.

75 "I am paying for": Percy Wyndham to Philip Webb, ca. January 1886, quoted in ibid., p. 82.

75 surveyed his new domain: Quoted in ibid., p. 83.

75 bearing "the Author's Compliments": Dakers, *Clouds,* p. 94; Asquith, *Haply I May Remember,* p. 42.

75 for the Wyndhams' guests: Mary Elcho to Evelyn de Vesci, 24 September 1889, De Vesci Papers, DD/DRU/87/3.

75 to Wilbury in 1884: Mary Elcho to Madeline Wyndham, 1 September 1884, Stanway Papers.

75 theorists of the day: Pamela Glenconner, *The Earthen Vessel: A Volume Dealing with Spirit-Communication Received in the Form of Book-Tests* (New York: John Lane, 1921), p. 138.

75 through the morning dew: Walburga, Lady Paget, *In My Tower,* 2 vols. (Hutchinson, 1924), 1:5–6.

75 "over the Western World": Samuel Hynes, *The Edwardian Turn of Mind: First World War and English Culture* (Pimlico, 1991), pp. 134–35.

76 "of our organized knowledge": Ibid., p. 139.

76 "through the front door": Ibid.

76 "sproits and spiris": Madeline Wyndham to Mary Elcho, September 1884, Stanway Papers.

76 "the life of Christ": Glenconner, *The Earthen Vessel,* pp. 136–37.

77 as she had arrived: Dakers, *Clouds,* p. 78.

77 house in their will: Ibid., p. 105.

77 percent of the workforce: Angela Lambert, *Unquiet Souls: The Indian Summer of the British Aristocracy* (Macmillan, 1984), p. 144.

77 less than eighteen months: Ibid.

78 "is it not horrid?": Madeline Wyndham to Mary Elcho, ca. September 1884, Stanway Papers.

79 "convulsions at 2:30 o'clock": Percy Wyndham to Mary Elcho, 14 March 1892, Stanway Papers.

79 commentary beneath, identifying each: Petworth Papers; Jeremy Musson, *Up and Down Stairs* (John Murray, 2009), pp. 148–49.

79 "a rub of soap": Ibid., p. 245. Horne's memoir was splendidly titled *What the Butler Winked At* (T. Werner Laurie, 1923), confirmation for suspicious employers of just how much their staff knew about their most intimate lives.

79 most certainly was not: Dakers, *Clouds,* p. 107.

CHAPTER 7: THE BIRTH OF THE SOULS

80 men to the electorate: Marquand, *Britain Since 1918,* p. 32.

81 "fears realized, says Papa": Mary Elcho to Hugo Elcho, n.d., Stanway Papers.

81 "to the devil again": Mary Elcho to Hugo Elcho, 28 January 1886, Stanway Papers.

81 had never been fond: See Mary Elcho to Madeline Wyndham, 21 March 1885, and 6 January 1886, Stanway Papers. The Cadogan Square house was initially numbered 36, and then renumbered 62 as the square expanded. Hugo's initial objection that the house did not come with stables was overcome when Mary found stables nearby that the Elchos could buy.

81 of seeing him again: Mary Elcho to Madeline Wyndham, 7 February 1886, Stanway Papers.

82 of fifty thousand unemployed: White, *London in the Nineteenth Century,* p. 376.

82 "windows in St. James's": Mary Elcho to Madeline Wyndham, dated 7 February 1886 (in fact, the riots were on 8 February), Stanway Papers.

82 "think about *nothing* else": Mary Elcho to Madeline Wyndham, 21 February 1886, Stanway Papers.

82 "yrs ago. f-rst k-ss": Mary Elcho to Arthur Balfour, 1 February 1906 (*Letters,* p. 231).

82 "tremendous love for Wash": Mary Elcho to Hugo Elcho, 27 February 1886, Stanway Papers.

82 "hardly since we married": Mary Elcho to Madeline Wyndham, 21 February 1886, Stanway Papers.

82 "too, dear old friend": Laura Lyttelton to Arthur Balfour, 2 April 1886, Whittingehame Papers, NRS GD/433/2/479/1, f. 6r.

82 possibility of anything more: Margot Asquith to Wilfrid Scawen Blunt, 10 and 28 May 1906, 27 January 1911, quoted in Longford, *Pilgrimage of Passion*, p. 375.

83 "makes one utterly miserable": Mary Elcho, diary entry, 24 April 1886, Stanway Papers.

83 "needed people are not": Mary Elcho to Madeline Wyndham, 26 April 1886, Stanway Papers.

83 "I have ever known": Asquith, *An Autobiography*, 1:63–64.

83 "it, as it were": Quoted in Ridley and Percy (eds.), *Letters of Arthur Balfour and Lady Elcho*, p. 24.

83 "you must forgive me": Mary Elcho to Arthur Balfour, 8 May 1886 (*Letters*, pp. 24–25).

83 Evan Charteris and Arthur: Ellenberger, "The Souls: High Society and Politics," p. 54.

84 (friend) and Harry Cust: Ibid.

84 that of anyone else: Mary Elcho to Arthur Balfour, 8 May 1886 (*Letters*, pp. 24–25).

84 the Whigs, now flourished: Wheatcroft, *The Strange Death of Tory England*, p. 33; Marquand, *Britain Since 1918*, p. 57; James, *Aristocrats*, p. 337.

84 "friendship to public politics": Asquith, *An Autobiography*, 1:207.

84 "heat and without reporters": Ibid.

85 would become Prime Minister: Ibid., 1:217; 2:14–15.

85 "fascinating, aristocratic, intellectual coterie": Robert Blake, quoted in Ellenberger, "The Souls: High Society and Politics," p. 1.

85 "charm" beyond the political: Frances Horner, *Times Remembered*, quoted in ibid., p. 5.

85 "in the same spirit": Quoted in Longford, *Pilgrimage of Passion*, p. 297.

85 "excellent thing for us": Quoted in Blow, *Broken Blood*, p. 202.

85 the sittings a "nuisance": Mary Elcho to Hugo Elcho, 28 October 1886, Stanway Papers.

85 "smartness all their own": Quoted in Abdy and Gere, *The Souls*, p. 12.

85 her in such finery: Arthur Balfour to Mary Elcho, 29 April 1892 (*Letters*, p. 69).

85 food, sustained their guests: Abdy and Gere, *The Souls*, p. 11.

85 his sense of humor: See MacCarthy, *The Last Pre-Raphaelite*, p. 478. Burne-Jones described Poynter, his brother-in-law, as filled with "dull excellencies."

85 quickness of her movement: Cynthia Asquith, quoted in Abdy and Gere, *The Souls*, p. 108.

85 "more pagan than soulful": Quoted in ibid., p. 11.

86 "of the social game": Ibid., p. 12.

86 vegetable, building or color: Lambert, *Unquiet Souls*, p. 93.

87 several times that season: Ellenberger, "The Souls: High Society and Politics," p. 5, and "The Souls and London 'Society,'" p. 133; see also Abdy and Gere, *The Souls*, p. 10.

87 "were bored with them": Arthur Balfour to Mary Elcho, [10 April] 1890 (*Letters*, pp. 67–68); also quoted in Ellenberger, "The Souls: High Society and Politics," p. 84.

87 vivacious "chaffing" of Hugo: Mary Elcho, diaries, 30 May 1887, Stanway Papers.

87 "talking [about] . . . Dickens etc": Ibid., 20 and 25 June 1887.

87 the company of men: Ellenberger, "The Souls: High Society and Politics," p. 85.

88 "(then) all day long": Lady Sibyl Lubbock, quoted in Abdy and Gere, *The Souls*, p. 169.

88 "direct heritage from them": Quoted in ibid., p. 15.

88 half-crown stakes with Hugo: Ridley and Percy (eds.), *Letters of Arthur Balfour and Lady Elcho*, p. 19; Blanche Dugdale, *Family Homespun* (John Murray, 1940), pp. 72–73.

88 "and ease are delightful": Lady Frances Balfour to Lady Betty Balfour, June 1889, Whittingehame Papers, NRS GD/433/2/301.

89 "a sample of idiocy!": Mary Elcho to Ettie Grenfell, 19 November 1890, Desborough Papers, HALS/DE/Rv/C477.

89 "of the elusive set": Mary Elcho to Ettie Grenfell, n.d. [ca. 1929], Desborough Papers, HALS DE/Rv/C477/101.

89 some point of debate: See, for example, Arthur Balfour to Mary Elcho, 28 February [1894] (*Letters*, p. 102), and Mary Elcho to Arthur Balfour, 15 May 1895 (*Letters*, pp. 124–25).

89 "died on the same day": Margot Asquith, *Off the Record* (Frederick Muller, 1944), p. 52.

89 Sibell was eight years older than George: Ellenberger, "Constructing George Wyndham," p. 497.

90 whose hand it was: Elizabeth, Countess of Fingall, *Seventy Years Young: Memories of Elizabeth, Countess of Fingall* (Dublin: Lilliput Press, 1991), p. 273.

90 "as upon a fairyland": Quoted in Egremont, *The Cousins*, p. 141.

90 his dark, "French" looks: Paget, *In My Tower*, 1:110.

90 "life at high pitch": Fingall, *Seventy Years Young*, p. 271.

90 "handsomest man in England": Abdy and Gere, *The Souls*, p. 92.

90 plain Mrs. George Wyndham: For an account of the episode, see Egremont, *The Cousins*, pp. 78–79.

91 "unstupid but ill-ballasted personality": Alfred Lyttelton to Mary Gladstone, 31 December 1886, quoted in Ellenberger, "The Souls: High Society and Politics," pp. 62–63.

CHAPTER 8: THE SUMMER OF 1887

92 "after Betsey at Panshanger": Mary Elcho to Hugo Elcho, 13 January 1887, Stanway Papers.

92 "in the family way": Ibid.

92 not have many children: Ridley and Percy (eds.), *Letters of Arthur Balfour and Lady Elcho*, p. 27.

92 "stuff its [*sic*] too naughty": Mary Elcho to Hugo Elcho, 12 January 1887, Stanway Papers.

93 "Migs propose Pints dispose": Mary Elcho to Hugo Elcho, 13 January 1887, Stanway Papers.

93 George acting as best man: *The Times*, 8 February 1887.

93 bun given to each child: Dakers, *Clouds*, p. 119.

93 driveway to Clouds themselves: Ibid.

93 "human life at all": Patrick Jackson, "Sir George Trevelyan," *Oxford Dictionary of National Biography.*

93 phrase "Bob's your uncle": For the suggestion, see Adams, *The Last Grandee*, p. 71. However, there does not appear to be an example in print of this phrase until Eric Partridge's *Dictionary of Slang and Unconventional English* (George Routledge & Sons, 1937), which would make it surprising if the phrase really dated back to 1887.

93 boasted the Irish crowds: Lambert, *Unquiet Souls*, p. 59; Ridley and Percy (eds.), *Letters of Arthur Balfour and Lady Elcho*, p. 33.

93 "in the political boat": Mackail and Wyndham, *Life and Letters*, p. 37.

93 in as many years: Adams, *The Last Grandee*, p. 76.

94 lives or possibly both: Mary Elcho to Arthur Balfour, 8 December 1921, Whittingehame Papers, NRS GD433/2/229/1, f. 29.

94 appear in his memoirs: Mary Elcho to Arthur Balfour, 7 March 1929 (*Letters*, p. 353).

94 "was a friend only": Quoted in Davenport-Hines, *Ettie*, p. 62.

94 "shall have his woman": Quoted in Longford, *Pilgrimage of Passion*, p. 297.

95 "I know she will": Arthur Balfour to Lady Frances Balfour, 6 March 1887, quoted in Ridley and Percy (eds.), *Letters of Arthur Balfour and Lady Elcho*, pp. 33–34.

95 "couldn't sleep from excitement": Mary Elcho, diary entry, 8 July 1887, Stanway Papers.

96 was a "great success": Mary Elcho to Madeline Wyndham, 4 July 1887, Stanway Papers.

96 "(or impurely) personal conversations": Mary Elcho to Hugo Elcho, 26 August 1887, Stanway Papers.

96 "[I] am getting uneasy": Mary Elcho to Hugo Elcho, 12 August 1887, Stanway Papers.

96 quelling one's hedonistic will: Mary Elcho to Hugo Elcho, 29 August 1887, Stanway Papers.

96 "stop to my Ethics": Mary Elcho to Hugo Elcho, 18 August 1887, Stanway Papers.

96 "a muff I think": Ibid.

96 honor to the Queen: Marie Adeane married, in 1891, Sir Bernard Mallet. Her recollections of her life with Queen Victoria were published under her married name.

96 "sweetness and social charm": Mary Elcho to Wilfrid Scawen Blunt, 27 March 1899, Blunt Papers, FM 492-1975.

96 month, and mean it: Adeane Papers.

96 her "Madeline the Mondaine": Madeline jokingly adopted the name herself: see her signature in a letter to Wilfrid Scawen Blunt, 21 February 1901, Blunt Papers, FM 258-1975.

96 "twitch! & wink! Terribly": Madeline Adeane to Madeline Wyndham, 19 August 1899, Adeane Papers.

97 but a comforting one: Madeline Adeane to Madeline Wyndham, 15 November 1887, Adeane Papers.

97 "We are not amused": Hibbert, *Queen Victoria,* p. 467.

97 conversation a little trying: Mary Elcho to Hugo Elcho, 18 August 1887, Stanway Papers; Pamela Tennant to Mary Elcho, 27 September 1903, Stanway Papers.

97 a confidence not kept: Hugo Elcho to Mary Elcho, 29 August 1887, Stanway Papers.

97 than his intended bride: Hugo was born on 25 August 1857, making him just short of five years older than Mary. Charles Adeane was born on 2 November 1863, making him about five and a half years older than Mananai, born on 31 March 1869.

97 letter "about fifty times": Charles Adeane to Madeline Wyndham, 29 August 1887, Adeane Papers.

98 "at all rich" either: Percy Wyndham to Mary Elcho, 18 May 1888, Stanway Papers.

98 "obedience to the law": Quoted in Brendon, *Decline and Fall,* p. 295.

98 interesting, said Balfour drily: Ibid.

98 to save "darling Ireland": Tynan Hinkson, *Years of the Shadow,* p. 256.

98 to do the same: See Constance Leconfield to Madeline Wyndham, 30 March 1898, 7 April 1898, Petworth Papers.

99 barbarity of the evictions: Longford, *Pilgrimage of Passion,* pp. 228–29.

99 "level of our sins": Quoted in ibid., p. 246.

99 "let us leave it": Quoted in Dakers, *Clouds,* pp. 126–27.

99 "how dull-witted he is": Quoted in Longford, *Pilgrimage of Passion,* p. 247.

99 "of a tame cat": Ibid.

99 "must govern herself too": Quoted in Lambert, *Unquiet Souls,* p. 62.

100 "caged bird to freedom": Mary Elcho to Hugo Elcho, 3 September 1887, Stanway Papers.

100 he were set free: Lambert, *Unquiet Souls,* p. 63.

100 Wyndhams as their wards: Madeline Adeane to Madeline Wyndham, 15 November 1887, Adeane Papers.

100 Percy was "splendid": Madeline Adeane to Madeline Wyndham, 10 November 1887, Adeane Papers.

100 of the London crowd: White, *London in the Nineteenth Century,* pp. 377–79.

100 bathing in children's blood: Brendon, *Decline and Fall,* p. 295.

100 "to my sanguinary character": Arthur Balfour to Mary Elcho, 24 December 1887 (*Letters,* p. 46).

101 "were you & Mamma!!!": Pamela Tennant to Mary Elcho, 13 August 1888, Stanway Papers.

101 against Balfour for assault: Longford, *Pilgrimage of Passion,* pp. 259–61.

101 it a "splendid commotion": Quoted in ibid., p. 252.

101 "out of his senses": Quoted in Egremont, *The Cousins,* p. 130; Lambert, *Unquiet Souls,* p. 63.

101 "brutal jailer of Irishmen?": Longford, *Pilgrimage of Passion,* p. 261.

CHAPTER 9: MANANAI

102 "is better isn't it?": Pamela Tennant to Mary Elcho, Good Friday (30 March 1888), Stanway Papers

102 "anything of that kind?": Percy Wyndham to Mary Elcho, 30 March 1888, Stanway Papers.

103 "as 'serene as oil!' ": Madeline Adeane to Mary Elcho, 26 November 1887, Adeane Papers.

103 to liven it up: Percy Wyndham to Mary Elcho, 18 May 1888, Stanway Papers.

103 "more I like him": Ibid.

103 not entirely indigent bridegroom: *Modern Society,* 4 August 1888, Adeane Papers.

103 "well . . . & perfectly comfortable": Charles Adeane to Madeline Wyndham, 26 July 1888, Adeane Papers.

103 for a "confidential chat": Madeline Adeane to Mary Elcho, 1 August 1888, Stanway Papers.

104 "how happy we are": Madeline Adeane to Madeline Wyndham, 4 August 1888, Adeane Papers.

104 "I owe my love": Charles Adeane to Madeline Wyndham, 26 July 1888, Adeane Papers.

104 luggage to the Continent: Madeline Adeane to Madeline Wyndham, 12 August 1888, Adeane Papers.

104 quite outnumbered by footmen: Madeline Adeane to George Wyndham, 25 August 1888, George Wyndham Papers.

105 "green river at Clouds": George Wyndham to Madeline Adeane, 31 August 1888, quoted in Mackail and Wyndham, *Life and Letters,* 1:226.

105 "*Italian Painters* by Jameson": Madeline Adeane to George Wyndham, 25 August 1888, George Wyndham Papers.

106 wept when they arrived: Marie Mallet, *Life with Queen Victoria: Marie Mallet's Letters from Court, 1887–1901,* ed. Victor Mallet (John Murray, 1968), p. xiv; Madeline Adeane to Mary Elcho, 27 March 1889, Stanway Papers.

106 Percy had recently built: Madeline Adeane to Percy Wyndham, 8 October 1889, Adeane Papers.

106 "feeble imitation of you": Madeline Adeane to Madeline Wyndham, 28 March 1889, Adeane Papers.

107 "tennis—walking, talking, reading": Charles Adeane to Madeline Wyndham, 6 September 1893, Adeane Papers.

107 puppy, everywhere she went: Madeline Adeane to Madeline Wyndham, 17 July 1889, Adeane Papers.

CHAPTER 10: CONFLAGRATION

108 and snapped at Dorothy: Pamela Tennant to Mary Elcho, 17 September 1893, Stanway Papers.

108 their first "grown-up" visit: Percy Wyndham to Mary Elcho, 8 March 1887, Stanway Papers.

108 "hearts ease purple": Pamela Tennant to Mary Elcho, 21 September 1888, Stanway Papers.

108 of her fellow guests: Ibid.

109 rather later than planned: Dakers, *Clouds,* p. 134.

109 "down to find them": Mary Elcho to Lady Frances Balfour, 21 January 1889, Whittingehame Papers, NRS GD/433/2/301, f. 11r.

109 not fade for weeks: Dakers, *Clouds,* p. 130.

110 part of the conflagration: Ibid., p. 131.

110 "the dear house burn": Wemyss, *Family Record,* p. 23.

110 "its beauty and terror": Olivier, *Four Victorian Ladies,* p. 89.

111 "tennis jersey & skirt": Mary Elcho to Lady Frances Balfour, 21 January 1889, Whittingehame Papers, NRS GD433/2/301, f. 11r.

111 dining room at breakfast: Ridley and Percy (eds.), *Letters of Arthur Balfour and Lady Elcho,* p. 58.

112 the rivalrous female Souls: Abdy and Gere, *The Souls,* pp. 160–61; and see Mary Elcho to Arthur Balfour, 3 April 1905 (*Letters,* p. 221).

112 "as anything can be": Mary Elcho to Arthur Balfour, 23 January 1889 (*Letters*, p. 56).

112 until the party ended: Ibid., p. 55.

112 "sponge or *burnt* away": Mary Elcho to Arthur Balfour, 13 January 1889 (*Letters*, p. 55).

112 "blotting self & sheets": Mary Elcho to Arthur Balfour, 23 January 1889 (*Letters*, p. 56).

112 "together we were drawn": Mary Elcho to Lady Frances Balfour, 21 January 1889, Whittingehame Papers, NRS GD433/2/301, f. 11r.

112 "stand and fall together": George Wyndham to Madeline Wyndham, 7 January 1889, Mackail and Wyndham, *Life and Letters*, 1:231.

112 the fire for years: Mary Elcho to Lady Frances Balfour, 21 January 1889, Whittingehame Papers, NRS GD433/2/301, f. 11r.; Pamela Tennant to Mary Elcho, 15 March 1889 and 7 February 1905, Stanway Papers.

112 entered into the house: Quoted in Dakers, *Clouds*, p. 134.

112 "loving and successful labor": Ibid.

112 Balfour, a "heart-breaking event": Lady Betty Balfour to Lady Frances Balfour, 14 January 1889, Whittingehame Papers, NRS GD433/2/301, f. 10r.

112 the existence of evil: Ibid.

112 "too ideal to live": Quoted in Dakers, *Clouds*, p. 131.

112 "making it lovely again": Mackail and Wyndham, *Life and Letters*, 1:231.

113 "of all their pains": Mary Elcho to Arthur Balfour, 13 January 1889 (*Letters*, p. 55).

113 £3,000 out of pocket: Dakers, *Clouds*, pp. 132–33.

113 "were in our own": Quoted in ibid., p. 135.

113 on 29 August 1891: Ibid.

CHAPTER II: THE SEASON OF 1889

114 "such a nice place": Madeline Adeane to Madeline Wyndham, 17 July 1889, Adeane Papers.

114 features and refined air: Percy Wyndham to Mary Elcho, 14 September 1888, Stanway Papers.

114 "literary and clever": Mary Elcho to Wilfrid Scawen Blunt, 27 March 1899, Blunt Papers, FM 492-1975.

114 "like an empty glass": Quoted in Philip Hoare, *Serious Pleasures: The Life of Stephen Tennant* (Hamish Hamilton, 1990), p. 8.

115 "read anything by them": Pamela Tennant to Mary Elcho, 14 June 1928, Stanway Papers.

115 "a time-sucker with you!": Pamela Tennant to Mary Elcho, 23 November 1891, Stanway Papers.

115 "I was so silent": Mary Elcho to Wilfrid Scawen Blunt, 16 November 1893, Blunt Papers, FM 1592-1976.

115 for her eighteenth birthday: Pamela Tennant to Mary Elcho, 10 February 1889, Stanway Papers.

115 "she thought was marvelous": Quoted in Hoare, *Serious Pleasures,* p. 22.

115 "but kept them going": Percy Wyndham to Mary Elcho, 14 September 1888, Stanway Papers.

116 friends with perfect respectability: Amy Milne-Smith, *London Clubland: A Cultural History of Gender and Class in Late Victorian Britain* (New York: Palgrave Macmillan, 2011), p. 162.

116 arms full of flowers: Lady Frances Balfour to Lady Betty Balfour, June 1889, Whittingehame Papers, NRS GD433/2/301, f. 42r.

117 "a *sine qua non*": *The World,* 16 July 1890, quoted in Ellenberger, "The Souls: High Society and Politics," p. 55; and in Lambert, *Unquiet Souls,* p. 10.

117 "He's got a cruet": Ellenberger, "The Souls and London 'Society,'" pp. 146–47.

117 from a wastepaper basket: Ibid.

117 "those sorts of crimes": Edith Lyttelton, quoted in Ellenberger, *The Souls: High Society and Politics,* p. 83.

117 "the usual hardy annual": Lady Frances Balfour to Lady Betty Balfour, June 1889, Whittingehame Papers, NRS GD433/2/301, f. 32r.

117 was returned to bed: Mary Elcho to Madeline Wyndham, 3 July 1889, Stanway Papers.

118 "two! Operas a week": Mary Elcho to Evelyn de Vesci, 28 April 1891, De Vesci Papers, DD/DRU 87/3.

118 the energy she expended: Madeline Adeane to Madeline Wyndham, 3 December 1899, Adeane Papers.

118 "looked 5 years younger!": Mary Elcho to Evelyn de Vesci, 28 April 1891, De Vesci Papers, DD/DRU/87/3.

119 "me a Kleine Pause": Mary Elcho to Hugo Elcho, 27 July 1900, Stanway Papers.

119 "it was doubly delightful": Pamela Tennant to Mary Elcho, 28 July 1889, Stanway Papers.

119 James were "really delightful": Pamela Tennant to Mary Elcho, 17 September 1890, Stanway Papers.

119 "*every* one admired it!!!": Pamela Tennant to Mary Elcho, 28 July 1889, Stanway Papers.

120 "most people unsatisfactory Earth!": Ibid.

120 receive Pamela's "capital" letter: Mary Elcho to Madeline Wyndham, 3 August 1889, Stanway Papers.

120 "them for a time": Mary Elcho to Evelyn de Vesci, 7 August 1889, De Vesci Papers, DD/DRU/87/3.

120 "& cats & clowns": Ibid.

120 *"so much* at first": Ibid.

120 yellow and pale blue: Madeline Adeane to Madeline Wyndham, 3 April 1889, Adeane Papers.

120 "if that is possible": Madeline Adeane to Madeline Wyndham, 25 September 1889, Adeane Papers.

120 the baby's first "fluff": Madeline Adeane to Madeline Wyndham, 4 October 1889, Adeane Papers.

120 "I knew nothing about": Pamela Tennant to Mary Elcho, 17 September 1893, Stanway Papers.

121 "cry to be lucky": Madeline Adeane to Pamela Tennant, 8 October 1889, Adeane Papers.

121 "one love the Queen": Marie Mallet to Lady Elizabeth Biddulph, 8 November 1889, quoted in Mallet, *Life with Queen Victoria,* p. 35.

CHAPTER 12: THE MAD AND THEIR KEEPERS

122 *Lippincott's* at its stalls: Neil McKenna, *The Secret Life of Oscar Wilde* (Arrow Books, 2004), pp. 185–86.

122 "temple of twopenny Rimmons": Curzon's reference is presumably to the quintessential false god of the Old Testament. See 2 Kings 5:18: "In this thing the LORD pardon thy servant, *that* when my master goeth into the house of Rimmon to worship there, and he leaneth on my hand, and I bow myself in the house of Rimmon: when I bow down myself in the house of Rimmon, the LORD pardon thy servant in this thing."

122 and his wife, Helen: Helen Kelsall Melland, Asquith's first wife, was the daughter of a Manchester doctor. The Asquiths married in 1877 and had five children: Raymond, Herbert, Arthur, Violet and Cyril. Helen died a few months after this visit, in the autumn of 1891, from typhoid fever.

123 while on the river: Quoted in Davenport-Hines, *Ettie*, pp. 57–58.

123 "suppose they weren't bored": Mary Elcho to Evelyn de Vesci, 28 April 1891, De Vesci Papers, DD/DRU/87/3.

123 his life and work: Wilfrid Scawen Blunt, Secret Memoirs XV, 1 July 1893 to 3 July 1893, Blunt Papers, FM 33-1975.

123 "future rulers of England": Quoted in David Gilmour, *Curzon: Imperial Statesman* (John Murray, 2003), pp. 103–4.

124 "for his red complexion": Quoted in Longford, *Pilgrimage of Passion,* p. 293.

124 "Cust bulged with sex": Lord Robert Vansittart, *The Mist Procession* (Hutchinson, 1958), p. 90.

124 His "harem": Arthur Balfour to Mary Elcho, 16 August 1893 (*Letters,* p. 14).

124 "content themselves with profligacy": Quoted in Ellenberger, "The Souls: High Society and Politics," p. 187.

125 "crudely expressed by him!": Pamela Tennant to Mary Elcho, 16 August 1892, Stanway Papers.

126 "clear their throats continually": Ibid.

126 defense was impossible, "ignore": Osbert Sitwell, *Laughter in the Next Room* (Macmillan, 1949), p. 100.

126 "deceived by outside views!!!": Pamela Tennant to Mary Elcho, 25 August 1893, Stanway Papers.

126 "foolishness on my part": Pamela Tennant to Mary Elcho, 16 August 1892, Stanway Papers.

126 man called Arthur Paget: Paget is remembered now as the inventor of sign language for the deaf and dumb, but his "engaging personal qualities"— his geniality, sympathy and "deep affection for the young and old alike"—as well as his eccentricity receive almost as much attention as his achievements in the *Oxford Dictionary of National Biography*: see Harry Lowery, "Paget, Sir Richard Arthur Surtees, second baronet (1869–1955)," rev. John Bosnell, *Oxford Dictionary of National Biography*, online ed., May 2008 (http://www.oxforddnb.com/view/article/35358, accessed 23 October 2013).

126 "of adjectives strung together!": Pamela Tennant to Mary Elcho, 31 August 1892, Stanway Papers.

128 "be nothing to you": Ibid.

128 "he really means it?": Mary Elcho to Madeline Wyndham, 5 September 1892, Stanway Papers.

128 daughter and Harry Cust: Percy Wyndham to Mary Elcho, 30 November 1892, Stanway Papers.

128 "He, Cust, is sane": Ibid.

CHAPTER 13: CRISIS

129 extended periods of time: By way of example, Mary spent almost six months of each of the years 1890 and 1891 apart from her children, whether at a house party, in London, ill or on a "cure": Nicola Beauman, *Cynthia Asquith* (Hamish Hamilton, 1987), p. 6.

129 was six years old: Asquith, *Haply I May Remember*, p. 59.

129 "he will get [it]": Mary Elcho to Evelyn de Vesci, 16 January 1891, De Vesci Papers, DD/DRU 87.

130 by marriage of Mary's: Lambert, *Unquiet Souls*, p. 78.

130 did not show it: Fingall, *Seventy Years Young*, pp. 179, 182.

130 "of her unhappy life": Hugo Elcho to Evelyn de Vesci, 20 March 1895, De Vesci Papers, DD/DRU 102.

131 "admire her courage intensely": Ettie Grenfell to Constance, Lady Wenlock, 8 December 1892, quoted in Davenport-Hines, *Ettie*, p. 54.

131 "I know, an angel": Lady Lyttelton, quoted in Tynan Hinkson, *Years of the Shadow*, p. 15.

131 phrase, an "unstable equilibrium!": Mary Elcho to Arthur Balfour, 13 August 1890 (*Letters*, pp. 71–72).

131 Arthur didn't: Ibid.

131 of sex than she: Ibid.

131 and her artistic skill: Arthur Balfour to Mary Elcho 16 July 1891 (*Letters*, pp. 73–74).

131 "quite her own master": Mary Elcho to Arthur Balfour, 30 October 1912 (*Letters*, p. 291).

132 "that seemed on fire": Asquith, *Haply I May Remember*, p. 134.

132 had asked for her: Beauman, *Cynthia Asquith*, pp. 6–7; Mary Elcho to George Wyndham, 3 January 1892, George Wyndham Papers.

132 her quiet darkened room: Pamela Tennant to Sibell, Countess Grosvenor, 28 December 1892, George Wyndham Papers.

132 "kiss her from me": Madeline Adeane to Madeline Wyndham, 28 December 1892, Adeane Papers.

132 faith to console them: Jalland, *Women, Marriage and Politics*, p. 181.

133 "her heart must break": Asquith, *Haply I May Remember*, p. 135.

133 "this of any child?": Arthur Balfour to Mary Elcho, 9 January 1893 (*Letters*, pp. 89–90); see also Mary Elcho to George Wyndham, 3 January 1893, George Wyndham Papers.

133 nothing could help her: Mary Elcho to Madeline Wyndham, 21 April 1893, Stanway Papers.

134 had first left it: Wemyss, *Family Record*, pp. 50–52.

134 that was undoubtedly Hugo's: Lambert, *Unquiet Souls*, pp. 64–65; Beauman, *Cynthia Asquith*, p. 15.

134 *Doubt*, published in 1879: Adams, *The Last Grandee*, pp. 34, 126.

134 "to the outside world": Arthur Balfour to Mary Elcho, 16 August 1893 (*Letters*, p. 14).

134 "endless arguments on Poetry": Madeline Wyndham to Mary Elcho, quoted in Dakers, *Clouds*, p. 160.

134 "for *thinking* it would': Percy Wyndham to Mary Elcho, 6 September 1893, Stanway Papers.

134 had been duly mollified: Wilfrid Scawen Blunt, Secret Memoirs XVI, 9 November 1893.

134 "extremely delicate weather glass": Pamela Tennant to Mary Elcho, 25 August 1893, Stanway Papers.

135 "comes down to breakfast": Pamela Tennant to Mary Elcho, 16 August 1893, Stanway Papers.

135 "lives outwardly perfectly matched": Pamela Tennant to Mary Elcho, 25 August 1893, Stanway Papers.

135 "in epigrams and aphorisms": Paget, *In My Tower,* 1:5–6.

136 "discussed civilization!": Pamela Tennant to Mary Elcho, 25 August 1893, Stanway Papers.

136 "thought herself with child": Wilfrid Blunt, Secret Memoirs XVI, 16 October 1893.

136 approval of their match: See Mary Lovell, *The Churchills: A Family at the Heart of History—from the Duke of Marlborough to Winston Churchill* (Little, Brown, 2011), pp. 49–50.

136 diary can be believed: Longford, *Pilgrimage of Passion,* p. 298.

136 "with great brutality": Wilfrid Blunt, Secret Memoirs XVI, 9 November 1893.

137 "sad errand after another": George Wyndham to Ettie Grenfell, 30 September 1893, Desborough Papers, HALS DE/Rv/C2800/39. All others found in NRS GD433/2/482, ff. 1–19r.

137 this day, accounts differ: Wilfrid Blunt heard the story from two different sources. Once the immediacy of the crisis had passed, George Wyndham gave him the fundamentals of the entanglement. Shortly afterwards, at what was doubtless a gossipy lunch with Lewis ("Loulou") Harcourt at 11 Downing Street (Loulou being the son of the Chancellor, Sir William Harcourt), Loulou, who had been present at the Derwent house party, told Blunt that George Curzon, upon receiving anonymous telegrams at the Derwent house party from a lady in distress "very foolishly shewed [them] around," thinking that they signified a crisis in Violet Granby's marriage. On then receiving a telegram from Harry Cust, at Sheffield, who had just seen the pregnancy certificate sent to him by Nina and Violet Granby, Curzon hastened to him, returning only briefly to enlist George Wyndham's help before the two hared off again to Harry (Secret Memoirs, 16 October and 9 November 1893). Ridley and Percy have Harry himself receiving letters from Nina Welby and showing them around as a joke (*Letters of Arthur Balfour and Lady Elcho,* p. 103), but it is likely that this is an example of the way in which the tale mutated as it filtered through society. Harry could be cruel, but he was surely not foolish enough to incriminate himself so completely as that. As subsequent events demonstrated, the Souls' morality could not extend to seducing unmarried women.

137 "time in perverting it": George Wyndham to Ettie Grenfell, 27 September 1893, HALS DE/Rv/C2800/38.

137 "so anxious so anxious": Pamela Tennant to Sibell, Countess Grosvenor, n.d. [September 1893], George Wyndham Papers.

137 flat all the way: Mary Elcho to Madeline Wyndham, 20 and 21 November 1893, Stanway Papers.

137 exile before he complied: Harry Cust to Arthur Balfour, 15 October 1893, Whittingehame Papers, NRS GD433/2/482, f. 4r.

137 "'to come back to'": Pamela Tennant to Mary Elcho, 13 March 1928, Stanway Papers.

137 "little saint as well": Harry Cust to Arthur Balfour, 15 October 1893, Whittingehame Papers, NRS GD433/2/482, f. 4r.

137 the *Ganges* in November: Madeline Adeane to Madeline Wyndham, 19 November 1893, Adeane Papers.

138 cut into the skin: Sitwell, *Laughter in the Next Room,* p. 99.

138 her to the skies: Wilfrid Scawen Blunt, Secret Memoirs XVI, 7 October 1893.

138 "kingdoms crumble down": Ibid.

138 "'married' to Miss Welby": Ibid., 16 October 1893.

138 England for the Continent: *The Times,* 16 October 1893.

138 "mouths of the public": George Curzon to Arthur Balfour, 16 October 1893, Whittingehame Papers, NRS GD433/2/482, f. 6r.

138 "thin veil at best": Charles Welby to Arthur Balfour, 16 October 1893, Whittingehame Papers, NRS GD433/2/482, f. 8r.

139 "refined and well-meaning": Quoted in Ellenberger, "The Souls: High Society and Politics," p. 214.

139 "they have many others": Wilfrid Scawen Blunt, Secret Memoirs XVI, 27 June 1894.

139 had had an abortion: Harry Cust to Arthur Balfour, n.d., f. 5r; Charles Welby to Arthur Balfour, 31 October 1893, f. 14r, and 3 November 1893, f. 15r, all Whittingehame Papers, NRS GD433/2/482.

139 "be the only solution": Quoted in Ellenberger, "The Souls: High Society and Politics," p. 214

CHAPTER 14: INDIA

140 "a separate little agony": Pamela Tennant to Mary Drew, 13 January 1894, BL Mary Gladstone Papers, vol. XXXIII, Add. MSS 46251.

140 "words can save them": Percy Wyndham to Mary Elcho, 20 October 1893, Stanway Papers.

141 Nina not at all: Harry Cust to Sibell, Countess Grosvenor, quoted in Egremont, *The Cousins,* p. 164.

141 "the next 10 years": Pamela Tennant to Madeline Adeane, n.d. [October 1893], Stanway Papers.

141 "dog was with him": Pamela Tennant to Sibell, Countess Grosvenor, 12 November 1893, George Wyndham Papers.

141 "than I ever expected": Ibid.

141 "people to amuse Papa": Madeline Adeane to Madeline Wyndham, 19 November 1893, Adeane Papers.

142 "of those 3 months": Pamela Tennant to Mary Drew, 13 January 1894, BL Mary Gladstone Papers, vol. XXXIII, Add. MSS 46251.

142 "in high mettalic [*sic*] tones": Madeline Adeane to Mary Elcho, 19 December 1893, Stanway Papers.

143 a noble, civilizing Empire: James, *Rise and Fall,* pp. 233–34.

143 "quiver instead of shine": Pamela Tennant to Mary Drew, 13 January 1894, BL Mary Gladstone Papers, vol. XXXIII, Add. MSS 46251.

143 "was anything but comfortable": Madeline Adeane to Madeline Wyndham, 7 December 1893, Adeane Papers.

143 "& tables . . . too dreadful": Ibid.

144 attracted by her vibrancy: Madeline Adeane to Madeline Wyndham, 14 March 1894, Adeane Papers.

144 "Eddie lacks *drive*": Quoted in Hoare, *Serious Pleasures,* p. 4.

144 what he looked like: Ibid., p. 17.

144 room at each other: Madeline Adeane to Madeline Wyndham, 14 March 1894, Adeane Papers.

144 "every line were extraordinary": Arthur Balfour to Mary Elcho, January 1894 (*Letters,* p. 94).

144 "*nimbus* of pure happiness": Pamela Tennant to Sibell Grosvenor, 1 February 1894, George Wyndham Papers.

144 "thoroughly, impossibly, cruelly unhappy": Pamela Tennant to Sibell Grosvenor, October 1894, George Wyndham Papers.

145 "happiness as one's birthright": Pamela Tennant to Mary Elcho, 28 August 1916, Stanway Papers.

145 "the hot sausages inside": Pamela Tennant to Sibell Grosvenor, 1 February 1894, George Wyndham Papers.

145 were evasive about Harry: In fact, Harry Cust had embroiled himself in another potential crisis by standing as Unionist parliamentary candidate for the seat of industrial North Manchester in a by-election planned for the spring of 1894. One prominent local activist, Millicent Fawcett, a radical Liberal Unionist and suffragist, caught wind of the "most ghastly story" of Harry, Nina and Pamela and began to circulate it around local political associations, demanding that Harry stand down, such a man not being a proper representative for the honest burghers of Manchester. Harry threatened Mrs. Fawcett with a libel suit: in turn, Mrs. Fawcett threatened to subpoena everyone involved in the scandal, including Arthur Balfour, in her defense. In June 1894, Balfour told Harry that he could not stand, fearing that otherwise the Souls' carefully hushed-up scandal would be revealed. Harry remained in political exile until he reentered Parliament as the Member for London's East End Bermondsey constituency in 1900.

145 "anything about that time": Ibid.

145 "best cabins on board": Madeline Adeane to Madeline Wyndham, n.d. [spring 1894], Adeane Papers.

145 "One can't do everything": Madeline Adeane to Madeline Wyndham, 14 March 1894, Adeane Papers.

145 "*better* she is again": Madeline Adeane to Madeline Wyndham, 5 May 1894, Adeane Papers.

CHAPTER 15: RUMOR

146 "contest of any arena": Roy Hattersley, *David Lloyd George: The Great Outsider* (Little, Brown, 2010), p. 72.

146 privilege of the Lords: Cannadine, *Decline and Fall,* p. 45.

147 capacity for manipulative intrigue: Patrick Jackson, "Harcourt, Lewis Vernon, First Viscount Harcourt (1863–1922)," *Oxford Dictionary of National Biography,* Oxford University Press, 2004; online ed., January 2008 (http://www.oxforddnb.com/view/article/33692, accessed 14 November 2013).

147 "amiable" and "instantly loveable": McKenna, *Secret Life of Oscar Wilde,* pp. 332–33.

147 peace to the town: Ibid., pp. 342–43.

148 unenthusiastic about the match: Pamela Tennant to Mary Elcho 30 October 1894, Stanway Papers.

148 "& without knowing why": Ibid.

148 "pain coming through sleep": Pamela Tennant to Sibell Grosvenor, 29 September 1894, George Wyndham Papers.

148 "bursting feelings": Pamela Tennant to Sibell Grosvenor, n.d. [October 1894]. Percy's policy regarding trials and difficulties had not changed since he outlined it to Madeline Wyndham thirty years before, and would not change thereafter. Some five years later, he briskly, albeit sympathetically, reproved his eldest daughter when she made reference to domestic troubles: "I know well all your trials and difficulties but don't allude to them as it only makes things worse putting them down in *black* and *white* and *underlining* them" (Percy Wyndham to Mary Elcho, 22 November 1900, Stanway Papers).

148 "I'm unhappy, or ill": Pamela Tennant to Mary Elcho, 30 October 1894, Stanway Papers.

148 wound through the mouth: McKenna, *Secret Life of Oscar Wilde,* p. 422.

148 fired was carefully overlooked: Ibid., p. 421.

149 "the 'one-moment-too-lateness' of Life": Pamela Tennant to Mary Elcho, 30 October 1894, Stanway Papers.

149 "when she is alone": Ibid.

150 Still hopeful for Baker-Carr: Madeline Adeane to Madeline Wyndham, 14 December 1894, Adeane Papers.

150 "man with money enough": Madeline Adeane to Madeline Wyndham, 10 December 1894, Adeane Papers.

150 "in the last 3 years": Pamela Tennant to Mary Elcho, 30 October 1894, Stanway Papers.

CHAPTER 16: EGYPT

151 the same regarding his: For discussion of the play, see Hynes, *Edwardian Turn of Mind*, pp. 174–78.

152 "retaliate secretly—and *lie!*": Ibid., pp. 177–78.

152 woman of her class: Longford, *Pilgrimage of Passion*, p. 295.

152 a more temperate climate: Fingall, *Seventy Years Young*, p. 184.

153 "take my children there!": Mary Elcho to Wilfrid Scawen Blunt, 16 November 1893, Blunt Papers, FM 1529-1976.

153 with Mary in mind: Longford, *Pilgrimage of Passion*, p. 308.

153 "went away to Arthur": Ibid., p. 307.

153 Sheykh Obeyd that winter: Wilfrid Scawen Blunt, Secret Memoirs XVI, 10 to 13 August and 5 October 1894.

153 "like riding a swallow": Mary Elcho to Madeline Wyndham, 22 November 1894, Stanway Papers.

154 of 5 January 1895: Wilfrid Scawen Blunt, diary entry, 5 January 1895, Blunt Papers, FM 343-1975.

154 "being in an hotel": Mary Elcho to Evelyn de Vesci, 17 January 1895, De Vesci Papers, DD/DRU/87.

155 "little less than love": Quoted in Longford, *Pilgrimage of Passion*, p. 311.

155 "will be far wrong": Arthur Balfour to Mary Elcho, 27 February 1895 (*Letters*, p. 120).

155 "extremest hopes were achieved": Wilfrid Scawen Blunt, diary entry, 14–15 January 1895, FM 344-1975.

155 "quite all that happened": Ibid.

155 taken advantage of her: Longford, *Pilgrimage of Passion*, p. 311; Mary Elcho to Wilfrid Scawen Blunt, 27 March 1899, Blunt Papers, FM 492-1975, and 5 May 1906, Blunt Papers, FM 559-1975.

156 "my true Bedouin wife": Quoted in Longford, *Pilgrimage of Passion*, p. 313.

156 "to me by instinct": Mary Elcho to Wilfrid Scawen Blunt, 6 April 1899, Blunt Papers, FM 493-1975.

156 "foot prints in it": Ibid.

156 "suppose it means nothing": Quoted in Longford, *Pilgrimage of Passion*, p. 311.

156 what was going on: Beauman, *Cynthia Asquith*, pp. 26, 30, 292–93.

156 "of beauty & romance": Mary Elcho to Wilfrid Scawen Blunt, 6 April 1899, Blunt Papers, FM 493-1975.

156 "living in the present": Mary Elcho to Evelyn de Vesci, 13 February 1895, De Vesci Papers, DD/DRU/87.

156 "pure gift from heaven": Quoted in Longord, *Pilgrimage of Passion*, p. 312.

157 "children, or her friend": Ibid., p. 313.

157 "be talking [about] them": Hugo Elcho to Evelyn de Vesci, n.d. [1895], De Vesci Papers, DD/DRU/102.

157 "not make any difference": Ibid.

158 "cut off her head": Longford, *Pilgrimage of Passion*, p. 313.

158 "Margate Sands straw hat!": Mary Elcho to Wilfrid Scawen Blunt, 6 April 1899, Blunt Papers, FM 493-1975.

158 earth with a bump: Harrison, *Autobiographic Memoir*, 2:173–79.

158 "night of our honeymoon": Longford, *Pilgrimage of Passion*, p. 313.

159 "soon & stay together": Hugo Elcho to Mary Elcho, n.d. [February 1895], Stanway Papers.

159 "stupidly anxious about Mary": Mary Elcho to Wilfrid Scawen Blunt, 6 April 1899, Blunt Papers, FM 493-1975.

159 "life for 15 days": Wilfrid Scawen Blunt, Diaries, 5 March to 13 March 1895, Blunt Papers, FM 344-1975.

160 "us & we it": Mary Elcho to Wilfrid Scawen Blunt 6 April 1899, Blunt Papers, FM 493-1975.

160 "when she woke up": Hugo Elcho to Evelyn de Vesci, 20 March 1895, De Vesci Papers, DD/DRU/102.

160 "go Grand Hotel Rome": Telegram from Hugo Elcho to Mary Elcho, 20 March 1895, Stanway Papers. It had been arranged in Hugo's previous letter to Mary that the two would meet in Rome: Hugo Elcho to Mary Elcho, 14 March 1895, Stanway Papers.

160 write or even speak: Hugo Elcho to Evelyn de Vesci, 20 March 1895, De Vesci Papers, DD/DRU/102.

160 "ought to live it": Mary Elcho to Hugo Elcho, 21 March 1895, Stanway Papers.

160 to bed before dinner: Mary Elcho to Madeline Wyndham, 9 April 1895, Stanway Papers.

161 "secret" of her pregnancy: Mary Elcho to Madeline Wyndham, 9 July 1895, Stanway Papers.

161 trouble to compare dates: Wilfrid Scawen Blunt, Secret Memoirs XVII, diary entry, 13 May 1895 (transcript of a letter from Mary Elcho), Blunt Papers, FM 34-1975; Mary Elcho to Madeline Wyndham, 9 July 1895, Stanway Papers.

161 "had had the opportunity": Wilfrid Scawen Blunt, Secret Memoirs XVII, diary entry, May 1895.

CHAPTER 17: THE FLORENTINE DRAMA

162 Saxon state's miniature court: Madeline Adeane to Madeline Wyndham, 6 April 1895, Adeane Papers.

163 "do what I ask": George Wyndham to Percy Wyndham, 7 April 1895, BL Eccles Bequest (unbound), vol. CXIV, Add. MSS 81732.

164 "prove himself a man": Ibid.

164 "every luck": Arthur Balfour to Mary Elcho, 20 March 1895 (*Letters*, p. 123).

164 asked for an update: Madeline Adeane to Mary Elcho, 6 May 1895, Stanway Papers.

164 "dropped on his side": Paget, *In My Tower*, 25 April 1895, 1:136–39.

165 took place that night: Blow, *Broken Blood*, p. 113.

165 "not common": Quoted in Ellenberger, "The Souls: High Society and Politics," p. 51.

165 "got reflected onto them": E. F. Benson, *Dodo—A Detail of the Day* (Lightning Source UK, n.d.), p. 27.

165 "you cannot make gentlemen": Quoted in Ellenberger, "The Souls: High Society and Politics," p. 64.

166 "Engaged E.T. still private": Pamela Tennant to George Wyndham, 21 August 1895, George Wyndham Papers; Madeline Adeane to Mary Elcho, 6 May 1895, Stanway Papers.

166 "world to the end": Edward Tennant to Charlotte, Lady Ribblesdale, 7 May 1895, Bodleian, Asquith Papers, MS. Eng. c. 6697, f. 156.

166 "only be deeply thankful": Madeline Adeane to Mary Elcho, 6 May 1895, Stanway Papers.

166 telegram of her own: Mary Elcho to Arthur Balfour, quoted in Dakers, *Clouds*, p. 163.

166 "no embrace for her": Edward Tennant to Charlotte, Lady Ribblesdale, 7 May 1895, Bodleian, Asquith Papers, MS. Eng. c. 6697, f. 156.

166 "coarse fiber in [Eddy]": Wilfrid Blunt, diary entry, 12 May 1895, Blunt Papers, FM 345-1975.

166 "nice simple letter": George Wyndham to Mary Drew, May 1895, quoted in Mackail and Wyndham, *Life and Letters*, 1:330–31.

166 "we have passed thro": Mary Elcho to Madeline Wyndham, 18 July 1895, Stanway Papers.

167 "emptiness & vain regrets": Mary Elcho to Madeline Wyndham, 16 May 1895, Stanway Papers.

167 "& capacity for enjoyment": Ibid.

167 " 'the man arx her?' ": Mary Elcho to Arthur Balfour, n.d. [spring 1895] (*Letters*, p. 124).

167 appeared no more unnerved: Percy Wyndham to Guy Wyndham, 23 May 1895, Stanway Papers.

168 of the "Florentine Drama": George Wyndham to Mary Drew, May 1895, quoted in Mackail and Wyndham, *Life and Letters,* 1:330–31.

168 at the wedding anyway: Mary Elcho to Madeline Wyndham, 9 July 1895, Stanway Papers.

168 "watches of the night": Mary Elcho to Arthur Balfour, 31 August 1895 (*Letters,* pp. 128–29).

168 while Hermione was dying: Wilfrid Scawen Blunt, Secret Memoirs XVII, 16 August 1895.

168 "me in a way": Ibid., 11 and 27 April 1895.

169 "it, to earn it": Ibid., 13 May 1895.

169 "nor finds it strange" Ibid., 28 June 1895.

169 all of the truth: Longford, *Pilgrimage of Passion,* p. 315.

170 "us and the Wyndhams": Wilfrid Scawen Blunt, Secret Memoirs XVII, 14 and 19 July 1895.

170 Sloane Street, in London: Order of Service for Pamela and Edward Tennant, kept and decorated by Mary Elcho, Stanway Papers.

170 "a bride so lovely": *The Lady,* 18 July 1895; and quoted in Blow, *Broken Blood,* p. 114.

171 girl, as Wilfrid insists: Wilfrid Scawen Blunt, Secret Memoirs XVII, 16 August 1895.

171 "a punishment to me": Ibid.

171 of the family only: Ibid., 9 December 1895.

171 birth, and recovered well: Edward Burne-Jones to Madeline Wyndham, 25 October 1895; unknown correspondent to Madeline Wyndham, 26 October 1895, Stanway Papers.

171 "fearlessly across the desert": Wilfrid Scawen Blunt, Secret Memoirs XVII, 9 December 1895.

171 Cheltenham the following year: Longford, *Pilgrimage of Passion,* pp. 318–19.

171 "might be very terrible": Mary Elcho to Wilfrid Scawen Blunt, 29 April 1896, Blunt Papers, FM 281-1975.

171 "at your own house?": Mary Elcho to Wilfrid Scawen Blunt, 27 March 1899, Blunt Papers, FM 492-175.

172 walk through Clouds' grounds: Mary Elcho to Wilfrid Scawen Blunt, 26 September 1901, Blunt Papers, FM 518-1975.

172 "distinctly rampageous young man": Mary Elcho to Wilfrid Scawen Blunt, 1 February 1906, Blunt Papers, FM 554-1975.

172 "as dull as anything": Ibid.

172 they had ever been: A full account of this is given in Longford, *Pilgrimage of Passion.*

172 "having to distress you": Mary Elcho to Arthur Balfour, 6 June 1893 (*Letters,* pp. 135–36).

CHAPTER 18: GLEN

173 "to take over Glen!": Quoted in Blow, *Broken Blood,* p. 116.

173 "rapturously . . . but perhaps sufficiently": Wilfrid Scawen Blunt, Secret Memoirs XVII, 19 July 1895.

173 had made in Florence: Pamela Tennant to George Wyndham, 22 October 1895, George Wyndham Papers.

174 "I did to you": Pamela Tennant to Marie Stopes, 14 July 1918, BL Stopes Papers, vol. CCXXXCCII, Add. MS. 58684.

174 "not—nor had been": Pamela Tennant to George Wyndham, 21 August 1895, George Wyndham Papers.

174 "it's his fault rather": Pamela Tennant to George Wyndham, 21 August 1895 and 24 August 1898, George Wyndham Papers.

174 "so formed & complete": Pamela Tennant to Mary Elcho, 23 October 1897, Stanway Papers.

174 away at weak spots: Pamela Tennant to Mary Elcho, n.d. [ca. 1900], Stanway Papers.

174 "to most other women": Pamela Tennant to Mary Elcho, 23 October 1897, Stanway Papers.

175 reform to poultry breeding: Edward Tennant to Pamela Tennant, 19 February 1896, Glenconner Papers, NRS GD510/1/30, f. 34.

175 sourcing and interviewing staff: See correspondence between Pamela Tennant and Edward Tennant in the course of autumn 1895 and spring 1896, Glenconner Papers, NRS GD510/26, 30, 31.

176 "[trimmed] Hat" ("sounds fascinating"): Edward Tennant to Pamela Tennant, spring 1896, Glenconner Papers, NRS GD510/1/30, f. 17.

176 flowers ("it is curious"): Edward Tennant to Pamela Tennant, 17 January 1896, Glenconner Papers, NRS GD510/1/31, f. 20.

176 framed and hung up: Edward Tennant to Pamela Tennant, 26 April 1896, Glenconner Papers, NRS GD510/1/31, f. 26.

176 politics in the newspapers: Edward Tennant to Pamela Tennant, 10 January 1896, Glenconner Papers, NRS GD510/1/30, f. 38.

176 to leave her again: Edward Tennant to Pamela Tennant, n.d. [ca. Easter 1896], Glenconner Papers, NRS GD510/1/30, f. 20.

176 "hang light on it": Madeline Wyndham to Pamela Tennant, 9 August 1897, Glenconner Papers, NRS GD510/1/26, f. 33.

176 "& gentle & nice": Mary Elcho to Arthur Balfour, n.d. [ca. November 1920], Whittingehame Papers, NRS GD433/2/229/1, f. 19.

176 to a steel fortune: Blow, *Broken Blood,* pp. 132–33.

176 children were not around: Harry Cust to Pamela Tennant, n.d., Tennant Papers, NLS 12143/4.

177   "with a bald top": Mary Elcho to Madeline Wyndham, 6 January 1886, Stanway Papers.

177   time she left Clouds: Madeline Wyndham to Pamela Tennant, 9 August 1897, Glenconner Papers, NRS GD510/1/26, f. 33.

177   "was well with me": Pamela Tennant to Wilfrid Scawen Blunt, 11 June 1922, Blunt Papers, FM 286-1976.

178   "I had before fish": Pamela Tennant to Mary Elcho, 23 October 1897, Stanway Papers.

178   "& the Babes also": Madeline Wyndham to Pamela Tennant, 9 August 1897, Glenconner Papers, NRS GD510/1/26, f. 33.

179   lack of civic virtue: Brendon, *Decline and Fall,* pp. 207, 209–10.

179   "by birth & conviction': Pamela Tennant to Mary Elcho, 7 June 1895, Stanway Papers.

179   "to make it intelligible": George Wyndham to Pamela Tennant, 19 January 1898, quoted in Mackail and Wyndham, *Life and Letters,* 1:323.

180   conversation before the fire: George Wyndham to Pamela Tennant, 5 March 1898, quoted in ibid., 1:334; 11 February 1898, ibid., 1:333.

180   she scarcely looked back: George Wyndham to Pamela Tennant, 11 February 1898, ibid., 1:333.

180   "they aroused in you": George Wyndham to Pamela Tennant, 10 January 1898, ibid., 1:320.

181   "and irresponsible and quaint": George Wyndham to Pamela Tennant, 23 April 1899, ibid., 1:352.

181   a typically breathless phrase: Cuttings all found in the Garden Book of Pamela Tennant, Stephen Tennant Papers.

181   "blow was 'pretty booklet' ": Pamela Tennant to Mary Elcho, 20 June 1900, Stanway Papers.

181   in her Wiltshire village: *The Times,* 20 November 1928.

181   disturbed by the squalor: Pamela Glenconner, *Edward Wyndham Tennant: A Memoir* (John Lane, The Bodley Head, 1919), p. 11.

CHAPTER 19: THE PORTRAIT, WAR AND DEATH

182   "painting your three daughters": John Singer Sargent to Percy Wyndham, 20 December 1898, quoted in Dakers, *Clouds,* p. 163.

182   "out of the picture": Percy Wyndham to Mary Elcho, n.d. [ca. May 1895], Stanway Papers.

183   "we are all gone": Mackail and Wyndham, *Life and Letters,* 1:67, 349–50.

183   confirmation of the news: Mackail and Wyndham, *Life and Letters,* 1:66.

183   "are all for war": Quoted in Egremont, *The Cousins,* p. 193.

183 "the House of Commons": Mallet, *Life with Queen Victoria,* 21 October 1898, p. 141.

184 "like a Neapolitan ice?": Mary Elcho to Madeline Wyndham, 18 January 1899, Stanway Papers.

184 "look well I think": Mary Elcho to Madeline Wyndham, 11 February 1899, Stanway Papers.

184 "is a *perfect fit!*": Mary Elcho to Madeline Wyndham, 1 February 1899, Stanway Papers.

184 "gown & curl papers": Mary Elcho to Madeline Wyndham, 7 February 1899, Stanway Papers.

184 "exactly like Miss Havisham!": Mary Elcho to Madeline Wyndham, 14 February 1899, Stanway Papers.

185 too dark to work: Madeline Adeane to Madeline Wyndham, 17 March 1899, Adeane Papers.

185 "demoniacal Influenza": Madeline Adeane to Percy Wyndham, 6 April 1899, Adeane Papers.

185 "problems presented to him": Mary Elcho to Madeline Wyndham, 28 February 1899, Stanway Papers.

186 "*curious* Miss Siddal was": Madeline Adeane to Madeline Wyndham, 29 March 1899, Adeane Papers.

186 for the Season in May: Charles Adeane to Madeline Wyndham, 21 April 1899, Adeane Papers.

186 "is a real drill-sergeant": Charles Adeane to Madeline Wyndham, 24 March 1899, Adeane Papers.

186 "there won't be war": Madeline Adeane to Madeline Wyndham, 16 August 1899, Adeane Papers.

186 "little 'individual' is'nt [*sic*] it": Madeline Adeane to Madeline Wyndham, 28 September 1899, Adeane Papers.

186 "we mobilize on Monday": Quoted in Egremont, *The Cousins,* p. 201.

187 "Well it has come": Mackail and Wyndham, *Life and Letters,* 1:71.

187 published in *The Times*: Egremont, *The Cousins,* p. 201.

187 "and no popery talk": Quoted in ibid., p. 188.

187 "ahead with our work": Quoted in ibid., p. 201.

187 "of the War nearer": Madeline Adeane to Madeline Wyndham, 31 October 1899, Adeane Papers.

188 "have warded it off": Madeline Adeane to Madeline Wyndham, 2 November 1899, Adeane Papers.

188 "about you & I!": Charles Adeane to Madeline Wyndham, 3 November 1899, Adeane Papers.

188 "*quietness* & *wonderful* resignation": Madeline Wyndham to Pamela Tennant, 4 November 1899, Glenconner Papers, NRS GD510/1/29, f. 38; 7 November 1899, Glenconner Papers, NRS GD510/1/29, f. 22.

188 "mind off the sorrow": Madeline Wyndham to Pamela Tennant, 7 November 1899, Glenconner Papers, NRS GD510/1/29, f. 22.

188 "& find us dead": Ibid.

188 words of H. G. Wells: H. G. Wells, *The New Machiavelli* (Duffield, 1910), p. 122.

189 comes to Black Week: See Chapter 9 onwards of Arthur Conan Doyle, *The Great Boer War* (Smith, Elder, 1900).

189 "the battle was over": Quoted in Brendon, *Decline and Fall*, pp. 218–19.

189 "banks of the river": Percy Wyndham to Mary Elcho, 16–17 December 1899, Stanway Papers.

CHAPTER 20: PLUCKING TRIUMPH FROM DISASTER

190 "men—paying for it": H. G. Wells, *The New Machiavelli*, p. 122.

190 urging root-and-branch military reform: Brendon, *Decline and Fall*, p. 219.

190 "come into the open": George Wyndham to Guy Wyndham, 6 January 1900, quoted in Mackail and Wyndham, *Life and Letters,* 1:386.

191 "bugle . . . sort of speech": Margot Asquith to Edward Tennant, 17 January 1900, Glenconner Papers, NRS GD10/1/42, f. 8.

191 "would never stop cheering": George Wyndham to Madeline Wyndham, 3 February 1900, quoted in Mackail and Wyndham, *Life and Letters,* 1:391.

191 "praise is not exaggerated": Arthur Balfour to Mary Elcho, 1 February 1900 (*Letters,* p. 166).

191 "it quite xtraordinarily [*sic*] well": Margot Asquith to Edward Tennant, n.d. [5 November 1900], Glenconner Papers, NRS GD510/1/42, f. 12.

191 "given him Cabinet rank": Percy Wyndham to Mary Elcho, 5 February 1900, Stanway Papers.

191 "the reach of fate": Arthur Balfour to Mary Elcho, 16 March 1900 (*Letters,* p. 167).

191 "richly sonorous voice": Newspaper cutting, n.d., among Glenconner Papers, NRS GD510/1/29, f. 7.

192 "*could* they have survived . . . ?": Madeline Adeane to Madeline Wyndham, 29 March 1900, Adeane Papers.

192 country were behind them: Mackail and Wyndham, *Life and Letters,* 1:72.

192 "best-hated man in Britain": *The New York Times,* 14 December 1913.

192 for over ten minutes: Madeline Adeane to Madeline Wyndham, 18 March 1900, Adeane Papers.

192 "they have been defaced": George Wyndham to Pamela Tennant, 11 September 1900, quoted in Mackail and Wyndham, *Life and Letters,* 1:405.

192 for the troops abroad: Charles Adeane to Madeline Wyndham, 1 February 1900, Adeane Papers.

192 "sometimes despair of the end": Madeline Adeane to Madeline Wyndham, 13 August 1900, Adeane Papers.

193 "blisters like a lemon": Madeline Adeane to Madeline Wyndham, 2 April 1904, Adeane Papers.

193 "Mafeking is well!": Madeline Adeane to Madeline Wyndham, 20 May 1900, Adeane Papers.

193 "bombardment. One dog killed": Quoted in Brendon, *Decline and Fall,* p. 220.

193 extravagant demonstrations of exultation: Jan Morris, *Farewell the Trumpets: An Imperial Retreat* (London: Faber & Faber, 1978), p. 86.

193 for her spectacular looks: Downes, *John S. Sargent,* pp. 54, 188–89.

193 to complement the portrait: Dakers, *Clouds,* p. 97.

193 appeared at the latter: Quoted in ibid., p. 165.

194 "as it *should be*": Mary Elcho to Hugo Elcho, 1 August 1900, Stanway Papers.

194 "lasts I make hay": Quoted in Mackail and Wyndham, *Life and Letters,* 1:72–73.

CHAPTER 21: THE 1900 ELECTION

195 "be content with failure": Quoted in Ellenberger, "The Souls: High Society and Politics," p. 91; Dakers, *Clouds,* p. 158.

195 Season, in late July: Abdy and Gere, *The Souls,* p. 106.

195 1895 Hugo was "chucked!": Mary Elcho to Madeline Wyndham, 16 July 1895, Stanway Papers.

195 "out of public affairs": Wilfrid Scawen Blunt, Secret Memoirs XVII, 16 July 1895.

195 "seeming" fell on deaf ears: Mary Elcho to Hugo Elcho, 1 August 1900, Stanway Papers.

195 "having nothing to do": Mary Elcho to Hugo Elcho, 13 September 1900, Stanway Papers.

196 "& never [had] been": Mary Elcho to Hugo Elcho, n.d. [ca. 1898], Stanway Papers.

196 roughly $1.07 million today: Ellenberger, "The Souls and London 'Society,'" p. 154. The $1.07 million figure is CPI. The equivalent employing GDP deflator is $952,000.

196 "and Hugo is undone!": Mary Elcho to Arthur Balfour, 30 August 1899, (*Letters,* pp. 158–59).

197 one of the trustees: Abdy and Gere, *The Souls,* p. 105.

197 "every way I can": Mary Elcho to Hugo Elcho, 13 September 1900, Stanway Papers.

197 "[Arthur] couldn't squash Long": Mary Elcho to Hugo Elcho, 25 September 1900, Stanway Papers.

197 "could have been found": Arthur Balfour to Mary Elcho, n.d. [September 1896] (*Letters,* p. 146).

197 "both high & low!": Mary Elcho to Percy Wyndham, 28 September 1899, Stanway Papers.

198 He gambled: Mary Elcho to Arthur Balfour, 30 August 1899 (*Letters,* pp. 158–59).

198 "nor give him up!": Mary Elcho to Arthur Balfour, 20 September 1904 (*Letters,* pp. 216–17).

198 "do a stupid thing": Margot Asquith to Edward Tennant, 10 October 1900, Glenconner Papers, NRS GD510/1/42, f. 9.

198 "dirty linen to herself": Margot Asquith to Edward Tennant, 31 July 1900, Glenconner Papers, NRS GD510/1/42, f. 11.

198 "many children I have!": Pamela Tennant to Mary Elcho, n.d. [1900], Stanway Papers.

198 "deglutition of hypocritical pledges": Quoted in Marquand, *Britain Since 1918,* p. 56.

199 "nervous excitement & terror": Pamela Tennant to Mary Elcho, n.d. [1900], Stanway Papers.

199 "lamentable mistakes & failures": Ibid.

199 more involved political role: Jalland, *Women, Marriage and Politics,* pp. 206ff.

199 "nothing but stupendous egotism": Ibid., quoted at pp. 209–10.

199 outweighing that to gender: Ibid., pp. 209–14.

199 the Scottish Anti-Suffrage League: See, for example, Edward Tennant to Pamela Tennant, 27 May 1896, teasingly suggesting that Pamela should show a prominent suffragist guest at Clouds, Lady Grove (a niece of the Wyndhams' friend Rosalind Howard), a letter in *The Times* presumably opposing women's suffrage: Glenconner Papers, NRS GD510/1/30, f. 32:2; and Clare Tennant to Edward Tennant, 15 November 1912, responding to her father's having sent her a printed copy of a recent speech he made opposing women's suffrage: "I'm sure the meeting will retard the 'vote' & when I read your speech I couldn't think *what* the suffragets [*sic*] could find to contradict reasonably the things you said . . .": Glenconner Papers, NRS GD510/1/41, f. 21.

200 "for all the meetings": Madeline Adeane to Madeline Wyndham, 21 and 1 September 1900, Adeane Papers.

200 "help them a little": Madeline Adeane to Madeline Wyndham, 23 September 1900, Adeane Papers.

200 "Imperial program of reform": James, *Rise and Fall,* p. 321.

200 "the next few years": Margot Asquith to Edward Tennant, 31 July 1900, Glenconner Papers, NRS GD510/1/42, f. 11.

200 "as traitors and pro-Boers!": Madeline Adeane to Madeline Wyndham, 5 October 1900, Adeane Papers.

201 for the next campaign: Pamela Tennant to Mary Elcho, n.d. [1900], Stanway Papers.

201 "charm will attract them": Margot Asquith to Edward Tennant, 5 November 1900, Glenconner Papers, NRS GD510/1/42, f. 12.

201 "of the Irish Government": Antony MacDonnell to George Wyndham, 22 September 1902, quoted in Mackail and Wyndham, *Life and Letters,* 2:760–61.

CHAPTER 22: GROWING FAMILIES

202 "spending of her time": Asquith, *Remember and Be Glad,* p. 192.

202 "heated . . . skirmish!": Mary Elcho to Ettie Desborough, 23 June 1915, Desborough Papers, HALS DE/Rv/C479/1.

202 "her extra out-of-the-way cleverness": Margot Asquith to Mary Elcho, ca. 1900, quoted in Blow, *Broken Blood,* p. 142.

202 "fashion to abuse Pamela": Mary Elcho to Ettie Desborough, n.d. [ca. 1918–19], Desborough Papers, HALS DE/Rv/C477/66.

203 "voice—peppery & imperative": Pamela Tennant to Mary Elcho, n.d. [July 1902], Stanway Papers.

203 "eyes shine like stars": Mary Elcho to Arthur Balfour, 2 January 1903 (*Letters,* pp. 193–94).

203 "women's problems": Francis Oke Buckland, *Health Springs of Germany and Austria* (W. H. Allen, 1890), p. 71.

203 "trust any other month": Madeline Adeane to Madeline Wyndham, 11 September 1900, Adeane Papers.

203 "son from darling Madeline!": Pamela Tennant to Mary Elcho, n.d. [July 1902], Stanway Papers.

203 Hall after his wife: Madeline Adeane to Madeline Wyndham, 1 January 1901 and 20 December 1900; Charles Adeane to Madeline Wyndham, 21 December 1900, Adeane Papers.

204 "being a 'grass widow'": Madeline Adeane to Madeline Wyndham, 17 January 1901, Adeane Papers.

204 son of Edward Grey: Blow, *Broken Blood,* p. 134.

204 under the title *Recreation*: Viscount Grey of Fallodon, *Recreation* (New York: Houghton Mifflin, 1920). These essays were drawn from an address given at Harvard University in December 1919.

204 of finance or politics: Their lengthy correspondence is in four large folders in the Glenconner Papers at NRS GD510/1/60.

204 Both quiet, unostentatious and honorable: See the picture of Edward Grey drawn by Prince Carl Lichnowsky, *My Mission to London, 1912–1914* (Toronto: Cassell, 1918), pp. 27–28.

205 "person in the world": Pamela Tennant to Mary Elcho, December 1903, Stanway Papers; Pamela Tennant to Sidney Cockerell, 22 January 1904, BL Cockerell Papers, vol. CXLVII, Add. MSS 52769, f. 157.

205 "it is so intimate!": Quoted in Marie Belloc Lowndes, *A Passing World* (Macmillan, 1948), p. 187.

205 public and private life: Edward Grey, Viscount Grey of Fallodon, *The Cottage Book: The Undiscovered Country Diary of an Edwardian Statesman,* ed. and introduced by Michael Waterhouse (Gollancz, 1999), p. 26.

205 having sex with Grey: Belloc Lowndes, *A Passing World,* p. 175.

205 "one—from your mother": Charles Adeane to Mary Elcho, 6 November 1905, Stanway Papers.

205 their striking good looks: Blow, *Broken Blood,* p. 165.

206 in the central role: Quoted in Hoare, *Serious Pleasures,* p. 7.

206 "family and immediate circle": Ibid., p. 23.

206 morning on their ponies: Edward Wyndham Tennant to Pamela Tennant, 23 August 1916, quoted in Glenconner, *Edward Wyndham Tennant,* p. 221.

206 for the first time: Ibid., p. 249.

206 "spiritually short-sighted": Pamela Tennant to Mary Elcho, 9 June 1928, Stanway Papers.

206 the family in 1906: Hoare, *Serious Pleasures,* p. 6.

206 he were an infant: Ibid., p. 6.

206 "children—let them go": Ibid., p. 7.

206 "children about like Pamela": Mary Elcho to Hugo Elcho, 31 October 1909, Stanway Papers.

206 "all in the *day*": Fanny Cliffe to Mary Elcho, 6 July 1906, Stanway Papers.

207 "ceiling and the plaster!": Wemyss, *Family Record,* p. 204.

207 "the minimum of possessiveness": Asquith, *Remember and Be Glad,* p. 20.

207 but never demanded them: Ibid.

207 "collar for her chow": Asquith, *An Autobiography,* 2:44.

208 "the creatures to Stanway": Asquith, *Remember and Be Glad,* pp. 42–43; *Haply I May Remember,* p. 14.

208 "most delightful old house": Beatrice Webb, *The Diary of Beatrice Webb: All the Good Things of Life,* vol. 2, *1892–1905,* ed. Norman and Jeanne MacKenzie (Virago, 1986), p. 254.

208 "outré people around her": Mary Elcho to Arthur Balfour, 1 October 1896 (*Letters,* p. 148).

208 "after dinner just to sleep": Mary Elcho to Hugo Elcho, 30 November 1912, Stanway Papers.

209   "really what I mean": Mary Elcho to Arthur Balfour, 18 February 1907 (*Letters*, p. 237).

209   dinner table at Stanway: Asquith, *Remember and Be Glad*, pp. 42–43; *Haply I May Remember*, p. 14.

209   "actually gone to church . . . !": Mary Elcho to Arthur Balfour, 18 February 1907 (*Letters*, p. 237).

210   "away radiant with satisfaction": Ridley and Percy (eds.), *Letters of Arthur Balfour and Lady Elcho*, quoted at p. 17.

210   "soul—the dinner bell": Asquith, *Haply I May Remember*, p. 13.

210   "shall all be prepared!": Madeline Adeane to Madeline Wyndham, 12 October 1905, Adeane Papers.

210   "moment it was gone!": Charles Adeane to Madeline Wyndham, n.d. [November–December 1905], Adeane Papers.

210   "wild with delight": Percy Wyndham to Madeline Wyndham, 3 November 1905, Stanway Papers.

210   "& mine . . . Bless you": Madeline Adeane to Madeline Wyndham, 1 December 1905, Adeane Papers.

211   "Isn't it a mercy?": Madeline Adeane to Mary Elcho, 21 November 1905, Stanway Papers.

211   "so grateful for him": Ibid.

211   "children under her care": Charles Adeane to Mary Elcho, 6 November 1905, Stanway Papers.

211   festivities in due course: Madeline Adeane to Madeline Wyndham, 12 December 1905, Adeane Papers.

211   "seems to radiate around": Madeline Adeane to Percy Wyndham, 31 December 1905, Adeane Papers.

CHAPTER 23: THE SOULS IN POWER

212   the House of Commons: Mary Elcho to Arthur Balfour, 15 July 1902 (*Letters*, pp. 188–89).

212   "took it as news": Ibid.

213   "Mary Elcho at Stanway": Asquith, *Remember and Be Glad*, p. 3.

213   "finished the Army thing": Mary Elcho to Arthur Balfour, 19 January 1904 (*Letters*, p. 210).

213   "up to the part": Ibid.

214   "quite a 'succès fou'": Mary Elcho to Arthur Balfour, 27 February 1904 (*Letters*, pp. 212–13). Lady Edward Cavendish was the widowed sister of Sir Frank and "hostessed" for her brother in Berlin.

214   the office of Commander-in-Chief: Ibid.

214   "by that Vampire Balfour": Arthur Balfour to Mary Elcho, 30 August 1897, quoted in Beauman, *Cynthia Asquith*, p. 17.

214 "harmless and most thrilling": Mary Elcho to Hugo Elcho, 1 August 1900, Stanway Papers.

214 "will destroy your letters": Mary Elcho to Arthur Balfour, 29 July 1898, quoted in Beauman, *Cynthia Asquith,* pp. 16–17.

215 is easy to believe: Nigel Nicolson, *Mary Curzon* (Weidenfeld & Nicolson, 1977), pp. 147–48.

215 "just a little selfish": Ibid.

216 "yr [Arthur's] own making": Mary Elcho to Arthur Balfour, 1 August 1900 (*Letters,* p. 171).

216 "knees at my feet": Mary Elcho to Arthur Balfour, 19 January 1904 (*Letters,* p. 209).

216 "grease (smells of peppermint!)": Mary Elcho to Arthur Balfour, 14 February 1907 (*Letters,* p. 236).

216 "things" were "talking business": Mary Elcho to Arthur Balfour, 19 January 1904 (*Letters,* p. 209).

216 where colleagues could not: Jalland, *Women, Marriage and Politics,* pp. 197, 204.

216 soon as she could: Arthur Balfour to Mary Elcho, 14 March 1894 (*Letters,* p. 105); Mary Elcho to Arthur Balfour, 23 September 1896 (*Letters,* p. 145).

216 "is in the Cabinet!": Mary Elcho to Arthur Balfour, 15 July 1907 (*Letters,* p. 190).

216 brought into the Cabinet: Arthur Balfour to Mary Elcho, 12 July 1902 (*Letters,* p. 186); Mackail and Wyndham, *Life and Letters,* 1:79.

217 old friends they were: Ridley and Percy (eds.), *Letters of Arthur Balfour and Lady Elcho,* p. 197.

218 "too bad seems doubtful": Arthur Balfour to Mary Elcho, 13 February 1903 (*Letters,* pp. 196–97).

218 "at not being there": Mary Elcho to Hugo Elcho, n.d. [1902], Stanway Papers.

218 "I have been living": Mary Elcho to Hugo Elcho, 20 February 1905, Stanway Papers.

218 "such injustice to yrself": Mary Elcho to Hugo Elcho, n.d. [1902], Stanway Papers.

220 "I'd tell you that": Mary Elcho to Arthur Balfour, 10 August 1903 (*Letters,* pp. 203–4).

220 "grateful for being told": Mary Elcho to Arthur Balfour, 18 September 1903 (*Letters,* p. 206).

220 "much of an experiment": Ibid.

221 "would be its last": Murray Hornibrook, in July 1924, quoted in Mackail and Wyndham, *Life and Letters,* 2:791.

221 "he could not stop": Mackail and Wyndham, *Life and Letters,* 1:91.

221 "over-engined for his hull": Ibid.

221 "or unsuited to deal": Ibid., 1:92.

221 "declaration for Home Rule": Ibid., 2:795.

222 demoralize the nationalist cause: Ibid.

222 behalf of the Government: Ibid., 1:93.

223 "that & the other": Mary Elcho to Wilfrid Scawen Blunt, n.d. [1913], Blunt Papers, FM 673-1975.

223 "atmosphere of sullen suspicion": Mackail and Wyndham, *Life and Letters,* 1:102.

223 "which he remains responsible": Ibid., 1:103.

223 merits of George's decision: Ibid., 1:105.

223 "will do me harm": Ibid.

225 close to the sun: Pamela Tennant to Mary Elcho, 8 March 1905, Stanway Papers.

225 "safety valve": Mary Elcho to Arthur Balfour, 24 February 1905 (*Letters,* pp. 219–20).

225 "help talking about it": Tynan Hinkson, *Years of the Shadow,* p. 257.

225 "Atlas all the world": Mary Elcho to Arthur Balfour, 24 February 1905 (*Letters,* pp. 219–20).

226 "you think of it": Percy Wyndham to Mary Elcho, 14 January 1906, Stanway Papers.

226 his perpetually weak back: Lambert, *Unquiet Souls,* pp. 128–29.

CHAPTER 24: PAMELA AT WILSFORD

227 "woman I ever saw": Hoare, *Serious Pleasures,* p. 4.

227 " 'intercourse of daily life' ": Pamela Tennant to Charles Tennant, 25 March 1908, Glenconner Papers, NRS GD510/1/41, f. 3r. The lines are from Wordsworth's "Tintern Abbey."

228 "privileges of my life": *The Times,* 5 February 1906.

228 teaspoon filled with sperm: Hoare, *Serious Pleasures,* p. 6.

228 the Bart's £3,151,976 estate: *The Times,* 4 January 1921. The current-day equivalent is $403,000,000 (CPI/RPI) and $369,000,000 (GDP deflator).

228 in shares and mining: Ridley and Percy (eds.), *Letters of Arthur Balfour and Lady Elcho,* p. 14.

228 on Wednesdays and Saturdays: *The Times,* 9 May 1910.

228 first two hours alone: Pamela Tennant to Charles Tennant, 26 May 1910, Glenconner Papers, NRS GD510/1/41, f. 9r.

230 ran through Wilsford's grounds: Blow, *Broken Blood,* p. 124.

230 belonged to the Tennants: Hoare, *Serious Pleasures,* pp. 5–6.

230 "has been worth doing": Pamela Tennant to Wilfrid Scawen Blunt, 12 April 1905, Blunt Papers, FM 553-1975 .

230   "of a noble size": Pamela Tennant to Sidney Cockerell, 22 April 1902, BL Cockerell Papers, vol. CXLVII, Add. MSS 52769, ff. 150–51.

230   "the open once more": Ibid. The lines are a misquotation of Wordsworth's "Lines Written in Early Spring": "The budding twigs spread out their fan, / To catch the breezy air."

231   "shout for my boots": *The Times*, 29 November 1920.

231   "untidy litter of books": Quoted in Hoare, *Serious Pleasures*, pp. 88–89.

231   "yes—but no luxury": Ibid., p. 32.

231   all other battleships obsolete: James, *Rise and Fall*, p. 336.

232   "and we won't wait!": John Biggs Davison, *George Wyndham: A Study in Toryism* (Hodder & Stoughton, 1951), p. 198; Egremont, *The Cousins*, p. 270.

232   "Empire of the English": George Wyndham to Sibell Grosvenor, 21 January 1906, quoted in Egremont, *The Cousins*, p. 259.

232   "bedroom over the kitchen": Margot Asquith, diary entry, 14 July 1906, Bodleian, Asquith Papers, MS. Eng. d. 4204.

232   "as a Muscovy duck": Raymond Asquith, diary entry of 1903, quoted in John Joliffe, *Raymond Asquith: Life and Letters* (Collins, 1980), p. 136.

232   annum after his death: Marriage Settlement of Margot Tennant, Glenconner Papers, NRS GD510/1/21, f. 4r.

232   the Bart had died: Edward Glenconner to Margot Asquith, 6 August 1919, Bodleian, Asquith Papers, MS. Eng. c. 6697. The current-day equivalent is $1,340,000 (CPI/RPI) and $1,310,000 (GDP deflator).

233   "own has been squeezed": Margot Asquith, diary entry, 14 July 1906, Bodleian, Asquith Papers, MS. Eng. d. 4204.

234   of his tales: Pamela Tennant to Sidney Cockerell, 26 February 1911, BL Cockerell Papers vol. CXLVII, Add. MSS 52769, f. 174.

234   "on the topmost bough": Sidney Cockerell to Pamela Tennant, 27 February 1911, Glenconner Papers, NRS GD510/1/35, f. 3r; F. W. Bain to Sidney Cockerell, 24 February 1911, Glenconner Papers, NRS GD510/1/37.

234   whom Pamela was close: N.d., Glenconner Papers, NRS GD510/1/32, f. 12r.

234   sleep at Stonehenge overnight: Asquith, *Remember and Be Glad*, pp. 191–92.

234   "water-drops": Pamela Tennant to Charles Tennant, 20 August 1908, Glenconner Papers, NRS GD510/1/41, f. 6r.

234   guests continued eating inside: Belloc Lowndes, *A Passing World*, p. 181.

235   the carpet in fury: Hoare, *Serious Pleasures*, p. 7.

235   demanding, vain and destructive: See Blow, *Broken Blood*; and Emma Tennant, *Strangers: A Family Romance* (Jonathan Cape, 1998), and *Waiting for Princess Margaret* (Quartet Books, 2009).

235 implacably face the wall: Blow, *Broken Blood,* p. 188.

235 the family's trade roots: Ibid., p. 117.

235 hint about her overspending: Ibid., p. 124.

235 "round hole, in Glasgow!": Pamela Tennant to Charles Tennant, 22 May 1908, Glenconner Papers, NRS GD510/1/41, f. 7r.

236 her goddaughter "Pammy" Adeane: Pamela Tennant to Charles Tennant, 7 October 1908, Glenconner Papers, NRS GD510/1/41, f. 5r.

236 "of *Wilsford* I believe!": Pamela Tennant to Charles Tennant, 25 March 1908, Glenconner Papers, NRS GD510/1/41, f. 3r.

236 "is only *just* done": Pamela Tennant to Charles Tennant, 7 October 1908, Glenconner Papers, NRS GD510/1/41, f. 5r.

CHAPTER 25: MR. BALFOUR'S POODLE

237 "the really worrying thing": Mary Elcho to Arthur Balfour, 9 July 1907 (*Letters,* p. 238).

237 "rather a darling": Mary Elcho to Arthur Balfour, 16 January 1906 (*Letters,* p. 229).

237 quietly humorous and diffident: *The Times,* 7 July 1916.

238 "a good Unionist Conservative": Mary Elcho to Arthur Balfour, 16 January 1906 (*Letters,* p. 229).

238 had endured since childhood: Mary Elcho to Hugo Elcho, 26 July 1911, Stanway Papers.

238 "crack up" under the strain: See for example Mary Elcho to Arthur Balfour, n.d. [January 1916] (*Letters,* pp. 334–35); and 22 May 1920, Whittingehame Papers, NRS GD433/2/228/1, f. 7r.

238 making Cincie overly religious: Ridley and Percy (eds.), *Letters of Arthur Balfour and Lady Elcho,* pp. 143–45.

238 resemblance to a squirrel: Asquith, *Haply I May Remember,* pp. 210–11.

238 in any other man: Ibid. pp. 2, 225–26.

239 "the same! whatever systems!!": Mary Elcho to Arthur Balfour, 9 July 1907 (*Letters,* pp. 238–39).

239 "*want* to please one": Mary Elcho to Arthur Balfour, 20 January 1906 (*Letters,* pp. 229–30).

239 "make you anti me?": Mary Elcho to Hugo Elcho, 12 January 1906, Stanway Papers.

240 "Tuscan, Romanesque Gothic style!": Mary Elcho to Arthur Balfour, 15 October 1907 (*Letters,* pp. 242–43).

240 policy in due course: Mary Elcho to Arthur Balfour, 16 November 1907 (*Letters,* p. 244).

241 mangled 1906 Education Bill: Hattersley, *Lloyd George,* p. 199.

241 "will save us now?": Percy Wyndham to Mary Elcho, 14 January 1906, Stanway Papers.

241 "sets it on to": Hansard 4, 176:1429, 26 June 1907.

241 the Lords could not veto: Hansard 4, 188:1908, col. 47.

242 (before) at his window: Asquith, *Remember and Be Glad*, p. 14.

242 "time to his music": George Wyndham to Percy Wyndham, 14 April 1908, quoted in Mackail and Wyndham, *Life and Letters*, 2:608.

242 "on the rug now": Pamela Tennant to Charles Tennant, 25 February 1909, Glenconner Papers, NRS GD510/1/41, f. 8r.

242 herself against the cold: Mary Elcho to Hugo Elcho, 26 May 1909, Stanway Papers.

242 "beneficial physically, mentally, spiritually": Mary Elcho to Arthur Balfour, 31 January 1909 (*Letters*, p. 255).

242 "the arms of Beb!": Mary Elcho to Hugo Elcho, 26 March 1909, Stanway Papers.

243 "I die of sickness": Ibid.

243 "*extreme* old age": Mary Elcho to Hugo Elcho, 7 March 1909, Stanway Papers.

243 and innovative agricultural college: The college, founded in 1907, was the brainchild of the reclusive Sir William Macdonald and his flamboyant sidekick James W. Robertson, the federal government's Commissioner of Agriculture and Dairying in the 1890s, who served as the college's first president. The college is now part of McGill University in Montreal.

243 "*I wish you would*": Mary Elcho to Hugo Elcho, 2 March 1909, Stanway Papers.

243 "*get* is positively El-Doradoish": Mary Elcho to Hugo Elcho, 7 March 1909, Stanway Papers.

243 had suffered a stroke: Mary Elcho to Hugo Elcho, 13 March 1909, Stanway Papers.

244 "against poverty and squalidness": Hansard 5C, 4:548, 29 April 1909.

244 "obviously intended as one": *The Times*, 22 June 1909

245 position is clear enough: Edward Tennant to Mr. Allard, 27 June 1909, Tennant Papers, NLS 1:0172.

245 not directly endorse it: *The Times*, 24 June 1909.

245 disregarding the country's wishes: Mary Elcho to Percy Wyndham, 21 January 1910, Stanway Papers.

245 "unwise and dishonest": Adams, *The Last Grandee*, p. 241.

245 "4,000 had done laughing": *The Times*, 11 October 1909.

246 the reformer Annie Besant: Ibid.

246 that he was hospitalized: *The Times*, 31 July 1909.

246 "cost to the ratepayers": *The Times*, 11 October 1909.

246   that preceded his stroke: Percy Wyndham to Mary Elcho, 3 October 1909, Stanway Papers.

246   "willing to do so": Mary Elcho to Hugo Elcho, 31 October 1909, Stanway Papers.

247   "rights of the Commons": *The Times,* 3 December 1909.

CHAPTER 26: 1910

248   "we may have achieved!": Mary Elcho to Percy Wyndham, 21 January 1910, Stanway Papers.

249   "be pretty well dead": Ibid.

249   "agitated at one time": Ibid.

249   "or none at all": Ibid.

249   "Labour members more likely": Percy Wyndham to Mary Elcho, 21 February 1910, Stanway Papers.

250   "*just* possible": Mary Elcho to Arthur Balfour, 23 March 1910 (*Letters,* p. 261).

250   "stem the Beb tide": Ibid.

250   "about it and about": George Wyndham to Mary Elcho, 15 February 1913, quoted in Mackail and Wyndham, *Life and Letters,* 2:737–38.

250   "will make him mad": Mary Elcho to Arthur Balfour, 23 March 1910 (*Letters,* p. 261).

250   "in our constitutional history": Roy Jenkins, *Mr. Balfour's Poodle: Peers v. People* (Papermac, 1999), p. 146.

250   by this terrible turn: Ibid., p. 145.

251   "Liberal?" and seated accordingly: Asquith, *Remember and Be Glad,* p. 127.

251   her gladioluses in triumph: Mary Elcho to Hugo Elcho, 10 July 1910, Stanway Papers. Mary's decision to abandon the full style may also have been due to Margot Asquith, who challenged Cynthia with the question: "Do you want your bridesmaids to look like twelve loaves of bread?" (Asquith, *Remember and Be Glad,* p. 127).

252   and Beb were present: Arthur Balfour to Mary Elcho, 26 July 1911 (*Letters,* p. 267).

252   at Clouds in October: George Wyndham to Mary Elcho, 6 October 1910, in Mackail and Wyndham, *Life and Letters,* 2:669.

252   was absent, from illness: Wemyss, *Family Record,* p. 208.

252   paint both their portraits: Dakers, *Clouds,* p. 172.

252   "various distressing infirmities": Quoted in ibid., p. 175.

253   "moment would be disastrous": Jenkins, *Mr. Balfour's Poodle,* p. 178.

254   not adopt it outright: Ibid., pp. 187, 190.

254   "near connections by marriage": Percy Wyndham to Mary Elcho, 8 December 1910, Stanway Papers.

CHAPTER 27: REVOLUTION?

255 "mind clear as crystal": George Wyndham to Philip Hanson, 5 April 1911, quoted in Mackail and Wyncham, *Life and Letters,* 2:687; Wemyss, *Family Record,* p. 209.

255 "can never forget it": Madeline Wyndham to Wilfrid Scawen Blunt, 6 December 1918, Blunt Papers, FM 894-1975.

255 "air with his Cries": Quoted in Dakers, *Clouds,* p. 176.

256 on Saturday, 18 March: *The Times,* 20 March 1911.

256 a green sandstone cross: George Wyndham to Madeline Wyndham, 11 December 1911, quoted in Mackail and Wyndham, *Life and Letters,* 2:710.

256 serving through paternalistic rule: *The Times,* 14 March 1911.

256 £26 16s. 6d., in total: Dated July 1911, Glenconner Papers, NRS GD510/1/21. The current-day equivalent is $3,140 (CPI/RPI) and $2,950 (GDP deflator).

256 else went to George: *The Times,* 11 April 1911. The current-day equivalent of the value of Percy's estate is $29.2 million (CPI/RPI) and $27.7 million (GDP deflation).

256 arching whitewashed ceiling overhead: George Wyndham to Madeline Wyndham, 1 October 1911, quoted in Mackail and Wyndham, *Life and Letters,* 2:707; and 21 December 1911, ibid., 2:712.

257 "his justice and generosity": George Wyndham to Charles Gatty, 16 March 1911, ibid., 2:686.

257 "of his own champagne!": Arthur Balfour to Mary Elcho, 19 July 1900 (*Letters,* pp. 168–69).

257 "having to create peers": Mary Elcho to Arthur Balfour, 12 January 1911 (*Letters,* pp. 263–64).

258 "behind his time": George Dangerfield, *The Strange Death of Liberal England* (New York, 1961), pp. 43–44.

258 flannels and straw hats: Arthur Balfour to Mary Elcho, 30 July 1911 (*Letters,* p. 269).

258 Club on Pall Mall: Viscount Grey of Fallodon, *Twenty-Five Years, 1892–1916,* 2 vols. (Hodder & Stoughton, 1926), 1:238.

258 and Balfour were present: Jenkins, *Mr. Balfour's Poodle,* p. 208.

258 "not a laborious week": Arthur Balfour to Mary Elcho, 16 July 1911 (*Letters,* p. 266).

258 "indeed most violent differences": Arthur Balfour to Mary Elcho, 23 July 1911 (*Letters,* pp. 266–67).

258 "ditch" defending the Lords: Adams, *The Last Grandee,* p. 252. The phrase has also been attributed to George Curzon: see David Gilmour, "Curzon, George Nathaniel, Marquess Curzon of Kedleston (1859–1925)," *Oxford Dictionary of National Biography,* online ed., January 2011 (http://www.oxforddnb.com/view/article/32680, accessed 23 October 2013).

258 "victims of a revolution": Jenkins, *Mr. Balfour's Poodle*, p. 226.

258 the House of Lords: Ibid., p. 227.

259 he too found "unpalatable": Ibid., p. 223.

260 "own kith and kin": Arthur Balfour to Mary Elcho, 30 July 1911 (*Letters*, p. 268).

260 "saviour of the Constitution": Jenkins, *Mr. Balfour's Poodle*, p. 233.

260 Strand two days later: Ibid., p. 236.

260 expire from the excitement: Ibid., p. 238.

260 "they would like that": Ibid., p. 234.

261 in his public life: Arthur Balfour to Mary Elcho, n.d. [11 August 1911] (*Letters*, pp. 269–70); Mary Elcho to Arthur Balfour, 14 August 1911 (*Letters*, pp. 270–71).

261 that it was required: Jenkins, *Mr. Balfour's Poodle*, pp. 252–53.

261 "prompt creation of peers": *The Times*, 11 August 1911; HL Deb., 10 August 1911, vol. 9, col. 1000.

262 Bill as sheer "revolution": HL Deb., 10 August 1911, vol. 9, cols. 1003, 1014.

262 "by our own enemies . . . ?": Quoted in Adams, *The Last Grandee*, p. 254.

262 "you up I think!": Arthur Balfour to Mary Elcho, n.d. [11 August 1911] (*Letters*, pp. 269–70); Mary Elcho to Arthur Balfour, 14 August 1911 (*Letters*, pp. 270–71).

262 plans from the first: Arthur Balfour to Mary Elcho, 8 October 1911 (*Letters*, p. 278).

262 "Leader—after so long": Mary Elcho to Arthur Balfour, 7 November 1911 (*Letters*, p. 282).

263 "it—voted for Revolution": George Wyndham to Sibell Grosvenor, 10 August 1911, quoted in Egremont, *The Cousins*, p. 278.

CHAPTER 28: 1911–1914

264 "downfall of the Peers": F. W. Bain to Pamela Tennant, 6 September 1911, Glenconner Papers, NRS GD510/1/37.

264 "sunshine" and "whipping wind": Pamela Tennant to unknown correspondent, 3 August 1911, Glenconner Papers, NRS GD510/1/35, f. 22:3r.

264 "doesn't express my need": Pamela Tennant to Charles Tennant, 3 August 1911, Glenconner Papers, NRS GD510/1/41, f. 14r.

265 "hair-pin for a paddle": Pamela Tennant to unknown correspondent (as before), 3 August 1911, Glenconner Papers, NRS GD510/1/35, f. 22:3r.

265 "I am in India": F. W. Bain to Pamela Tennant, 1 May 1911, Glenconner Papers, NRS GD/510/1/37.

265 "of no value anywhere": Pamela Tennant to Charles Tennant, 3 August 1911, Glenconner Papers, NRS GD510/1/41, f. 14r; Pamela Tennant to

unknown correspondent (as before), 3 August 1911, Glenconner Papers, NRS GD510/1/35, f. 22:3r.

265 gave her "essence . . . cheaply": Elizabeth Asquith to Mary Charteris, 27 December 1914, quoted in Blow, *Broken Blood,* p. 143.

265 the Church of Scotland: *The Times,* 4 March 1911.

265 fish for trout there: Glenconner, *Edward Wyndham Tennant,* p. 101.

265 took to Peebles Ball: Pamela Tennant to Charles Tennant, 7 October 1908, Glenconner Papers, NRS GD510/1/41, f. 5r.

265 (Charlie) for their ballgowns: Madeline Adeane to Mary Elcho, 22 March 1911, Stanway Papers.

266 "ever be in debt!": Edward Tennant to Margot Asquith, 8 April 1910, Bodleian, Asquith Papers, Oxford MS. Eng. c. 6676, f. 160.

266 "both owe Henry *everything*": Bodleian, Asquith Papers, MS. Eng. c. 6676, f. 163 (n.d.).

266 "do nothing at all": Margot Asquith to Edward Tennant, 5 November 1911, Glenconner Papers, NRS GD510/1/42, f. 12r.

266 entertained far too little: Edward Tennant to Margot Asquith, 15 January 1917, Bodleian, Asquith Papers, MS. Eng. c. 6697, ff. 164–65.

266 "me than any other": Pamela Tennant to Sidney Cockerell, 26 February 1911, BL Cockerell Papers, vol. CSLVII, Add. MSS 52769, f. 174.

266 "*that kill the soul*": "Fantasia—of a London House Closed," in Glenconner, *The White Wallet,* pp. 211–12.

266 "study of, wild birds": Asquith, *Remember and Be Glad,* p. 192.

267 disliked guests to Stanway: Ibid.

267 vitriol against the world: Mary Elcho to Arthur Balfour, 2 June 1923, Whittingehame Papers, NRS GD433/2/229/3, f. 4r.

267 Bosie as a gift: Blow, *Broken Blood,* p. 125; and see *The Times,* 13 June 1913, reporting on Bosie's bankruptcy that year, in which it is explained that in 1907 Eddy had created a company, Wilsford Press Limited, and had immediately then assigned all its shares to Bosie for a nominal sum.

267 they had been subjected: Belloc Lownes, *A Passing World,* p. 178; Philip Hoare, *Oscar Wilde's Last Stand* (New York: Arcade Publishing, 1998), pp. 20–21.

267 "the price of fish": Susan, Lady Tweedsmuir, *The Edwardian Lady* (Duckworth, 1966), pp. 87–88.

267 adjacent to the Palace: Blow, *Broken Blood,* p. 172.

268 "last withdrew in despair!": Wemyss, *Family Record,* p. 234.

268 bird, it recognized Pamela: Ibid., p. 235.

268 "in the dining room fire?": Edward Grey to Pamela Tennant, 18 December 1911, Glenconner Papers, NRS GD510/1/35, f. 12r.

268 in her keepsake box: Pamela Tennant to Sibell Grosvenor, 25 January 1912, George Wyndham Papers.

268 not include his wife: F. W. Bain to Pamela Tennant, 1 April and 18 August 1911, Glenconner Papers, NRS GD510/1/37.

268 beneath her serene face: Edward Grey to Pamela Tennant, 23 March 1913, Glenconner Papers, NRS GD510/1/60/3, f. 10r.

268 "more than Mary-Queen-of-Scots beautiful?": Edward Grey to Pamela Tennant, 8 December 1911, Glenconner Papers, NRS GD510/1/35, f. 12r.

268 "evening to other attractions": Ibid., and 5 March 1913, ibid., f. 22:7r.

269 " 'bulbs' he called it": Edward Grey to Edward Tennant, 25 February 1912, Glenconner Papers, NRS GD510/1/60/2, f. 8r.

269 in that family's life: Tennant, *Waiting for Princess Margaret,* p. 72.

269 dull father looked like: Hoare, *Serious Pleasures,* p. 17.

270 across the North Country: Clare Tennant to Edward Tennant, 25 February 1912, Glenconner Papers, NRS GD 510/1/42, f. 18r.

270 "one's life for months": Asquith, *Diaries,* 8 May 1915, p. 17.

270 "want to fight them": Mary Elcho to Arthur Balfour, 31 October 1912 (*Letters,* pp. 291–92).

270 "(rag to Balf) side!": Mary Elcho to Arthur Balfour, 30 October 1912 (*Letters,* pp. 290–91).

270 "our marriage Lucky Bag": Mary Elcho to Arthur Balfour, 24 February 1913 (*Letters,* p. 294).

270 "fitted to your personality": Arthur Balfour to Mary Elcho, 16 September 1912 (*Letters,* p. 288).

270 "swarming in and out": Mary Elcho to Arthur Balfour, 12 September 1912 (*Letters,* p. 287).

271 "founded a watering place!": Ibid.

271 "clean as they do": Philip Ziegler, *Diana Cooper* (Harmondsworth: Penguin Books, 1981), p. 41. Diana was the child of her mother's affair with Harry Cust and was the infant born at the time that Harry first started courting Pamela in 1892.

271 "tired she moves furniture": Mary Elcho to Arthur Balfour, 15 October 1907 (*Letters,* p. 242).

271 "my Scotch champion": Mary Elcho to Arthur Balfour, 29 March 1922, Whittingehame Papers, NRS GD433/2/229/2, f. 5r.

271 out of her grasp: Mary Elcho to Arthur Balfour, 19 March 1913 (*Letters,* pp. 297–98).

271 "house for the sane": Mary Elcho to Arthur Balfour, 12 September 1912 (*Letters,* pp. 286–87).

271 mistress, Lady Angela Forbes: Mary Elcho to Arthur Balfour, 24 February 1913 (*Letters,* pp. 294–95).

271 which lay about thirty miles: Mary Elcho to Hugo Elcho, 24 January 1913, Stanway Papers.

272 "very hard nut ahead": Mary Elcho to Arthur Balfour, 24 February 1913 (*Letters*, pp. 294–95).

272 "shriek like a mandrake!": Ibid.

272 "pleased with each other": Katharine Tynan Hinkson *The Middle Years* (Constable, 1919), p. 233.

272 "Pamela, Guy and *all*": Mary Elcho to Arthur Balfour, 24 February 1913 (*Letters*, p. 294).

272 "give them their heads": Ibid.

272 "how few women understand?": George Wyndham to Hilaire Belloc, 4 June 1913, quoted in Mackail and Wyndham, *Life and Letters*, 2:749.

273 prostitute in a brothel: Ellenberger, "Constructing George Wyndham," p. 501. For a more colorful account, see Joan Wyndham, *Dawn Chorus* (Virago, 2004), pp. 12–13.

273 "be borne and endured": Perf Wyndham to Sibell, Countess Grosvenor, 10 June 1913, Stanway Papers.

273 "& the big sweep": Mary Elcho to Wilfrid Scawen Blunt, n.d. [1913], Blunt Papers, FM 673-1975.

273 "I loved and admired": Longford, *Pilgrimage of Passion*, p. 390.

273 "great tragedies of life": Mackail and Wyndham, *Life and Letters*, 1:126.

273 "honesty in public life": Longford, *Pilgrimage of Passion*, p. 390.

274 "together in the past": Madeline Adeane to Mary Elcho, 2 August 1914, Stanway Papers.

274 He promptly sold it: *The Times* 29 July 1914.

274 personal allowance to £2,000: Asquith, *Diaries*, 23 August 1915, p. 71.

274 year for eight years: Ibid.

275 "my old *pretty* name!": Mary Elcho to Wilfrid Scawen Blunt, 28 September 1914, Blunt Papers, FM 719-1975.

276 "yet have to unfold": *The Times* 4 August 1914.

276 "again in our lifetime": Simon Blow says that this was Eddy Tennant (see *Broken Blood*, p. 134). It seems more likely that it was, as claimed by himself, John Spender, editor of the *Westminster Gazette*: see J. A. Spender, *Life, Journalism and Politics*, 2 vols. (New York: Frederick A. Stokes, 1927), 2:14–15.

CHAPTER 29: MCMXIV

277 "great issues before them": *The Times*, 5 August 1914.

278 was with their children: Davenport-Hines, *Ettie*, p. 180; see also Wemyss, *Family Record*, p. 240.

278 "ready," said Sibell, ashen-faced: Wemyss, *Family Record*, p. 241.

278 Expeditionary Force (the BEF): The terminology was alien to people at

the time. In 1918, Pamela reminded Margot with relish of "your [Margot] exclaiming one early day in the War '"B.E.F.?" What does "B.E.F." mean?' " (Pamela Glenconner to Margot Asquith, Bodleian, MS. Eng. c. 6676, ff. 144–48).

278 1914 alone was 174,901: Niall Ferguson, *The Pity of War* (Penguin Books, 1999), p. 198.

278 Home Defense in 1913: Newspaper cutting dated 1 December 1913, reporting Eddy's address to the Liverpool Liberal Federal Council on Home Defense, Glenconner Papers, NRS GD510/1/51, f. 1r.

279 "dismissed all the servants": Asquith, *Diaries,* p. xvi.

279 helplessly, seeking his advice: Mary Elcho to Arthur Balfour, August 1914 (*Letters,* p. 311).

279 son not to go: Ibid.

279 in that first wave: Mary Elcho to Wilfrid Scawen Blunt, 28 September 1914, Blunt Papers, FM 719-1975.

279 West Lancashire Territorial Association: Cannadine, *Decline and Fall,* p. 72.

279 official age for enlistment: Glenconner, *Edward Wyndham Tennant,* p. vi.

279 pasted to a lamppost: Wemyss, *Family Record,* pp. 240, 242.

280 Grenadier Guards as well: Asquith, *Diaries,* 16 October 1915, p. 88.

280 "of its greatest trial": Cannadine, *Decline and Fall,* pp. 73–74.

280 "like a big picnic": Julian Grenfell to Ettie Desborough, 24 October 1914, quoted in Nicholas Mosley, *Julian Grenfell: His Life and the Times of His Death, 1888–1915* (Weidenfeld & Nicolson, 1976), p. 239.

280 on caps and aprons: Lady Angela Forbes, *Memories and Base Details* (2nd ed., Hutchinson, 1922), p. 153.

280 the arriving Belgian refugees: Ibid., p. 171.

280 were induced to move: Mary Elcho to Arthur Balfour, 1 January 1915 (*Letters,* pp. 315–16).

280 "charming Belgian notaire": Ibid.

280 notable for their "ingratitude": Forbes, *Memories and Base Details,* p. 171.

280 "a cup of tea": Ibid., p. 76.

281 largesse with her Woodbines: Ibid., pp. 174–75.

281 and a roaring success: Ibid., p. 171.

281 the days of peace: Ibid., p. 161.

281 ambulance units and canteens: Cannadine, *Decline and Fall,* p. 73.

281 get the best cases: Forbes, *Memories and Base Details,* p. 161.

281 unsuitable for a hospital: Mary Elcho to Arthur Balfour, August 1914 (*Letters,* p. 311).

282 "do wonderful things here": Wemyss, *Family Record,* p. 285; Pamela Adeane to Mary Elcho, 1 October 1917, Stanway Papers.

282 end of the war: Wemyss, *Family Record,* p. 286.

282 taking convalescents for drives: Ibid.

282 the spring of 1915: Mary Elcho to Arthur Balfour, 13 April 1915 (*Letters*, p. 323).

282 feuds with Eliza Wedgwood: Mary Elcho to Hugo Elcho, 7 October 1915, Stanway Papers.

282 "about everything Angela does": Ibid.

282 less glamorous than Angela's: Ibid.

282 "tired as they became" Glenconner, *Edward Wyndham Tennant*, pp. 119–20.

283 of her own experience: Ibid., p. 118.

283 "Trussler's zeal from Stephen": Pamela Tennant to Mary Elcho, 9 October 1914, Stanway Papers.

283 in addition to Oliver: Tennant, *Waiting for Princess Margaret*, p. 125.

283 the bigamous curate's son: Pamela Tennant to Charles Tennant, 25 February 1909, Glenconner Papers, NRS GD510/1/41, f. 8r.

283 at the War Office: Pamela Tennant to Edward Tennant, n.d. [postwar], Glenconner Papers, NRS GD510/1/51, f. 16r. The child was an artistic prodigy—Pamela had hung some of her paintings in Queen Anne's Gate. Pamela took her down to Wilsford: "My idea is to put the child at the Bishops school in Salisbury for the winter as her surroundings in London are very objectionable. She is a nice mannered quiet little child. She draws all day long," she told Eddy.

283 fifty pounds per annum: Tennant, *Waiting for Princess Margaret*, pp. 115, 128.

283 when he was adopted: Ibid., p. 120.

283 birth in Salisbury Infirmary: Hoare, *Serious Pleasures*, p. 13.

284 is telling the story: Ibid.; Blow, in *Broken Blood*, notes that his grandmother had adopted a child who "had run away to sea in his early teens," but gives his date of adoption as nearer that of Stephen's birth, and his name as Barnaby (p. 173).

284 know of his existence: See Tennant, *Waiting for Princess Margaret*, and Blow's version in *Broken Blood*.

284 little more than fifteen: Tennant, *Waiting for Princess Margaret*, p. 128.

284 advanced for his years: Glenconner, *Edward Wyndham Tennant*, p. 85.

284 the actress Hermione Baddeley: For an account of this episode see Hermione Baddeley, *The Unsinkable Hermione Baddeley* (Collins, 1984), pp. 54–58.

284 "*dead* through the head": Madeline Adeane to Mary Elcho, 18 September 1914, Stanway Papers.

284 "*knowing* he must die": Ibid.

284 "*for such an Englishman!*": Edward Wyndham Tennant, "Percy Wyndham," Stanway Papers.

284 "best as we can": Arthur Balfour to Mary Elcho, 17 September 1914 (*Letters*, p. 312).

284 "and glamorous for ever": Asquith, *Diaries,* 20 October 1915, p. 91.

285 "such a sickening waste": Mary Elcho to Arthur Balfour, September 1914 (*Letters,* p. 313).

285 "in our *united* family": Madeline Adeane to Mary Elcho, 29 September 1914, Stanway Papers.

285 "everywhere, like a soldier": Mary Elcho to Wilfrid Scawen Blunt, n.d., Blunt Papers, FM 724-1975.

285 "was a wonderful evening": Ibid.

286 flapping in the wind: Wemyss, *Family Record,* p. 256.

286 "Salon" to amuse Yvo: Mary Elcho to Arthur Balfour, 13 April 1915 (*Letters,* p. 323).

286 "very worried about it": Wemyss, *Family Record,* p. 292.

286 Hugh on every point: Asquith, *Diaries,* 16 May 1915, pp. 29–30.

286 "Howitzers on cement floors!": Mary Elcho to Wilfrid Scawen Blunt, 28 September 1914, Blunt Papers, FM 719-1975.

286 for her own sons: Mary Elcho to Hugo Elcho, 7 October 1915, Stanway Papers.

286 "we have not got": Mary Elcho to Arthur Balfour, 17 May 1915 (*Letters,* pp. 324–25).

286 " 'sorts' mentally and physically": Wemyss, *Family Record,* p. 287.

287 "the Steward of Glamis?": Ibid., p. 252; Asquith, *Diaries,* p. xvii.

287 "the Gallant Glittering Gloucesters": Wemyss, *Family Record,* p. 264.

287 fellow officer Tom Strickland: His real name was Algernon Walter, but he was known always as Tom.

287 "a very large wound": Wemyss, *Family Record,* p. 263.

288 "their horses are fit": Mary Elcho to Arthur Balfour, 13 April 1915 (*Letters,* p. 322).

288 the "deplorable" munitions output: Arthur Balfour to Mary Elcho, Easter Saturday 1915 (*Letters,* p. 320).

288 disgraced after the Dardanelles: Ridley and Percy (eds.), *Letters of Arthur Balfour and Lady Elcho,* p. 326.

289 "the nation trusts him": Quoted in ibid., pp. 325–26.

289 clothes in red pen: Pamela Tennant to Margot Asquith, 12 March 1918, Bodleian, MS. Eng. c. 6676, ff. 144–48.

289 "tyranny of little things": Glenconner, *Edward Wyndham Tennant,* pp. 119–20.

289 Both Yvo—"a joy-dispenser": Asquith, *Diaries,* 19 October 1915, p. 90.

289 "and purpose" for Bim: Glenconner, *Edward Wyndham Tennant,* p. 119.

289 two-seater crammed with people: Ibid., p. 118.

289 dinner, the next play: Ibid., pp. 157–58.

290 "Rome" in their antics: Quoted in Ziegler, *Diana Cooper,* p. 80.

290 morphine and "chlorers" (chloroform): Duff Cooper, *The Duff Cooper Dia-*

ries, 1915–1951, ed. John Julius Norwich (Phoenix, 2006), 9 January and 18 February 1916, pp. 24, 25.

290   "ridicule" to the Coterie: Asquith, *Diaries,* 15 September 1915, p. 79.

290   Peter's Church, near Babraham: Sibell Adeane married Edward Kay-Shuttleworth in December 1914. Madeline Adeane married Denis Wigan in October 1915.

290   "like scum on ham": Pamela Tennant to Margot Asquith, 12 March 1918, Bodleian, Asquith Papers, Add MS. Eng. c. 6676, ff. 144–48.

290   "Summer Holidays, just beginning": Glenconner, *Edward Wyndham Tennant,* pp. 121–22.

291   "Oliver—2st 4lb": Tennant, *Waiting for Princess Margaret,* p. 119; see also Hoare, *Serious Pleasures,* p. 12.

291   "all may be well": Edward Grey to Edward Tennant, 7 August 1915, Glenconner Papers, NRS GD510/1/60/4, f. 18r.

291   "even for a moment": Wemyss, *Family Record,* p. 303.

291   "living in two houses": Asquith, *Diaries,* 23 August 1915, p. 71.

291   "guns are quite inadequate": Ibid., 9 September 1915, p. 77.

291   the theater with friends: Forbes, *Memories and Base Details,* p. 201.

292   "out cold and dead": Wemyss, *Family Record,* pp. 305–6.

292   "seeing things in perspective": Forbes, *Memories and Base Details,* p. 201.

292   both knew the odds: Lambert, *Unquiet Souls,* p. 190.

292   in their mother's bed: Asquith, *Diaries,* 9 September 1915, p. 77.

292   "enthusiasm of their boys": Forbes, *Memories and Base Details,* p. 201.

293   "if he wanted anything": Wemyss, *Family Record,* p. 307.

293   "of his beloved face": Ibid.

CHAPTER 30: THE FRONT

294   shortly after Yvo's departure: Madeline Wyndham to Wilfrid Scawen Blunt, 6 October 1915, Blunt Papers, FM 772-1975.

294   "to get a telegram": Wemyss, *Family Record,* p. 281.

294   "salt of my earth": Sir Alan Lascelles, *End of an Era: Letters and Journals of Sir Alan Lascelles from 1887 to 1920,* ed. Duff Hart-Davis (Weidenfeld & Nicolson, 2006), 12 July 1912, p. 128.

294   note to his grandsons: Those grandsons include my father; his mother is Tommy's eldest daughter.

295   "God, were there too": Lascelles, *End of an Era,* p. 162.

295   from the barbed wire: Wemyss, *Family Record,* p. 312.

295   with almost daily letters: Ibid., pp. 315–16; Edward Wyndham Tennant to Pamela Tennant, 18 August 1915, quoted in Glenconner, *Edward Wyndham Tennant,* p. 127.

295   brother, David, in September: Ibid., p. 130.

295   "the 4th of June": Yvo Charteris to Hugo Elcho, 6 October 1915, quoted in Wemyss, *Family Record*, p. 322. The "4th of June" is a reference to the day of celebrations held each year by Eton College, Yvo's school, to mark the birthday of its long-dead royal supporter, George III. To this day, the fourth of June (although never now held on the actual date but earlier, in May) is marked annually by speeches, a cricket match, a boat procession and elaborate picnics hosted by the parents of the pupils at the school.

295   "before George [Gordon] Moore": Yvo Charteris to Cynthia Asquith, 7 October 1915, ibid., p. 324.

296   "Mort aux Boches!": *The Times*, 21 June and 7 August 1915.

296   "is natural to man": Quoted in Lambert, *Unquiet Souls*, p. 190.

296   could during the day: Glenconner, *Edward Wyndham Tennant*, p. 172.

296   rattle of machine guns: Lambert, *Unquiet Souls*, p. 190.

296   "in a second line": Quoted in Wemyss, *Family Record*, p. 326.

296   "how to give up": Quoted in ibid., p. 312.

297   his commanding officer said: Lambert, *Unquiet Souls*, p. 191; Asquith, *Diaries*, 24 October 1915, p. 93.

297   "thank him for it": Glenconner, *Edward Wyndham Tennant*, p. 145.

297   irony of this juxtaposition: In September 1915, Bim had written to Pamela of the generals commanding his Guards brigade, division and army corps and the First Army, "respectively . . . Brigadier General Hayworth, General Lord Cavan, General Haking, and Haig at the head of the list. They are all very fine generals and I could wish for no one else." Just a month later, from Vermelles, Bim wrote in his poem "*A Bas la Gloire!*" of those:

> *who didn't die*
> *Although they were in France—these sat in cars,*
> *And whizzed about with red-band caps, awry,*
> *Exuding brandy and the best cigars.*
> *With bands and tabs of red, they could defy*
> *The many missives of explosive Mars*

(Glenconner, *Edward Wyndham Tennant*, pp. 134, 151). The contrast shows the change wrought in Bim, or at least the extent to which he concealed his true thoughts from his parents in favor of the cheerful trusting son they wished to see.

297   "and hopeful about him": Asquith, *Diaries*, 22 October 1915, p. 92.

298   " 'What a bore!' ": Ibid., 19 October 1915, pp. 90–91.

298   "till all is blue": Ego Charteris to Mary Elcho, 25 October 1915, quoted in Wemyss, *Family Record*, p. 352; Asquith, *Diaries*, 3 July 1916, p. 186.

298   "It hurts me physically": Asquith, *Diaries*, 20 October 1915, p. 91.

298 "Not little Yvo": Quoted in Davenport-Hines, *Ettie*, p. 202.

298 "was rocking round one": Mary Elcho to Arthur Balfour, 8 December 1921, Whittingehame Papers, NRS GD433/2/229/1, f. 29r.

298 "has wearily to take": Mary Elcho to Wilfrid Scawen Blunt, 5 December 1915, Blunt Papers, FM/779-1975.

298 "& prove herself indestructible": Davenport-Hines, *Ettie*, p. 202.

298 "worldly hopes & aspirations': Mary Elcho to Wilfrid Scawen Blunt, 5 December 1915, Blunt Papers, FM 779-1975.

299 "is for the best!": Mary Elcho to Arthur Balfour, 22 December 1915 (*Letters*, p. 322).

299 "about Bim & Xtopher": Pamela Tennant to Mary Elcho, 9 June 1916, Stanway Papers.

299 "*in a golden haze*": Glenconner, *Edward Wyndham Tennant*, Appendix III.

299 (Brigade), away from action: Ibid., p. 184.

299 "the General the date": Ibid., p 189.

300 "stand up against it": Pamela Tennant to Mary Elcho, 9 June 1916, Stanway Papers.

300 favorite books and pictures: For an illustration, see Dakers, *Clouds*, p. 175, plate 94.

300 "the sorrows of others": Pamela Tennant to Mary Elcho, 9 June 1916, Stanway Papers.

300 "have you any orphans?": Hoare, *Serious Pleasures*, p. 13.

301 "to get good news": Pamela Tennant to Mary Elcho, 9 June 1916, Stanway Papers.

301 "What *can* one do?": Asquith, *Diaries*, 22 April 1916, p. 158.

302 "the level of consciousness": Wemyss, *Family Record*, p. 372.

302 "like his pathetic luck": Asquith, *Diaries*, 22 April 1916, p. 160.

303 of mist and fog: *The Times*, 25 and 27 April 1916.

303 "were killed & taken": Mary Elcho to Evelyn de Vesci, 26 September 1916, De Vesci Papers, DD/DRU/87.

303 Elcho's body for hours: Lambert, *Unquiet Souls*, p. 194.

303 "kept me outwardly calm": Wemyss, *Family Record*, p. 372.

303 "worried, over-tired and nervy": Asquith, *Diaries*, 19 May 1916, p 166.

303 "so maddening not knowing": Mary Elcho to Arthur Balfour, 7 May 1916 (*Letters*, p. 337).

303 had become a nun: Asquith, *Diaries*, 20 May 1916, p. 167.

303 "wild with joy": Wemyss, *Family Record*, p. 375.

303 sent the wrong name: Ridley and Percy (eds.), *Letters of Arthur Belfour and Lady Elcho*, p. 339; Wemyss, *Family Record*, p. 373; Asquith, *Diaries*, 28 June 1916, p. 181.

303 "he'll never come back?": Asquith, *Diaries*, 1 July 1916, p. 182.

303 Mary was at Clouds: Mary Elcho to Arthur Balfour, 3 July 1916 (*Letters,* p. 339).

304 "course I didn't *know*": Mary Elcho to Madeline Wyndham, July 1916, Stanway Papers.

304 the second of July: Wemyss, *Family Record,* p. 373. In fact, as Cynthia's diary shows, the news came on 1 July 1916.

304 he now could not: Mary Elcho to Arthur Balfour, 3 July 1916 (*Letters,* p. 339).

304 "sick of the word": Ibid.

304 "other word for it": Asquith, *Diaries,* 4 July 1916, p. 187.

304 *Times* in September 1916: *The Times,* 26 September 1916.

304 "simple, unsuperlative sergeant": Mary Elcho to Ettie Desborough, 26 September 1916, Desborough Papers, HALS DE/Rv/C477/49; see also Wemyss, *Family Record,* p. 376, where Mary recounts these words asking, "Could a finer epitaph be given by one soldier to another than these two words . . . ?"

304 "in March or April": Mary Elcho to Arthur Balfour, January 1916 (*Letters,* pp. 334–35).

305 "Generals don't look ahead": Quoted in Lambert, *Unquiet Souls,* p. 196.

305 of the German trenches: Ibid., p. 198.

305 eggs in three hours: Cannadine, *Decline and Fall,* p. 76.

305 "it for genuine 'poesie'": Glenconner, *Edward Wyndham Tennant,* p. 222.

305 a photograph of her: Ibid.

306 "and so did I": Ibid., p. 210.

306 "six months' rest now": Ibid.

306 men—even officers—thought: Lambert, *Unquiet Souls,* p. 205.

306 "they taught him double-entry": Quoted in ibid., pp. 199–200.

306 "God rest his soul": Glenconner, *Edward Wyndham Tennant,* p. 166.

307 "*an' higher every day*": Ibid., p. 293.

307 blow to her worldview: Lambert, *Unquiet Souls,* p. 199.

307 "'other chaps' hellish good shoot'": Glenconner, *Edward Wyndham Tennant,* p. 229.

308 "if you remember him?": Ibid., p. 223.

308 made headlines in England: Lambert, *Unquiet Souls,* p. 202.

308 "last remains of courage": Asquith, *Diaries,* 19 September 1916, p. 217.

308 "guide the future here": Davenport-Hines, *Ettie,* p. 212.

309 "there has ever been": Glenconner, *Edward Wyndham Tennant,* p. 234.

309 "Apologies for the dust": Ibid., p. 115.

309 "heart of triple bronze": Ibid., p. 234.

309 "absolutely instantaneously": Ibid., p. 238.

310 battle of the Somme: Lambert, *Unquiet Souls,* p. 202.

310 had advanced six miles: Ibid., p. 199.

310 "great day for me": *The Times*, 27 September 1916.

310 "what a perfect place!": Ibid., 29 September 1916.

CHAPTER 31: THE REMAINDER

311 of the fighting services: Cannadine, *Decline and Fall*, p. 83.

311 in total, fourteen died: Quoted in ibid., p. 81; Lambert, *Unquiet Souls*, p. 221.

311 "and who is dead": Asquith, *Diaries*, 11 November 1915, p. 97.

312 "not just invented afterwards": Cannadine, *Decline and Fall*, p. 80.

312 "to save the world!": Mary Elcho to Wilfrid Scawen Blunt, 5 December 1915, Blunt Papers, FM 779-1975.

312 saccharine and utterly sanitized: Davenport-Hines, *Ettie*, p. 209.

312 "(the Souls!) Golden Age": Mary Elcho to Arthur Balfour, 12 September 1916 (*Letters*, p. 341).

312 "which could be had": Quoted in Davenport-Hines, *Ettie*, p. 212.

312 "again, a moral parturition": Glenconner, *The Earthen Vessel*, p. 82.

313 "bleeding in the dust": Mary Elcho to Arthur Balfour, 21 January 1916 (*Letters*, pp. 342–43).

313 "track of little Yvo": Ibid.

313 "up to the holocaust": Ibid.

313 of cliché and hyperbole: Mary Elcho to Ettie Desborough, 23 October 1931, Desborough Papers, HALS D/ERV/C477/102.

313 them inadvertently to criticism: Mary Elcho to Arthur Balfour, 21 January 1916 (*Letters*, pp. 342–43).

313 "in heart's blood . . . !": Mary Elcho to Ettie Desborough, 23 October 1931, Desborough Papers, HALS D/ERV/C477/102.

313 as she had hoped: Mary Elcho to Arthur Balfour, 21 January 1916 (*Letters*, pp. 342–43).

313 "have fought & lived?": Mary Elcho to Ettie Desborough, 23 October 1931, Desborough Papers, HALS D/ERV/C477/102.

313 events that took place: Edward Grey to Edward Tennant, 22 January 1916, Glenconner Papers, NRS GD/510/1/60/4, f. 33r.

313 "whenever you want me": Edward Grey to Edward Tennant, 26 September 1916, Glenconner Papers, NRS GD510/1/60/4, ff. 31 32r.

314 and at Itchen Abbas: Edward Grey to Edward Tennant, 27 April 1917, Glenconner Papers, NRS GD510/1/60/2, f. 19r.

314 "'war' he would repeat": Blow, *Broken Blood*, p. 157.

314 "quarter of the globe": Glenconner, *The Earthen Vessel*, p. 138.

314 "it were almost indelicate": Asquith, *Diaries*, 11 November 1915, p. 97.

314 her spirit guide, Feda: Glenconner, *The Earthen Vessel*, p. 141.

315 "match the endeavor somehow": Pamela Tennant to Mary Elcho, 23 January 1918, Stanway Papers; Glenconner, *The Earthen Vessel,* p. 79.

315 "so uplifted & happy": Hoare, *Serious Pleasures,* p. 129.

315 as giving her hope: Pamela Tennant to Mary Elcho, 9 June 1916, Stanway Papers.

315 waiting list for sittings: Glenconner, *The Earthen Vessel,* p. 79.

315 stormed out of court: *The Times,* 8 January 1917. Pamela would appear as a witness for the defense in similar trials on subsequent occasions, such as the case of "The Medium in the Mask" (*The Times,* 16 March 1920), and was one of those to attend the opening of *Earthbound,* an American motion picture dealing with spiritualism, at the Covent Garden Opera House, which was released early in the UK due to popular demand (*The Times,* 26 October 1920).

315 across the submarine-infested Atlantic: Barbara McKenzie, "James Hewat McKenzie: November 11th 1869–August 29th 1929," *Quarterly Transactions of the British College of Psychic Science* 8:3 (October 1929): 159–68.

316 "the existence of God": Quoted in Ellenberger, "The Souls: High Society and Politics," p. 157.

316 encouraged those still unsure: Glenconner, *The Earthen Vessel,* p. 153.

316 "of Yvo than Ego": Asquith, *Diaries,* 19 November 1916, p. 236.

316 "husband had been killed": Ibid., 16 December 1916, pp. 245–46.

316 Yvo made an appearance: Pamela Tennant to Mary Elcho, n.d., Stanway Papers.

316 "to offer much hope": Marie Stopes, *Married Love* (New York: The Critic and Guide Company, 1918), pp. 67–68.

316 "been violated": Ibid.

317 "acquire a great vogue": Ibid., p. 68.

317 "I was somehow responsible?": Marie Stopes to Pamela Tennant, 14 July 1918, BL Stopes Papers, vol. CCXXXVIII, Add. MS. 58684, f. 152.

317 "misguided in my confidence?": Pamela Tennant to Marie Stopes, 14 July 1918, BL Stopes Papers, vol. CCXXXVIII, Add. MS. 58684, ff. 153–54.

317 at Traquair near Glen: Blow, *Broken Blood,* p. 150.

318 "who had gone before": *The Times,* 9 March 1920.

318 with her sons' spirits: Mary Elcho to Arthur Balfour, n.d. [spring 1917] (*Letters,* p. 344).

318 Ego's two small sons: Mary Elcho to Madeline Wyndham, 22 September 1916, Stanway Papers.

318 "(one cannot tell them)": Mary Elcho to Madeline Wyndham, July 1916, Stanway Papers.

318 "friends who were dead": Quoted in Lambert, *Unquiet Souls,* p. 222.

318 "the same—flat depression": Quoted in ibid.

318 "have lost your generation": Quoted in Cannadine, *Decline and Fall,* p. 81; Lambert, *Unquiet Souls,* p. 221.

318 "vain for our Victors": Davenport-Hines, *Ettie,* p. 225.

318 "the hour of victory": Quoted in Cannadine, *Decline and Fall,* p. 79.

318 "duration of the war": Asquith, *Diaries,* 7 October 1918, p. 480.

CHAPTER 32: THE GREY DAWN

319 "to have it continued": Glenconner Papers, NRS GD510/1/51, f. 24r.

320 "body of darling Mamma": Mary Elcho to Arthur Balfour, 10 October 1919, Whittingehame Papers, NRS GD433/2/229/1, ff. 3–6r.

320 "birth into *another* world": Mary Elcho to Arthur Balfour, 23 September 1919, Whittingehame Papers, NRS GD433/2/229/1, f. 1r.

320 "concerned with food production": *The Times,* 28 November 1917.

320 "be running the kitchen": Madeline Adeane to Mary Elcho, 18 January 1920, Stanway Papers.

320 and all mod cons: Christopher Simon Sykes, *Private Palaces: Life in the Great London Houses* (Chatto & Windus, 1985), pp. 325–26.

320 "light and modern drainage?": Ibid., quoted at pp. 321, 322.

321 "under which I stand": Edward Tennant to Margot Asquith, 6 August 1919, Bodleian, Asquith Papers, MS. Eng. c. 6697, ff. 152–53.

321 undoubtedly precipitated by her: Earl Haig would also be buried there in 1928.

321 itching to reopen Gosford: Mary Elcho to Arthur Balfour, 22 May 1920, Whittingehame Papers, NRS GD433/2/229/1, f. 7r.

321 "people come in October": Quoted in Ridley and Percy (eds.), *Letters of Arthur Balfour and Lady Elcho,* p. 351.

321 the next twenty years: Asquith, *Diaries,* 30 July 1918, p. 464.

321 "one's back to it": Mary Elcho to Arthur Balfour, 22 May 1920, Whittingehame Papers, NRS GD433/2/229/1, f. 7r.

321 "bungalow" on financial grounds: Ridley and Percy (eds.), *Letters of Arthur Balfour and Lady Elcho,* p. 351; Nicola Beauman, *Cynthia Asquith,* p. 273.

321 "tea together every day!": Mary Elcho to Arthur Balfour, 13 May [1924], Whittingehame Papers, NRS GD433/2/229/3, f. 22r.

322 "a great deal better!": Quoted in Ridley and Percy (eds.), *Letters of Arthur Balfour and Lady Elcho,* pp. 351–52.

322 private secretary since 1918: Mary Elcho to Arthur Balfour, 22 May 1920, Whittingehame Papers, NRS GD433/2/229/1, f. 7r.

322 acting as his hostess: Ibid.

322 "home will be here": Mary Elcho to Arthur Balfour, 8 December 1921, Whittingehame Papers, NRS GD433/2/229/1, f. 29r.

323 "few that are left": Ibid.

323 "pie of the universe": Mary Elcho to Arthur Balfour, December 1921, Whittingehame Papers, NRS GD433/2/229/1, f. 28r.

323 "looking after my . . . grandchildren": Quoted in Ridley and Percy (eds.), *Letters of Arthur Balfour and Lady Elcho*, p. 349.

323 "time of my life": Mary Elcho to Arthur Balfour, 23 September 1919, Whittingehame Papers, NRS GD433/2/229/1, f. 1r.

323 "coat & riding boots": Mary Elcho to Arthur Balfour, 14 January 1922, Whittingehame Papers, NRS GD433/2/229/2, f. 1r.

323 she told Arthur stoutly: Mary Elcho to Arthur Balfour, n.d. [1923], Whittingehame Papers, NRS GD433/2/229/3, f. 17r.

323 streamed the disembarking hordes: Lambert, *Unquiet Souls,* p. 57.

323 Hugo's valet was auctioneer: Mary Elcho to Arthur Balfour, n.d. [1921–22], Whittingehame Papers, NRS GD433/2/229/2, f. 27r.

323 thirteen years Bibs's senior: See Mary Charteris to Wilfrid Scawen Blunt, 13 May 1921, commenting that the "great question" had been whether Bibs and Ivor were in love with each other, and that she, Mary Charteris, used to find Ivor "rather a cold fish . . . but I expect Bibs will transform him." Blunt Papers, FM 190-1975.

323 "rejoiced—and my mother": Mary Elcho to Wilfrid Scawen Blunt, n.d. [1921], Blunt Papers, FM 193-1976.

324 "has been too wonderful": Mary Elcho to Dorothy Carleton, 1 March 1920, Blunt Papers, FM 988-1975.

325 while she was away: Pamela Tennant to Mary Elcho, 17 March 1920, Stanway Papers.

325 (to make the journey): Hoare, *Serious Pleasures,* p. 16.

325 "thought of her joy": Pamela Tennant to Mary Elcho, 17 March 1920, Stanway Papers. Stephen had gone with Pamela, and was impressed by the reading. One medium had told them "things unknown to us both, which we checked in England. She couldn't have read our minds." Hoare, *Serious Pleasures,* p. 16.

325 "table groans under cards": Quoted in Hoare, *Serious Pleasures,* p. 16.

325 (New York's Sulgrave Institution): *The New York Times,* 7 January 1920.

325 recitals at their hotels: Hoare, *Serious Pleasures,* p. 16.

325 be a routine operation: Pamela Tennant to Margot Asquith, 13 January 1921, Bodleian, Asquith Papers, MS. Eng. c. 6676, f. 154.

326 annuity to Nanny Trussler: Hoare, *Serious Pleasures,* pp. 17–18.

327 "and a Fragonard": Pamela Tennant to Dorothy Carleton, 1 October 1921, Blunt Papers, FM 248-1976.

327 "'one's husband to death'": Mary Elcho to Ettie Desborough, 29 November 1920, Desborough Papers, HALS DE/Rv/C477.

327 Margot at dinner parties: Pamela Tennant to Margot Asquith, 17 January 1921, Bodleian, Asquith Papers, MS. Eng. c. 6676, f. 155.

327 "Yours, in utter sincerity": Pamela Tennant to Margot Asquith, 11 January 1921, Bodleian, Asquith Papers, MS. Eng. c. 6676, f. 151.

327 to eat and change: Pamela Tennant to Margot Asquith, 17 January 1921, Bodleian, Asquith Papers, MS. Eng. c. 6676, f. 155; Margot Asquith to Pamela Tennant, n.d., Bodleian, Asquith Papers, MS. Eng. c. 6676, ff. 152–53.

327 "quarrel for Eddy's sake": Pamela Tennant to Margot Asquith, 17 January 1921, Bodleian, Asquith Papers, MS. Eng. c. 6676, f. 155.

327 "and made me happy": Pamela Tennant to Mary Elcho, 28 February 1921, Stanway Papers.

328 night's conversations with Bim: Blow, *Broken Blood,* p. 164.

328 from her spiritualist tract: Hoare, *Serious Pleasures,* p. 97.

328 summer of that year: *The Times,* 17 February 1922.

328 until it was over: *The Times,* 6 June 1922.

328 "Press had worried me": Pamela Tennant to Lucy Graham Smith, n.d. [summer 1921], Bodleian, Asquith Papers, MS. Eng. c. 6676, f. 157.

328 "NO Spring till now": Pamela Tennant to Wilfrid Scawen Blunt, 1 October 1921, Blunt Papers, FM 248-1976.

328 "pronounced dead by surgery": "The Romantic 'Miracle' of England's Loneliest Man," *American Feature Press,* 1922.

329 Smith Square in Westminster: Hoare, *Serious Pleasures,* p. 63.

329 (Mary saw her sister): Wemyss, *Family Record,* p. 235.

329 waiting by the car: Baddeley, *The Unsinkable Hermione Baddeley* p. 47.

329 "very perfect friendship": Pamela Tennant to Lucy Graham Smith, n.d. [summer 1921], Bodleian, Asquith Papers, MS. Eng. c. 6676, f. 157.

329 been unable to reply: Pamela Tennant to Wilfrid Scawen Blunt, 11 June 1922, Blunt Papers, FM 286-1976.

329 to a political meeting: Belloc Lowndes, *A Passing World,* p. 175.

329 "hope for the future": Pamela Tennant to Marie Stopes, 1 February 1923, BL Stopes Papers, Add. MSS 58693, ff. 31–32.

329 "made known to them": Pamela Tennant to Marie Stopes, 9 February 1921, BL Stopes Papers, Add. MSS 58688, f. 7; see also letters of 27 May 1921, Add. MSS 58689, f. 69; and 27 June 1921, Add. MSS 58689, f. 139.

330 "invented? If so where—": Pamela Tennant to Marie Stopes, June 1922, BL Stopes Papers, Add. MSS 58691, f. 224.

330 (Havelock Ellis and Balfour): Founded as the Eugenics Education Society in 1906, it changed its name to the Eugenics Society in 1926.

330 "depraved, and the feeble-minded": Marie Stopes, *Radiant Motherhood* (G. P. Putnam's Sons, 1921), p. 220; *The Times,* 29 October 1918 Glenconner, *The White Wallet,* pp. 372–75.

330 "of use to her": Pamela Tennant to the Stopes Society, 10 November [post-1922], BL Stopes Papers, Add MSS 58702, f. III.

331 "& admires your work": Pamela Tennant to Marie Stopes, June 1922, BL Stopes Papers, Add. MSS 58691, f. 224.

331 "life of an invalid": Madeline Adeane to Mary Elcho, 11 December 1925, Stanway Papers.

331 *Letters* a decade before: Grey of Fallodon, *Twenty-Five Years,* 1:xxii.

331 his life and work: See Keith Robbins, *Sir Edward Grey: A Biography of Lord Grey of Fallodon* (Cassell, 1971).

331 ("gift of beauty, darling"): Baddeley, *The Unsinkable Hermione Baddeley,* p. 13.

331 written especially for her: Ibid., pp. 44–49 and 53–54; Hoare, *Serious Pleasures,* p. 52. In this, David resisted Pamela's attempts to match him more successfully than Christopher, whom Pamela persuaded to marry her goddaughter Pamela Paget (offspring of her erstwhile suitor, Arthur). Stephen Tennant designed the bride and bridesmaid's medieval-themed dresses for the Paget-Glenconner wedding, which was billed by *Vogue* as one of the "most important social events of 1925." The marriage was a disaster and ended in divorce a decade later (see Hoare, *Serious Pleasures,* p. 51).

332 (looked like an iceberg): Hoare, *Serious Pleasures,* p. 63.

333 "advantage from the picture": Dakers, *Clouds,* p. 219.

333 go towards supporting Guy: Ibid., p. 220.

333 "a lack of *touch*": Pamela Tennant to Mary Elcho, 13 March 1928, Stanway Papers.

334 "D'you hear me?": Baddeley, *The Unsinkable Hermione Baddeley,* p. 48.

334 "wanted my baby too": Ibid., pp. 57–58.

334 " 'gave it to me' ": Ibid., p. 62.

334 press went to town: *Miami News,* 4 January 1931.

334 "they invent long interviews": Pamela Tennant to Mary Elcho, 14 May 1928, Stanway Papers.

334 "papers in this company": Quoted in Hoare, *Serious Pleasures,* p. 114.

334 be her third husband: Beck had been one of the speakers at the luncheon that Pamela and Eddy had attended on their American tour in 1920, promoting Anglo-American relations. It seems likely that when Pamela had advocated extending the arm of friendship, this was not quite what she had meant.

335 "by any emotional strain": Pamela Tennant to Mary Elcho, 14 June 1928, Stanway Papers.

335 "cried out against me": Pamela Tennant to Mary Elcho, 14 May 1928, Stanway Papers.

335 fashionably new psychoanalytical slant: Pamela Tennant to Mary Elcho, 14 June 1928, Stanway Papers. Doubtless the biography was Romer Wilson's *All Alone: The Life and Private History of Emily Jane Brontë* (1928).

335 when told the news: Blow, *Broken Blood,* p. 172.

335 that Pamela was dead: *The Times,* 20 November 1928.

336 the widowed elder statesman: Hoare, *Serious Pleasures,* pp. 125–26.

336 "rained messages on me!": Ibid., p. 128.

336 hair standing on end: *Ogden Standard-Examiner,* 17 February 1929.

336 "to wish us goodnight": Baddeley, *The Unsinkable Hermione Baddeley,* p. 68.

CHAPTER 33: THE END

337 "the blow first fell": Madeline Adeane to Mary Elcho, 5 December 1928, Stanway Papers.

337 "would our family happenings": Madeline Adeane to Mary Elcho, 2 January 1929, Stanway Papers.

337 "modern house The Rectory": Madeline Adeane to Mary Elcho, 21 December 1925, Stanway Papers.

337 child to full term: Ibid.

338 "know why—*Robert's* child": Madeline Adeane to Mary Elcho, 19 November 1929, Stanway Papers.

338 of massage already existing: Ibid.

338 not long to live: See, for example, Mary Elcho to Arthur Balfour, 7 March 1929 (*Letters,* p. 353).

338 "tomorrow without a tremor": Quoted in Ridley and Percy (eds.), *Letters of Arthur Balfour and Lady Elcho,* pp. 351–52.

338 "her gentle gracious sway": Ibid.

338 "shone with inexhaustible fun": *The Times,* 3 May 1937.

338 "controversial maelstrom": Arthur Balfour to Mary Elcho, 17 November 1920, Whittingehame Papers, NRS GD433/2/229/1, f. 12r.

339 "but not intentionally malevolent": Ibid.

339 "was on balance good": *The Times,* 17 January 1929.

339 "different ambitions and different politics": *The Times,* 21 January 1929, letter from "X"; 26 January 1929, letter from "Q"; Ettie Desborough to Mary Elcho, 25 January 1930, Desborough Papers, HALS DE/Rv/C1100/257, and 9 November 1935, DE/Rv/C1100/166.

339 claimed had never existed: *The Times,* 21 January 1929, letter from "X"; 26 January 1929, letter from "Q."

339 Souls, as of old: Ridley and Percy (eds.), *Letters of Arthur Balfour and Lady Elcho,* p. 352.

339 "truth about these things!": Quoted in ibid., p. 353.

339 thrown into his grave: Ibid., p. 354.

339 "the blank will be": Quoted in Abdy and Gere, *The Souls,* p. 41.

339 "unfailing friend": Mary Elcho to Arthur Balfour, 7 March 1929 (*Letters,* p. 353).

339   Souls memoir in earnest: Ettie Desborough to Mary Elcho, 25 January 1930, Desborough Papers, HALS DE/Rv/C1100/257.

339   in Surrey for tea: Ettie Desborough to Mary Elcho, 16 June 1936, Desborough Papers, HALS DE/Rv/C1100/176.

340   "but not *too* bad": Dakers, *Clouds,* p. 226.

340   to make it manageable: Ibid., pp. 225–27, 239–44.

340   "Friendship's Garland": Ettie Desborough to Mary Elcho, n.d. [1935], Desborough Papers, DE/Rv/C1100/167.

340   that Mary had admired: Evelyn de Vesci to Evan Charteris, n.d. [summer 1936], De Vesci Papers, DD/DRU/5/3/2.

340   names and "unsubstantiated assertions": Evan Charteris to Evelyn de Vesci, n.d. [summer 1936], De Vesci Papers, DD/DRU/5/3/2.

340   "criticism . . . a *saddening* document": Evelyn de Vesci to unknown correspondent, n.d., De Vesci Papers, DD/DRU 5/3/2.

340   "& agonized & distracted": Dorothy Charteris to Evelyn de Vesci, 18 August 1936, De Vesci Papers, DD/DRU/5/3/2.

341   "commonly regarded as doomed": Evan Charteris to Evelyn de Vesci, n.d. [summer 1936], De Vesci Papers, DD/DRU/5/3/2.

341   "my last visit there": Ibid.

341   "get her own way": Ibid.

341   "out all other considerations": Ibid.

341   "ought to say no": Madeline Adeane to Mary Elcho, 3 February 1937, Stanway Papers.

342   "spirit has passed away": *The Times,* 3 May 1937.

342   "there . . . cannot be filled": Ibid., 4 August 1941.

342   "social and intellectual center": Ibid., 2 August 1941.

343   "unto the perfect day": Pamela slightly misquoted this, as she so often did, as "the Light of the Just shineth more & more unto the perfect Day."

343   only he could see: Again, Pamela misquotes, giving the boy's name as "Hans."

344   "gates of Dublin Castle": Pamela Tennant to Mary Elcho, 13 March 1928, Stanway Papers.

BIBLIOGRAPHY

MANUSCRIPT SOURCES

Where an abbreviation is used for a publicly accessible manuscript source in the Notes, it is appended in square brackets.

Papers in Publicly Accessible Archives

Bodleian Library: papers of Margot Asquith, Countess of Oxford and Asquith, 1862–1945 [Bodleian, Asquith Papers, MS. Eng.]
British Library:
  Avebury Papers
  Papers of Arthur James Balfour
  Burns Papers
  Cockerell Papers
  Eccles Bequest of Manuscripts (Lady Eccles Oscar Wilde Collection)
  Papers of Allan Fea
  Papers of Viscount and Viscountess Gladstone
  Papers of Mary Gladstone (Mrs. Drew)
  Letters to John Lane
  Papers of Robert Ross
  Society of Authors Archive
  Stopes Papers
  Watts-Dunton Papers
  Papers of Douglas Young
  Fitzwilliam Museum, Cambridge: papers of Wilfrid Scawen Blunt [FM]
  Hertford Archives and Local Records Office: papers of Lady Desborough [HALS DE/Rv]

National Census Archives: http://www.nationalarchives.gov.uk/records/census
  -records.htm
National Library of Scotland: Tennant Papers [NLS 12143/4]
National Records of Scotland (formerly the National Archives of Scotland):
  Glenconner Papers: Papers of the Tennant Family of the Glen, Peebleshire,
    Lords Glenconner [NRS GD510]
  Whittingehame Papers: Papers of Arthur James Balfour, 1st Earl of Balfour,
    and Viscount Traprain of Whittingehame [NRS GD433]

Somerset Records Office: Papers of Evelyn, Lady de Vesci [DD/DRU]
The Times Archive: http://www.thetimes.co.uk

Papers in Private Collections

Adeane Papers: papers of Madeline and Charles Adeane
Petworth Papers: papers of Percy and Madeline Wyndham, by kind
  permission of Francis Wyndham and the Earl of Egremont
Stanway Papers: papers of Mary, Countess of Wemyss, held at Stanway
  House, Gloucestershire, in possession of the 13th Earl of Wemyss and
  March
Stephen Tennant Papers: formerly in the possession of Hugo Vickers, now
  predominantly at the Beinecke Rare Book and Manuscript Library, Yale
  University
George Wyndham Papers: papers of George Wyndham and Sibell, Countess
  Grosvenor

SECONDARY SOURCES

Books

Place of publication is London, unless otherwise stated.

Abdy, Jane, and Charlotte Gere. *The Souls* (Sidgwick & Jackson, 1984).
Adams, R. J. Q. *Balfour: The Last Grandee* (John Murray, 2008).
Adelman, Paul. *Great Britain and the Irish Question, 1800–1922* (Hodder &
  Stoughton, 1996).
Adler, Kathleen, Erica Hirshler and H. Barbara Weinberg (eds.). *Americans in
  Paris, 1860–1900,* accompanying the exhibition *Americans in Paris, 1860–1900* at
  the National Gallery, London; Museum of Fine Arts, Boston; and the Metro-
  politan Museum of Art, New York (National Gallery Company, 2006).

Airlie, Mabell, Countess of. *Thatched with Gold: The Memoirs of Mabell Countess of Airlie,* ed. and arranged by Jennifer Ellis (Hutchinson, 1962).

Aldous, Richard. *The Lion and the Unicorn: Gladstone vs. Disraeli* (New York: W. W. Norton, 2007).

Appignanesi, Lisa. *Mad, Bad and Sad: A History of Women and the Mind Doctors from 1800 to the Present* (Virago, 2008).

Asquith, Lady Cynthia. *Diaries, 1915–1918,* ed. E. M. Horsley (New York: Alfred A. Knopf, 1969).

——. *Haply I May Remember* (James Barrie, 1950).

——. *Remember and Be Glad* (James Barrie, 1952).

Asquith, Margot. *An Autobiography,* 2 vols. (Thornton Butterworth, 1920–22).

——. *The Autobiography of Margot Asquith,* ed. with an introduction by Mark Bonham Carter (Weidenfeld & Nicolson, 1995).

——. *More Memories* (Cassell, 1933).

——. *Myself When Young* (Frederick Muller, 1938).

——. *Off the Record* (Frederick Muller, 1944).

——. *Places and Persons* (Thornton Butterworth, 1922).

Baddeley, Hermione, with Muriel Burgess. *The Unsinkable Hermione Baddeley* (Collins, 1984).

Bagehot, Walter. *The English Constitution,* ed. Miles Taylor (Oxford: Oxford University Press, 2001).

Balfour, Arthur James. *Chapters of Autobiography,* ed. Blanche Dugdale (Cassell, 1930).

Ball, Stuart. *The Conservative Party and British Politics, 1902–1951* (Longman, 1995).

Beauman, Nicola. *Cynthia Asquith* (Hamish Hamilton, 1987).

Begbie, Harold (as "A Gentleman with a Duster"). *Mirrors of Downing Street: Some Political Reflections* (Mills & Boon, 1920).

Bell, Quentin. *A New and Noble School: The Pre-Raphaelites* (Macdonald, 1982).

——. *Victorian Artists* (Routledge & Kegan Paul, 1967).

Belloc Lowndes, Marie. *Diaries and Letters, 1911–1947,* ed. Susan Lowndes (Chatto & Windus, 1971).

——. *I, Too, Have Lived in Arcadia: A Record of Love and Childhood* (Macmillan, 1941).

——. *A Passing World* (Macmillan, 1948).

——. *Where Love and Friendship Dwelt* (Macmillan, 1943).

Bennett, Alfred Rosling. *London and Londoners in the Eighteen-Fifties and Sixties* (T. Fisher Unwin, 1924).

Biggs Davison, John. *George Wyndham: A Study in Toryism* (Hodder & Stoughton, 1951).

Blow, Simon. *Broken Blood: The Rise and Fall of the Tennant Family* (Faber & Faber, 1987).

Boyce, D. G. *Decolonization and the British Empire, 1775–1997* (Macmillan, 1999).

———. *The Irish Question and British Politics, 1868–1996* (2nd ed., Macmillan, 1996).

Brandon, Ruth. *The Spiritualists: The Passion for the Occult in the Nineteenth and Twentieth Centuries* (Weidenfeld & Nicolson, 1983).

Brendon, Piers. *The Decline and Fall of the British Empire* (Jonathan Cape, 2007).

Brooke, Rupert. *1914 and Other Poems* (Solihull: Helion Books, 1993).

Bryant, Barbara (ed.). *G. F. Watts Portraits: Fame & Beauty in Victorian Society,* accompanying the exhibition *G. F. Watts Portraits: Fame & Beauty in Victorian Society* at the National Portrait Gallery (National Portrait Gallery Publications, 2004).

Buckland, Francis Oke. *Health Springs of Germany and Austria* (W. H. Allen, 1890).

Byatt, A. S. *The Children's Book* (Chatto & Windus, 2009).

Calloway, Stephen, and Lynn Federle Orr (eds.). *The Cult of Beauty: The Aesthetic Movement, 1860–1900,* accompanying the exhibition *The Cult of Beauty: The Aesthetic Movement, 1860–1900* at the Victoria and Albert Museum (V&A Publishing, 2011).

Cannadine, David. *Class in Britain* (New Haven: Yale University Press, 1998).

———. *The Decline and Fall of the British Aristocracy* (rev. ed., Penguin Books, 2005).

Chesterton, G. K. *Autobiography* (Hamish Hamilton, 1986).

Clifford, Colin. *The Asquiths* (John Murray, 2002).

Colquhoun, Kate. *Taste: The Story of Britain Through its Cooking* (Bloomsbury, 2007).

Conan Doyle, Sir Arthur. *The Great Boer War* (Smith, Elder, 1910).

Cooper, Duff. *The Duff Cooper Diaries, 1915–1951,* ed. John Julius Norwich (Phoenix, 2006).

Crathorne, Nancy. *Tennant's Stalk: The Story of the Tennants of the Glen* (Macmillan, 1973).

Cunningham, Hugh. *The Challenge of Democracy: Britain, 1832–1918* (Harlow: Longman, 2001).

Dakers, Caroline. *Clouds: The Biography of a Country House* (New Haven: Yale University Press, 1993).

———. *The Holland Park Circle: Artists and Victorian Society* (New Haven: Yale University Press, 1999).

Dangerfield, George. *The Strange Death of Liberal England, 1910–1914* (New York: Capricorn Books, 1961).

Darwin, John. *The Empire Project: The Rise and Fall of the British World System, 1830–1970* (Cambridge: Cambridge University Press, 2009).

Davenport-Hines, Richard. *Ettie: The Intimate Life and Dauntless Spirit of Lady Desborough* (Weidenfeld & Nicolson, 2008).

Davidoff, Leonore. *The Best Circles: Society, Etiquette and the Season* (Croom Helm, 1974).

Davies, Philip. *Lost London, 1870–1945* (Croxley Green: Transatlantic Press, 2009).

Downes, William Howe. *John S. Sargent: His Life and Work* (Thornton Butterworth, 1926).

Dugdale, Blanche E. C. *Arthur James Balfour: First Earl of Balfour, K.G., O.M., F.R.S.* (Hutchinson, 1936).

——. *Family Homespun* (John Murray, 1940).

Eccleshall, Robert, and Graham Walker. *Biographical Dictionary of British Prime Ministers* (New York: Routledge, 1998).

Eden, Emily. *Miss Eden's Letters*, ed. Violet Dickinson (Macmillan, 1919).

——. *The Semi-Attached Couple* and *The Semi-Detached House* (Virago, 1979).

Egremont, Max. *Balfour: A Life of Arthur James Balfour* (Collins, 1980).

——. *The Cousins: The Friendship, Opinions and Activities of Wilfrid Scawen Blunt and George Wyndham* (Collins, 1977).

——. *Siegfried Sassoon: A Biography* (Picador, 2005).

Ferguson, Niall. *The Pity of War* (Penguin Books, 1999).

Fingall, Elizabeth, Countess of. *Seventy Years Young: Memories of Elizabeth, Countess of Fingall* (Dublin: The Lilliput Press, 1991).

Fitzgerald, Penelope. *Edward Burne-Jones* (Stroud: Sutton Publishing, 2003).

Flanders, Judith. *A Circle of Sisters: Alice Kipling, Georgiana Burne-Jones, Agnes Poynter and Louisa Baldwin* (Viking, 2001).

——. *Consuming Passions: Leisure and Pleasure in Victorian Britain* (Harper Perennial, 2007).

Fletcher, Sheila. *Victorian Girls: Lord Lyttelton's Daughters* (Hambledon Press, 1997).

Forbes, Angela, Lady. *Memories and Base Details* (2nd ed., Hutchinson, 1922).

Foster, R. F. *Modern Ireland, 1600–1972* (Penguin Books, 1989).

Gardiner, Juliet. *The Thirties: An Intimate History; Britain in the Thirties* (Harper Press, 2010).

Gere, Charlotte. *Artistic Circles, Design and Decoration in the Aesthetic Movement* (V&A Publishing, 2010).

Gilmour, David. *Curzon: Imperial Statesman* (John Murray, 2003).

Girouard, Mark. *Life in the English Country House* (New Haven: Yale University Press, 1978).

——. *The Victorian Country House* (New Haven: Yale University Press, 1979).

Glenconner, Pamela. *The Book of Peace: Made by Pamela Tennant* (Chiswick Press, 1900).

——. *The Children and the Pictures* (London, William Heinemann; New York, Macmillan, 1907).

——. *The Earthen Vessel: A Volume Dealing with Spirit-Communication Received in the Form of Book-Tests* (New York, John Lane, 1921).

——. *Edward Wyndham Tennant: A Memoir* (John Lane, The Bodley Head, 1919).

——. *The Sayings of the Children: Written Down by Their Mother* (Oxford: B. H. Blackwell, 1918).

——. *Shepherd's Crowns: A Volume of Essays* (Oxford: Basil Blackwell, 1923).

——. *Village Notes: and Some Other Papers* (William Heinemann, 1900).

——. *The White Wallet* (T. Fisher Unwin, 1912).

——. *Windlestraw: A Book of Verse with Legends in Rhyme of the Plants and Animals* (Chiswick Press, 1910).

Green, E. H. H. *The Crisis of Conservatism: The Politics, Economics and Ideology of the British Conservative Party, 1880–1914* (Routledge, 1995).

Greensted, Mary. *An Anthology of the Arts and Crafts Movement: Writings by Ashbee, Lethaby, Gimson and Their Contemporaries* (Aldershot: Lund Humphries, 2005).

Grey of Fallodon, Viscount. *The Cottage Book: The Undiscovered Country Diary of an Edwardian Statesman*, ed. and introduced by Michael Waterhouse (Gollancz, 1999).

——. *Recreation* (New York: Houghton Mifflin, 1920).

——. *Twenty-Five Years, 1892–1916*, 2 vols. (Hodder & Stoughton, 1926).

Harris, José. *The Penguin Social History of Britain: Private Lives, Public Spirit: Britain, 1870–1914* (Penguin Books, 1993, Kindle ed.).

Harrison, Frederic. *Autobiographic Memoirs*, 2 vols. (Macmillan, 1911).

Hattersley, Roy. *David Lloyd George: The Great Outsider* (Little, Brown, 2010).

Hazelgrove, Jenny. *Spiritualism and British Society Between the Wars* (Manchester: Manchester University Press, 2000).

Hibbert, Christopher. *Queen Victoria: A Personal History* (HarperCollins, 2000).

Higgin, Letitia. *Royal School of Needlework, Handbook of Embroidery (1880)* (East Molesey: Royal School of Needlework, 2010).

Hill, Georgiana. *A History of English Dress from the Saxon Period to the Present Day*, 2 vols. (Richard Bentley, 1893).

Hoare, Philip. *England's Lost Eden: Adventures in a Victorian Utopia* (Harper Perennial, 2006).

——. *Oscar Wilde's Last Stand: Decadence, Conspiracy, and the Most Outrageous Trial of the Century* (New York: Arcade Publishing, 1998).

——. *Serious Pleasures: The Life of Stephen Tennant* (Hamish Hamilton, 1990).

Hobsbawm, Eric. *The Age of Empire, 1875–1914* (Abacus, 1994).

Holmes, Richard. *Footsteps: Adventures of a Romantic Biographer* (Harmondsworth: Penguin Books, 1985).

——. *Sidetracks: Explorations of a Romantic Biographer* (Flamingo, 2001).

Hunt, Tristram. *Building Jerusalem: The Rise and Fall of the Victorian City* (New York: Metropolitan Books, Henry Holt, 2005).

Hynes, Samuel. *Edwardian Turn of Mind: First World War and English Culture* (Pimlico, 1991).

Illustrations of the Sargent Exhibition, Royal Academy, 1926 (Royal Academy of the Arts, 1926).

Jackson, Lee. *A Dictionary of Victorian London: An A–Z of the Great Metropolis* (Anthem Press, 2006).

Jackson, Margaret. *What They Wore: A History of Children's Dress* (Allen & Unwin, 1936).

Jalland, Pat. *Women, Marriage and Politics, 1860–1914* (Oxford: Oxford University Press, 1988).

James, Henry. *The Ambassadors* (New York: Signet Classic, 1960).

——. *The Awkward Age* (Macmillan, 1899).

——. *The Portable Henry James*, ed. John Auchard (Penguin Books, 2004).

——. *The Spoils of Poynton*, ed. David Lodge (Harmondsworth: Penguin Books, 1987).

James, Lawrence. *Aristocrats: Power, Grace and Decadence—Britain's Great Ruling Classes from 1066 to the Present* (Little, Brown, 2009).

——. *The Rise and Fall of the British Empire* (Abacus, 1995).

Jenkins, Roy. *Mr. Balfour's Poodle: Peers v. People* (Papermac, 1999).

Jennings, Humphrey. *Pandaemonium: The Coming of the Machine as Seen by Contemporary Observers, 1660–1886* (Icon, 2012).

Joliffe, John. *Raymond Asquith: Life and Letters* (Collins, 1980).

Keating, Peter (ed.). *The Victorian Prophets: A Reader from Carlyle to Wells* (Fontana, 1981).

Keay, John. *India: A History* (HarperCollins, 2000).

Kinealy, Christine. *This Great Calamity: The Irish Famine, 1845–52* (Dublin: Gill & Macmillan, 1994).

Kipling, Rudyard. *Plain Tales from the Hills*, ed. H. R. Woudhuysen (Harmondsworth: Penguin Books, 1987).

Lambert, Angela. *Unquiet Souls: The Indian Summer of the British Aristocracy* (Macmillan, 1984).

Lascelles, Sir Alan. *End of an Era: Letters and Journals of Sir Alan Lascelles from 1887 to 1920*, ed. Duff Hart-Davis (Hamish Hamilton, 1986).

——. *King's Counselor: Abdication and War; The Diaries of Sir Alan Lascelles*, ed. Duff Hart-Davis (Weidenfeld & Nicolson, 2006).

Laver, James, *Taste and Fashion: From the French Revolution to the Present Day* (George G. Harrap, 1945).

Levine, Joshua. *Forgotten Voices of the Somme: The Most Devastating Battle of the Great War in the Words of Those Who Survived* (Ebury Press, 2008).

Lichnowsky, Prince Carl Max. *My Mission to London, 1912–1914* (Toronto: Cassell, 1918).

Liddell, Adolphus. *Notes from the Life of an Ordinary Mortal* (John Murray, 1911).

Lomax, James, and Richard Ormond. *John Singer Sargent and the Edwardian Age: An Exhibition Organized Jointly by the Leeds Art Galleries, the National Portrait Gallery, London, and the Detroit Institute of Arts* (Leeds: Leeds Art Galleries, 1979).

Longford, Elizabeth. *A Pilgrimage of Passion: The Life of Wilfrid Scawen Blunt* (Weidenfeld & Nicolson, 1979).

Lovell, Mary. *The Churchills: A Family at the Heart of History—from the Duke of Marlborough to Winston Churchill* (Little, Brown, 2011).

Luke, Michael. *David Tennant and the Gargoyle Years* (Weidenfeld & Nicolson, 1991).

MacCarthy, Fiona. *The Last Pre-Raphaelite: Edward Burne-Jones and the Victorian Imagination* (Faber & Faber, 2011).

———. *William Morris: A Life for Our Time* (Faber & Faber, 1994).

Mackail, J. W., and Guy Wyndham (eds.). *Life and Letters of George Wyndham*, 2 vols. (Hutchinson, 1925).

Mackay, Ruddock F. *Balfour: Intellectual Statesman* (Oxford: Oxford University Press, 1985).

MacKenzie, Jeanne. *The Children of the Souls: A Tragedy of the First World War* (Chatto & Windus, 1986).

Makari, George. *Revolution in Mind: The Creation of Psychoanalysis* (Duckworth, 2008).

Mallet, Marie. *Life with Queen Victoria: Marie Mallet's Letters from Court, 1887–1901*, ed. Victor Mallet (John Murray, 1968).

Mansel, Philip. *The Levant: Splendour and Catastrophe on the Mediterranean* (John Murray, 2010).

———. *Paris Between Empires, 1814–1852: Monarchy and Revolution* (John Murray, 2001).

Marquand, David. *Britain Since 1918: The Strange Career of British Democracy* (Orion, 2008).

Marr, Andrew. *The Making of Modern Britain* (Macmillan, 2009).

Masters, Brian. *Great Hostesses* (Constable, 1982).

Mayhew, Henry. *London's Underworld*, ed. Peter Quennell (Feltham: Hamlyn, 1950).

———. *Mayhew's London: Being Selections from "London Labor and the London Poor,"* ed. Peter Quennell (Pilot Press, 1949).

McKenna, Neil. *The Secret Life of Oscar Wilde* (Arrow Books, 2004).

Milne-Smith, Amy. *London Clubland: A Cultural History of Gender and Class in Late Victorian Britain* (New York: Palgrave Macmillan, 2011).

Morris, Jan. *Farewell the Trumpets: An Imperial Retreat* (Faber & Faber, 1978).

———. *Heaven's Command: An Imperial Progress* (Faber & Faber, 1978).

———. *Pax Britannica: The Climax of an Empire* (Harmondsworth Penguin Books, 1979).

Mosley, Nicholas. *Julian Grenfell: His Life and the Times of His Death, 1888–1915* (Weidenfeld & Nicolson, 1976).

Moyle, Franny. *Constance: The Tragic and Scandalous Life of Mrs. Oscar Wilde* (John Murray, 2011).

Musson, Jeremy. *Up and Down Stairs* (John Murray, 2009).

Nevill, Lady Dorothy Fanny. *The Reminiscences of Lady Dorothy Nevill*, ed. Ralph Nevill (Edward Arnold, 1906).

Nicholson, Virginia. *Singled Out: How Two Million Women Survived Without Men after the First World War* (Viking, 2007).

Nicolson, Juliet. *The Great Silence: 1918–1920; Living in the Shadow of the Great War* (John Murray, 2009).

———. *The Perfect Summer: Dancing into Shadow in 1911* (John Murray, 2007).

Nicolson, Nigel. *Mary Curzon* (Weidenfeld & Nicolson, 1977).

Olivier, Edith. *Four Victorian Ladies of Wiltshire* (Faber & Faber, 1940).

Oppenheim, Janet. *The Other World: Spiritualism and Psychic Research in England, 1850–1914* (Cambridge: Cambridge University Press, 1985).

Paget, Walburga. *In My Tower*, 2 vols. (Hutchinson, 1924).

Pankhurst, E. Sylvia. *The Suffragette: The History of the Women's Militant Suffrage Movement, 1905–1910* (New York: Sturgis & Walton, 1911).

Pearce, Edward. *Lines of Most Resistance: The Lords, the Tories and Ireland, 1886–1914* (Little, Brown, 1999).

Pearce, Malcolm, and Geoffrey Stewart. *British Political History, 1867–1995: Democracy and Decline* (Routledge, 1992).

Perkin, Joan. *Women and Marriage in Nineteenth-Century England* (Routledge, 1988).

Porter, Roy. *London: A Social History* (Penguin Books, 2000).

Powell, David. *The Edwardian Crisis: Britain, 1901–1914* (Macmillan, 1996).

Powell, Margaret. *Tales from Below Stairs* (Sidgwick & Jackson, 2012).

Pugh, Martin. *The Making of Modern British Politics, 1867–1939* (2nd ed. Oxford: Basil Blackwell, 1993).

Ridley, Jane, and Clayre Percy (eds.). *The Letters of Arthur Balfour and Lady Elcho, 1885–1917* (Hamish Hamilton, 1992).

Sackville-West, Vita. *The Edwardians* (Virago, 1983).

Seaman, L. C. B. *Victorian England: Aspects of English and Imperial History, 1837–1901* (Methuen, 1973).

Sitwell, Osbert. *Great Morning: An Autobiography.* Vol. 3 (Macmillan, 1948).

———. *Laughter in the Next Room: An Autobiography.* Vol. 4 (Macmillan, 1949).

———. *Left Hand, Right Hand! An Autobiography.* Vol. 1 (Macmillan, 1945).

———. *The Scarlet Tree: An Autobiography.* Vol. 2 (Macmillan, 1946).

Spender, John. *Life, Journalism and Politics*, 2 vols. (New York: Frederick A. Stokes, 1927).

Steinbach, Susie. *Women in England, 1760–1914: A Social History* (Weidenfeld & Nicolson, 2004).

Stevenson, David. *1914–1918: The History of the First World War* (Penguin Books, 2005).

Stone, Lawrence, and Jeanne C. Fawtier. *An Open Elite? England, 1500–1880* (Oxford: Clarendon Press, 1984).

Stone, Norman. *World War One: A Short History* (Allen Lane, 2007).

Stopes, Marie. *Married Love* (New York: The Critic and Guide Company, 1918).

———. *Radiant Motherhood* (New York: G. P. Putnam's Sons, 1921).

Strachey, Lytton. *Eminent Victorians* (The Folio Press, 1979).

Sykes, Christopher Simon. *Private Palaces: Life in the Great London Houses* (Chatto & Windus, 1985).

Taylor, D. J. *Bright Young People: The Rise and Fall of a Generation, 1918–1940* (Chatto & Windus, 2007).

Tennant, Emma. *Girlitude* (Jonathan Cape, 1999).

———. *Strangers: A Family Romance* (Jonathan Cape, 1998).

———. *Waiting for Princess Margaret* (Quartet Books, 2009).

Tennant, Harold John. *Sir Charles Tennant: His Forbears and Descendants* (privately printed, 1932).

Thirkell, Angela. *Wild Strawberries: A Novel* (Hamish Hamilton, 1934).

Thompson, Paul. *The Edwardians* (Paladin, 1979).

Thorold, Peter. *The London Rich: The Creation of a Great City from 1666 to the Present* (Viking, 1999).

Tillyard, Stella. *Citizen Lord: Edward Fitzgerald, 1763–1798* (Chatto & Windus, 1997).

Trevelyan, G. M. *English Social History* (Longmans, Green, 1944).

Tromans, Nicholas (ed.). *The Lure of the East: British Orientalist Painting*, accompanying the exhibition *The Lure of the East: British Orientalist Painting* at Tate Britain (Tate Publishing, 2008).

Tweedsmuir, Susan. *The Edwardian Lady* (Duckworth, 1966).

Tynan Hinkson, Katharine. *The Middle Years* (Constable, 1916).

———. *Twenty-Five Years: Reminiscences* (John Murray, 1913).

———. *The Years of the Shadow* (Constable, 1919).

Vansittart, Robert, Lord. *The Mist Procession: The Autobiography of Lord Vansittart* (Hutchinson, 1958).

Walkley, Christina, and Vanda Foster. *Crinolines and Crimping Irons: Victorian Clothes; How They Were Cleaned and Cared For* (Peter Owen, 1978).

Watts, Mary S. *George Frederic Watts: The Annals of an Artist's Life*, 2 vols. (Macmillan, 1912).

Webb, Beatrice. *The Diary of Beatrice Webb: All the Good Things of Life*, vol. 2: *1892–1905*, ed. Norman and Jeanne MacKenzie (Virago, 1986).

Wells, H. G. *Ann Veronica: A Modern Love Story* (Virago, 1980).

——. *The Correspondence of H. G. Wells*, ed. David C. Smith (Pickering & Chatto, 1998).

——. *The New Machiavelli* (Duffield, 1910).

——. *Tono-Bungay* (Macmillan, 1914).

Wemyss, Mary, Countess of. *A Family Record* (Plaistow, Curwen Press, 1932).

West, Julius. *G. K. Chesterton: A Critical Study* (Martin Secker, 1915).

Wheatcroft, Geoffrey. *The Strange Death of Tory England* (Penguin Books, 2005).

White, Jerry. *London in the Nineteenth Century* (Vintage, 2008).

Wilde, Oscar. *The Complete Works of Oscar Wilde* (New Lanark: Geddes & Grosset, 2001).

Wilson, A. N. *The Victorians* (Hutchinson, 2002).

Wyndham, Joan. *Dawn Chorus* (Virago, 2004).

Wyndham (afterwards Adeane) Madeline Pamela Constance Blanche. *The Sad Story of a Pig and a Little Girl*, illustrated by Richard Doyle (Walker & Cockerell, 1901; reprinted from the 1st ed., Isel, Cumberland, 1876).

Young, Kenneth. *Arthur James Balfour: The Happy Life of the Politician, Prime Minister, Statesman and Philosopher, 1848–1930* (G. Bell, 1963).

Ziegler, Philip. *Diana Cooper* (Harmondsworth: Penguin Books, 1981).

Chapters, Journal Articles and Unpublished Theses

Cannadine, David. "The Context, Performance and Meaning of Ritual: The British Monarchy and the 'Invention of Tradition' circa 1820–1977." in Eric Hobsbawm and Terence Ranger (eds.), *The Invention of Tradition* (Cambridge: Cambridge University Press, 1992).

Ellenberger, Nancy Waters. "Constructing George Wyndham: Narratives of Aristocracy in Fin-de-Siècle England," *Journal of British Studies* 39:4 (October 2000): 487–517.

——. "The Souls: High Society and Politics in Late Victorian England," PhD thesis, University of Oregon, 1982.

——. "The Souls and London 'Society' at the End of the Nineteenth Century," *Victorian Society* 25:2 (winter 1982): 133–60.

McKenzie, Barbara. "James Hewat McKenzie: November 11th 1869–August 29th 1929," *Quarterly Transactions of the British College of Psychic Science* 8:3 (October 1929): 159–68.

INDEX

Page numbers in *italics* refer to illustrations.

ILLUSTRATION CREDITS

A NOTE ON THE TYPE

This book was set in Adobe Garamond. Designed for the Adobe Corporation by Robert Slimbach, the fonts are based on types first cut by Claude Garamond (c. 1480–1561). Garamond was a pupil of Geoffroy Tory and is believed to have followed the Venetian models, although he introduced a number of important differences, and it is to him that we owe the letter we now know as "old style." He gave to his letters a certain elegance and feeling of movement that won their creator an immediate reputation and the patronage of Francis I of France.

Composed by North Market Street Graphics, Lancaster, Pennsylvania

Printed and bound by Berryville Graphics, Berryville, Virginia

Designed by Iris Weinstein